Jun 2013

FRAGILE EMPIRE

BEN JUDAH

FRAGILE EMPIRE

HOW RUSSIA FELL IN AND OUT OF LOVE WITH VLADIMIR PUTIN

YALE UNIVERSITY PRESS
NEWHAVEN AND LONDON

For information about this and other Yale University Press publications, please contact:

U.S. Office: sales.press@yale.edu   yalebooks.com
Europe Office: sales@yaleup.co.uk   www.yalebooks.co.uk

Set in Janson Text by IDSUK (DataConnection) Ltd

Printed in Great Britain by TJ International Ltd, Padstow, Cornwall
Library of Congress Cataloging-in-Publication Data

Judah, Ben.
   Fragile empire: how Russia fell in and out of love with Vladimir Putin / Ben Judah.
      pages; cm
   ISBN 978-0-300-18121-0 (cloth: alkaline paper)
   1. Putin, Vladimir Vladimirovich, 1952- 2. Presidents—Russia (Federation)
   3. Russia (Federation)—Politics and government—1991- I. Title.
   DK510.766.P87J83 2013
   947.086′2—dc23
                                                                              2012048007

A catalogue record for this book is available
from the British Library.

10 9 8 7 6 5 4 3 2 1

2017 2016 2015 2014 2013

CONTENTS

LIST OF ILLUSTRATIONS

ACKNOWLEDGEMENTS

IN RUSSIA, my first and foremost thanks are to Yekaterina, Oleg and Anton Zykov. Your hospitality was the one thing that allowed me to spend enough time in Moscow to begin to understand Russia. I am deeply grateful. Polina Eremenko was the hand that pulled this project together, organizing the meetings, trips and interviews that make it come to life. I cannot thank her enough. In becoming a reporter, my thanks go to Ilya Arkhipov, who has been a mentor in showing me how to cover Russia since we met in the mayhem of a collapsing Kyrgyzstan. By no means least, I want to thank Garrett Pappas. Had it not been for his hospitality, I would not have been able to cover the winter protest movement and its fate the year Putin returned. It is truly appreciated.

In Britain, I want to thank my mother Rosie Whitehouse not only as an editor, but the one who inspired me from an early age to travel and learn about Russia. No one could have helped me more, or taught me more about writing. Then, my father Tim Judah, for always being there and showing me in a hundred little ways how to be a real journalist. They add up to everything. My brother and sisters have lived with this project and the obsessions it entailed for a long time. Their kindness and tolerance helped make it happen. I also want to thank Claire Judah, Mary Gilbert and Marion Judah for helping me get started.

I want to thank all those who have helped me reach this point. Dan Perry, who helped me get to Moscow, Daniel Johnson, who sent me around Russia, and Daniel Korski, who brought me into the European Council on Foreign Relations and inspired me to aim for analysis. Above all, Nicu Popescu, whose enthusiasm made him the best teacher I ever had. I am indebted to Elena Gnedina for carefully reading and commenting on this manuscript. All along the way Edward Lucas was a source of constant encouragement and invaluable guidance. I am deeply thankful to Phoebe Clapham and Robert Baldock for taking this gamble. Without them, this book would not be here.

Amongst my friends, James Schneider helped me formulate my ideas by always knowing what the right questions were to ask over the years. This book began in those conversations. Dylan Chadha had an uncanny ability to point my thoughts in the right direction. Max Seddon never failed to share his time or brilliant observations as this came together. Theo Gibbons was a constant source of support. David Patrikarakos was always there when I needed advice. Special thanks go to William Rice, for sharing not only analytical notes but also meetings, and with whom conversations in the Scarsdale Tavern were as important to the thinking of this book as they were to the reporting. I am extremely grateful.

London, December 2012

For my mother
with love and thanks

Two hundred years ago the historian Nikolai Karamzin visited France. Russian émigrés there asked him, 'What is happening back home, in two words?' Karamzin didn't need two words. 'Stealing,' he replied. And they really are stealing. On a broader scale every year. People carry off beef carcasses from meatpacking plants. Carders from textile factories. Lenses from photographic firms. They swipe everything – tile, gypsum, polythene, electric motors, bolts, screws, radio tubes, thread, glass. Often this takes on a metaphysical character. I'm talking about the completely mysterious thefts without any rational goal. This can only happen within the Russian state – of that I'm convinced.

Sergei Dovalatov, *The Suitcase* (1986)

INTRODUCTION
THE WEAKEST STRONGMAN

THINGS LIKE this were not supposed to be happening anymore. In November 2010, a Russian family were celebrating in their new, proud brick house on Green Street. They were successful people, farmers, and this was a quiet town called Kushchevskaya on the fertile black earth plains of the south. There was much to fete: they were together, on National Unity Day, and the new baby not yet a year old. As they gathered round the table for a toast, their guard dog outside was shot with a tranquilizer dart. Right then, the house was broken into. Eleven armed men pushed in. They began to kill everyone. First they went for the men, then the women and children. They strangled and stabbed them. Soon there were twelve bodies around the dining table, four of them children. They doused the bodies in petrol and set them alight. As they fled, they threw the bodies on top of the nine-month-old baby and left her screaming in the flames, to choke on the smoke. Afterwards they went to the local fast-food joint for a beer as if nothing had happened.

The provincial governor shrugged. 'Unfortunately, on some levels, such gangs exist in every region and in every city.'[1]

He was right. These were very ordinary Russian criminals. They were not only psychopaths, but bandits who, in hock with officials, had infested the state. Their boss was not an outlaw. His name was Sergey Tsapok and he was the law – a member of the local council, tied to the tax agencies, the regular police and the prosecutor, let off from offences by these authorities over a hundred times. He liked to boast that he had been a guest at the President's inauguration in the Kremlin. He was there to watch the children being strangled.

The murders horrified Russia, because they smelt of something worse than murdered children – a rotting state. The dead farmer had been trying to resist Tsapok's demands for a feudal 'tribute'. He was standing up to the extortion racket that Tsapok imposed on those weaker than him across the area. The state, permeated by the mafia, could do nothing to protect him.

Back in Moscow, the government tried to find out what had happened, to calm a hysterical gutter press, but found nobody at the end of the line whom it could trust to tell the truth. None of the local bureaucrats was untainted. The circumstances were so suspicious and the state so weak that the Kremlin had no choice but to send the chief prosecutor himself to run the investigation 'manually' on site.

Vladimir Putin was forced to admit that in Kushchevskaya 'all the organs of power have failed'.[2] But this was no isolated incident. These were only the latest victims of Putin's failure. He had promised to end the 'wild 1990s' with what he called a 'dictatorship of law' and a 'vertical of power'. Yet his stability had turned out to be corrosive. His statement was an admission that the corruption and lawlessness of the 1990s had not gone away. The great and the good, like Valery Zorkin, the chief justice of the constitutional court, were horrified. 'One has to admit, honestly, that the disease of organized crime has too deeply infected our country,' he wrote. 'If the mafia isn't pushed back it will raise the question of whether Russia can survive beyond the next ten years.'[3]

This book asks how such a murder can still happen in twenty-first-century Russia. To find the answer, it shines the interrogator's lamp not just on Putin's face but on the nation and his system as a whole. This is a study of Putin's triumph as a politician and his failure to build a modern state. This book asks what is wrong with Putin's Russia – how such a weak state manages to steal so much from its people, and why they allow it to do so. Previous books have told the story of the rise of the Putin system; this one aims to start telling the story of its decay. It explores how botched state building created neither a 'dictatorship of law' nor a 'vertical of power' but sowed the seeds for the slow disintegration of Putin's once unchallengeable popularity.

Putin's failure has turned Russia into a country of gigantic contradictions. It has modernized as a society but degenerated as a state. It has grown wealthier, but more fragmented and feudalized. Russia has globalized and real incomes have soared by over 140 per cent, but institutions have slid into racketeering and fraud. This book investigates how people see politics in a country where Moscow has more billionaires than New York, whose economy grew faster than that of Brazil through the 2000s, which has the biggest online presence in Europe and one of the most engaged social media followings in the world; but where in 2010 indicators warned it was as corrupt as Papua New Guinea, with the property rights of Kenya, as easy to do business in as Uganda and as competitive as Sri Lanka.

This is an anguished, broken society and Putin is not shaping it. His initiatives to meld it such as the Nashi youth movement and ideologies such as 'sovereign democracy' have flopped. In spite of the state, this nation is going its own way – finding itself in new churches and supermarkets, as it crystallizes into a twisted civil society that venerates vigilantes and demonizes corrupt officials. This is a country pulling apart, in the grips of a culture war – where the Russian Patriarch calls the Putin era 'a miracle of God', but the heroes of the wild Moscow underground, the hippest scene in Europe, are the brightly coloured balaclavas of the Pussy Riot girl band who said a 'punk prayer' in the main cathedral.[4]

It was not always like this. This book asks why Putin was once as popular as a true Russian hero like Yuri Gagarin, gathering an immense fortune in political capital, only to squander it. I show how Putin found a sophisticated way both to 'manage democracy' and censor the media – but also seduced millions of Russians by telling them what they desperately wanted, even needed him to say. This book illustrates how the Putin court was corrupt and dysfunctional from the very beginning, but explains why Russians supported him as he failed to build the modern, fully functioning state that they desperately wanted.

I saw the peak of Putinism. At the end of the 2008 war in Georgia I watched Russian troops mourn the dead and celebrate victory in South Ossetia as the approval rating of the 'national leader' hit 83 per cent.[5] They believed Putin had restored Russia as a great power. Yet at the end of 2011 I watched huge rallies in Moscow as protestors called for him to dismantle this same system. They believed he had stolen the elections and even the state. On the streets, it looked as if Putin had lost control of events.

Between those two moments in Russian history the consequences of this regime have become clear and the changes that are now undermining it began. This book tells the story. It asks how Putin could squander that dizzying peak of popularity after his victory in 2008. It shows how he only entrenched his tsar-like power when demonstrators took to the streets in winter 2011–12 denouncing as illegitimate what they now called his 'party of crooks and thieves'.

A new era is being born. The old Putin model is bust and Putinism by consent slowly coming to an end. To understand what is happening to Russia I have travelled from St Petersburg to Vladivostok to find the consequences of the Putin regime and the contours of this new era. I wanted to understand the opposition and their unnerving heroes. What promising and troubling things do they say about the Russian future? I try to explain how this movement has started to undermine the regime, but is not as powerful a force as one might expect them to be. Across the country discontent is enormous, but resistance still marginal. I wanted to find out why, although the regions can barely tolerate the status quo because they feel like Moscow colonies under the 'vertical of power', even in the most remote and suffering cities many people still feel there is no alternative to Putin. Regime legitimacy has collapsed, but nothing has yet replaced it in people's hearts.

The book ends with a look into Russia's nightmares in the Far East – to ask if this ramshackle system is strong enough to resist the rise of China.

To write this book I travelled 30,000km over five years. I crossed Russia from the Baltic to the Pacific twice, interviewing hundreds of people in places where most Western journalists never go: catching rides in the trucks of wild gold miners on the ice road between Yakutsk and Magadan, travelling down Siberian rivers with Old Believers to find unelectrified villages, talking to the shamans and witches of Tuva. I even travelled on a Russian military truck over the ceasefire line into South Ossetia at the end of the Georgian war. I tried to spend as much time as possible with ordinary Russians in unglamorous places, from the grease-bars of Kaliningrad, to the roadside cafeterias of Nizhny Tagil and the minimarkets of Khabarovsk; it is their views and fears that have done more to shape my analysis than any other. From criminals to conscripts and cadres, I have tried to interview people from every walk of life about their country. When I talk about Russia, or the regions, I am referring to these thousands of interviews as a whole.

I criss-crossed Moscow hundreds of times on Stalin's clattering underground, rushing to meet opposition leaders, analysts, politicians and officials. I found in Moscow a city that resembled Berlin and Chicago in the 1930s, with a seasoning of Paris in the 1960s – a place where my generation had defined itself against its elders, like nowhere else in Europe, with the same fizzing romantic resistance of the 1960s baby-boomers. They will inescapably assume power. I cannot remember the Cold War or the Soviet Union – I come from a new generation, the generation of the anti-Putin protesters on the street. I hope my new perspective mirrors theirs: not post-Soviet, but non-Soviet.

Inside the state, I had the chance to speak to ministers, governors, officers and even the Federal Security Service (FSB), who in detaining me and confiscating an early manuscript became by accident the first readers of this book. Picking up a draft, the FSB officer interrogating me asked if I realized how volatile and close to disintegration Russia really was ('Russia can collapse again! Into a bloodbath of civil war without us to stop it . . .'). This book is about this apocalyptic fear, which shapes Russia – how it brought Putin to power, how he uses it to stay in power and how it is now being turned against him.

Only when something starts to fall apart, can we understand how it really worked. To answer the question 'what is wrong with twenty-first-century Russia?' we need to know why Russia fell in love with Putin, the man who now epitomizes the country's ills, whose name is a synonym for the state. Why Putin? What was the Russia that made him? What had it come to for a man like him to be handed power? Who was this sullen lieutenant colonel from the swamps of St Petersburg?

PART ONE

The Rise of the Lieutenant Colonel

CHAPTER ONE

THE PRESIDENT FROM NOWHERE

PUTIN'S MOTHER is dead. So is his father. His wife Lyudmila is eerily absent. She is no longer by his side at the goose-step parades or the never-ending animal shoots. On the rare occasions that she appears in public, to show she is still alive, the woman is unsteady on her feet and seems to flinch at his touch. His daughters are a state secret. This television tsar seems lonely, exercising alone in echoing halls, as if terrified of physical decay.

But in St Petersburg, an elderly woman with concerned, maternal eyes still watches him strut on the evening news. Vera Gurevich, old but not frail, is the person who remembers his childhood best. Her voice wavers, suddenly on the edge of a cackle, then suddenly speeds up. Her eyes are bright blue, a pasty colour that you only seem to find among the very old. To everyone but her, he has become the state. In 2012, once the protests and jeers that shook the regime as he retuned himself the title of President abated, I felt I needed to speak to someone like this. I can imagine a day when there will be nobody who really knows Putin left.

Late one afternoon we sat and talked on a bench in Victory Park in beautiful summery weather. Not inside, of course not inside, anyone could be listening inside. We were in St Petersburg, surrounded by ugly brutalist architecture. These avenues are where the recent history of the place really is, where the front line was – no piecrust architecture or tour groups of elderly Germans in sight, only the concrete conformism of Soviet blocks, or bullying Stalinist baroque that renders it indistinguishable from anywhere else in Russia.

Vera was Putin's teacher and she thinks about him every day. Devoted to him, she talks about 'Putka', in a disorganized, aged way, as if he was her own son. We sat on a bench and talked. A bruised alcoholic dozed on another bench nearby. She says, 'The government is something that should have nothing to do with you ... it should be almost invisible. This government, it stays out of my way, it doesn't ask anything of me . . . you could say it was the best of governments.'

She tells me everything she remembers. When we started to walk towards the metro, the interview over, I ask her if she had voted for the governing party, United Russia in the rigged 2011 parliamentary elections that detonated mass protests. 'Pah! I did not vote for United Russia. I voted for Just Russia . . . because I believe in justice.'

The conversation is confused. She is suspicious, her thoughts twist and turn back on themselves, but she clings to her memories of the little Putin she taught as his form teacher from age nine to seventeen. 'I am so proud of him, I am proud of him like a son.' Then she jerks her hand. How she wishes he was her son. 'You have to understand what it was really like.' But you can somehow tell that her thin memories of the boy fifty years ago have become mixed up with the man she has seen on television.

Her eyes suspect me of something, and as she put back on her baseball cap with 'CHESS' emblazoned on it, we turned back towards the noise of the main road. And Putin? Did she still see that little boy in him? Vera had voted for him, not for his party, but there was something she no longer recognized. For a second, she paused. 'Now there is a sadness in his eyes . . . It is the harshness of it all. It wasn't always there.'

Little Putin

She met him when he was almost ten years old. It was 1962 and it seemed the Soviet Union might beat the Americans to the moon. She was a young schoolteacher and in the staff meeting Vera Gurevich was handed over the role of form teacher to Putin's class. She was warned that it was full of rough, ill-disciplined little boys. One of them she was told to watch out for was the one called 'Putka' by classmates. This was the Soviet 1960s and teachers were being told to pay more attention to individual pupils and not 'the mass of the class'. With this in mind, she saw this disruptive boy as a child who needed special attention. 'He was so stubborn. He was trouble.' The boy tore in and out of the classroom shouting 'coo-coo it's me' and seemed never to do his homework. Or even realize that he should:

'He did nothing. He didn't care about the results. He just scribbled something down on the paper during the test and then . . . ran away! He didn't care. He just ran away. He didn't care about the consequences.'

There were also fights – and he fought back: 'But if people hurt him he reacted immediately, like a cat . . . He would fight like a cat – suddenly – with his arms and legs and teeth.'

Her concerns reached the point that she was visiting the boy's apartment regularly, to implore his parents to put him on the straight and narrow. She found 'Putka' had a weak mother:

'She was not a very literate person. She didn't have a secondary school education. She'd only been to primary school. She was from the village. So I had to go and check on his homework, sometimes two or three times a week, to see they were paying attention. Putin's mother always said, "This is a topic for his father. He is a boy and this is a man's job." She didn't see this as a woman's role . . . She was from the village you see. And Russia has always been a patriarchy.'

This boy had been born in 1952 and grown up in a hungry, crumbling post-war Leningrad: the 'hero city' of the blockade, where almost every adult he knew had lived through it. His childhood, even his physique, was shaped by the siege – he shares his slight frame with those whose mothers were also malnourished. Putin is the grandson of a chef who served Stalin, Lenin and even Rasputin, the mad monk who wielded enormous influence in the court of Nicholas II. This grandfather was not just a cook, but almost certainly a spy. The chef's job in the state dachas he worked in was reserved for NKVD agents, the political police later known as the KGB, to snoop on the guests. As a child Putin was taken to visit him, still cooking in his old age at a guesthouse of the Moscow party elite. Putin's father worked as a factory foreman, but fought in the war in an NKVD unit behind enemy lines. The war never left him. He suffered extensive wounds at the front but likely remained in the NKVD 'active reserves' throughout his career. This was the opposite of a family of dissidents. The Putins were conformists.

In Soviet Leningrad, a city of communal apartments, gossip travelled at lightning speed and personal privacy was near impossible. Families had a quasi-rural existence in tenement buildings, putting out their washing together, knowing all of each other's business and, on summer evenings, sitting out in the sun in a line of cheap deckchairs. The apartment that the Putins lived in was cramped, shared accommodation, with a communal kitchen and bathroom. By Western standards Putin grew up in poverty – but not by Soviet ones. 'Out of my students,' remembers Gurevich, 'the apartment was far from the worst. He had a little desk to do his work. Many didn't even have that. He had everything he needed.' It was a typical working-class childhood. This world of *komunalka* apartments was one without urban anonymity. 'Putin's mother didn't want a child,' smirks Gurevich. 'He was born when she was forty-two. The others had died. She told her husband she didn't want another, and he replied, "But who will be there, who will look after us when we are old, we must have a child." She indulged him. She fed him for two years on breast milk.'

As Putin's teacher, Gurevich fretted that his father was not disciplining him properly. She respected Vladimir Spiridonovich Putin ('He was such an intelligent man'), but she found him odd and disturbingly introvert. 'I once asked his father, "Why are you such a closed person?", to which he replied: "In the ways we need to be we are open. But only a fool would open his soul to the world. You have to know who you are talking to." ' These were wise words, from a man who knew the NKVD well and had grown up during Stalin's terror. Yet his son was growing up in a rough city. Leningrad was overrun with street kids, hungry, violent gangs of near illiterate children brawling and skirting the edge of crime. Gurevich became increasingly worried that Putin was on the verge of joining them:

'No one ever beat him. I know this because I once grabbed Putin by the scruff of his neck and he stammered: 'How dare you, this is not your role, my father has never beaten me.' He was in the courtyard, I saw him and said 'go and do your homework'. He stayed there playing with these boys that had made a ball out of some cloth. He was the youngest – about eleven – and the rest were already fifteen or seventeen. They were street boys. Already drinking beer and smoking. It was dangerous to be with street boys. They were doing things like spitting to see who could spit the furthest. I asked him why he was hanging around with street boys and he replied, "In life you have to know everything." '

It was at this point that Putin did the strangest, most reckless thing of his childhood. Maybe, because he wanted to experience 'everything'. He went to the KGB headquarters and asked how he could join. Was he play-acting his father, or grandfather? Politely, those in the office told him to study hard at school and read law at university. 'You see, he was obsessed by the patriotic spy films that were being screened all over the city at the time. They got under his skin,' remembers Gurevich. 'But he kept it a secret from me. He never told us he had done this until he was grown up.'

Putin did not become a street urchin. He grew closer to his teacher, to the point that he was taken along on her family holidays. In his early teenage years he discovered what were to be his two passions – judo and German. 'After he found these he really became better and better until he was really a well-behaved – but closed – young man.' Martial arts gave Putin the discipline he needed. He quickly became obsessed by it, eventually going on to win all-city prizes in the sport. Yet, he was more reticent to take to German. This was the subject Gurevich taught and Putin's resistance was overcome by her insistence:

'He once announced to me: "I don't want to study German anymore." I asked, "Why?" He said, "My uncle died at the front and my father was made an invalid at the front by the Germans. I can't study German. I want to study English instead." So, I said to him, "But all Germans are different."

I explained to him that the Germans at the front were just following orders, doing their patriotic duty. I said that there was not just the war to talk about but also German culture, German philosophy and that Germany was always a very cultured country. I said that if he studied German he would become a more learned person. To which he replied: "Fine then, so not all Germans are the same, so tell me about some interesting Germans then." So I told him about the German communists. I asked, "Karl Marx, have you heard of him? You know he was German." And Putin was surprised: "But I thought he was a Jew." I said, "Yes, but he lived in Germany." '

The nation whose war crimes hung over his childhood Leningrad came to fascinate him. Much later he would tell an audience: 'I have two natures and one of them is German.'[1] By that, he meant ordered, clean, organized and philosophical. By the time Putin left school he had turned from 'Putka' into a disciplined, if dour, careerist. He was admitted to Leningrad State University to study law – following the advice of the KGB headquarters. He was becoming ambitious. Gurevich, no longer his teacher but now a family friend, went to visit her former student to see how he was getting along:

'When he was twenty-three I went to see him. He had a political map of the world on his wall. And I asked: "What do all these little flags you've stuck on this mean?" He replied: "The more I learn, the faster I mature." What I did not know is that he was studying both to become a lawyer – but also trying to join the KGB. He claimed he was training to be a policeman. I suspected he was now training up for the KGB, as once I saw him with a military-style band running down his trouser leg. I thought – a regular copper, like you say you are . . . you most certainly are not.'

Conformists from this generation thought the Soviet Union was a successful, even wealthy country, albeit with profound problems. They knew it had ramshackle food supplies, appalling shortages and dreadful consumer goods, but they thought this could be fixed. Russians could not comprehend that a country with space stations, an intervention in Afghanistan and one-quarter of the world's scientists was a fragile empire on a precipice. They did not know that the central planners had made the budget so dependent on the booming price of oil that the latter's collapse would turn into a balance of payments crisis, then a fiscal crisis, then a food crisis as the USSR could not afford the imports that fed its cities, leaving it begging the West for credits – for which it would do anything in return. Worse still, even in the midst of this crisis, they were so confident that Russia was a first-rank nation that they believed the collapse of the USSR in 1991 meant everyone would be 'living like an American' in a few years.

The collapse of the Soviet Union was surrealist and ironic. The scientific-technical intelligentsia that had hoped for it, the shallow middle class, would live through a decade that could have come from the dystopian imagination of J.G. Ballard – turbo-consumerism amid the collapse of society. The end goal they had wished for, the economic programme they had wanted and the bureaucratic implosion they had cheered, suddenly turned Russia into a partially third-world country with memories of the space age.

The Double Disaster

Grainy footage focuses in on a young civil servant sitting on an uncomfortable chair, in 1996. He awkwardly looks at the floor, then away, just not into the lens. He eats his first words, then makes himself clear: 'However sad and however frightening it may sound . . . I think that in our country a return to a certain period of totalitarian rule is possible.' He sighs. Then for a second, a second too long, he can't seem to find the words. 'The *danger* . . . is not to be found in the organs that provide order, the security organs, the police or even the army. It is a danger at our summit, in the mentality of our people, our nation . . . our own *particular* mentality.' A poor jump cut takes us to the next frame:

'We all think in a way . . . which we don't try and hide . . . and *I sometimes think in this way* . . . that if only there was a firm hand to provide order we would all live better, more comfortably and in safety. In fact . . . this comfort would be short-lived, because this firm hand will be tight and very quickly strangle us and . . . It will be instantly felt by every person, then in every family. Only in a *democratic* system where all the workers of the intelligence services, which we call KGB, MVD, NKVD and all the rest . . . when they know that within a year this political hand can change nationally, regionally and locally . . . will they ask themselves what are the laws of the country in which we live?'[2]

The interview is over. The young Putin's eyes fall to the floor. The world-view of this man is a pure product of the double disaster. He is a man whose career was defined by his experiences working in the KGB in Dresden in a failing authoritarian bloc, then by working as a senior official in St Petersburg town hall in a failing democracy.

Putin's rebaptized home town, like almost every other Russian city, was in social chaos in the 1990s. Euphoria gave way to an overwhelming feeling of anarchy. There was no promised, no anticipated, prosperity. Instead Russia was a country that felt so lost and confused that quack 'faith healers' became staggeringly popular. In the late 1980s and early 1990s one silent faith healer, who claimed to 'charge' creams, liquids and ointments, would make mute and packed halls of the sick and frightened hold up jars of water, to be electrified with his 'healing' power. He even had a daily morning show on television, during which tens of thousands of families in their living rooms held up pots and jars in front of their screens when he ordered them to. This could happen because St Petersburg and countless other cities shuddered through the winter of 1992, fearing famine – for the first time since the rule of Stalin.

Statistically the situation was terrifying, even if one accounts for fraudulent Soviet accounting. GDP officially fell by 44 per cent, deeper than 1930s depression America, even Weimar Germany.[3] Nationally the number of murders peaked at over 30,500 a year, as the poverty rate reached 49.7 per cent.[4] But the grimmest statistics concern people's stomachs. Meat consumption fell by 40 per cent through the decade.[5] 'The wild nineties' is what these years are still called. Today, 'the nineties' is a synonym in Russian for a decade that left practically every family with stories of deprivation, unpaid wages, economic humiliation and diminished status. Even by the standards of the time, St Petersburg was struggling. Once a naval hub of the military–industrial complex, the city lost its economic livelihood. Its whole economic purpose, as prescribed by Soviet planners, was switched off and spending on cruisers and submarines virtually ceased. What made this all the worse, was that in 1991 the city thought 'democracy' could be reached as quickly – and would be as bountiful – in the same way their grandparents had once believed in the promise of true and plentiful communism.

Early 1990s St Petersburg was the city that made Putin a politician. Because he has stuffed the Russian government and the oligarchy with his friends and colleagues, it also defined the Putinist elite. The future 'national leader' returned home in 1990 from an undistinguished career in foreign intelligence in East Germany with neither the status nor the security he thought he had bought into with the KGB. The collapse of a dreamed of vocation as an agent abroad was harder for Putin than just losing a job when you're a father of two little girls. It was like losing a father, losing his life's whole goal.

He had lived the life of a second-rate spy – in Dresden where he drank too much and got fat. His first thirty-five years were lived with little success at all. He had trouble communicating and left a woman at the altar. Putin never rose to more than the rank of lieutenant colonel. Perhaps it's not surprising how few of the stories Putin has told about his early life have any emotion in them at all. Apart from one, in Dresden in 1989, when an anti-communist mob is massing outside the offices the KGB worked from. It was at that moment he realized things were falling apart. Unsure how to react, but convinced something had to be done, immediately, Putin made frantic calls:

I was told: 'We cannot do anything without orders from Moscow. And Moscow is silent.' After a few hours our military people did finally get there. And the crowd dispersed. But the business of 'Moscow is silent' – I got the feeling that the country no longer existed. That it had disappeared. It was clear that the Union was ailing. And that it had a terminal disease without a cure – a paralysis of power.[6]

This shock, this feeling of being orphaned, crept up the spines of millions in Soviet state service during that vast and irreparable breakdown. For Putin and his generation, those who did not come from intellectual families, believed what they were told about the USSR's superpower success; they did not question propaganda, or want what they did not have – that moment is their defining scar. Putin has spent a career trying to overcome that paralysis. But his horror that night in Dresden was not just philosophical. It was the realization that he was about to lose his livelihood in foreign intelligence, which had been his childhood dream, and with it his place in the world. The collapse was about to turn him from a privileged foreign agent into a personal failure, even a moral pariah, in the new Russia.

Putin is from a lost generation. Not every Russian was a dissident, a democrat or felt oppressed. Putin was one of millions who had never seriously questioned the system, never sought its dismantlement – and who lost their privileges and sense of self when it collapsed. Putin admits that he did not reflect on the repression carried out by the KGB when he entered the service and is proud that he even tried to 'join' as a child: 'My notion of the KGB came from romantic spy novels. I was a pure and utterly successful product of Soviet patriotic education.'[7] This was not abnormal, but perhaps a bit of a throwback. As early as 1961 only 25 per cent of Soviet youth listed 'building communism' as one of their life goals.[8]

The consequence of such successful indoctrination being utterly exposed is that Putin and his generation have cynicism as their world-view. The system's unravelling disproved every notion that the authorities had drilled into them. Putin, like millions of Russians who dedicated their lives to the Soviet state, found themselves irrelevant, mocked for having a 'Soviet mentality'; those in the KGB were shunned and told they had been the 'enemy of the people' all along. From here stems a sense of betrayal, even viciousness, against idealism and moralizing democrats. Strangely enough, it was none other than the former dissident Andrei Sinyavsky, whose trial in the 1960s had initially rallied together the first Soviet human rights 'defenders', who expressed this lost generation's utter disorientation:

What did Soviet power give the man in the street? Freedom, land, wealth and food? Nothing of the sort. All it gave was a sense of righteousness and a sense we lived in a properly run and logical world.

We have now fallen out of that logical Soviet cosmos into chaos and have no idea what to believe in. The meaning of the lives of several generations has been lost. It looks as though they lived and suffered in vain. After all it is hard to believe in the dawn of capitalism, particularly such a criminal and wild capitalism, which smacks of criminal lawlessness.[9]

Putin returned to St Petersburg to find the night crackling with gunshots as well-armed gang warfare was edging the city into anarchy. Calm and crumbling, if slightly creepy, during the late Soviet period – with then typically low crime rates and few sources of entertainment – the city experienced an avalanche of crime, discos, prostitutes, pole dancers, machine-gun killings and corruption after the fall. Contract-killings became commonplace, gangsters were elected to the town council and 'privatization' saw local oligarchs emerge, often by force, as power brokers. The 1990s saw the city dominated by mafia groups who quickly corrupted the city's culture into one of sleazy nightclubs, misogyny and anti-intellectualism. Even the gravediggers were said to be part of an extortion racket. St Petersburg acquired a reputation as the 'bandits' capital' after a string of high-profile murders: an oil executive was blown apart with a rocket-propelled grenade during rush hour, a city council member was indicted for running a ring of contract-killers and another was beheaded by a car bomb. This is the environment that made Putin believe that 'Russia needs strong state power and must have it.'[10]

With such a stark and disappointing transition, men of Putin's age were left obsessed by stability and burnt out. This was a decade of dizzying overload. The Soviet Union had frozen out modernity and got itself trapped in a dated 1930s heavy-industry fantasy with a police state. So, Russia was forced to go through all of the spasms of post-modernity – the sexual revolution of the 1960s, the consumer revolution of the 1970s, the 'greed is good' of the 1980s and the electronic takeover of the millennium – all at once in the 1990s. This is why Putin's generation have been called 'generation emptiness'.[11] They are men shaped by a tsunami of shopping, PR and state collapse, their thinking warped by post-modern philosophy amid ideological bankruptcy. It is a generation for whom too many lost their ability see right from wrong, and with it went all their certainties apart from cynicism.

Servant Putin

Perhaps no one lived 1990s St Petersburg quite like Arkady Kramarev, the city's chief of police from 1991 to 1994. He knew Putin well: 'We were neighbours, lived next door to each other, said "hello, how are things?"

most mornings and because of what I did, worked closely together.' His white, thinning hair still has hints of the gold shock it once was. His upper lip droops and his cheeks are worn and blotched. His blue eyes have hints of cataracts. Kramarev is an old man who never stops smoking. 'The crime wave was like a hurricane,' he remembers, vividly. The late 1980s were 'calm years', where only a hundred or so murder cases would drop on his desk a year. 'The funny thing is that the first thing I felt when the Union collapsed was simple euphoria.' But within eighteen months of the collapse, six hundred to eight hundred murder cases were piling up in his paper stacks: 'At first we had no idea how to deal with this. We were Soviet policemen. We knew how to deal with organized crime only in theory.'

As the West cheered the withdrawal of the Soviet army from Berlin, Prague and Kabul, millions of its AK-47s turned up at car-boot sales across Russia. Killings soared but Kramarev's police were in disarray. Inflation dissolved wages. The experienced officers left in droves. He still feels bitter that he was not allowed to deploy military or vigilante patrols: 'There were no functioning courts to solve disputes between the new capitalists. So, in the conflicts that came the main judge was the Kalashnikov.' Friends who went into business were murdered and, he laughs, 'We used to say a bandit had a four-year lifespan.' One day contract killers gunned down a businessman with machine guns and sped off. By the time the police found the car it was already riddled with bullets; the killers had already been killed. Every morning Kramarev would storm into the office feeling 'furious, always looking . . . *for a way out*'.

Putin's political technique is the product of working in this St Petersburg for its local Boris Yeltsin – the 'democrat' Anatoly Sobchak – a man whose name came to echo in the city all the hopes and failures of those years. A perestroika darling of the intelligentsia, who stood out as an orator in Mikhail Gorbachev's semi-elected Congress of People's Deputies, with gushing speeches denouncing 'greedy and incompetent leaders who could reduce our lives to absurdity', he was to fail the democracy test in office.[12] Sobchak ruled the city like Yeltsin ruled Russia. The same man who had stood on the steps of the Winter Palace defying the hardliner coup in 1991 preferred to rule by decree, treated the legislature with disdain and awarded himself the right to hand out city properties. Under his watch, the town hall was accused of skyrocketing corruption and bribery. 'He said he was this great democrat, but he had such strong authoritarian tendencies,' remembers Kramarev. 'He once asked me to ban a book written about him by a deputy, who is now jailed for murder. I said that's impossible . . . and besides, a job for the KGB, not the police.'

The St Petersburg democrats were ambiguous about democracy and stuffed their offices with KGB men. They were behaving just like Yeltsin in Moscow. Like Sobchak in St Petersburg, he was locked in combat with parliament as his support evaporated in an economic depression. The situation was so bad that a report by the International Labour Organization warned: 'there should be no pretence. The Russian economy and the living standards of the Russian population have suffered the worst peacetime setback of any industrialized nation in history.'[13]

In the capital it was the liberal intelligentsia who called on the 'great democrat' to rule by decree, to use force against parliamentary rebels and suggested postponing the elections. If Putin had picked up the 'liberal' *Literaturnaya Gazeta* in 1992 he might have read letters from the great and the good shouting:

> Mr. President,
>   As citizens of Russia we consider it our duty to express our firm support for the policy of radical reforms. Do not let yourself be stopped by the hysteria of temporary favourites, who, standing at the side of the road of Russian history, sense the fragility of their existence. Pyotr Arkadyevich Stolypin did not hesitate to put his country's welfare above the reverence for parliamentary forms, forms which not a single people have ever acquired instantly.[14] We believe that Russians support the government of the republic. We are convinced a direct appeal to them is an essential step. It can brook no delay.[15]

In 1992 as Putin and Sobchak sat in St Petersburg town hall, the parliament that had once greeted Yeltsin with applause, turning into an ovation as he pulled down the USSR, moved into outright rebellion. It wanted to stop radical reform after the disaster of price liberalization. The situation was akin to wartime – the average monthly wage had fallen to $6 and over 60 per cent of wages were in arrears.[16] The International Labour Organization calculated that 85 per cent were now in poverty.[17] Russia seemed about to shatter. One-third of all governors were withholding their taxes and, even in St Petersburg, 74.43 per cent had voted 'yes' in a referendum on making the city a 'republic'.[18]

When fighting broke out in Moscow between militia loyal to the parliament and Kremlin forces, Yeltsin convinced the military to storm parliament. It was shelled into a smouldering ruin and a new super-presidential constitution rushed through, untying the executive from effective checks and balances. Sobchak mimicked Yeltsin in his treatment of the St Petersburg assembly, ordering a part-time and toothless body into existence as its replacement. As the liberals and democrats applauded, only a few ostracized thinkers such as Dmitry Furman realized what was happening:

What will happen now is more or less clear – a new authoritarian system headed by Yeltsin, who cannot be blamed for anything, because he is being carried along by a wave of history that has caught him, racing through the democratic-populist stage, and is now pushing him towards the role of 'Grand Prince', who relies on the democratic movement that is devoted to him and is increasingly dominated by rhetorical anti-Communism and Russian nationalism.[19]

As Yeltsin's writ was weak beyond Moscow in the early 1990s local power brokers had to improvise their own transitions. Cities such as Nizhny Novgorod became the strongholds of anti-communist democrats, whilst some provinces – like Bashkortostan – became starkly authoritarian; meanwhile, others including Yakutia became de facto controlled by local ethnic clans that excluded native ethnic Russians from the spoils. Sobchak copied Moscow.

The West liked the idea of Yeltsin being surrounded by dashing 'young reformers', but in fact he brought the military and FSB into government. They held as little as 5 per cent of top government posts under Gorbachev in 1998 but by 1993 occupied 33 per cent, climbing to 46 per cent by the end of his term.[20] He liked them as drinking partners. Like Yeltsin, Sobchak chose to build his 'liberal' power base in close cooperation with the local KGB–FSB. Sobchak made many of their agents – in order not to challenge him – partners in his administration. This is why he chose Putin to be his right-hand man. Putin was one of his former students from St Petersburg State University Law Faculty, where Sobchak still taught – who now washed up back on campus as its KGB 'curator'. This must have been a humiliatingly minor job for a man who dreamed of being the Soviet Bond. It was here that they first politically hooked up. This was the start of Putin's second life as a powerful but municipal official, the deputy mayor responsible for foreign trade.[21] He soon became Sobchak's effective deputy for everything, and officially became the first deputy mayor. The two were in tandem almost from the start – with Putin being trusted to such an extent by the boss that he would be acting mayor in his absence, to the shock of his colleagues. Putin was a hit on local TV. He spoke neither in the old party language, nor like a moralizing new democrat – but straight from the wild 1990s. To the cameras, Putin once coldly insisted:

'If the criminals have attacked authority there must be an appropriate punishment. It's a policemen's duty to be severe and cruel if necessary. It is the only way to reduce criminality – the only way. We hope to eliminate ten criminals for each officer killed . . . within the law, of course.'[22]

Kramarev, the police chief, is certain that Sobchak thought this was good politics: 'He thought having a KGB number two would be good for ratings, give him support from their system and be a strong sign he was willing to work with them.' This is when he started working closely with Putin. Kramarev recalls:

'I thought he was just an insignificant official at the time who always stood up when I went into his office to tell him frankly – "is Sobchak crazy? What the hell is this? Can you just stop that?" – but the young Putin really knew what was going on. Unlike Sobchak, he had his feet on the ground. He saw the collapsing economy, the crime wave. He saw that the country was at death's door. He grasped that . . . The essential fact.'

Kramarev and all the other people who were working with Putin, from hostile democratic deputies in the St Petersburg assembly to rival mayoral candidates, remember a quiet, efficient man, who in the words of one 'meant no when he meant no, meant yes when he meant yes, and always explained that no. Unlike the other incoherent officials.'[23] He came across as a cut above the other officials. Well-spoken, loyal and a man who meant what he said. Kramarev remembers countless moments when Putin defused rows he was having with Sobchak – including dissuading him from banning politically damaging books. He remembers a good negotiator who knew how to make friends. But of course making friends – and winning men's trust – are the skills of a spy. 'I'm a specialist in human relations,' is how Putin would hint to friends that he was in the KGB.[24]

'There were rumours from the start that Putin was a KGB insertion to keep an eye on Sobchak.' This is the commanding voice of Igor Kucherenko, who was the deputy chairman of St Petersburg assembly of which Sobchak was the chairman, before becoming mayor. Kucherenko is the kind of man whose hopes have been disappointed the most by the 1990s: a real revolutionary, anti-Soviet liberal. A portrait of the neoliberal former prime minister Yegor Gaidar, the zealous grandson of a savage Bolshevik general, is pinned to the side of his cramped office, the three-volume *History of the New Russia*, with Gaidar emblazoned on it, sits ostentatiously in his display cabinet. He first met Putin in the heady 1989 days after he was hired by Sobchak as an assistant. 'But those are only rumours,' says Kucherenko:

'You have to remember the KGB itself was in a state of collapse at that time – like everything else – it was divided between groups of young agents that knew better than anyone else that the country needed reform, needed to change, groups of older conservatives that wanted nothing to change, and groups of people that knew that privatization was inevitable and wanted to manage, to control this process. When I met Putin he was in the first category and he ended up in the third.'

Kucherenko pauses to point to a 15cm framed photo of himself to the right side of his cluttered desk. 'That's Boris Nikolayevich Yeltsin and I.' You get the impression he looks at it quite often during the working day.

They are in front of a train station; an almost unrecognizably healthy Yeltsin is smiling and slightly blurred. He looks fiercely into and beyond the lens. 'But the very fact Putin was in the KGB was one of the reasons Sobchak chose him. He knew the KGB would oppose him and he thought Putin would make them easier to deal with.'

He smokes heavily, trying to remember the young man in his peripheral vision who became omniscient. 'Putin would disappear out of photographs. When he became President I threw open my photo album to see us together – I knew he'd be there next to me at one of so many events we were at together. But he wasn't in a single one. He'd slipped out of every frame. I sometimes wonder if he even has a reflection in the mirror.'

Quite a few of the regular democratic deputies – enthused pioneers of perestroika – found it very strange that such an 'impeccable democrat' as Sobchak should have employed a KGB agent as deputy mayor. At a cocktail party thrown by the German Embassy to celebrate the first anniversary of the fall of the Berlin wall, Yury Vdovin, an outspoken democratic deputy from St Petersburg assembly, found himself at the corner of a table next to the young Putin. They took some shots, Putin only raising the glass to his lips. Vdovin is open about the fact that he'd had a few more than that. 'Don't you think it's a bit strange, Vladimir Vladimirovich, that you as a KGB agent should be working in democratic St Petersburg town hall?' He looked back, then retorted:

'Yury Innokentevich, first of all I worked in foreign intelligence and I never spied on or persecuted any dissident, I never watched them. And you must know us officers in foreign intelligence, we had all the information on the real situation in our country and in the world, and it was the ones in East Germany who were the most progressive and liberal of them all. And I was one of them! That's why I'm fighting for democracy and liberal economics.'

But at the time Vdovin, a human rights activist, did not see anything particularly wrong with Putin: 'He knew how to get along with people. He got things done.'

But whatever Putin said were his intentions, whatever he came across as – was he passing on information to the KGB about Sobchak? Had Sobchak not just made a gesture to the KGB but picked his own handler in appointing him? Kramarev is suddenly coy: 'It is possible. I do not have this information. But you have to remember a KGB officer always stays a KGB officer. I cannot exclude that Putin was also . . . *always spying on me.*' But the former police chief has no respect for such agents: 'They were never fighting real crime, they were just wasting their time following some person who'd said a joke about Brezhnev. The whole KGB was sent to stop those Solzhenitsyn books circulating . . . and they failed even at that.'

Putin probably was a 'handler' – but one double-timing his loyalties, like so many others in an entire KGB system that was so infested with closet democrats it was paralyzed and spasmodic when it was most needed, failing to impose martial law during the 1991 coup. Yet he did really grow close to Sobchak. He cried at his funeral. This explains why, over the years, Sobchak's daughter Ksenia found it so easy to prance around first as Russia's answer to Paris Hilton, despite her plain looks in country with no shortage of supermodels, before hatching into an anti-Putin glamour-activist. She has never been harmed. 'I never understood why Putin looked up to that man as a leader', groaned Kramarev. 'When my guys were following around some bandit oligarchs taking pictures, Sobchak's wife would often turn up in the pictures too – you see . . . she got around socially.'

Sobchak's regime operated in a similar manner to the one Putin would one day run. It was outrageously corrupt and incredibly clannish. For most of the Soviet period, officials had privileges – a holiday on the Black Sea at a special resort or a good car – but not astounding levels of wealth. To now watch a 'new Russian elite' acquire fortunes during the 1990s only served to embitter the nation. Locally it was clear that the transition had not worked out as expected. 'Sobchak's town hall always had this odour of corruption, he was not controlling what any of his deputies were doing,' recalled one 1990s local committee chief.

The blue-eyed and slight Vantanyar Yaiga saw Putin almost every day in the town hall. Whilst Putin was Sobchak's chief deputy he was also his chief advisor. 'You see we felt besieged,' says Yaiga. 'We were frightened that if we split, that if we broke up, the communists could come back, and it would all be ruined.' Yaiga stammers and forgets his words with age. 'This besieged feeling gave both Sobchak and Putin a high degree of commitment and loyalty to the people they employed. It would take them a very, very long time to throw out a bad person. You can still see this in the way Putin behaves.' This mild-mannered man wears a badge of the ruling United Russia party on his lapel. He was a friend of Putin. Twenty years later he has an unclear job as a 'foreign affairs advisor', quite something for such an elderly man who cannot speak English, in the tsarist glory of the Mariinsky Palace in St Petersburg. We met in a hall of suitably tsarist grandeur – which only exacerbated his slightness and his vaguest of roles:

'Oh, Putin had such a wicked sense of humour. During the time we were working together and meeting almost every day – and one day I said to him, "Vladimir Vladimirovich, I have a problem, I'm being harassed by these businessmen for a good deal but I'm only an advisor and have no administrative functions." He said, "Tell them you eat with us."'

Even today, Yaiga still finds this 'joke' extremely funny, but nationally escalating impunity and embezzlement left Andrei Sinyavsky, the former dissident, full of fear: 'In the eyes of the people, democracy has become synonymous with poverty, the embezzlement of public funds, and theft. This disappointment with democracy is extremely dangerous for a country without a stable democratic tradition.'[25]

One possible incident of embezzlement and abuse of power pointed straight at the young Putin. As the official responsible for trade and investment, he had hatched a scheme in 1991 to ship raw materials abroad to 'save St Petersburg from famine', signing $122 million worth of deals with nineteen foreign companies, with him as the middleman, in exchange for food. The food never arrived and members of the local legislature campaigned for his resignation.

Alexander Belyaev was then the head of city assembly. He was so disturbed by the food scandal that he called for Putin's head. Twenty years later this white-haired man with strangely long legs and eyes that never stop moving tries to choose his words carefully. He remembers Putin's faltering first speech – fending off food accusations – with stumbling pauses. Putin was then nervously speaking in his own defence, as Belyaev was trying to have him fired. We talk as Belyaev smokes Marlboro Reds one after another, with unconscious drags, in a gloomy corridor – not in his office, I presume, for fear of bugs. He whispers hoarsely:

'When the assembly discussed these Putin matters we decided that it was either corruption or unprofessionalism. This is why we called on Mr Sobchak to dismiss Mr Putin. He didn't. He stood by him and we didn't have the power to get rid of him. But all these facts gave us the impression that corruption could have been involved.'

He remembers Putin as no unprofessional fool. 'You see this man had good qualities too. He was an expert at making friends, of being loyal to those friends. He is a brilliant observer of human nature, and he is very good at tactics.' Embezzler or not, he saw Putin behaving no differently from the other officials:

'You need to understand that there were no anticorruption laws, there were no clear rules how anything should be done, no code of conduct for any of these state officials. They were flying abroad on the expense accounts of banks, taking huge 'gifts', on which there was no limit in monetary value, they were going on vacations on other's expenses. This was the time of "privatization". Putin was enjoying all this too.'

Sobchak protected Putin from the assembly. The deputy mayor claimed he was being persecuted 'for being a KGB agent'.[26] Incidents like this explain the extent to which the Sobchak–Putin team discredited themselves. They ended up being despised, like the Yeltsin cabal, and lost the mayoral race in 1996 to a group of politicians who were even more brazenly corrupt and in hock with the mafia. More importantly, Sobchak had fallen out with Yeltsin's then blood brother and moonshine drinking partner Alexander Korzhakov, his KGB chief bodyguard, who wielded enormous power in court. He threw his weight against them. Anti-Sobchak leaflets were dropped from helicopters. This election was Putin's only real, traumatic, experience of running a competitive vote as the losing side's campaign manager. He refused to serve the new mayor and withdrew dejected to his dacha, to train dogs. A personal failure.

Operation Successor

The year that Sobchak lost his election was the year that Boris Yeltsin, unsteady on his feet after five heart attacks, but desperate not to lose power, began to turn Russia into a 'managed democracy'. He had grabbed a conductor's baton next to Chancellor Helmut Kohl on live TV, uncontrollably drunk, and waved it wildly at the brass band playing as Russian forces withdrew from Germany. At home his bodyguard's wife was watching and burst into tears of shame. He then sent over 7,500 soldiers to die in a botched war against Chechen rebels, which he lost, humiliating the remains of the army that had trained to defeat NATO by dashing through the Fulda Gap. His ratings were in single figures and, had the 1996 election been free and fair, he would never have won.

Yeltsin forgot his promise to serve only one term, but knowing full well how loathed he was, he dithered in his decision, mired in depression. Then he woke up one morning and, in a barely audible voice, told bodyguard Korzahkov: 'I've decided to run.'[27] To win the Kremlin he made a pact with the new tycoons, known as the oligarchs. These coarse, half-bandit multi-millionaires were epitomized by Boris Berezovsky, who would boast (inaccurately) how he and seven bankers controlled over 50 per cent of Russian GDP.[28] They called him 'the comet', because he thought so fast, a man who had been festering in late socialism as a mathematician dreaming of winning the Nobel prize. But by the time I met him, in summer 2012, Berezovsky had lost the will to defend his past. His mind was back in the nineties. 'At first,' he said, 'nobody understood what was business.' He barely made eye contact; the bombast was gone. Eight months later he was found dead on his bathroom floor.

In his glory days, he radiated power and menace. He and the other oligarchs had made every right call in a country falling to bits. These men had just started going to Davos, the annual gathering of the world's super-elite in the Alps, when they realized that Yeltsin might actually lose the election. They saw the Western elites rushing to shake hands with Gennady Zyuganov, the leader of the opposition Communist Party of the Russian Federation (KPRF), which seemed poised to return to power, like its rebranded ex-siblings had already done in parts of Eastern Europe.

'We were shocked at Davos,' remembered Berezovsky in the gloom of his London office, decorated with portraits of Lenin, Gorbachev and Khrushchev. There was also one of himself, poking his grinning face round a column, as Yeltsin spoke at a podium. 'We had a very short psychological experience of the West and we were shocked. We had expected the West to help us. We thought they were now scared of new competition.' His eyes were fixed on a repulsive silver statuette of Picasso in his meeting room, which he seemed particularly proud of. Its stomach opened up to reveal a miniature silver woman bathing in gold coins. He spoke almost comically fast:

'We didn't think about others. About those who were not ready for the transition, or who couldn't make it at all. We didn't recognize at the time how dangerous it was to split society – how much jealousy and violence that would engender. Those left behind were not as *sophisticated* or as *creative* as us, but they were not bad. We, the class that was more advanced in feelings, creativity and understanding of the future, did not take responsibility. We just focused on making more and more money.'

Under the Alpine peaks the richest oligarchs made the 'Davos Pact'. If the West was not going to save Yeltsin, they would. This was the moment the Kremlin began to build a power system based on patronage. In exchange for bankrolling a media blitz, importing every PR and campaigning technique they could afford and pushing any positive coverage of Zyuganov off their TV stations, they were allowed to 'privatize' the 'crown jewels' of the Russian economy at knocked-down prices for their loyalty, in a corrupt scheme known as 'loans-for-shares'. This way, nearly 60 per cent of the state's industrial assets were handed to the oligarchs despite the resistance of the left-dominated parliament.[29] These included the gigantic Siberian oil, mining and mineral mega-complexes – the heart of the Soviet economy.

By this point all respect for democratic procedure was secondary to staying in power for Yeltsin. He was so frightened of losing the election that he came within inches of a decree suspending it for two years, banning the Communist Party and imposing emergency rule. The decrees drawn up, he was talked out of this move at the last minute, as the first part of his conspiracy went into action, a 'bomb alert' in parliament that sent the frightened deputies running into the street.

The night of the first round of the presidential election, after weeks of hysterical propaganda warning of civil war and the Bolshevik menace, dubious returns came in from the provinces. There were many results so statistically improbable, they seemed to point only to fraud. Yeltsin suffered another heart attack before the second round. To the end, Berezovsky denied there was outright vote rigging, but recalled: 'If you ask me whether the Yeltsin government used administrative resources to win, the answer is yes.' By this he meant the government used the bureaucracy to campaign for the government candidate.

No one really knows who won the 1996 election, as fraud was so widespread and also used by the opposition. What we know for sure is that it was an unfair vote that paved the way for a new era of 'no-alternative' elections. Not sticking to the rules has consequences. 'There is hardly any doubt who won,' the future president Dmitry Medvedev is reputed to have said, 'it was not Boris Nikolayevich Yeltsin', fending off an accusation of rigging the 2011 parliamentary election.[30]

Russia already had a monarchical presidency, where what really mattered was court politics around Yeltsin, who could not be dislodged by elections, had neutered parliament, and had surrounded himself with former KGB officers, military men and neoliberal economists. Institutions were in disarray, or had ceased to matter.

Yeltsin's second term began to collapse barely after it had got going. It discredited Russian liberalism for a generation. 'Liberals' as a group have never really been in power in Russia. They were powerful in Yeltsin's Kremlin, but jostled with free-market KGB types and pro-business military men. Their only real taste of power was the 1998 government of the 'young reformers' dominated by Sergei Kiriyenko, Anatoly Chubais and Boris Nemtsov, then favoured as Yeltsin's successor, which was out and out for radical reforms, without a party backing, representing the kind of neoliberal agenda that only 4 per cent of the electorate had backed in the parliamentary vote.[31]

Under them, Russia's economic situation and accounts were deteriorating so badly that by 17 August 1998 there was no alternative left but to default. That night they invited the oligarchs one by one, to alert them. The millions about to lose their deposits were given no warning and no scheme was thought up to insure them. They woke up to the news that the International Monetary Fund (IMF) director Michel Camdessus had cut the country off from further credit and announced: 'I alerted President Yeltsin that Russia would be treated no differently from Burkina Faso.'[32]

That night was the second founding of the state. This was when Yeltsin lost control of events. It was the moment when the elite got scared and moved further towards authoritarianism. According to Grigory Satarov, Yeltsin's former aide, it was then the president ditched the idea of Nemtsov as the successor and decided Russia needed a robust, military man. Intellectuals began to debate the need for a 'Russian Pinochet' to defend the market, with the famous talking head Mikhail Leontyev even travelling to Chile to interview the ageing general for national TV – as a model for Russia. The act of defaulting washed out the remaining dregs of hope for democratic capitalism. Scores of banks folded, millions lost their savings, inflation hit 84 per cent and food prices soared.[33] Kaliningrad in the west halted financial transfers to Moscow; Vladivostok in the east suspended food deliveries outside the city.

For ordinary Russians, the 'transition' seemed to have led nowhere – nothing undermines faith in democracy more than losing your life's savings. Miners blocked the railroads; inside the government the fear was palpable. The country's most famous anti-Soviet dissident and its moral authority, Alexander Solzhenitsyn, refused an award from Yeltsin's government, which he said had 'taken Russia to such dire straits'.[34] In a moment of honesty, Yeltsin's own prime minister, Viktor Chernomyrdin, blurted out what many truly felt inside the Kremlin: 'There is still time to save face, but then it's going to be necessary to save the rest of the body.'[35]

The feeling that Russia was approaching calamity was heavy and omnipresent. The mayor of Moscow, Yuri Luzhkov, and the former prime minister, Yevgeny Primakov, after he was dismissed by a Yeltsin nervous at his growing popularity, raised an alliance of governors and swung the national NTV channel behind him. There was real fear inside the inner circle known as the 'family' that they would put Yeltsin on trial if they seized power.

This circle needed a protector who could win the next election. This was the Kremlin that Vladimir Putin, then a young, impressive former KGB bureaucrat from St Petersburg, first started work in. His friends helped him get there. Yeltsin's powerful minister for privatization, Anatoly Chubais, had worked for Sobchak in St Petersburg and brought his fellow Sobchakite, the economist Alexey Kudrin, with him. When Putin stuck by Sobchak and refused to serve under his successor, the 'St Petersburg set' helped him find work in the Kremlin too. He rose quickly, but the jobs he was assigned for – head of the notoriously corrupt property department, the presidential monitoring service, deputy head of the presidential administration charged with the regions, and then director of domestic intelligence (FSB) – taught him one thing: the Russian 'federation' was practically a fiction.

In the eighteen months after the default, the situation was bleak and the 'family' knew it. Sensing the changing political wind, even the loyal Boris Nemtsov was pushing Yeltsin to 'throw the oligarchs out of the Kremlin'.[36] 'The Russian economy was near collapse,' remembered Berezovsky, barking this out in his Mayfair boardroom to stress the point. Yeltsin's daughter, her husband, his chief of staff and their favourite oligarch – Berezovsky – began scrambling to find a successor. They had to find one who would neither imprison Yeltsin, nor confiscate their assets but also be strong enough to stop the collapse of Russia. This was 'Operation Successor'.

Berezovsky had known Putin for a while. They had been introduced in his St Petersburg days by the oligarch Pyotr Aven. By now he was the rising bureaucratic star, and Berezovsky had been impressed that Putin had demonstratively attended his wife's birthday party whilst he was fighting for influence with Yevgeny Primakov, the first of Yeltsin's three ex-KGB prime ministers. Berezovsky thought he could trust this former KGB agent. But the 'family' had some misgivings about him: his rank was too low and he was quite short. But he had major selling points. He was impressed by Putin's loyalty to his former boss, the 'Yeltsin of St Petersburg'. This had gone as far as providing a government plane to help him flee to France when a corruption case (which presumably might have touched Putin himself) was opened against Sobchak.

Berezovsky felt he had hard evidence that this loyal servant would be a bulldog protector. Putin had been made head of the FSB and was using that position to be the 'family' bodyguard. He had purged it of their enemies, sacked as many as one-third of FSB officials and sealed it shut from incriminating leaks. He stymied investigations into corruption inside the Kremlin. Putin even released a graphic sex-tape discrediting the state prosecutor who had gone after Yeltsin's daughter. When the prosecutor saw the video of himself with prostitutes on national TV, he suffered a heart attack.

Even better, this effective man, Putin, had no financial resources at all and was thus completely dependent on the 'family' money. Yeltsin started to like him a lot. Berezovsky was then charged with convincing him to accept life as the successor, visiting him several times including when Putin was on holiday with his family in the south of France. He looked loyal. Berezovsky remembered: 'We were not friends, but Putin made a series of impressive steps, which were unusual – when Sobchak lost the election, he refused to serve under the new mayor.' More importantly Putin held appeal to each part of the elite – he was ex-KGB, but he had worked for democratic Sobchak, he had shown himself to be loyal and he had shown himself able to lead. The oligarch was impressed, forgetting that strangers can be dangerous:

'He looked brave. He was a good team player. He accepted the rules. He never played any political dirty tricks, nor did he play games with Yeltsin's opponents like the previous prime minister, Sergei Stepashin, had been doing. He was young and many people wanted youth in power after years of old and frail Yeltsin. He did strictly as agreed. Putin looked like a normal, natural Russian.'

Berezovsky was by now aggressively trying to persuade Putin to be Yeltsin's heir:

'I said, "So what do you think?" We were at his dacha, and Putin said, "I don't want to be President . . . I want to be Berezovsky." '

Dreaming of Pinochet

'Operation Successor' was set to the music of the huge apocalyptic psycho-drama playing out on Russian TV chat shows – the fear of collapse part two – as insurgent attacks multiplied in the Caucasus and the screeching guests called for Chechens to be ethnically cleansed and a Russian Pinochet to make sure Moscow was open for business, by means of the military police.

Putin inherited a monarchical presidency that was turning into a 'managed democracy' (the term is alleged to have been invented by Yeltsin's chief of staff, Alexander Voloshin). He also inherited a country on the brink of war that he thought was about to dissolve into blood. The fighting in the Caucasus was escalating and Moscow's control over the regions was unravelling in a hundred little acts of insubordination. Siberian Yakutia, mother of one-quarter of the world's diamonds, had declared English an official language.[37] There had even been an attempt to create a 'Urals Republic'. The Siberian coal-mining province of Kemerovo was even building up its own hard currency and gold reserves. Regions were throwing up trade barriers between each other, the kind of which are usually seen between states. In Muslim Tatarstan on the Volga, not only had its President won the rights for special Russian passports with a separate Tatar identity page, but threatened loudly that if Russian volunteers were sent to fight in Kosovo in 1999 alongside Orthodox Serbs, his Tatars would volunteer to fight against them with Muslim Albanians.[38]

The fact that default, disorder and depression had happened under the banner of democracy made the desire for reaction inevitable. This is why more than three-quarters of Russians now regretted the fall of the USSR and 70 per cent said they were ready to put order over democracy.[39] Between 1991 and 2000 at least 150,000 people were murdered, the fourth highest rate in the world, whilst over 150,000 cars were stolen a year.[40] Demographics tell the darkest story – soaring death rates and slumping birth rates saw the population collapse at a faster rate than it had even during the Russian Civil War. Male life expectancy plunged to fifty-seven years: a teenage boy had less chance of reaching sixty than had his great-grandfather born in 1900.[41]

Russia's biggest problem was not even in the cities falling to pieces but in the cold flatlands and bogs of western Siberia – its oil fields. The crisis of the state reflected the collapse of the Russian oil industry. In a cruel conjunction of geology, financial markets and bore-hole maintenance, everything had gone wrong in the industry that government revenues depended on. From its Soviet peak, oil production had collapsed almost 50 per cent, the oil price had fallen 60 per cent, and investment into the fields themselves had sunk 70 per cent.[42] The pumps and drills of western Siberia, once the envy of the West, were now ramshackle piles and operated in line with defunct practices, degrading the fields themselves. Russia was not only producing much less oil, but the oil was worth far less and the industry itself urgently needed any profits to be reinvested, simply to keep it going. To make matters worse, the new oil tycoons were barely paying taxes, but hiding their revenues down 'onshore offshore' tax holes in Russian regions that Moscow was too weak to plug. Even the fields themselves seemed exhausted, as if geologically dying. The industry that Russia depended on looked ruined.

However, not everything was in implosion. The country was engulfed in a surreal explosion of consumerism, television and advertising as it was sociologically disfigured. The once forbidden West – in the form of Pepsi, Levis and Veuve Clicquot was pouring in. The number of telephones, apartments, refrigerators, cars, radios and trips abroad soared – along with the murder rate, drug abuse, alcoholism, prostitution and violence. For all the social pain inflicted, the reformers did lay the technical–legal basis for a consumer society, within such a steep decline in overall living standards. The 1990s caught the small Russian middle class in a strange bind: they were accumulating more and more stuff, but the system to secure all their stuff was falling to bits. To protect their fridges and their holidays abroad, more and more were tempted by the idea of a Russian Pinochet.

Most Russians were impoverished. As many as 40 per cent had sunk below the official poverty line, which had been lowered from the Soviet version in order to hide the fact that, by old measurements, a majority were now impoverished.[43] They were desperate for wages and pensions to be paid, and were terrified that public services were about to collapse completely. Their old discontent at the USSR's breadlines and bureaucrats had been eclipsed by anger at Yeltsin. For them, the collapse of the Soviet Union was also the collapse of the welfare state.

The final delirious twist was that the intelligentsia, newspapers, magazines and 'thick journals' – Russian culture itself – was in free fall as commercial TV was exploding. The very class that had wanted the revolution had lost out from it, with violent entrepreneurs and oligarchs – the people they disdained – rising to the top. The circulation of all Russian titles had imploded from over 37 million in 1990 to fewer than 7.5 million the year of the default, and of these the USSR's flagship semi-intellectual publication *Argumenty i Fakty* saw its readership shrunk from over 30 million in 1990 to just 3.5 million five years later.[44] Mass TV news was making Yeltsin look more and more like a senile alcoholic, creating ever more demand for a Russian Ronald Reagan, who would be the first true actor-politician on screen who knew how to work the viewers. Meanwhile,

the TV sets in almost every home left by the Soviet Union were retuned
to a cacophony of over ten new channels broadcasting uncensored, licen-
tious advertising. Dissident intellectuals gave way to TV hosts – and even
Solzhenitsyn got himself a talk show.

The result was hysteria, a crashed Russia dangerously vulnerable to
deviant messiahs and well-intentioned psychopaths. It should be no
surprise, then, that Russia's favourite film that decade was *Brother*. It is a
bleak portrait of a criminal time. Danila, a demobbed conscript, arrives in
St Petersburg to start a new life but finds the city lawless, dilapidated, a
place where the strong crush the weak. Here, in Putin's city of cracked
paint, crumbling buildings and claustrophobic apartments, Danila goes
into 'business' with his brother, a contract killer. He is the film's hero. He
forces North Caucasian fare dodgers to pay for their tickets on the buses.
He hunts down gangster after gangster, killing 'the Chechen' and the other
bandits who terrorize downtrodden ethnic Russians. He is no friend of the
Jews. He is a bandit but, unlike the others, one who stands up for the weak.
This 1997 film was a sensation. It was as if subconsciously the country
wanted a man like Danila to mete out raw justice from Yeltsin's chaos.

The Nervous Breakdown

'Elections, I just hate them,' is what Yeltsin remembers Putin replied when
he asked him to become his prime minister and successor. On 9 August
1999 the old man appointed somebody he liked and trusted, but who had
the popularity of a statistical error: 1 per cent.[45] National politicians
dismissed Yeltsin as insane, ludicrous or bizarre. Inside the political castle,
many of his top aides were aghast. It looked as if the man who had gone
through three prime ministers in as many years had finally lost it completely.
Even Putin's dying father was astonished at his rise: 'My son is like a tsar!'[46]

He was the man from nowhere, but Putin thought his career could go
up in flames. Yeltsin had made his decision the day after Arab-led Islamist
fighters had crossed out of rebel Chechnya into Russian-controlled
Dagestan. The new prime minister was convinced that the country was on
the verge of an all-out Christian–Muslim conflagration, akin to that raging
in Yugoslavia. He claims that when the fighting broke out again in the
Caucasus he tried to calculate how many Russian refugees the United
States and Europe could absorb:

> My evaluation of the situation in August, when the bandits attacked
> Dagestan, was that if we did not stop it immediately, Russia as a state
> in its current form was finished. We were threatened by the
> Yugoslavization of Russia.[47]

In the last year of the Yeltsin regime, the Kremlin began preparing to rein-
vade Chechnya. In a state of paranoia, Russia was preparing for war. The
widespread belief that the first war in Chechnya was started to boost
Yeltsin's popularity fed rumours of extensive collusion between the 'family'
and the militant band that attacked Dagestan, led by Shamil Basayev.[48]
These include allegations, which some scholars claim to have verified, of a
meeting in a villa in the south of France 'agreeing' on the incursion, as the
pretext to help the self-styled emir to take Grozny as his own and to give
the 'family' the event it needed to install its heir.[49] When I met Anton
Surikov, the military intelligence agent alleged to have organized the
meeting, he told me: 'You have to realize that all Russian politicians today
are only bandits from St Petersburg.' A few months later he was dead. The
facts themselves are murky, but the conspiracy theory points to something
very real: not official collusion, but the complete collapse of trust in
Russian authorities.

The fighting that began in Dagestan and turned into the second
Chechen war became Putin's campaign, but it began as his inheritance.
Yeltsin took a shine to his steely support for the war plans. The public,
however, had not. In mid-September only 5 per cent said they planned to
vote for Putin in the 2000 presidential elections, less than wanted to vote
for 'against all'.[50]

The invasion only went ahead after Russians began dying in their beds.
The carnage turned Putin from a nobody into the most popular politician
in the country. Between 4 and 16 September 1999 the country was hit by
a series of bomb attacks that blew apart mostly suburban apartment blocks,
claiming the lives of 305 and injuring over 1,000 in Moscow and the
provincial cities of Volgodonsk and Buynaksk.

These mysterious bombings killed sleeping families in the city outskirts.
For a few unsteady weeks, normal folk patrolled their stairwells and courtyards in vigilante gangs against an enemy that was attacking the most
nondescript, suburban apartment blocks. Who was behind these blasts is
unclear. Another in provincial Ryazan was foiled by vigilant residents. They
had spotted men of 'Slavic appearance' acting suspiciously in their basement. They claim they were placing explosives under the apartment block
in sacks labelled 'sugar'. When the local police arrived they announced they
had defused a live bomb. Yet days later the head of the FSB Nikolai Patrushev
made a statement – rather oddly – that it had been a 'training exercise' to
test popular vigilance. The FSB claimed that they themselves had placed
the sacks of 'sugar' there. The local police and city FSB were shocked: they
believed they had found a live bomb. Had Patrushev, desperate for positive
coverage, said something stupid – or revealed something sinister?

These explosions were not a complete surprise. For weeks, the gutter press – hostile to the regime – had been filled with hysteria that 'state terror' was being planned.[51] There was an atmosphere of conspiracy and dread in the country. One Duma deputy even claimed he was warned from within the FSB that there was a plot.[52] Yeltsin's enemies such as General Alexander Lebed accused the 'family' of the bombings in order to: 'create mass terror, a destabilization which will permit them at the moment to say you don't have to go to the election precinct, otherwise you'll risk being blown away by the ballot boxes'.[53]

As many as 40 per cent of Russians polled have suspected the Kremlin.[54] They felt this way as, after the shelling of parliament in 1993 and the near cancelling of the 1996 elections, it was clear Yeltsin's cabal were ready to kill to stay in power. The mystery of the explosions, and the conspiracy theories surrounding them, are as important as who actually carried out the attack. They show either the complete state of disrepair, uncoordination and clownish unprofessionalism of the country's security services, or something far darker, their utter disregard for Russian blood. The widespread belief amongst Russian journalists that the FSB, Putin and the 'family' are responsible is telling. It shows how the Kremlin had by the decade's end become so intensely distrusted by its own people that it could conceivably have carried out mass murder to fix an election result. All of the possible scenarios – part of the establishment 'blackmailing' Yeltsin–Putin, the 'family' planting the bombs themselves as a false flag to win the vote, the authorities ignoring the warnings on purpose or agents 'faking' a prevention in order to restore their shredded reputation, or even the security services simply being outstandingly incapable – tell the same story: that of a broken-down state.

Hexogen is at the heart of this story: this is the explosive found in the basement in Ryazan. Researchers have claimed that it was only found in Russia at the time in tightly guarded FSB installations. But is this evidence that the FSB itself planted a 'false-flag' or that it could no longer secure its own stockpiles?[55]

The key people investigating the explosions have died in suspicious circumstances. These deaths have been gruesome. Several members of the investigative commission died in apparent assassinations, others in hit-and-run incidents, one from a tropical disease that caused his skin to peel off. Under any of the likely scenarios a 'cover-up' would have been carried out by the security services. They have as much need to avoid embarrassment as not being exposed in a conspiracy

These questions remain unanswered, but the consequences were clear. A new era had begun, blurred in the uncertainties between incompetence and amorality that defined it. The only beneficiary of the apartment bombings was the Kremlin's chosen successor. Russia reinvaded Chechnya;

Putin acted the part of a macho-saviour in front of the cameras and his popularity exploded. 'We will waste them in their outhouses,' he snarled at the perpetrators in salty criminal slang. As he said it, his popularity rating was soaring up to 79 per cent in December 1999 and the pro-Kremlin faction Unity which had been cobbled together to support him came second to the Communist Party in the race for parliament.[56]

In the 2000 presidential elections Putin was swept into the Kremlin atop a shaky wave of nationalist fear, the crescendo of the double disaster that made the new Russian state. The bombings seemed to change everything, even the language of politics itself. Now liberal TV anchors were the ones calling for the 'carpet bombing' of Chechnya and for the army to use 'napalm'.[57] This wave was the exact inverse of the tsunami of liberal euphoria that had crowned Yeltsin in 1991. Fear of terrorism was so intense in Russia – greater than the hysteria in the USA after 9/11 – that Putin took control of the government with ease.

His performance of calm fury throughout these atrocities meant that Putin now had an approval rating of almost 80 per cent and Yeltsin resigned early on 31 December 1999. Shuddering, he asked Russia to forgive him: 'For many of our dreams did not come to pass.' That night, Berezovsky had every reason to uncork imported champagne. He had found a man who was all things to all people: he was loyal but he was brave, he was KGB but a Yeltsin–Sobchak democrat, and he was essentially martial but economically liberal. He was grey – you could project your dreams onto him. But as it would turn out, this is exactly what Berezovsky himself was doing . . .

Putin was not a break from Yeltsin but the culmination of his choices and mistakes. But was there still an escape from entrenched authoritarianism? Had the man Russian democrats so feverishly supported doomed them to Putinism? One advisor in the current government's closest circle, who asked to remain anonymous, only sighs:

'Yes, I think there still was a chance to avoid a return to full authoritarianism. Putin inherited this half-built system. It was up to him, he would determine its shape – just imagine Putin had been a good man, not corrupt and not wanted to rule forever. There was still a way out. It all depended on who Putin really was.'

That was the question that nobody – not even Berezovsky – really knew the answer to. Not that they cared on the night of 31 December 1999 as he assumed his post as acting president. The inner circle were too busy creating a TV Putin. In the first telepopulist stunt, Putin was flown to a Russian front-line position in Chechnya to celebrate the millennium with the troops. All the way there, he drank champagne from the bottle. The spin doctors had been planning the shot carefully for weeks, working out how Putin would raise a plastic cup of vodka with the troops, to show that he was fearless, one of the people, but then suggest they not finish the vodka shot until the job was done – showing he was not Yeltsin, he was not a drunk and he would not tolerate failure. It went straight to the head of a vulnerable and scarred nation, desperate to be saved.

In the same way as the PR 'political technologists' attempt to cast Yeltsin's chosen heir as a 'break with the past' was the opposite of the truth, so the national mood could not have been further away from Putin's tele-populist posturing. Inside, Russians had far more in common with the characters of their pre-eminent, reclusive writer Victor Pelevin than with their new president. Pelevin is a writer in search of a metaphor. He is looking for the metaphor for Russia. In his early novels the USSR is a locked train speeding nowhere, or a rocket where cosmonauts must release each stage by hand, then burn up on re-entry with them, if it is to reach the moon at all and keep pace with the Americans, who have the luck of possessing automatic release buttons. In 1999, Pelevin's metaphor for the unstable, shape-shifting and beliefless country was *The Lives of Insects*. At the edge of a Russian forest, these fragile, parasitical little creatures, whose wings are easily torn, are trying to do a business deal with an American insect. The proud Soviet Russia that frightened the West had woken up as a wounded and pathetic fly.

CHAPTER TWO

THE VIDEOCRACY

As PUTIN'S rule was about to begin, on 29 December 1999 his team posted a manifesto outlining his goals for Russia. The dense essay announced to the people that Putinism was a project. 'Russia was and will remain a great power,' it asserted.[1] 'This is preconditioned by the inseparable characteristics of its geopolitical, economic and cultural existence. They have determined the mentality of the Russian people and the policy of the government throughout the history of Russia and they cannot but do so at present.'[2] But in the closing paragraph it raised the spectre of this identity, this Russia, being extinguished for good. 'Russia is in the middle of one of the most difficult periods in its history. For the first time in the past 200–300 years, it is facing a real threat of sliding to the second, possibly even the third, echelon of states. We are running out of time left to remove this threat.'[3]

Putin did not just inherit the Kremlin and the crisis. He inherited Yeltsin's people, the Yeltsin agenda and Yeltsin's war in Chechnya. Putin's first term, between 2000 and 2004, was not fully Putin's own – but was shaped by the Yeltsin legacy. Putin's challenge looked Sisyphean – but Yeltsin had actually left behind one immense advantage. It was Putin's luck to take over just as an economic boom took off. The year he began as prime minister growth hit 10 per cent thanks to a 75 per cent lower exchange rate following the default. Russian exports were competitive again and the state was no longer burdened by crippling debt. The country had rebounded from rock bottom. This legacy defined 'early Putinism'. From his appointment as prime minister to the beginning of 2003, Putin's politics were set on a road not entirely of his own choosing.

The man whom the Russian public associate with this period is Mikhail Kasyanov, a fallen political star. Dismissed from his post in 2004 and now pushed from the power elite, Putin's first prime minister has not let go of the manners of a minister. Or – as the framed antique map of the empire above his desk hints – ambitions to return as one. Today, the entrance to Kasyanov's office has an illuminated wall-size photo of him at an opposition march, standing behind a banner that heckles 'Russia without Putin!' His respectful, hushed staff give his office – or 'party headquarters', as they refer to it – the airs and graces of a government in exile. He likes to call himself an 'opposition leader' but I have not met one person who is 'led' by him.

Kasyanov had neither expected to rise so high – nor to be cast out so suddenly. Ten years before his appointment to high office he had been a Soviet central planner. Like so many others, he was convinced until the last moment that the USSR was as solid as the United States. Looking back, he says:

'I, like most citizens, believed the Soviet Union to be inviolable, that no one would ever be able to destroy it. As an exemplary bureaucrat already in a high position, I thought that the State Planning Commission and the body of Lenin would live forever and for all time. And then everything that was made collapsed in three days!'[4]

Kasyanov then did two things common for his generation of top bureaucrats. First he swapped one orthodoxy for another – axiomatic thinking about central planning was replaced with a textbook neoliberal outlook. He then tried to turn his position in the Soviet nomenklatura into the most politically (they said financially) profitable position in Yeltsin's new Russia. Unlike the vast majority – he succeeded. He was suave, with that certain charm needed in a courtier. The ailing leader took a shine to him. Yeltsin liked 'bright young things', people like Kasyanov in whom he saw the minimum of a 'Soviet mentality'.

This helped Kasyanov rise quickly to be deputy finance minister by 1995, and made him responsible for Russia's foreign debt and IMF loans. In the Yeltsin government – with debt to GDP ratio reaching 140 per cent in 1998 – there were few jobs that were more important. Kasyanov was the man holding the strings to Russia's IMF life support, which was keeping the state alive. 'The default was just killing news for me,' he says, 'I was shocked. I had been fighting it so hard. I was opposed to this decision to default.' Like all other junior members of the government, he claims he was not informed until the decision had been taken – 'by a tiny group of people, without any consultation'. But it was not bad news for his career. The same month that Yeltsin made Putin his prime minister, Kasyanov was promoted to be his last finance minister.

When Putin called Kasyanov a year later, asking if he would become his prime minister, he was the clear continuity candidate. In choosing Kasyanov, Putin's government signalled that a Yeltsin 'young reformer' would run it on a day-to-day basis. With almost fluent English and close to a decade of experience closely cooperating with the IMF, Kasyanov was a soothing choice for foreign creditors. He was, however, seen rather differently inside Russia. Kasyanov had two reputations in the Kremlin – one for competence, another for corruption.

Kasyanov had a nickname that stuck like glue – 'Misha 2 per cent'. He has never been able to shake off a reputation in Russia for kickbacks and taking a cut. The name goes back to the period when he was charged with negotiating Russia's IMF loans. There were repeated allegations that these loans were being transferred into politically favoured banks, slush funds or simply disappearing.[5] The money was urgently needed to pay wages – some months in arrears, leaving whole single-industry towns unpaid and in crisis – and to prevent vital public services from ceasing completely. He was the official who might have known how so much money could have disappeared. Though it has never been proved, corruption accusations touching Kasyanov surfaced daily in the press and were mentioned in a report for the US congress.[6] He fiercely denies them as 'black PR', but when Putin placed him in charge of an anticorruption body, Grigory Yavlinsky, the liberal leader of the anti-Chechen-war Yabloko Party, growled that it was like 'putting a vampire in charge of a blood bank'.[7]

This was the CV of Putin's choice. The two made a deal immediately on how to share power. As Kasyanov recalls the decisive phone call:

'He asked me if I wanted to be his prime minister. I said "yes" – and laid out the following conditions. I enumerated a list of economic reforms that I felt were absolutely necessary for the development of the country. Putin answered: "I accept. Just stay out of my side." So, we orally divided power like this. I would manage the implementation of economic reforms and state finances and he would concentrate on Chechnya, security, foreign policy and managing certain domestic groups.'

Kasyanov also asked for Putin not to repeat Yeltsin's habit of dismissing the government without any explanation to the public. He agreed.

Putin needed a competent hand to manage the bulk of the government's economic affairs. Not only was he untrained in them but, for his first few months in office, the new president had no choice but to prioritize Chechnya. Defeat in war would have turned him immediately into a lame duck. Military planning and then invasion of the rebel region itself was the immediate business of his office. The first six months of Putin's presidency was one of all-out war in the North Caucasus. He viewed its success as his making or breaking. 'At first Putin was concentrating overwhelmingly on Chechnya,' says Kasyanov, who claims this left him and the ministers room to draw up a reform agenda.

The early Putin was a war president. His main focus was the tank columns and ground forces he dispatched to Grozny. This has had a huge effect on his world-view. Putin was as shaped by the apartment bombings and the Chechen war as George W. Bush was by 9/11 and his wars in Iraq and Afghanistan. Nothing mattered more to Putin in his first year in power. 'My mission,' he declared, 'my historic mission – it may sound lofty, but it's true – is to resolve the situation in the Northern Caucasus.'[8]

Putin fought this war in an apocalyptic state. His conviction that without him Russia stands on the verge of Yugoslav-style wars has not dissipated. During his first months in office, the Russian Army laid siege to Grozny. The result was described by the United Nations as 'the most destroyed city on earth'.[9] At every stage Putin was constantly receiving updates from the front. The war hung over his mind and government. His economic advisor Andrei Illiaronov remembers that when Putin received the news that one of the last Chechen strongholds had fallen during a routine meeting, he burst out, 'Well, we have rolled over Shatoy.'[10]

Kasyanov looks back: 'You must understand that I really believed, we really hoped that Putin could stop people dying from terrorist attacks on the streets when he assumed power after the apartment bombings. This is why we tolerated measures that in retrospect were too much and too harsh.' As a result, their initial politics were sold to the country as something akin to a 'state of emergency'. Yet tolerance for 'temporary measures' to stabilize the state, which then became permanent features, is a common way in which authoritarian regimes come about.

War put the first clamps on the media. These new rules were applied first to Russian war correspondents. Their graphic, brave but sensationalist reporting had swung the public against the first Chechen war. Putin would not let it happen again. Reporters and editors were first told, then pressured, to be 'patriotic'. Then they were warned. In the liberal newspaper *Kommersant* a Kremlin spokesman made it clear, 'When the nation mobilizes its forces to achieve some task, that imposes obligations on everyone, including the media.'[11]

It wasn't long before an example was made of someone: the passionate and pro-Chechen reporter Andrei Babitsky. He had enraged the authorities with comments excusing rebel atrocities. Born in Moscow and a Russian citizen, Babitsky was apprehended by Russian forces while trying to report from the siege of Grozny. He was detained, then swapped with Chechen rebels for captured troops as if an enemy combatant. The new president shrugged, 'So you say that he is a Russian citizen. Then he should have acted in accordance with the laws of your country, if you want to be protected by those laws.'[12]

According to Putin, this war was not just about Chechnya – but about Russia, about ending an epoch: 'What's the situation in Northern Caucasus and in Chechnya today? It's a continuation of the collapse of the USSR.'[13]

This time the army was not bogged down and defeated. Russian forces recaptured Grozny by February 2000 and direct rule from Moscow was re-established by May. The last towns and villages held by Chechen insurgents were brought under Russian control by the following winter. Chechen fighters retreated to the mountains to begin a long guerrilla war – but by the time a rigged 'referendum' in 2003 installed Akhmad Kadyrov as Moscow's Chechen in Grozny, it looked like Putin had succeeded where Yeltsin had failed. He had stopped Russia falling apart.

The Putin Consensus

In their first few months in office Putin and Kasyanov were waging a two-front war for legitimacy: one a battle for Chechnya and the other a struggle to push through economic reforms that had stalled in the late 1990s. Their work was Putin's first 'tandem' and their quick victories on these two fronts secured the new regime's legitimacy amongst the elite. Putin was no longer seen as a 'man from nowhere' but as a man with achievements. Kasyanov recalls:

'The consensus was based on two things: order and reforms. We felt that Putin was the man strong enough, that he was the solution that could bring order to the country. The other element was reform – to implement reforms that had been blocked. Putin really did capture hopes then – hope for order and hope for reform.'

Kasyanov himself was troubled by Putin, but not troubled enough to quit. In conversation he is coy about why he remained in government, but admits he was unnerved by the moves against the media. He says, 'at times I could have done more'. Perhaps he did not heed the signs. Kasyanov says he first felt real unease at a 1999 banquet hosted in the FSB headquarters, the notorious Lubyanka. Putin proposed a toast with 'great enthusiasm', before solemnly declaring: 'Dear Comrades, I would like to announce to you that the group of FSB agents that you sent to work undercover in the government has accomplished the first part of its mission.'[14]

The hall exploded in cheers. Kasyanov recalls, 'There, at the banquet, I took it as a not too successful joke in a traditional style for the audience. But, later that day, the thought flashed through my mind: 'But what if in the words of the President, perhaps, lay a deeper meaning?'[15]

That Kasyanov should not have resigned or challenged this authoritarian drift is unsurprising. He felt he had been given the power he asked for. Kasyanov says Putin stuck to their 2000 deal – with Putin taking high politics, security and foreign policy, and Kasyanov focusing on reform until the second half of 2003. 'He did not interfere in 90 per cent of what I was working on. The 10 per cent he did interfere in was the gas sector.

He repeatedly told me not to initiate any reforms in the gas sector and anything related to Gazprom. This was his key intrusion.' Traumatized by the default, Kasyanov felt that economically, the situation was as fraught as in the Caucasus:

'The treasury was empty, the price of oil almost reached $20 per barrel. There was still a high level of private capital outflows. Many experts also believed [that] in the absence of access to external sources of funding we would require a new devaluation of the Ruble. All of these problems needed to be urgently addressed. And most importantly – it was obvious that the socio-economic mechanism of Russia was hopelessly out-dated and needed a major upgrade.'[16]

Putin asked Kasyanov to push the reform agenda in close cooperation with Alexander Voloshin, his chief of staff who had held the same job under Yeltsin, and appointed his St Petersburg associate German Gref as Minister of Economic Development to head an expert group on reforms. Gref, as the head of the Centre for Strategic Development, a think-tank specially created in the run-up to the 2000 election, had drafted a 200-page report as the basis for the policy agenda. It was an ambitious, if in places vague roadmap. Together with the economist Alexey Kudrin, with whom Putin had shared an office in Sobchak's town hall, these men formed the kernel of the reformist group in government. 'We must pay tribute to Putin,' Kasyanov said: 'I could contact him at any time. If I had something to clarify or inform the President about, I never had a problem; we could discuss everything in person or by telephone.'

After Yeltsin's hangovers and disappearances, Putin's work ethic over-joyed the bureaucracy. Beyond it both the government's policy vectors appealed to different parts of society – the campaign for order in the Caucasus calmed a frightened country. Putin's 'tough measures' won respect with working families craving an end to 'chaos', whilst his reforms appealed to big business and the tiny middle class. Those Russians who had started businesses – big or small, from shopkeepers to oligarchs – were struggling in a half-reformed business environment. The changes that Putin's govern-ment brought in were far-reaching and some immediately beneficial.

Putin's first term saw an impressive roll call of results. 'What we really wanted to do was to implement the policies we had not been able to imple-ment under Yeltsin,' explains Kasyanov. They mostly succeeded. In 2001 the maximum social security tax was cut from 35 per cent to 26 per cent. In 2002, the corporate profits tax was cut from 35 per cent to 24 per cent. The government was especially pleased that it had scrapped the 35 per cent top-rate progressive incomes tax for a flat tax of 13 per cent. Calculated at a rate that Russians would actually pay, it increased revenues and stimu-lated the economy. The long-stalled Land Privatization Bill was finally put on statute. In 2004, a stabilization fund was created and VAT was shaved from 20 per cent to 18 per cent. All the while, business-friendly legal changes were ushered in. After decades of imports, improvements in agriculture even saw the country become a net exporter of grain.

This won Putin the establishment's confidence – as a man who got things done. This dovetailed with the positive economic legacy of the default. The devalued ruble made exports both cheaper and more competitive. There was finally recovery and growth: now the worst was over. The government was no longer forced to spend up to one-quarter of its budget servicing its debt. 'Most people now believe that the default had a positive impact,' admits Kasyanov. The clearest indicator of a return to solvency was that Russia started to run balanced budgets. A return to confidence could be measured in high GDP growth, which was sustained at over 7 per cent a year until 2008.

Consequently, the inflation rate declined and the rate of foreign and domestic investment rose. Overall this enabled the government to return to financing regular public services – wages, pensions and funding from the state was now on time. Salaries no longer went unpaid for months at a time. This was the single most important factor undergirding Putin's legitimacy.

Yet alongside liberal economics came the muzzling of TV. Kasyanov claims that he did not see what was coming. Sitting with him I wondered how great his share of historical blame actually was. No fool, he was prime minister from 2000 to 2004 – as the decrees creating an authoritarian state were issued. He did little to stop this progression as he prioritized order and reform, power and growth, over the rights of Russians. No, I thought, it would be wrong to signal out Kasyanov. His mistakes and misconceptions were those of the elite as a whole. At the time, both rich and poor saw Putin as behind them. A fragile consensus had been established. It was unclear where it might lead.

Robbery and Videocracy

TV had undone Putin's predecessors. Every night the Soviet evening news had framed Brezhnev in senile degeneration. It had built up Gorbachev as a charismatic saviour only to expose him as a confused failure when he couldn't compete with a rambunctious, then sober Yeltsin. It destroyed the reputation of this 'great democrat' with a hundreds clips of his slurring and shaking, demeaning peasant alcoholism. The power of TV turned Yeltsin into nothing better than the drunken Brezhnev of a failed democracy. This is why within weeks of his inauguration Putin began to build a 'videocracy' – his autocracy over the airwaves to the masses that mattered.

The oligarchs who controlled TV knew how powerful they were – powerful enough to extort the state. Especially Vladimir Gusinsky, a failed theatre director and the emotional owner of NTV, a channel that had more than 100 million viewers and reached nearly every corner of Russia. It could make or break election campaigns. Its 'pundits' and 'commentators' were screeching guard dogs for their master's interests, hounding politicians into concessions. They were not impartial journalists; Gusinsky thought he could do the same to Putin, shouting to his inner circle, 'I'll destroy him.'[17] In October 1999 he arrived at the terse new prime minister's office for lunch. He was angry that the government had just handed over $100 million to Berezovsky's TV channel, ORT, in order to tide it through an advertising slump. Gusinsky thought he was powerful enough to deserve the same. According to the Kremlin and his own associates, he said at lunch:

'I understand you have very little chance of becoming president, but if we work with you and you do what we say, we'll try to make you win. And we need $100 million in credit.'[18]

Gusinsky denies this version of events, but has admitted he asked for 'funding' at the same level as ORT from Putin at a subsequent meeting.[19] He may have asked for what looked like a bribe to support the out-of-focus successor, because this is how he had done business with Yeltsin. That tawdry Kremlin had been so desperate to get the 'media oligarchs' on side to win the 1996 elections that it had effectively subsidized their empires. The sums were enormous for a bankrupt country. Gusinsky alone had been given more than $1.5 billion in state support over the years.[20] In the months before the 1996 election, Gazprom had started buying shares in his Media-Most company. This was the beginning of the state company making a series of economically senseless loans to Gusinsky worth over $1 billion. It ended up owning 30 per cent of Media-Most. To prop up the regime, the state-controlled gas giant seemed to be investing in everything apart from its own pipelines and reserves. It was being used like a giant government slush fund and not a natural resource company. It was feeding the oligarchs when it should have been saving the collapsing mining cities of the north.

When Putin first sat in Yeltsin's chair, the Kremlin lived in fear of the two great 'media oligarchs': Vladimir Gusinsky of NTV and Boris Berezovsky of ORT. Both thought Putin was a provincial bureaucrat who they could push about. They were archetypal oligarchs – both brilliant, both Jewish, both excluded from the 'Slavs only' club of the inner sanctums of the KGB, the finest Soviet research institutes and the upper echelons of the party itself. Whilst Putin was preparing for his dream job as foreign intelligence officer, they were festering in dead ends in the run-up to perestroika. Gusinsky was an illegal 'gypsy cab' driver; Berezovsky was a frustrated mathematician without his own car.

Then the tables turned. Both had sussed the financial promise of post-communism whilst Putin was still shell-shocked, watching the unravelling of Soviet power in Dresden. By the time Yeltsin was considering Putin as his successor, the old Soviet power dynamics were topsy-turvy. These formerly fringe men now had TV channels with the ability to make or break government policy by whipping up their millions of viewers to such an extent that they thought they could pitch up in government offices and ask for $100 million. Putin feared these stations. They had such huge audiences they could have undermined a fragile regime if he botched his relationship with them.

After conniving to install Putin, Berezovsky felt strong enough to publicly boast that he was the manipulator of Moscow. 'It is acceptable,' he claimed, 'indeed necessary to interfere directly in the political process to defend democracy.'[21] Yet in the weeks after his inauguration, the new president made a comment flatly contradicting him. It confused and unnerved Moscow. 'These people who fuse, or who help a fusion of power and capital, there will be no oligarchs or the like as a class.'[22] It sounded eerily Stalinist. It was a promise to 'liquidate the oligarchs as a class'.[23] This surprised the shabby city, where the tycoons still had the wardrobes of bandits – which had expected Yeltsin's heir to be the protector of Berezovsky and the oligarchy against those they painted as unreconstructed communists or ex-KGB revanchists. Berezovsky had admired Putin for being 'brave'. He had not understood that he was also ruthless.

Off the airwaves, Putin behaved rather differently. He was conscious of the limits of his power over the oligarchs. They had funded his campaign. They hoped to influence him as they had Yeltsin. Yet the public saw them as little better than thieves. Inside the security establishment that had reared the new president, it was considered criminal, even absurd, that a bunch of businessmen could have been handed over control of the country's natural resources for next to nothing. Whatever Putin's personal feelings towards the oligarchs, he offered them a compromise in July 2000. Gathering the country's twenty-one leading tycoons in the Kremlin he made a simple deal – they could keep their businesses, if they stayed out of politics. Two men were not invited – Berezovsky and Gusinsky.

What was happening to the uninvited oligarchs was an example of how expensive it would be to refuse Putin's offer. He had already gone after Gusinsky. He despised him. Gusinsky had refused to support Putin in the elections and his channel had dedicated only 5 per cent of its coverage to the pro-Kremlin party Unity, almost all of it negative, in the 1999 vote for the Duma.[24] To make matters worse, Gusinsky had shown a documentary two nights before the presidential elections hinting at FSB involvement in the apartment bombings.[25] And he had asked for more money.

Putin wanted to illustrate in the plainest financial terms that the era of an extorted government subsidizing oligarchs was over. So, he asked for Gusinsky's company to pay back the 1996 loan from Gazprom. It was nothing less than asking him to return Yeltsin's bribe. The tycoon at first didn't understand what was happening. He was arrested, thrown into the overcrowded and flea-ridden Butyrka jail and under duress made to sign over stakes in NTV to Gazprom. It was the beginning of a legal assault to grab the channel through its debts to the state. In June 2000, less than five weeks after Putin's inauguration, Gusinsky fled the country – and the twenty-one businessmen invited to meet Putin the following month to hear the terms of 'his deal' took note.

It appeared everyone had understood – apart from Berezovsky – that they had made a mistake. Putin was the protector of no class. But Berezovsky was busy coming up with more fantastic ideas. He mused that Russia should be converted into a confederation of independent states.[26] He was beginning to fight with Putin, criticizing his policies and preparing to throw ORT into battle against him. This is how Berezovsky had always operated under Yeltsin, supporting him only then to swivel and undermine him. The former president even once lamented that he wished he could send Berezovsky on a business trip abroad – 'forever'.[27] Yet Berezovsky underestimated Putin.

The end came for Berezovsky when his TV station wounded Putin. It happened when it exposed the new leader as a bad communicator. Just months after Putin's inauguration he made his first gaffe, in August 2000. It could have proved fatal. The *Kursk* – the pride of the Russian fleet, one of the nation's most modern submarines, which only a year before had been tracking the US Sixth Fleet during the bombing of Kosovo – suffered a crippling explosion and sunk to the bottom of the Barents Sea. The sailors called for help; they were asphyxiated when none came. That nothing could be done stunned the country – the submarine had been on a training exercise. The event saw the public seized with mass grief, not unlike the response in Britain to the car crash that killed Princess Diana. But at the time of the sinking Putin was on holiday; he did not return for five days. It was as if Tony Blair had refused to return to London for almost a week after Diana had died.

Berezovsky's ORT began rolling out negative coverage. In a panic, the key PR hands in the Kremlin convinced Putin to act. He flew to the scene but, without a crowd of carefully preselected people, he completely mishandled the genuine grieving families. Dressed in black for mourning, but coming across as a shifty mobster in a polo neck, he showed his stress and found difficulties in communicating. At times he seemed wide-eyed. He offered only the most pitiful of excuses:

'There have always been tragedies at sea, including in the time we thought we were living in a very successful country. There have always been tragedies. I just never thought that things were in this kind of condition.'[28]

ORT's cameras caught all of this. The channel blamed him for the deaths of the 118 sailors, accusing him of preferring to let them die rather than accept the foreign help that had been offered. It was media disaster for Putin and a demonstration of the power of Berezovsky's ORT. But his protégé was determined that a TV station would never hurt him again. After this humiliation, Putin chose to confront his former patron, venomously saying in October 2000, 'If necessary we will destroy these instruments of blackmail.' This is exactly what he did in the months that followed. At that moment Leonid Parfyonov, one of the most famous journalists in the country and the face of Russian television, realized that every TV screen in the country was about to be turned into a Kremlin megaphone, recalling:

> It was between the Kursk and the NTV affair that the realization dawned on me that we were moving into an authoritarian regime based on control of TV. These events showed that you could say power was bad or dysfunctional. But now you could no longer say power could make a mistake.

The last time Berezovsky met Putin it was in the offices of his chief of staff, Alexander Voloshin. Putin accused him of putting up prostitutes in front of the cameras as the wives and girlfriends of the sailors. He then told Berezovsky: 'I want to control ORT. I will manage it.'

The oligarch recalled that once Putin left the room he turned to the bearded and bald Voloshin and said, 'I think we have made a mistake . . . We have let the black colonels in.' Berezovsky claimed that Voloshin blew off his comparison of ex-KGB colonel Putin to the South American and Greek 'colonel' regimes that had seized power during the Cold War. Yet it was men like Voloshin who had once craved 'a Russian Pinochet'.

Regardless of the right historical analogy, Putin had no intention of being exposed. Picking them off, one after the other, he managed to force both Gusinsky and Berezovsky into exile. The key to his success was how utterly unexpected his power grab was. No one had prepared for it. That day in the Kremlin, the last thing Putin said to Berezovsky was this: 'You were one of those that asked me to become President. So how can you complain?'

No one had expected anything like this from the lieutenant colonel. The next episode in the hostile takeover of the media was the end of the NTV affair. In September 2000 Gazprom sued Media-Most for the non-repayment of its 1996 'bribe'. By April 2001, after lengthy legal manoeu-vring, the exiled Gusinsky's TV channel was finally brought under full Gazprom control by means of its outstanding debts. Its home in the Ostankino TV tower, a Moscow icon taller than New York's Empire State Building, was entered by force. The new 'editorial' team then ousted all its popular government critics.

The ease with which Putin seized the main television stations reflected the weakness of society, of journalism and the oligarchs. The 1990s had produced few strong non-governmental organizations (NGOs) or civic movements, as the economic depression had ravaged the civil society that had sprung up during the perestroika years. Moscow's journalists were far from a community, but a fragmented, inexperienced demi-monde full of hired columnists, hysterical TV hosts and paid-for agitators. Oligarchs such as Berezovsky were themselves despised by the public, to the extent that even when they started telling the truth about creeping authoritari-anism they were doubted. There was little for resistance to form around.

In November 2000 Berezovsky had fled first to France, then to Britain. It was there that he received the news that the man that he had done so much to help was issuing an international arrest warrant against him. 'I felt when I first heard the news – how small is Putin to behave like this? I thought he was above using the instruments of pressure and oppression. I thought he was not so weak. I thought he could use the power of persuasion, of explanation, not those of oppression.' Nevertheless, in what Berezovsky did not say, and in the regret of what he did, I could tell that he felt he had been a fool. Months before his death, he left an emotional post on Facebook: 'I repent and ask forgiveness for what led to the power of Vladimir Putin.'

The man who Berezovsky had thought was the 'family' bodyguard had robbed him. He had been destroyed as a Russian politician. Putin had asserted his independence in the boldest way. He had devoured his patron. Criminal investigations were opened against Berezovsky who, under pres-sure, sold his share of ORT to Roman Abramovich, who promptly handed it over to the state. By taking over ORT and NTV Putin had achieved exactly what he wanted – he had become Berezovsky. It was the beginning of a massive redistribution of assets. By 2008, some 90 per cent of all Russian media was directly or indirectly under Putin's control.[29]

Putin called this asset grab the 'war on the oligarchs'. With the creation of two oligarch-exiles all federal TV stations were easily brought under Kremlin supervision. News coverage or satire that could undermine the regime would disappear from the screens. But it was something more than pulling puppet shows that lampooned Putin – it installed a modernized form of authoritarianism in Russia.

Putin had created a 'videocracy'. This is an ascendancy where hegemony over national broadcasting underwrites political dominance, a style of power that eschews relying on mass parties or arresting men for telling anti-regime jokes or distributing leaflets. This was not unique to Russia, but in step with the changes new technology had brought to power in Europe as a whole. In Italy, Silvio Berlusconi dominated Rome as he controlled the country's most powerful media holding, whilst in London Tony Blair governed as much through spin as through a grip on the House of Commons. Like Blair and Berlusconi, Putin realized that power now sprung from an ability to dominate 24-hour news. The difference was that in this regime TV editors would get calls from 'up top' setting the agenda; the secret services would call reporters to tell them they had gone too far, and journalists were frequently murdered.

In the early 2000s the new men in the Kremlin had every reason to feel pleased with themselves. To their satisfaction, the public appeared to agree, with 50 per cent of those polled believing that the TV channels belonging to the exiled oligarchs were attacking Putin, due to their owners' financial interests.[30] Without much fuss or the need for any of the clumsy censorship of the Soviet Union, they had their message coming out of the airwaves. Their position looked sophisticated, almost unassailable. In March 2000, as many as 83 per cent of Russians had learnt about the election campaign through TV compared to just 19 per cent in the national press.[31] With less than 2 per cent of the country having either access to satellite TV or the Internet the Kremlin seemed to have done the impossible: it had provided censorship for the masses and media freedom for the intelligentsia. This meant it never needed to lock up many people.[32] Putin has never imprisoned as many journalists as his contemporary Tayyip Erdogan in Turkey. Technology, however, never stands still.

The Cult of Personality

The Kremlin seized the airwaves by creating a TV tsar, through telepopulism. Putin was not 'born' but 'made'. As the doyen of Russian journalism, Leonid Parfyonov puts it:

> Putin is really a collective product of the key spin doctor Gleb Pavlovsky, the deputy Kremlin chief of staff Vladislav Surkov, the press team, editors of national TV, which insulate him from the

world – the defining image of which is Putin under HD cameras directing a minister to get into action – it's a complete creation.

It was not always so slick. In some of his earliest television appearances with Yeltsin, Putin seemed nauseous and mousey. It was his lack of charisma, his 'greyness' that meant the PR 'political technologists' had to go into overdrive to create an action figure image out of him. After some initial fluffs, it was wildly successful. Parfyonov thinks the hidden ingredient was Putin's endlessly changing costumes:

> The success of Putin was that he never repeated the mistake of Brezhnev who was there ageing on TV, the same static image capturing the decay of the state. He understood that he had to be multiple Putins – Putin diving into the sea to rescue amphorae, Putin driving a yellow car through Siberia, Putin racing a sports car. It was about not being Brezhnev, not being Yeltsin. Not having the image stuck.

The infamous Kremlin spin doctor Gleb Pavlovsky himself recalled: 'Putin, of course spoiled us. Rather, we used Putin to spoil ourselves. The Presidency was so quickly filled with the gas of absolute charisma that the answer to any question quickly became – like Putin.'[33] What Pavlovsky means by *spoiled*, is the increasingly extravagant acts of media-blitz that he invented, infecting almost all aspects of Russian TV. Moments that gradually made Putin seem almost absurd, just like this: Putin saunters onstage. His smile is insincere. Wearing a blue zip-up jumper over a beige turtleneck, Pavlovsky's agents have made it look like he has come straight from the gym. The tune from MC Hammer's 'U Can't Touch This' announces him; a crowd of teenagers clap and scream as he makes his entrance on the country's most popular hip-hop show, *The Battle for Respect*. Standing in front of a giant screen, Putin extols the martial values of rap. For viewers across Russia's nine time zones, the sight is as striking as seeing Margaret Thatcher on *Top of the Pops*. There are cries of 'Respect, Vladimir Vladimirovich, Respect!' The shaven-headed winner of the rap challenge bellows: 'This man is a legend . . . he is our icon . . . let's make some noise so everyone can hear!'[34] And the viewers at home, mostly young people in factory towns far from Moscow, are left feeling that Putin is 'with it'.

Telepopulism was deployed in a relentless, never-ending PR campaign throughout the country's state-controlled television channels, spinning the 'national leader' into various guises designed to appeal to different groups across Russia's fractured society. Putin appeared on television as the defender of the thrifty housewife: bursting into a supermarket to inspect the prices, then humiliating the chain's owner over the price of sausages and demanding they be sold for less. For the unemployed, he was cast as the worker's friend: helicoptering into town to demand an oligarch reopens a factory. For those nostalgic for the USSR, there were photo-shoots of Putin's holidays: dressed in camouflage and prowling the hinter-land, he was the picture of Russia's strength. Rural Russians were encouraged to identify with Putin swimming bare-chested in a river. Military men could connect with images of the leader dressed up as a fighter pilot or a sailor. Selections of calendars devoted to Putin's judo skills were made widely available, whilst those who might have been tempted by extremism were offered the sight of Putin shooting a Siberian tiger with a sedative dart. Characteristically, after one Moscow metro bombing, Putin sought to shore up his image by tagging a polar bear.

But why was Putin's posturing such a hit? The truth was that his popu-larity in the 2000s was both manipulated but also – it must not be forgotten – genuine. Yes, the state influenced all major television news outlets. Critical journalists were hounded by pro-Putin youth groups and occa-sionally murdered. Opposition activists were repressed and elections rigged, but in the 2000s Putin genuinely enjoyed the respect of ordinary Russians. They admired his command of the language. Yeltsin was a bumbling alcoholic, Gorbachev spoke with a peasant drawl, Brezhnev with a senile lisp, Khrushchev like a hick – and Stalin had such a heavy Georgian accent that he was frightened to address the nation.[35]

Telepopulism worked because Putin reflected a wounded Russia just as it would like to see itself: athletic, healthy and proud – the antithesis of a nation plagued by a demographic crisis, heroin addiction and social rot. It was a Russian version of the Berlusconi popularity trick, which drew force on 'Il Cavaliere' being the Italian that many of his compatriots wished they were. In Britain, this is why Boris Johnson, the bumptious mayor of London, is the nation's favourite politician – he is the TV sensation everyone wishes was their friend. Crowning this were Putin's live mara-thon annual 'phone-ins'. Building on the legacy of Russians writing letters to the tsars, or to Stalin, this show implicitly projected Putin as listening to each and every Russian, if only they got their question in on time. Pavlovsky gushed that in the media world Putin created, 'TV news smelled of incense, holy oil poured on the work of the government and its leader.'[36]

After the 'wild 1990s' Russia wanted to believe in heroes. This was one of the reasons why Putin's popularity astounded opinion pollsters, staying above 60 per cent for twelve years. This was the kind of majority that his contemporaries such as Blair, Berlusconi or Bush could only dream of. Even the golden youth at the elite MGIMO University in Moscow told me that they had found Putin's appearance on the rap show a little cringeworthy, but far from risible. When I smirked that Putin 'the Kremlin action hero' was ridiculous, one A-grade student snapped back, 'Men here can expect to live to the age of fifty-nine on average – below the life expectancy of Pakistanis! The president has to promote health and exercise at any cost. And if that means bare-chested calendars, swimming shoots, judo or being on a rap show – so be it.'

The other side of his popularity was that Putin has always been what the opposition calls 'the great promiser'. In a manner at times reminiscent of Soviet propaganda that offered up a 'radiant future', Putin said his mission was nothing less than 'an effective state capable of guaranteeing the rules of the game translated into rules for everyone'. In his three 'state of the nation' addresses in 2003, 2007 and 2012, closing down each four-year political cycle, Putin made almost verbatim promises: these included a pledge to double GDP, transform the military, strengthen civil society, build an efficient state, battle corruption and construct a country where democracy, competition with fully protected property and human rights would all flourish. He promised everything that Russians could have wanted and more. This is what his party called for in 2003:

> Russia must become an equal member of the international community. This entails a minimal acceptable standard of living for the entire population of Russia, which should be, on average, as it is in the countries of the EU. We are talking not just about European wage levels, but also to have on the same level as the EU provisions for housing, healthcare and social protection.[37]

For those waiting for payday in Siberian auto-cities or Arctic mining colonies, this constant barrage of propaganda and promise calmed them, and coaxed them for ten years into playing the part of Putin's people. The Kremlin did not realize it at the time but this overreliance on the leader's personality was leaving the regime extremely vulnerable to the 'Putin trick' no longer working. Strutting around as the 'alpha male', he sold himself as nothing short of a superhero. It was only a matter of time before the image would boomerang. But, of course, those in the Kremlin at the time never saw him that way. 'No, no, the alpha male – it's all a load of crap,' admitted Pavlovsky, 'It was important against Yeltsin. He was weak, sick and old, but *he* was – young, a sportsman and so on.'[38]

The Putin Majority

Though as a child Putin had dreamed of being something like the Soviet James Bond, this propaganda was not only about vanity – but sociology.

His Kremlin was using telepopulism to turn Russia into the 'Putin majority'. They looked over their shoulders, many of them simply onto their previous jobs, and saw Yeltsin. They believed he had been deserted by the masses and been manipulated by the oligarchs, the IMF and the West. Russia, like the Soviet Union, had to have 'an absolute majority'.

Telepopulism was to serve it up perfectly cooked, as Pavlovsky remembers. Jewish from Odessa, he had been a dissident but cracked under interrogation and grassed up others to the KGB, before being exiled for three years in the Arctic land of Komi, where he wrote frenzied letters to the authorities, but which were read only by the local alcoholic police detective. Having lost his faith in democracy, he was certain Putin had to become the president of the wounded:

> What made it possible for us to create such a long-fixed Putin majority? The victorious majority of the 2000s was built on vengeful losers – state employees, pensioners, workers, and the unanimously cursed and universally despised bureaucratic power structures. And most importantly, the democrats had neglected women – who became the most faithful part of the Putin coalition. The losers of the 1990s would become winners; the zeroes and the socially worthless would ascend the pillars of statehood. This is how the Putin majority merged yesterday's outcasts and losers. The memory of nothingness made their teeth grab onto the new status quo. We called this stitch-up stability.[39]

To secure the 'Putin majority', they deployed all the techniques of subterfuge and monopoly that officials liked to call 'managed democracy'. What this meant, to quote the regime ideologist Sergey Markov, is a system where: 'all problems that can be solved through democratic means, are solved through democratic means, but those that cannot are solved by other means'.[40] In practice, this meant campaigning like in a democracy, but with all the fraud of an authoritarian regime.

First they had to make Putin sound like his voters – the only social class really present in Russia in the early 2000s, a formless lower middle class – earning a living from payday to payday, dipping in and out of poverty. The tone, gesture and vernacular that made Putin seem as down to earth as possible was systematically prioritized. Putin even occasionally slips into the slang language known as 'fenya' – thieves' slang. This resonated in a brutalized Russian society. According to research by Vladimir Radchenko, the former deputy chairman of the Supreme Court, between 1992 and 2007 over 15 million Russians received a criminal record – over 30 per cent of all adult males – and, in a country of only 142 million citizens, over

5 million have spent at least some time in custody or the prison system, leaving Russia with the second largest prisoner population per capita in the world.[41]

Watching Putin in the moment that clinched his popularity, threatening to chase Chechen insurgents and 'waste them in their outhouses', sends a chill down the spines of those who have read the *Gulag Archipelago*. There, Solzhenitsyn had warned that the day Gulag slang was heard in Moscow State University would be the day the camps had infected all Russia. Putin's coarse bar-humour would unsettle Moscow's diplomatic corps. He once remarked when informed that the former Israeli president, Moshe Katsav, was facing trial for sexual assault: 'He raped ten women. We never knew he had it in him. We all envy him.'[42]

Being a real man of the people, even an orator, was essential but not enough. Yeltsin was always, even in his trembling later years, more of a 'muzhik' – a peasant, 'son of the earth', than his successor – and at his best was always more charismatic than Putin has ever been. So how did the poles of Putin's big tent hold together for over a decade?

It was not only posturing. Yeltsin had told Russians what he wanted them to hear – that the Soviet Union had been a catastrophe and the lives they had led under it had been a deceit. Putin reversed this. He started telling Russians what the majority of normal people desperately wanted, even needed him to say.[43] They had not lived decades of their lives in vain. The sacrifices and cults of the Soviet dream had been cruel, hopelessly flawed, but it had not all been a stupid mistake that could now be mocked. Soviet heroes and Soviet triumphs were still glorious even if the Union was gone. This is why Putin said, 'Those who do not regret the fall of the USSR have no heart. Those who want to restore it have no brain.'[44]

The Kremlin was also at last providing them with the payslips they needed most. The Putin majority were simply grateful that their wages and state benefits were paid on time due to the economic upswing and stabilization of government finances. This was something that radically improved the lives of Russians – in a country where over 53 per cent are 'budgetniki', or reliant on state salaries, pensions or benefits.[45] Within two to three years of Putin taking office, protests against withheld salaries and benefits had dried up. The most critical 'stability' Russians needed was provided for. The impact this had for normal people cannot be overestimated – the last time state paychecks and benefits had been stable and secure was in the first few years of Gorbachev.

TV never let them forget it. 'Generous Putin' was a propaganda staple. Campaigning for the Putin majority saw the regime consistently resort to high-PR spending campaigns. Here the regime defined itself against the perceived 'heartlessness' of Yeltsin. These included consistent efforts to redirect taxes from the energy sector into increased spending. These policies were sold to normal Russians as defending lower-middle-class interests. Starting in the early 2000s there were consistent salary raises for bureaucrats and state employees, pension increases, and rising investment in healthcare and education.

As the videocracy took shape, the teams around the deputy chief of staff, Vladislav Surkov, and the spin doctor Pavlovsky created Putin as a symbol very different from Vladimir Vladimirovich, the grey man from St Petersburg. The idealization of the leader as the nation's father, friend, fighter and pride echoed disturbingly with the past. The opposition screamed that Russia was returning to a Stalinist leader cult. But they were creating an embodiment of the state, as much as glorifying a man, for exactly the same reasons as the 1930s developers of 'agitprop'. By glorifying the state as a leader they covered up its shortcomings. There were also unnerving echoes to the cult of personality in the 1930s. As the historian Simon Sebag-Montefiore recounts:

> His adopted son Artyom Sergeev remembers Stalin shouting at his son Vasily for exploiting his father's name. 'But I'm Stalin too', said Vasily. 'No, you're not', said Stalin. 'You're not Stalin and I'm not Stalin. Stalin is Soviet power. Stalin is what he is in the newspapers and the portraits, not you, not even me.'[46]

Looking back at what Pavlovsky and Surkov had done, Boris Mezhuev, the pale and piercing-eyed conservative philosopher from Moscow State University, only sighed. A decade later, with a cheap whisky in his hand in a grubby chain cafe frequented by his students in a rundown mall above the metro station, Mezhuev tried to half sum up and half excuse what had happened to them: 'You see for a man of my generation, the 1990s left us with only two routes – one, to the border to Europe, the other to become a character out of Generation P.'

Generation P – which in Russian alludes to both 'Generation Lost', or 'Generation Fucked', is the book by the reclusive writer Victor Pelevin. It comes up again and again when normal Russians try to explain what the post-Soviet period was like to live through. It is seen in Russia as a self-portrait of the generation that went from perestroika idealists dreaming of democracy to Putinist cynics thinking everything is only PR. For them, the new regime was the end point of their failure and loss of faith. These were the same people that had gathered in their hundreds of thousands on Red Square against communism. Now they barely stood up for independent TV as disorientated, exhausted and disappointed by their dreams – they had lost the will to fight. What for?

Generation P is about an everyman called Babylen Tatarsky, who fell in love
with Pasternak poems one summer in the countryside and enrolled in a
Moscow literary institute, but whom the collapse has turned not into a
poet but an impoverished shop assistant. Chance throws him into his true
calling – tuning Western advertising to fit Soviet tastes. Grilled by his first
boss to come up with a way to promote a cigarette brand called 'Parliament'
he suddenly realizes that his whole diploma on Russian parliamentari-
anism was just a prelude for the chaos of post-communist consumerism:

> Tatarsky had realized quite clearly that the entire history of parlia-
> mentarianism in Russia amounted to one simple fact – the only thing
> the word was good for was advertising Parliament cigarettes, and
> even there you actually could get by quite well without any parlia-
> mentarianism at all.[47]

He is a cipher for the burnt-out Moscow media men that began as
Berezovsky's hacks and ended up putting the make-up on Putin. But
certainly, what Mezhuev meant was not that he and Pavlovsky had turned
into drug-fuelled wrecks, gorging on vodka and cocaine like Pelevin's
Tatarsky, who discovers that all Russian politicians are just 3D holograms
made by advertising executives who kill each other for contracts. Neither
of them tried to have a conversation with Che Guevara on a Ouija board
or (to our knowledge) stumbled around on LSD coming up with branding
strategies to make more money. What Mezhuev meant, what made Putin's
TV coup so easy, was that the 1990s left men his age living by the book's
morality, by these two phrases:

> Tatarsky, of course, hated most of the manifestations of Soviet power,
> but he still couldn't understand why it was worth exchanging an evil
> empire for an evil banana republic that imported its bananas from
> Finland. But then, Tatarsky had never been a great moral thinker, so
> he was less concerned with the analysis of events (what was actually
> going on) than with the problem of surviving them.[48]

CHAPTER THREE

THE GREAT TURN

RUSSIAN HISTORY beats to the years in which the leader makes a great turn. Stalin overhauled his agenda in 1929 and set the party on a road to super-industrialization and terror. Gorbachev came out as a radical in 1988 when he announced 'glasnost' – the openness the system could not survive. Yeltsin the 'impeccable democrat' turned in 1993, when he ordered the Alfa commando force to storm the same parliament he had barricaded himself within – in the name of 'democracy' – from these same commandoes in 1991.

The year that Putin made his great turn was 2003. It closed the era where he ruled like Yeltsin's heir. It was the moment when Russia lurched decisively into an authoritarian regime. This was the year that those who had gone along with 'the Russian Pinochet' first got a taste of what that meant, the year when those who trusted in Yeltsin's judgement first sat up in shock. Even Boris Nemtsov was stunned. 'At first I thought because he was a Yeltsin man – he was a man like me! I had no idea what he would turn into.'

The Conservative Thug

Putin is not an intellectual and not a romantic. He does not, like many Russian politicians, come from the ranks of the intelligentsia. His family home in a Leningrad *komunalka* was not a home to books, hushed conversations about repression or whispers of doubt. His mother was a janitor. Once describing his childhood, he mentioned an orthodox Jew who would read the Talmud in the communal apartment, but said, 'I am not interested in such things.'[1] His eldest brother died in infancy, and his second older brother died of diphtheria in the war. His father survived the conflagration but with extensive wounds. Putin brawled in the streets; summing up his childhood, he recalls, 'I was a real thug.'[2]

Putin has a harsh, uncompromising view of the world. Those close to the German intelligence agency, which watched his time in Dresden, claim that he beat his wife.[3] From time to time, his disdain for the doctrinaire thinking of Soviet communists or Russian liberals seeps out, neither of whom he sees as genuine problem-solvers but blames for the double disaster. Putin thinks he is a practical man.

He is obsessed by history and considers himself a Russian conservative. He is fond of recalling the words of the reformist authoritarian minister between 1906 and 1911, Pyotr Stolypin: 'Give the government twenty years of stability and you will no longer recognize Russia.' Stolypin brooked no dissent and in the slang of the day the hangman's noose was known as 'Stolypin's tie'. Putin has built a statue to him in Moscow. After a century of passionate commissars and dissidents, cosmonauts and novelists, his hero is an unemotional bureaucrat whose mission in life was to keep Russia's ideological, animal spirits down, so that it could get on with its development. In a reversion to tsarist conservatism, rejecting the revolutionary spirit of 1917 and 1991, stability is sacred.

Putin's tone is close to that of Alexander Solzhenitsyn, the inheritor of the Russian conservative tradition beloved of the West. Towards the end of the writer's life, a stroke left his right hand paralyzed and his hand gnarled, but he had found a ruler he could praise. He had spent the 1990s with a biweekly talk show with a lot of screaming – 'it's a nightmare!', 'this is terrible!', 'outrageous!'. This enemy of the Soviets, with a low opinion of Gorbachev, Yeltsin and the West, admired Putin despite his KGB past. For Solzhenitsyn, under his leadership Russia was 're-discovering what it meant to be Russian'.[4] He had returned to the motherland in 1994 from his Soviet-imposed exile in the United States, embarking on a journey, or perhaps a pilgrimage, from the Pacific to Europe. Meeting with anxious families and the hungry he found a 'poor and demoralized country,' which he did not consider suited to Western democracy.[5] Like Putin, he came to believe that only a long-term, distinctively Russian form of liberal authoritarianism, where Church and state are partners, could restore the nation. 'Putin inherited a ransacked and bewildered country,' said Solzhenitsyn, 'and he started to do with it what was possible – a slow and gradual restoration.'[6]

He accepted from Putin the highest honours of state, which he had refused from the hands of Yeltsin. There in the Kremlin, Solzhenitsyn spoke his mind – 'Of course Russia is not a democracy yet and it's only just starting to build a democracy so it's all too easy to take it to task with a long list of omissions, violations and mistakes.' His vision of reconstruction was uncannily similar to Putin's frequent invocation of the nineteenth-century tsarist foreign minister Alexander Gorchakov's line, 'Russia is calm, Russia is concentrating', as the empire built up its forces after humiliation in the Crimean War.

Like Putin, Solzhenitsyn considered the development of a party system 'irrelevant' for Russia and believed 'human duties' were as important as human rights.[7] After traversing the country in 1994, Solzhenitsyn published a pamphlet, republished in millions of copies, titled 'How to Rebuild Russia'. He argued that Russia needed to rebuild itself around a Slavic-Orthodox core of Ukraine, Belarus and northern Kazakhstan – 'for we do not have the strength for the periphery'.[8] It is a pamphlet that every politician of his generation claims to have read. Trying to integrate with these countries, whilst ignoring the Muslim ex-SSRs yet refusing to let them fall out of a Russian sphere of influence, has dominated Putin's foreign policy. Like Solzhenitsyn, Putin has a world-view that is old fashioned for his country. He claims to not use the Internet as he thinks, '50 per cent is porn material', believes Russia needs a 'strong hand' and that he is beloved by an abstract 'real Russia' in the heartland.[9] Putin is distrustful of international organizations and liberal Muscovites alike. Solzhenitsyn, of course, due to his post-Soviet politics, is not universally revered in Russia, but mocked for his faux-tsarist diction and as an anti-Semitic sham-sage.

At a dinner in Paris, Putin was asked who his heroes were. He said that in his office he had the portraits of two tsarist legends, Peter the Great and Alexander Pushkin, and a European one – General Charles de Gaulle.[10] This point is both flattery and something more. Like de Gaulle, who sought to bridge France's schizophrenic traditions of revolutionary republicanism and monarchism, Putin sees himself as bringing together both tsarist and Soviet traditions. This is how Putin imagines himself.

Putin's economic thinking is also an attempt to bridge Soviet and free-market techniques. This is clear from his only piece of book-length political writing. Putin did not in fact write this, his 'dissertation'. It was partly plagiarized and almost certainly ghost written. The text comes from his unemployed interlude between St Petersburg and Moscow, when Putin was anxious to burnish his credentials and find a new job. After Sobchak's 1996 election defeat he turned to the St Petersburg Mining Institute. He had engaged in discussions at the institute on the post-Soviet economy with associates throughout the 1990s. He had friends there. So, Putin used his contacts to obtain a 'candidate's dissertation', the equivalent of a PhD.

In the 140-page research paper that bears his name, at least 16 pages are lifted verbatim from the 1978 American textbook *Strategic Planning and Policy* by William King and David Cleland. Putin's thesis, entitled 'The Strategic Planning of Regional Resources and the Formation of Market

Relations', may not be original research, but this point hardly matters in trying to understand his thinking. It is the clearest statement of his economic intentions before assuming power – one to which he has remained remarkably consistent. Putin's text argues:

> Mineral and raw material resources represent the most important potential for the economic developments of the country . . . In the 21st century, at least in its first half, the Russian economy will preserve its traditional orientation towards raw materials . . . Given its effective use, the resource potential will become one of the most important pre-conditions for Russia's entry into the world economy.[11]

The dissertation suggests that this is not to be achieved using the free-market alone but with state guidance: 'The development of the extracting complex should be regulated by the state using purely market methods; yet the state has the right to regulate the process of their development and use, acting in the interests of society as a whole.'[12] Russia should commit to: 'comprehensive state support and the creation of large financial–industrial corporations which span several industries [focusing] on the resource-extracting enterprises, which should [then] compete as equals with the transnational corporations of the West'.[13] Essentially, the argument Putin puts forward is that:

• Russia will remain a resource-driven economy but a free-market one.
• The state must support the creation of giant raw materials corporations.
• These corporations will compete on the free market with the West.
• These corporations must act in the interests of Russia as a whole.
• Russian capitalism will be raw materials driven and guided by the state.

It represents a crude vision for the Russian economy. 'Putin has an X axis and a Y axis,' says Sergei Aleksashenko, the former deputy head of the Russian central bank. 'You can plot how he will react to a given threat. He operates – even if you don't agree with them – by values and principles.' The cardinal of these, is that when challenged by men empowered by gigantic assets, be they TV channels or oil companies, Putin has lashed out and confiscated them. This is how he puts it:

> One should never fear such threats. It's like with a dog, you know. A dog senses when somebody is afraid of it, and bites. If you become jittery, they will think they are stronger. Only one thing works in such circumstances – to go on the offensive.[14]

The Opposite Man

To become truly president, Putin had to rob Berezovsky. To become the undisputed master of Moscow, he had to destroy Russia's richest man. Standing in his way, trying to pull the country in another direction, was Mikhail Khodorkovsky, and he had more oil than Norway.[15] The battle with Gusinsky and Berezovsky determined that Putin, and not businessmen, was the master of TV. The clash with Khodorkovsky determined who had the final say over oil.

Putin believed that booming crude oil should be heavily taxed to fund state power and that whoever pumped it out should follow his orders. Khodorkovsky did not agree and tried to block the Kremlin's plans to fund a strong state by 'lobbying'.

When the oligarch refused to back down, the two fought. This struggle finalized the shape of the post-Soviet state. It was a battle over who really controlled Russia's resources. It decided whether the unexpected 2000s oil boom would fuel the power of the state or private corporations. Khodorkovsky was the greatest of the oligarchs and he had wanted to set the political tone for Russia. He had wanted to be as influential as Putin. But it was Putin who became Khodorkovsky, taking his hydrocarbons and throwing him into a Siberian prison colony, into a zone where sometimes thieves' law prevails, or sometimes no law at all.

Khodorkovsky was never a dissident. He was intelligent, ambitious and, yes, ruthless, whilst being at the same time somewhat temperamental to the point of being volatile. Always something of an actor, more than a commander, in the end someone foolish despite his superior, mocking grin. But he was never a dissident.

He came from the other side of Russia. The half-Jewish Khodorkovsky was from the Moscow lower middle class. He dreamed of being a captain of industry, of being the boss. Putin's breaks had come because he was loyal and calculating; Khodorkovsky always got lucky as the gambler. Putin could go on one knee and say something he didn't believe, because these were only tactics; Khodorkovsky would never do this, because what mattered to him was his pride. Putin had clung to his superiors; Khodorkovsky had never held back from risk.

In the late 1980s, he was not distributing copies of *The Gulag Archipelago* but a leading agitator at his university in the Komsomol, the communist youth league that fed the party with recruits. This organization was so unpopular that polls showed it was loathed by Soviet youth more than the party, the KGB or even the emerging neo-fascist street thugs. 'I know now my parents always hated the Soviet state,' remembered Khodorkovsky, but he did not think twice about being part of an organization that photo-graphed 'refusnik' Jews outside their synagogue for the authorities.[16]

The collapse of the Soviet Union was the collapse of authority. This meant the crumbling of state power over its own property rights. Khodorkovsky was smart. He understood this. The party youth were encouraged to experiment with 'self-financing' business, in the name of market socialism. So, Khodorkovsky opened a small cafe that was one of thousands of Komsomol businesses popping up across Russia. Yet all around them, the bureaucratic eyes that looked after those assets in the name of the people, were starting to look elsewhere. Just as Khodorkovsky was experimenting with business, the party apparatchiks felt this anaemia of authority, especially over what they ran in the name of the state, real-izing that if they were quick they could make off with it before the bureau-cratic doors slammed shut.

As administration itself imploded, Vladimir Putin picked up the phone in Dresden and was informed – 'Moscow is silent.' The USSR had not been hit by a nuclear strike but 'Soviet institutions were victimized by the organizational equivalent of a colossal 'bank run', to quote the political scientist Steven Solnick.[17] As it dawned on Putin that the country was gripped by 'the paralysis of power', the cadres at the other end of the tele-phone were rushing to claim as many assets as they could.

At the last all-Union Komsomol meeting in 1990 there was such chaos that they forgot to sing the Soviet national anthem. The brightest people in Komsomol were not there. Together with their superiors, they were turning the state assets they had access to into private assets. Khodorkovsky was one of those men stealing little bits of the state. As more and more officials sensed impending doom, this star cadet was given the privilege by the party, with backing from the highest level, to turn the 'non-cash' that was a hypo-thetical accounting unit between state enterprises, into 'cash' that could be used in real life. They gave him the right to create a bank and *the right to create money out of nothing* in a country where almost 50 per cent were about to be plunged into poverty. Many said he was the 'party's experimental capi-talist', others that he had a relationship with the KGB. By now, the failed 1991 coup had turned the 'bureaucratic bank run' into a stampede. The last two treasurers of the Communist Party mysteriously fell from windows, as the cash and gold they administered ran out the door. There was specula-tion, which Khodorkovsky has denied, that he knew where it had gone.

The Komsomol disappeared. What it had owned did not. This made Khodorkovsky rich; he grew richer still by trading in computers and boot-legging counterfeit cognac. They said that he and his friends, most of them Jews, traded in much, much more. The year Putin returned to St Petersburg a depressed lieutenant colonel and the father of two small girls, uncertain how he was going to pay for them, Khodorkovsky was in love with this new world. He had learnt how to live in a country where everyone else was drowning. Nothing expressed his pleasure in the new Russia more than his 1993 manifesto called *Man With A Ruble*, which crowed: 'Our idol is his financial majesty the capital.'[18]

Khodorkovsky was never a man like Sakharov, the anti-Soviet dissident. He did not grow up in opposition to the system that created Putin but was one of its architects. Khodorkovsky was one of the oligarchs who did more to discredit liberal and Western-looking politics in the country than all the propaganda that came afterwards. He is one of the culprits of the historic failure of Russian liberalism. This man was an insider at the heart of the Yeltsin regime, the advisor to the Russian prime minister in 1991, the deputy minister for fuel and energy in 1993, a regular guest in the Kremlin – whilst Putin was a provincial official. Looking back after it had all gone wrong, he remembered the 1990s:

Into this chasm, through media and bureaucratic channels, they pumped pretty liberal ideas about reality, manipulating information. By the way, it was in the 90s when the concept of the all-powerful Political Technologist first arose — a person who is supposed to be able to make up for the absence of real politics in one or another area with clever 'virtual' throwaway products.[19]

Khodorkovsky was speaking with experience when he spoke of political technologists. It was he who had first employed Vladislav Surkov, the greatest of them all. He discovered this cynic in velvet trousers, who became Kremlin deputy chief of staff and Putin's key 'controller' of domestic politics, creating fake parties, rigging elections and screaming at Duma deputies to vote this way or that in his office. Surkov was working for him as a bodyguard, when Khodorkovsky recognized he had a talent. Together they would put the first advert on Soviet TV.

This kind of politics was not atypical, and is not considered a travesty. What Khodorkovsky is loathed for is that he was on the inside of the infamous 'loans for shares' deal. This was the rigged auction that sold much of Russia's oil, gas and mining infrastructure to Yeltsin's 1996 backers – not mere companies but gigantic Soviet mega-complexes built by armies of geologists, slaves and 'heroes of labour'.

Khodorkovsky was one of those swindlers. For a mere $350 million he got the Yuganskneftegaz complex in western Siberia, with proven oil reserves far larger than Mexico, Angola or Norway. Just two years later his stake would be worth twenty times more than he had put up for it. To the rest of the country this auction was considered a crime.

This discredited 'democrats' in Russian eyes. It tainted the liberalism that the oligarchy claimed for its own. This made it all too easy to vilify 'democracy' itself. That the tycoons had abused their access to a desperate, sick president of a weak state so that they could privatize the nation's mineral wealth at a fraction of its real value, became one of the main propaganda points of the Putin regime. Much later, Khodorkovsky would come to see that 'my sinful self', a leader in that alliance of giant money and the neoliberal reformers, had lost society. He wrote in one bilious open letter on 'Russians liberals':

> They lied to 90 per cent of the people when they generously promised that a privatization voucher would buy two cars. Sure, an enterprising player on the financial market with access to private information and with the ability to analyse this information could turn a privatization voucher into as many as ten cars. But the promise was that everyone would be able to do it.[20]
>
> They kept their eyes shut to Russia's social conditions, while conducting privatization and ignoring its negative social consequences, coyly calling it painless, honest and fair. It's well known what people think of that 'great' privatization now.[21] . . .
>
> The election campaign of 1995–96 showed that the Russian people had already rejected liberal government. As one of the 1996 presidential campaign's major sponsors, I, of all people, should remember quite well what a monstrous effort it took to make the Russian people 'choose with their hearts'.[22]

But by the time he had grasped this, it was already much too late. The oligarchs and the liberal politicians had not only come to be seen as heartless, but incompetent too. It is not as though the young tycoon had acted like he understood what 'a monstrous effort' it was at the time – or maybe, we should just presume, he understood all along.

Two years after Khodorkovsky and his gang grabbed those immense oil fields that became the core of Yukos oil company, Russia itself went bankrupt. The country defaulted, the currency was devalued and the savings of the middle class decimated. The night before the default, nobody thought of informing the millions of financial victims, but Khodorkovsky was in the White House, being briefed on what shape the decree would take. Once it was all over for him, he could see the mistakes of his own Yeltsin elite with crystal clarity. He wrote:

> They didn't force themselves to think of the catastrophic consequences of the devaluation of Sberbank [Russia's largest, state-owned

savings bank] deposits. Then, it would have been possible to come up with a very simple solution — by securing deposits through government bonds that could be paid back by taxes on capital gains (or for example stocks in Russia's best companies transferred to private ownership). But the powerful liberals didn't want to waste their precious time; they didn't want to exercise their grey matter.[23]

Did he push for that plan on the night he was there in the White House? Neither Khodorkovsky nor any of the Yukos executives were acting with a social conscience in 1998. The moment that the default struck they moved funds offshore and threatened to dilute the value of the company's shares to zero if minority shareholders would not sell at the price they wanted. A truckload of important financial documents ended up at the bottom of a river.

This behaviour left his company notorious. Yukos was a by-word in business circles for atrocious corporate governance. In 1998 Khodorkovsky was seen as the moral equal of the other oligarchs – little better even than Berezovsky. The company had huge debts and he the reputation of a card sharp. In 1998 someone murdered the mayor of Nefteyugansk, the oil town by the Yukos fields, on Khodorkovsky's birthday. There is a Russian mafia tradition to deliver a birthday 'gift' to the person who commissions a kill. Khodorkovsky was immediately suspected. But was someone trying to frame him, as the oligarch's men claimed, with the murder in fact the work of local Chechen bandits?

The months after the crash left Khodorkovsky with two stark options. The first was to do nothing and live off the cash from exporting Yukos's oil, but with the barrel trading at its lowest value in decades, this did not seem too attractive to an enormously ambitious man. The second option was to turn to PR, convince shareholders and investors he was reinventing his company, improving his production techniques and driving up its share price and thus his fortune. He chose the second option. The insight that had struck him was that his company was undervalued simply because it was a Russian company. So much oil would be valued at as much as ten, maybe twenty times more, if it were a Western company. This is where the drive to change Yukos began.

The rashness of Khodorkovsky, his susceptibilities to moods and changes of heart, perhaps even to acting, gripped him like a mania. He started dressing differently – out went the 1990s thick-rimmed glasses, the moustache and the dress sense that seemed so laughably Soviet. In came new-century style rimless glasses, turtleneck jumpers, jeans and an apparent zeal for fighting corruption and turning Yukos until a model company. At first, Moscow laughed. Had Khodorkovsky undergone a change of heart? Or was he playing the lead role in an elaborate, expensive, PR show? It was both. Genuine attempts were made to improve the company – but he had cottoned on that even reputations can be laundered, and that there were Western accountants, Western lawyers and image-makers all too happy to do it. He drafted in global management consultancies to rebuild the Yukos interior and began spending more and more time in London, Washington and New York, talking about his charity work.

The man who began as Komsomol's experimental capitalist came up with a new slogan: 'Honesty, Openness, Responsibility'. He wasn't the only one trying to rebrand himself. The only difference was that, unlike the other oligarchs, he began to believe his own PR. Khodorkovsky began to genuinely think that he was a moral actor, a value-creator, a strategic genius – that he had 'built' Yukos rather than having been 'given' Yukos.

He had good reasons for this. Khodorkovsky had become obsessed with efficiency and was convinced of his own magnificent genius, as he had achieved nothing less than a production miracle in the part of Russia that matters most – the oil fields of western Siberia. Destructive and inept Soviet techniques had damaged the fields to such an extent that production had almost halved in the 1990s. Russia simply did not have the technology or the competence to exploit the oil that remained. It was Khodorkovsky who first decided to cut through the Russian hydrocarbons establishment and import Western advisors and techniques wholesale.

Through new fracking, flooding and pump techniques Yukos reversed the production decline in western Siberian. The old Soviet fields were losing less oil and new fields were pumping out far more effectively. The results were spectacular. The average flow rate from Khodorkovsky's wells doubled between 1997 and 2002.[24] He was at the heart of a revolution as his techniques were copied across the industry. Russia's growth in oil production was so steep that it constituted half the growth in oil production in the whole world between 1998 and 2004.[25] The country that had been exporting just 3.3 million barrels a day in 1998 was exporting over 6 million in 2005.[26]

And Khodorkovsky knew full well that the government couldn't have done this. Private companies had seen production rise by two-thirds but state-controlled ones rose only by a quarter.[27] Not only was Russia producing more, but what it was producing was worth more. There was now no stopping Khodorkovsky's addiction to efficiency and booming sense of self-worth. In 1998 the country had been making only $28 billion from oil and gas – it would hit $243.6 billion by 2005.[28] He felt he was the one turning Russia's fortunes around.

In this convinced, contemptuous mood, Khodorkovsky was the first to see right through Putin's telepopulism as pure PR, that it was all stunts not state building. Putin had done nothing to increase oil production. Khodorkovsky was the first person to realize that Russia had exited economic crisis, but was still in a governance crisis. The things that could be solved by an economic upswing were getting better, but the things that needed government competence to solve – such as corruption, terrorism and extortion – were as bad as before. When Khodorkovsky looked at the way Putin ran Russia, he saw the way that Yukos had been run ten years earlier. He saw the President as a shoddy manager.

This irked Khodorkovsky, because he was now gripped by an efficiency mania as oil prices soared. He started to want to do for the country what he had done for his company. Especially since he knew exactly what was going on inside the Kremlin. He had sources, former employees and friends right up to Putin's office. He was also their neighbour: the Yukos gang lived together in exquisite villas in the new Russia's Beverley Hills, the exclusive Zhukovka gated communities off the Rublevka highway to the west of the city – this was Putin's home too. Khodorkovsky would complain that the President's morning escort that closed the highway to traffic made him late for work. Who did this Putin think he was anyway – closing the lanes like a tsar?

Who Is Sovereign over Oil?

Khodorkovsky thought he was better than this St Petersburg 'chinovnik' – this bureaucrat. By now he was the richest man in Russia, worth $8 billion; he was also the richest person in the world under forty. He expressed such thoughts privately, then he started dropping the hint publicly. He no longer wanted money. Khodorkovsky increasingly wanted power. Rumours began to circulate that he wanted to be president. Then he made an announcement that he would quit business when he turned forty-five in 2008, exactly in time for what was supposed to be the first 'post-Putin' presidential election. The hiss was growing louder that he wanted Putin's job. His comments did the bare minimum to dissuade people. Referring to himself and his long-time business partner, he quipped:

> Leonid Nevzlin and I have reached the conclusion that we have enough personal money to keep us happy. In that sense, money plays absolutely no role. Money is an instrument to be used for other things. It is an instrument like ammunition in the military – you have to constantly replenish it.[29]

They had already taken aim at the Duma – and were winning the battle for influence in the notoriously chaotic, corrupt chamber. As late as 2003 the

Putin clan were, like team Yeltsin, struggling to control it. They did not have a majority. In 1999, the government party only had 64 seats out of 450 in parliament and had only secured 23.32 per cent of the vote. The Kremlin had forged the United Russia party out of factions adding up to 235 seats, but its hold was shaky. Symbolic of their lack of control in Putin's first term, fist fights even broke out in the Duma as angry, chanting communist deputies blocked German Gref from reaching the speakers' podium to present the Land Privatization Bill.

This lack of control gave the oligarchs (especially Khodorkovsky) the ability to rent, buy and bribe the deputies. The Kremlin was not the only source of political financing in town, as Khodorkovsky had a rival patronage system. Yukos had bankrolled the liberal and pro-American opposition parties, Grigory Yavlinsky's Yabloko and Boris Nemtsov's Union of Right Forces. Khodorkovsky had made hefty donations to Putin's party. Donations to Fatherland all-Russia, the party that had hoped to challenge Unity, had made the Yukos executive Vladimir Dubov a deputy on its list. He was soon made chairman of the Duma's taxation committee.

This was the way the Moscow elite saw Khodorkovsky putting his politics into practice. It was discrediting the stand he took publicly. It did not look like publicly interested liberal politics, but the politics of big oil, pure and simple. Khodorkovsky, of course, admitted he was engaged in 'lobbying', but the Kremlin did not see it this way. They were furious. The speaker of parliament bemoaned that on oil legislation it seemed 'as if there are 250 Vladimir Dubovs in the chamber'.[30]

This was no hysterical remark. The government was repeatedly defeated in its attempts to increase taxes on the oil sector. Putin and his men wanted to increase the state take in oil profits as high as possible, whilst Khodorkovsky was fighting for it to stay as low as it had been in the 1990s. The reform-minded German Gref was distraught, having calculated that this cost the treasury $2 billion a year.[31] It would be wrong to see the Yukos affair as Putin's overreaction to aggressive lobbying. This was not lobbying, but a battle over who would grow rich on the new oil boom – private companies or the state.

Khodorkovsky was practising extensive tax avoidance and throwing everything he had to stop taxes on oil profits going up. This left the government spitting at his grandiose speeches about how his charity work was going to educate 2–3 per cent of students in Russia who had been left behind by an 'inefficient state'. Even the old Yeltsin man, Mikhail Kasyanov, who saw nothing wrong with Khodorkovsky's plans to merge with either of the Western oil majors ExxonMobil or Chevron said: 'The fact that Khodorkovsky was allegedly buying up the deputies, I once angrily told Putin myself.'[32]

Putin had warned the oligarchs to stay out of politics if they wanted to carry on in business. In 2000, when he had gathered the twenty-one tycoons in the Kremlin to spell this out to them, Khodorkovsky had been there. Putin had showed what happened – through Berezovsky and Gusinsky – if they didn't. Most tycoons did not see this 'offer' as an attack. Most were relieved and did the best they could to comply: they were moneymakers uninterested in politics. They were not real businessmen, who had built up the oil fields, but courtiers who lived in fear of losing their cash cows.

Khodorkovsky was different. He not only interfered but tried to block Putin from turning the oil boom into state power. His lobbying was to show Putin that he held the property rights to Yukos, that he was strong enough to stop his profits being turned into tax – that he was sovereign over oil. Khodorkovsky had always been different. At the very beginning he had been warned – that the last time when young men in the Komsomol were encouraged to dabble in business, in the 1960s, some of them had ended up arrested. 'I did not remember this,' he once boasted, looking back gleefully laughing at that moment when he had followed his instinct.[33] He was not a man who listened to the cautious – not when every risk had brought massive returns. It was simply too late for him to stop taking them.

I Am Powerful Enough to Insult You

At the time the oligarchs, like most Russians, were more frightened of a weak state than an overbearing one. Moscow was paranoid that the Russian Federation could go the way of the Soviet Union. Putin's assertion that a 'weak state is a threat to democracy', rang true.[34] To be more precise – most oligarchs were convinced that a weak state was a greater threat to their property rights than an authoritarian one they got on with. Most were happy to exchange less room for manoeuvre for increased asset security.

Not Khodorkovsky. By 2003 it looked like he was breaking the 'deal' to stay out of politics in exchange for his fortune. He was increasingly promoting an agenda at odds with Putinism. Khodorkovsky began to campaign across the eleven time zones with his 'Open Russia' foundation. As the Kremlin tried to co-opt elites, Khodorkovsky was building an alternative institutional network of think-tanks and charities, funding political parties and paying for ever more Duma members. He wanted to educate 2–3 per cent of students in his charity schools. So, people began to ask – how many relatives did those 2–3 per cent of students have? So, how many voters does that turn into?

As the head of Russia's biggest company Khodorkovsky was the only businessman who felt he could stare down the state. In fact, in 2003 he was nothing less than the most powerful businessman in Russian history. Neither under Yeltsin nor the tsars had a tycoon ever openly flouted the supreme interests of the Kremlin in such a way before. And all this on barrels of oil that many officials felt they had given to him for $350 million in exchange for loyalty.

The President had not 'liquidated' the oligarchs as a class. Their wealth grew exponentially during his first term. In 2000, zero Russians featured on the *Forbes* billionaires list, by 2003 there were seventeen. Should Putin be unable to show himself stronger than the richest of them, it would have left him vulnerable to them all. 'Khodorkovsky was playing politics in the way it had been played before,' observed Sergey Aleksashenko, the former deputy head of the Central Bank, 'And he expected to get the same results as before.' With the arrogant swagger of a kingmaker, boasting of his hired deputies, Khodorkovsky wanted to be the new Berezovsky.

Putin was considered weak. This is why Putin felt he needed to do something that would be so damaging to Russia's reputation and so contested within the Kremlin itself. The endgame for Khodorkovsky risked being the endgame for Putin if he botched it. There is an expression in Russia – if a pack of wolves is following you in the forest, remember you only have to kill one, otherwise they will devour you.

Reflecting frayed nerves inside the government, the Kremlin-linked pamphleteer Stanislav Belkovsky published a 'paper', which argued that the oligarchs were not only increasingly powerful but also were plotting to stage a constitutional coup. First, they would buy up the Duma, then turn Russia into a parliamentary republic, before overturning the FSB security elites once and for all as they gloriously installed Khodorkovsky as a new, all-powerful, prime minister. This 'research' reflected real unease. When Belkovsky published his 'analysis', Putin was still considered to be just another president. It read:

> In circumstances where the country has virtually no real political parties, where the institutions of civil society are weak or in the pocket of the powerful, where the systems of mass communication and the media are under the control of the oligarchs, such a radical transformation of the system of government is not in the interests of Russia or the Russian people. It would mean that oligarchs would be even further freed from any constraint connected with the objective interests of the nation. Such a weakening of the influence of the President would mean power flowing directly into the hands of big business,

which would be freed from any real mechanism of control . . . *we are in fact talking about the prospect of an oligarchical coup in Russia.*[35]

It was a warning to the tycoon. Khodorkovsky may not have been positioning himself for the presidency per se, but he was positioning himself as the leader of pro-American and liberal forces in Russia. He was so politicized that he had to make a declaration in 2003 that he was not intending to stand in the 2004 presidential election. Charles Krause, his American former spokesman, who was glued to Khodorkovsky at the time, explains his motives like this:

'He never intended to run for president. That's a complete fabrication. I saw him say repeatedly "I have a Jewish surname I can never be President." But if you ask whether he intended to have some form of public life after 2008 when the Putin era was supposed to end, I think that he was.'

The authorities felt under attack – and they were. Khodorkovsky had started publicly insulting Putin – accusing his government of being corrupt and incapable. On 19 February 2003, the shadow-boxing between the richest and the most powerful two men in Russia came into the open – *in a meeting broadcast nationally.* Putin had summoned the country's most powerful businessmen to the Kremlin to discuss with them the challenge of mounting corruption. Khodorkovsky had prepared a slideshow of opinion polls on the topic and its content as he revealed it in the domed hall – was explosive.

- *Slide Two*: 27 per cent of Russians thought corruption was the most serious threat to the nation.
- *Slide Three*: 49 per cent of Russians thought corruption had spread to the majority of state officials including 'the highest levels of federal power'.
- *Slide Four*: 32 per cent of Russians felt that the leadership was powerless to tackle corruption; 29 per cent of Russians felt the leadership chose not to tackle corruption; 21 per cent of Russians felt the leadership neither wished nor is capable of tackling corruption.
- *Slide Five*: Independent auditors suggested 30 per cent of the state budget was being lost to corruption.
- *Slide Six*: 72 per cent of Russians thought it was a waste of time to pursue a complaint through the official justice system as it was corrupt or they could not afford the bribe.
- *Slide Seven*: Amongst students, low-paid jobs such as tax inspectors were more popular than professions as they were viewed as having huge potential for corruption.

'Please . . .' interrupted Putin. 'Let us not apply the universal presumption of guilt to our students.' At this Khodorkovsky then made one final, immense accusation:

'We need to make corruption something that is universally ashamed of. Let us take for example the purchase by the state oil company Rosneft of the firm Northern Oil . . . Everyone knows the Northern Oil deal had an ulterior motive. I must tell you that corruption is spreading in this country. You could say that it started *right here*. And now is the time to end it.'

Khodorkovsky had not just said that in the Kremlin itself – he had said it on camera. This was the greatest mistake made by a man carried away by his own performance and convinced that he had the power to insult anyone, without any consequences. He had underestimated Putin, who glacially defended Rosneft before smiling, like a coiled, poised snake:

'But some companies like Yukos have got themselves fantastic, excessive reserves of oil. I think the real question is: how did they get them? *The ball is in your court*. And another matter. I believe that Yukos has got into a few problems with tax affairs. You may claim that you are dealing with those problems. But the question that needs to be addressed is, how did they arrive in the first place?'[36]

Watching the TV at home with his wife, the former KGB general hired by the oligarch to run his security operations burst out, 'We are finished!'[37] Just days later, the tycoon summoned his men and warned them that tough times lay ahead. He had gone to war.

Capturing General Yukos

Khodorkovsky was growing even more brazen as his business plans were becoming ever more grandiose. The tycoon was bragging to Western oil executives about those in his pay in the Duma. He was discussing his own pipeline plans to China; indifferent to the Kremlin view that this was foreign policy and not a matter for businessmen. He wanted to turn Yukos into the biggest conglomerate in the country by far. He wanted to swallow the oil firm Sibneft. He wanted to merge with a Western oil major. With a company so large, so integrated into global capital, he believed he would then be powerful to the point of being untouchable.

As long as Khodorkovsky continued like this, Putin had a rival: Putinism was not going to be secure. His final crime was that Putin came to believe he was preparing to sell a majority stake in Yukos, the crown jewels of Russian hydrocarbons, to the American oil titan ExxonMobil. This would have put him – and the best part of Russia's oil – out of the Kremlin's reach. There were those inside the government who felt furious and even betrayed. The way they understood 'loans for shares', was that these men had been awarded resources in order to become the loyal capitalist class that Russia lacked. They reasoned to themselves that, at a time when only foreigners could have coughed up the real value of these mega-complexes, it had been reasonable to award them to trustworthy Russian businessmen. And now Khodorkovsky wanted to sell to the Americans. Days before Putin sent the FSB to get him, he told one Western executive, 'I have eaten more dirt than I need to from that man.'[38]

Yukos executives began to be arrested. In the weeks leading up to Khodorkovsky's arrest two of the richest oligarchs, Mikhail Friedman and Mikhail Potanin, told him to stop. They warned him he was endangering himself, endangering them and the whole country. He didn't. So why did Khodorkovsky feel so secure? Berezovsky and Gusinsky were already in exile. Putin had already clamped down on TV. The regime had shown that it reacted to threats by tightening the screws.

Inside the government itself the challenge mounted by Khodorkovsky was causing rifts and strain: many at the very top were opposed to the drastic measures being planned against him, including the prime minister, Mikhail Kasyanov. He had sensed a change in his relationship with Putin for months. 'The breakdown of our agreement [to divide power] came in 2003. At first the pressure began on business, then the plot to take Yukos took shape with increased pressure being placed on the oil industry as a whole.'

Khodorkovsky thought he was better than Berezovsky or Gusinsky. He thought he had better intelligence. Those close to him say that, at the time, Khodorkovsky felt he was safe as he had sources at the very heart of the Kremlin. These sources had been reliable up to this point. His family and his advisors claim this was none other than Alexander Voloshin, Putin's chief of staff, the same man who had told Berezovsky not to worry that they had 'let the black colonels in'.

Khodorkovsky's son Pavel blames Voloshin for intrigues that led to his father's arrest: 'Voloshin was trying to use my father in an internal Kremlin power struggle.' He claims that Voloshin had suggested Khodorkovsky present the infamous slides on Russian corruption to Putin. 'I have from several sources,' insists Pavel, 'that Voloshin now feels remorse. He did not intend it to lead to an arrest.'

Khodorkovsky was better than other oligarchs. He had a wife and unlike the others was not a shameless womanizer. For fun he did not fly a plane load of women to 'party' in a ski chalet, but took all his children to Paris, to walk them round the Louvre, stopping to explain what each artefact was. This makes hearing Pavel talk about 'my father' unsettling. What was about to happen was not only a man's political catastrophe but a personal one.

In public the oligarch was refusing to show fear, but in private his sense of tomorrow had darkened. In 2003 Khodorkovsky went on what would be his last visit to the United States to show his American colours. This was the year US forces stormed into Baghdad. He visited his son Pavel at Babson College, where he was studying. Pavel remembers; 'My father said to me, "The final thing they will do now is arrest me." He seemed to know this was coming.'

Yet Khodorkovsky still had time to flee the country, as Berezovsky had done. Why he did not do this is a question he has never fully answered. In his letters from prison he alludes to himself as a martyr, that he chose to be arrested, that he had resisted temptation and been purified by prison.

> I could have foreseen things. When I understood things, it was already too late. I had the choice of going onto my knees or going to jail. And maybe I could have gone onto my knees. The temptation was very great.[39]

Was he trying to be a martyr? Or is this the self-valediction of an imprisoned egomaniac who cannot admit he made a mistake? To many it seemed he had developed an almost messianic complex. His writings from jail brimmed with biblical references and insinuations that he had been reborn:

> Yes, that sweet word 'freedom' has many meanings. But its spirit cannot be eradicated nor extirpated. It is the spirit of the titan Prometheus who presented man with fire. It is the spirit of Jesus Christ who spoke as the one who was right and not like the scribes and Pharisees. Hence, the reason for the crisis of Russian liberalism lies not in the ideals of freedom, albeit perceived differently by everyone. This is not about the system, but people, as the last Soviet prime minister Valentin Pavlov used to say. Those who were entrusted by fate and history to guard the liberal values in our country have failed in their task. Today we must sincerely admit that, because the times of slyness are over, and to me, here in a dungeon of remand centre No. 4 this is, perhaps, a bit more obvious than to those in more comfortable conditions.[40]

Those working closely with the oligarch do not believe he intended to be a martyr. This sense of self was to come later. According to his then spokesman Krause:

'I think that he misjudged. He knew that he would be arrested and he had been told by sources he thought were very reliable in the Kremlin that he would be arrested for two to three days, but then he would be let out on bail. So then, at that point, he could decide whether or not he wanted to stay and fight or quietly leave. At that point I think he misjudged. He thought he was more powerful than he was. He had what he thought were very reliable sources. The question is whether or not those sources were misled or deliberately misleading Khodorkovsky.'

Voloshin resigned with the news of the arrest. But the whole Khodorkovsky story is not just a story of intrigue, nor is it a morality play. It is a story about Russian power, and like all Russian political stories – it is about PR. What made Khodorkovsky different from the other oligarchs is that he had invested hugely into his image, especially in the United States. This meant that his arrest would strain relations between Russia and the West, unlike the Gusinsky and Berezovsky affairs, which were ignored in Brussels and Washington. As his former spokesman, Krause identifies his work at the PR firm that Yukos hired, as fundamental:

'The work that we did with him at APCO is also a very important part of the story. Had someone not started working with him in the early 2000s and managed to really communicate to people in the West that he was really trying to change his game, his arrest would have been viewed as a long overdue act by the government to go after crooks. He had a very good trip to the United States right before his arrest. So much so that the President's wife Barbara Bush asked me about this case.'

I made contact in summer 2012 with some of Khodorkovsky's 'people' in London. They agreed to ask his lawyers to carry a letter from me to his prison colony. When I sat down to write it I felt odd, like I was writing to a ghost, even a myth. The question that dogged me most of all was this: Did the tycoon understand he was risking so many years in jail, not merely a few nights in a fetid cell like Gusinsky had experienced back in 2000? For months – nothing. Then I received a call. 'He's written back.' Touching on the question that was gnawing at me, Khodorkovsky had given me half an answer:

I had been told already at the beginning of 2003 that Putin had willed they give me eight years. Although at first I did not believe them.

The night before his arrest the oligarch was flying on a private jet across Russia, visiting politicians and inspecting fields. Officially it was to 'promote the company in the regions'. But why would a Russian oil company need to 'promote the company in the regions', by delivering political speeches at universities and meeting local governors? Those whose parties he was funding knew this was simple cover.

Boris Nemtsov says unofficially that the head of Yukos wanted to speak to local leaders about their political frustrations and drum up support amongst students. In the Kremlin, that bureaucrat on a throne, that 'chinovnik', had already given the order, the order most thought he would never dare give; for what would the West do if he gave that order?

The night before Putin's men came, Khodorkovsky's plane had been delayed in taking off for his destination in Siberia. He had half-jokingly asked the pilot if they had enough fuel to reach Finland. The following morning, they came for him on his jet. 'Nobody move.' They had 'FSB' stitched on their tundra uniforms and they were all heavily armed. In Moscow, his wife had been dreaming she was lost in a collapsing city. 'Put your guns down.' In his letter, Khodorkovsky recalls his emotions the moment the FSB barged in:

> When armed people entered into the airplane, if anything I felt a sense of calm. At last the energy-sapping waiting was over and certainty had appeared.

In Siberia, the richest man in Russia was thrown into an unheated cell, then forced into a black canvas hood and marched in handcuffs onto a military aircraft. In that first week inside the prison system, his first cell-mates remember him lying in his cot, shocked, refusing food. 'He seemed to be thinking very hard about something.'[41]

It was already over. There is no rule of law in such political cases; here the law does not really exist until it is made a weapon. In Moscow, the stock exchange was forced to close for an hour to stabilize trading. In newsrooms and in political circles there was also shock. The only ones who did not really understand were his youngest children, twin boys.

Prime Minister Kasyanov spoke out against it. No one, not even he, had quite believed until the last minute that Putin was capable of such an outrageous, ruthless, assertion of power. But he was. The show trial started within months. The once mighty oligarch was soon sitting in a cage waiting to be tried. No longer in shock – he seemed composed, even elegant behind bars. Khodorkovsky wrote to me about his feelings in that cage:

> The formal arrest took place later, in the [Moscow] Basmanny Court, where I first looked into the craven roguish eyes of a bureaucrat in the robes of a judge.

Khodorkovsky writes that as he smiled, crossing his arms in relaxed defi-ance, looking straight into the cameras and the flash photography of all Russia:

I was only thinking about my close ones. I was looking at my mother, at my wife; I was endeavouring to catch their gaze and to hold it, to convey my composure. It seemed to me this was important to them.

For the other tycoons, this was terrifying political theatre. TV repeatedly replayed this image of the powerless Khodorkovsky to impress upon his fellow billionaires who was the power in Russia. The day after he was arrested, the seven richest men in Russia flew out of Moscow. Inside the government those such as Kasyanov were in despair:

> Frankly, I felt after the arrest . . . along with my colleagues in the government, a diminished enthusiasm for reform [from Putin]. All took it as a signal that the liberal reforms will be phased out. Kudrin, Gref, other ministers were in a gloomy mood, they were morally depressed.[42]

Putin allegedly refused to answer Kasyanov's demands for an explanation. Even the prime minister did not understand. Why did Khodorkovsky have to be arrested?

> I asked Putin three times to tell me what was the reason for the arrest of Khodorkovsky. When he finally told me he said that he had been financing parties in the Duma that he had not permitted him to do – in particular the Communist Party. That was what Putin said was the reason for the arrest. The logical deduction you could make was that Putin was frightened of Khodorkovsky.

Many in Moscow believed that this fear was being stoked in Putin by someone. Inside the Kremlin, there were cunning tacticians, trying to turn Khodorkovsky's power play into their own – and fingers pointed at Igor Sechin, the deputy chief of staff. This was an old friend Putin trusted. He had hired Sechin to work for him in St Petersburg in 1991. Through the years Sechin had prospered by controlling access to 'the Boss', even drawing up morning 'reports' to be read by Putin first thing. Khodorkovsky wrote in his letter to me that he thinks Sechin brought about his downfall:

> Nobody in our country has any doubt that 'approval' for my arrest was received personally from Vladimir Putin . . . But the initiator of everything that happened – and today this can be said with a high degree of certainty – was Mr Sechin, who knows his 'patron' very well indeed, and was able to successfully manipulate him and a significant

part of his retinue. I was shown, as the most dangerous political adversary, and into the bargain as representing the interests of Americans [. . .] the conspiracy-theory mentality easily accepted the idea of a large-scale conspiracy, taking into account facts of financial assistance to opposition parties; the activity of the Open Russia foundation; once again, the problem of the need to get away from a super-presidential model of the regime to a parliamentary one, something I had been discussing widely; the call to reject systemic corruption, which has today become one of the foundations of the regime; and so on.

It is impossible to say precisely which of the arguments that was being advanced by Sechin through various people ended up being the decisive one for Putin to arrest me. Most likely he was dared to – or be exposed as a weakling.

The Consequences of Khodorkovsky

The arrest was the defining act. It imposed the Putin consensus on the oligarchs. The rival political patron was finished. It established once and for all that Putin would not tolerate open challenges to the executive. It made it clear that the presidency had powers akin to a tsar. It was Putin's 1929, his 1988, his 1993. Within the government not everyone was pleased with this new turn. Kasyanov in particular continued to speak out against the arrest until January 2004. This was not appreciated:

At the next cabinet meeting, he [Putin] made us sit there for more than an hour while the prosecutor read out all the charges against Khodorkovsky, as if hearing them spoken proved their legitimacy. All the cabinet members sat there stone-faced, with no clue why it was being done. As for me, I couldn't keep from cracking a smile now and then as I listened to the blatant absurdities and fabrications. And, of course, throughout Putin was closely watching the reaction of the cabinet members, and mine was the only one at variance. When it ended, of course, nobody had any questions or comments, and everybody walked out in silence.[43]

Out in western Siberia the arrests continued. To show that Khodorkovsky was never coming back, more than 370 Yukos workers were hauled before the police. Then the nationalizations began. This, according to Putin, is why: 'I want to say once again that the state should manage only the property it needs to carry out its public functions, ensure state power and guarantee the country's security and defence policy.' Reality was cruder. When threatened by Berezovsky and Gusinsky, the President had grabbed what made them powerful – their assets. Now, he nationalized Khodorkovsky's resources.

To the despair of men like Kasyanov, this remade Russia as an economy and a state. Putin allies started to 'double-hat' on the boards of big state companies. All talk of the privatization of the state oil giant Rosneft vanished. Within two years, the share of Russian GDP produced by private enterprise fell from 70 per cent to 65 per cent.[44] Within four years the share of Russian oil production in private hands fell from 90 per cent to 45 per cent.[45]

More importantly the Yukos affair established who the oil boom would fuel – the state. There would be no more 'lobbying'. By 2005 the state was taking 83.8 per cent of oil companies' profits in tax, where in 1999 it had taken just 45.1 per cent.[46] By the end of the decade, mass tax avoidance from the oil companies was a thing of the past and the Kremlin was taking in over 90 per cent of their profits as taxes.[47]

Not only had Putin seized oil rents back from the oligarchy, the state had seized a huge share of the assets. Corporate stock controlled by the government jumped from 11 per cent in 2003 to 40 per cent in 2007.[48] Berezovsky had boasted that seven oligarchs controlled over 50 per cent of Russian GDP (who in reality controlled around 15 per cent) but in 2006 it was five government officials who chaired companies that produced 33 per cent.[49] They had become the oligarchs.

The losers inside the government were the free-market types and the Yeltsin-era officials such as Kasyanov and Voloshin. The winners were the 'siloviks', the Russian for those who command 'sila' or strength – military and security men. The others that came out on top were the St Petersburg team that had stuck magnetically to their boss under pressure, even the neoliberals such as Alexey Kudrin. The dramatic weakening of Kremlin liberals was clear to Khodorkovsky:

> The main thing for Sechin was the abrupt weakening of the demo-cratic wing of the President's retinue, with a simultaneous strength-ening of the role of repressive mechanisms in running the country. Thus it was that he is the one who became the main principal benefi-ciary of the changes that took place as a result of the 'Yukos trial'.

The former oligarch is not the only person to argue that conservative forces inside the Kremlin wanted to take his personal wealth and return it to state hands, where they could embezzle from it with ease. Prominent conservatives admit former KGB agents in the government were pushing for nationalizations. 'More or less, those that favoured more state control of the economy were the siloviks,' reminisced Grigory Rapota, a former lieutenant general in Russian foreign intelligence, a minister at the time.

Yet the tycoon repeatedly said they offered him the chance to go on 'one knee' and keep his company, until almost the very end. His failure to do so unlocked the door for Sechin and his men. The renationalization of Northern Oil, which Khodorkovsky had criticized in the Kremlin, was thus the first of many.

The great turn sent a clear message to the oligarchs not to interfere in politics – and to foreign investors that Russia was no level playing field. The arrest warned Westerners never again to even think of major oil deals without Putin's express blessing. They could only play as subordinate partners in the energy game.

With Khodorkovsky eliminated, the Kremlin felt it had achieved full authority over energy. It began to talk itself up as nothing less than an energy superpower, the Saudi Arabia of the north, where Russia's resources served its geopolitical aims. This was no idle fantasy – the country had the largest natural gas reserves in the world and would overtake Saudi Arabia as the world's largest oil producer.

Yet the show of disunity – even disloyalty in the government, unnerved Putin. Much of the government was opposed to the turn, leaving it at risk to damaging cracks. Within six months of the Khodorkovsky arrest, the entire Kasyanov cabinet was dismissed in spring 2004. The prime minister had been on holiday with Boris Nemtsov, the opposition leader Khodorkovsky had funded, and is alleged to have discussed the possibility of a move against Putin. When confronted with this rumour Kasyanov later cryptically recalled:

> When Putin announced my resignation, he did not say why. But that evening I was told the same story you just mentioned [the plot with Nemtsov] by people close to the president, and I came to believe it. I remembered what happened the day before, February 23rd, when we attended a gala concert at the Kremlin. That night the President behaved strangely. During the intermission, he stood in a corner whispering with [Nikolai] Patrushev [the head of the FSB] and avoiding everybody. The next day, the 24th, Putin suddenly cancelled a cabinet meeting and told me to come alone.[50]

The sacking of Kasyanov was the climax of a purge. This had begun in Gazprom and at the bottom ranks. By 2003 as many as 70 per cent of officials inside the Kremlin had been appointed by Putin himself.[51] This continued throughout the rest of his first presidential term. By 2008, he had personally appointed 80 per cent of the top 825 positions in the country, most of them military and intelligence roles.[52]

The crushing of Khodorkovsky caused this tectonic shift. It would be to blame the victim to suggest that his ambitions upset the balance within the Russian elite, resulting in victory for the forces of reaction – and thus he should never have attempted this. That, however, was the result. A good general picks battles he intends to win. Khodorkovsky's hubristic sense of power resulted in the sidelining of pro-American free marketers. He misjudged his enemy and misunderstood the battle. It resulted in the elimination of the main alternative source of patronage for the country's politicians.

Even now Putin still sees him as an enemy. A decade later his views have not changed. In 2010 when asked what would happen to the former CEO of Yukos he snarled: 'A thief should sit in jail.'[53] At the time of writing Khodorkovsky's jail term is set to expire in 2014 – but this is far from certain.

The trouble for Khodorkovsky was that outside the liberal intelligentsia in the capital, because of the crimes of the 1990s – as he now claimed to painfully see from his bunk in the penal colony – the country more or less agreed with Putin. In deepest Russia he was seen as little better than a better-dressed Berezovsky. The President's popularity, on the other hand, only climbed.

The irony of the injustice – for all those in the factory towns who smiled at the news of an oligarch getting what in their minds he deserved – is that given the scale of corruption in the Putin court, these resources that had been nationalized were going to be used for private gain in much the same way they had been when they belonged to a private company.

The man who had an army of bodyguards, and his own former KGB generals on staff, ended up behind barbed wire in a penal colony in outer Siberia, attached to a uranium mine, not far from the Chinese border, in a camp that in Soviet times few returned back to Europe from alive. There he was made to sew gloves with the inmates, lost all parole for refusing to sew ever more of them, and one night his cellmate would stab him in the face with a cobbler's knife. There, he wrote that he had realized what had jailed him: 'the authoritarian project, a direct consequence of "Yeltsin-1996"', which had been his project.

This is not a 'morality play'. Ideas about 'redemption' in prison are not the way to judge the consequences of Khodorkovsky's actions on Russia, only on himself. If we take this man at face value, if we believe that he did not want to be president, but wanted to rally democratic Russia, we need to judge him as a politician. So what were the results? In less than a year of his incarceration in Siberia: his company was lost to the state and with it went the main funder for the opposition. The liberal parties he backed failed to make it back in to the Duma in the 2004 elections and defeat left them in disarray, squabbling as their money ran out. The bottom line was that the huge Yukos supporter of a pro-American Russia had disappeared. Khodorkovsky had, in the end, helped neither Nemtsov nor Yavlinsky, or even Zyuganov, but only Sechin.

So let us ask: if a general fighting for a democratic Russia, who views his oil company as 'ammunition' for his forces, leads his men into a forest, refuses to 'go on one knee' (no matter if it would have been good tactics), gets surrounded then captured, has his ammunition stolen from him, his men scattered and is imprisoned in the Gulag – is this general a hero, or is he a failure?

As I sat reading Khodorkovsky's letter from his faraway cell for the first time it was these words that struck me. They came from a man who considered himself both:

> My impression of Russia has not particularly changed in jail. Actually, I did not have any illusions before either. It is a huge backward country with a very segmented, weak society and an atomised population, the majority of whom feel themselves not to be citizens, but serfs to various kinds of 'bosses'.
>
> Of the new things I now feel – only that of my own personal responsibility for what is happening, which weighs very heavily on me. The responsibility of a person who could and can change something, and this means I must at least try. The older I get the more frightening it becomes to face the Creator. I believe more and more: He gave us strength, and He will ask us to account for how we have thoughtlessly wasted it on secondary things. Someone who does not believe has it easier in this sense, perhaps.

Authoritarianism is Weakness

Putin's circle has never felt fully secure for long. Shocks have constantly left them on the defensive, cobbling the system together in an ad hoc, unplanned manner, as threats to power emerged. This is a government that spends vastly more of its time in crisis management mode than the White House.

Crisis makes the personality of a leader central. When a problem suddenly explodes and engulfs the agenda, what matters are not his beliefs or his programmes but gut instincts, the way he improvises. Politics under pressure is how you react on your feet, not how you implement a plan. Gorbachev's instincts were ultimately democratic. Yeltsin's were those of a megalomaniac. Putin's instincts proved anti-democratic, paranoid and authoritarian. They could even be called Chekist – the Russian expression for a secret serviceman's world-view.

Kasyanov's tenure as prime minister saw the Putin government evolve from one that was considered liberal by the Russian elite into entrenched authoritarianism. He believes there was no plan – this was the product of cumulative reactions:

> Putin's authoritarianism was about eliminating risks to his power – free TV became a risk, it was eliminated, when elections became a risk, they were eliminated, when parliament became a risk, it was eliminated – this is all because Putin was frightened of genuine competition. It moved step by step, as each risk appeared he reacted forcefully to it. Putin was frightened of being exposed.

Kasyanov is right – Putin's turning points came when he felt hunted. TV and Khodorkovsky, the two things that had threated to expose him, were destroyed. Yet why did a regime with virtually no effective opposition in the early 2000s fear criticism so intensely? Why did a hugely popular president – who had conquered Grozny and passed effective reforms – fear open competition?

The answer is that Khodorkovsky was right. Russia's economic crisis was over but its governance crisis was not. And the reason Putin became so frightened of him is that he was exposing that in his speeches. The government was failing in basic tasks – behind the telepopulism there was no let up in corruption, terrorism and lawlessness. Khodorkovsky knew that had Putin's real record been discussed on national TV it would not have shone. His popularity was not in sync with his performance. Contrary to what the public was being told during Putin's first presidency, the country actually saw more murders, more terrorist attacks and greater corruption than under Yeltsin. This grim record is what made TV censorship and silent oligarchs so important for the Kremlin.

Despite the counter-terror bravado of 'wasting them in their outhouses', Russia's rising numbers of victims stood out internationally. Between 2001 and 2007 the country lost 1,170 lives to terrorist attacks, making it the third most terrorist-prone country in the world after Afghanistan and Iraq. In those same years Israel lost 'only' 158 lives and Pakistan 'just' 222.[54]

Every attack uncovered incapable officials, corruption and trails of collusion. The 2002 Dubrovka theatre siege in central Moscow shocked Russia, both because its crack troops proved cack-handed and because, despite all the military efforts in the Caucasus, some forty terrorists with large amounts of weapons could still be casually driving around the capital. In the Dubrovka theatre more than 1,000 theatregoers were held hostage by Chechen terrorists and 140 killed in a bungled assault. Unconscious bodies, knocked out by a mysterious gas used by Russian special forces, were left in piles outside the theatre, many choking on their own vomit. This horror could not be kept off TV. One expert estimated that it left 30 million people needing 'psychological help'.[55]

Nor was this the end of it. Attacks with the impact of London's 7/7 bombing kept on coming. In 2004, two passenger jets exploded after leaving Moscow's main airport. The dismal cause of the security breach was that both of the suicide bombers had bribed airport staff $140 to be let aboard.

Yet the most graphic illustration of Putin's failure took place in a Christian town in the North Caucasus. Beslan is a synonym for carnage in Russian. Here the rain comes down from the mountains and the air is filled with the tension of a frozen conflict. Local North Ossetian security forces spit at neighbouring Chechens and Ingush. They are not seen as fellow people of the Russian federation, but enemy tribes. Moscow is not spoken of like a modern federal centre, but as the imperial centre – the armed pacifier, policeman and arbiter of the mountains. 'When I was in Russia,' is the way the locals talk; 'over in Russia things are different'.

In their wide cemetery are the faces of hundreds of murdered children engraved on the stones. Toys, sodden teddy bears and rotting plastic play-things are left on the graves. And bottles of water, dozens of bottles of water. The cemetery is enormous for a sleepy town – it has to be, to bury an entire generation.

In September 2004, almost a year after Khodorkovsky was arrested, a Chechen and Ingush militia stormed the school of this poor ethnic Ossetian town, where posters shouting 'Brotherhood and Unity for the people of the Russian Federation' suggest that things are otherwise. The militia held the children hostage. When Russian forces assaulted it over 385 of them died. Beslan lost a generation in the cruellest of ways – for days they were given no water. That is why there are bottles of water on their graves. 'They will not be thirsty in the afterlife,' coughed an Ossetian official at the cemetery gates. The traces of flame-throwers used by Russian troopers inside the school smelled of incompetence as much as savagery.[56]

Five years after Putin had come to power, Beslan was proof that he was failing to keep Russians safe. The child massacre, with its subplots of official bungling, callous indifference and missed opportunities to negotiate, pushed Putin further into authoritarianism as a way of 'limiting risk' to his authority. After the slaughter, government rhetoric now began to sound dark and anti-Western, implying that foreign powers were behind the attacks. Speaking about foreign power in a way that had been little heard in Russia since the early 1980s Putin warned:

Some would like to tear from us a 'juicy piece of pie'. Others help them. They help reasoning that Russia still remains one of the world's largest nuclear powers, and as much still represents a threat to them. And so they reason that this threat needs to be removed. Terrorism is just an instrument to achieve these aims.

He sounded like a hysteric but was in fact being sensible. Putin was trying to distract Russia from the obvious: the FSB was failing. This inability to stamp out the threat opened the way for the Putin elite to be challenged by the opposition – hence the need to take preventative measures.

'Putin was frightened after Beslan of real competition,' says Kasyanov, 'which is why he launched a raft of anti-constitutional reforms – to eliminate any risk of losing power.' First, Putin abolished regional governors' elections. Instead they would now be appointed by him and rubber-stamped by local legislatures. Being elected to the Duma as an independent MP was rendered impossible by new laws insisting that all had to be elected on party lists.

Simultaneously the rules for registering parties were tightened. It was now necessary to get over 40,000 signatures, which could be thrown out easily by the authorities on 'authenticity' grounds. The threshold to enter the Duma was also raised from 5 per cent to 7 per cent. These laws meant that the Duma had ceased to be a place for either fist fights or real debates. Boris Gryzlov, the speaker, summed up perfectly what had happened when he said: 'the State Duma is not the arena where you have to carry out political battles'.[57]

Putin had a slogan – 'the dictatorship of law'. This is what he promised. This is why he said Khodorkovsky had gone to Siberia. Yet anyone in the know knew that this was PR. In 2006 every major position still had a price tag on it. The going rate for a minister's post was $10 million, or that of a governor $8 million. Seats in the Duma cost roughly $2 million with a seat in the Federation Council between $1.5 and $5 million.[58] The only difference was that with Khodorkovsky in jail, there was no overtly rival patronage system to the Kremlin's with its sinews inside the political system. Out on the streets it was still lawless: the average annual murder rate under Yeltsin's rule and Putin's first presidency is virtually identical at 26 and 27 deaths per 100,000 people respectively.[59]

'We have proved ourselves to be weak,' Putin growled after the Beslan massacre, 'and the weak get beaten.' After each humiliation Putin blamed the bureaucracy and lack of central control, even foreigners. He was left feeling that the facts had been hidden from him, or that his officials were deliberately deceiving him. The chronic incapacity to deal with corruption and crime convinced him that more control and greater state capacity was needed. The greatest threat Khodorkovsky posed to Putin was not some fictitious oligarchic plot – but that the richest and one of the most respected men in Russia was saying that this regime was incompetent, that Putin was not a strongman but an incompetent 'chinovnik' – a mere bureaucrat out of his depth.

The Collapse of Managed Democracy Next Door

'Russia has and will always be a great power': these are the words with which Putin began his presidency. But what kind of 'great power' cannot get what it wants – *in Ukraine?* This country, for Russians, is not really a country. Going there is not really going abroad; being from there is not really being foreign. Russians are as intermarried with Ukrainians as the English are with the Scots; they feel like the Germans would towards a sovereign Bavaria – that it is something abhorrent, and surely temporary. There are as many born Ukrainians in the Kremlin as there are native Scots in Westminster. Here in Kiev, in the beginning, was the baptism of the Rus – the common forefathers of both Russians and Ukrainians.

Nobody is really nostalgic for the days when Russian tanks ruled in Budapest. 'But Ukraine . . .' says Alexander Verkhovsky, the leading voice on Russian nationalism: 'It was not like Tbilisi or Yerevan. Those places were always different. But Ukraine . . . In the Soviet Union it was practically the same place! There was real shock that a border was put up and even today if you ask your average Russian where a border town is, in which country is – say Belgorod – most people will have no idea if it is in Russia or Ukraine. The mental map of the borders is blurred.'

Power in Ukraine is considered so important in Moscow that the last twist of the great turn that began with the Khodorkovsky affair took place not in Russia but in Ukraine. Powerful Kremlin officials were sent to win the election for the pro-Russian candidate using all the tools of managed democracy. They botched it so badly, in a country that Russians do not really consider to be 'abroad', that it was worse than a disaster: it was the foreign policy equivalent of what the 1998 default was for economics – rock bottom.

They threw at it the best 'political technology' that rubles can buy. Their candidate, Viktor Yanukovych, was given a makeover and Putin quality TV advertising, whilst a travelling circus blocked main squares across the country to obstruct the opposition from holding rallies. Their hopeful – Viktor Yushchenko – was mysteriously poisoned with a gigantic dose of dioxin. Later, a mysterious tape surfaced connected to the poisoning, which appeared to implicate Kremlin officials. With the campaign in full swing even Putin himself visited. On the night, massive fraud called the victory for Putin's man in an 11 per cent defiance of the exit poll.

The opposition denounced the election as stolen and protests broke out across Kiev, given backbone and direction by Western-funded NGOs. Before long the city was paralyzed. Putin was shocked and hinted to the outgoing Ukrainian leader that he thought he should send in the tanks. When it came to the point of round-table talks between the two sides Putin even suggested sending Boris Yeltsin out of retirement as his representative.

The protesters won as a million people flooded onto the streets. As Putin's men fled humiliated, the Bush administration and those that dreamt of a European Union that can dominate over Moscow in former 'fraternal republics', which in Brussels had begun to be called 'the shared neighbourhood', were delighted. The Arabs were vomiting up the neo-conservative 'Freedom Agenda' but in Eastern Europe something that looked like the good old days of 1989 was under way. For a moment Ukraine forgot that it is as overshadowed by Russia as Mexico is by the USA and fantasized about being in NATO. London, Brussels and Washington indulged them.

Moscow was aghast. Into this, the deepest of Russia's historical wounds, the Americans were keen to push the NATO alliance. Ukrainians see this as their right as an independent country, but real horror gripped the Kremlin. 'This was our 9/11,' says Pavlovsky – or a moment Moscow realized its defences simply weren't there. Rewinding back to 1991, when the intelligentsia clapped as Yeltsin cut loose the other SSRs, as the country as a whole shrugged off the independence of the Ukraine – *because nobody wanted to pay to keep these people* – there was an overriding conviction that it didn't matter if they became independent. People thought, 'They will just stay where they are.' The foreign policy establishment thought an expensive empire would be converted into a cost-effective sphere of influence, not truly independent. Had Russians thought at the time that Ukrainians could join a NATO alliance led by George W. Bush they would have gone to war to stop it exiting the USSR.

Not only did Putin's foreign policy machine look completely kaput, but key figures in the establishment, the same men who were supposed to be keeping his regime afloat, failed as well. The outcome in Kiev was considered so vital that the Kremlin assigned its most experienced agents to the task. None other than Dmitry Medvedev (then almost unrecognizably pudgier), the Kremlin chief of staff, ran the case. He had dispatched the spin doctors who had manufactured Putin's own election victory – Gleb Pavlovsky and his sidekick Sergey Markov – off to Kiev.

Putin's agents failed so utterly in 2005 that his leading spin doctor Gleb Pavlovsky was forced to flee his hotel and the rest of Kiev like a thief. He had been assigned by the Kremlin to swing the election for the pro-Moscow candidate, but flopped so miserably that the Western-looking opposition had triumphed. This was the Orange Revolution and Kiev was ecstatic, but Pavlovsky was terrified. He needed to get out of the country of his birth, Ukraine, as quickly as he could. But Pavlovsky did not want to leave anything to chance. So, he slipped on an orange scarf and an orange hat, and disappeared into the throng as it shouted pro-American slogans, among a crowd dizzy with delight that they had wrestled back a rigged election. This is when Pavlovsky drew the obvious conclusion – they needed their own protesters.

Walking Together

Moscow changed tack. They reinstalled the old soundtrack of Soviet prop-aganda. Out went screeching about 'international terrorism', in came campaigns against 'the enemy within'. Then they began rebuilding the Komsomol, the youth league that had fed recruits into the party and mobi-lized red youths to parade through the streets.

The Kremlin likes to have outfits on the shelf in case it needs them – and in January 2005 it whipped out a small sponsored rabble it had toyed around with and sent the spin doctors who had failed in Ukraine to give it a massive upgrade. The outfit in question was called 'Walking Together' and had flickered in and out of importance as a Kremlin experiment in Putin's first term. These were nasty people. The guy in charge was Vasily Yakemenko, the government's favourite 'youth'. This was a man who had grown up in the gyms and gangs of Lyubertsy, a working-class Moscow commuter slum, synonymous with the mob. According to the former head of Russian Interpol, this friend of the Kremlin had been an active gang member in a circle of criminal weightlifters who carried pictures of Hitler in their wallets.[60] He was certain some gang members had being raping the local girls and staging robberies across Moscow.

From what we know about their techniques, the KGB, then the FSB always found a use for such thugs. What we know for certain is that in 2000 Yakemenko became the head of 'Walking Together', a youth group that was supposed to bring toughs out onto the street to cheer Putin. At first it received only a limited amount of attention and cash, but jumped to notoriety nevertheless. Yakemenko, destined to be a minister, and a posse that included several future members of parliament, began a campaign against writers. In particular they took against Vladimir Sorokin, the *enfant terrible* of Moscow post-modernism, who writes about endless queues in which nobody knows what is being queued for, a Russia whose citizens are every day required to eat a daily ration of cellophane-packed human faeces, or a gay sex scene between none other than clones of Khrushchev and Stalin.

The Kremlin-supported 'Walking Together' began suing the country's leading satirist, harassing Sorokin for being a 'pornographer' and distributing the offending passages as leaflets on street corners. In a scene worthy of the artist's work, the Putin youth mounted a gigantic papier-mâché toilet, brimming with foam, before ceremoniously throwing in some of the 6,700 books by 'pornographic' authors they had assembled: Vladimir Sorokin, Viktor Pelevin and Karl Marx. The following morning, this 'book toilet' was exploded with 400 grams of TNT. Nevertheless, the organization had neither proved particularly useful or able to mobilize the 'youth' and it sunk into disrepute. Members in St Petersburg were exposed as trading in pornographic tapes.

The Kremlin was too desperate to care about this. What had been a marginal experiment after the Orange Revolution went mainstream. This scandalous flop was earmarked a $17 million budget and was converted into a mass organization that is now synonymous with Putinism: Nashi, 'Ours'.[61] Yet the atmosphere inside Russia was jittery after what had happened in Ukraine, jittery enough for Surkov himself to arrange a meeting with the biggest names in Russian rock to ask that, if Orange unrest ever broke out, they would at least stay neutral.

Top officials were not being paranoid about protests. There really was unrest bubbling across Russia. In 2000, the state statistical service had recorded only 80 strikes, falling to 67 in 2003 before exploding to 5,993 the following year.[62] With all eyes in the government focused on Kiev on 1 January 2005, few would have thought about Federal Law 122 coming into force that day. The reform replacing in-kind benefits with cash also stripped pensioners of their Soviet right to free public transport. This sparked the biggest protest wave since the 1990s. It was huge. Some estimates suggest over 300,000 people demonstrated across the country.[63] Superficially these protests were against Federal Law 122, but in reality they were about post-Soviet injustice and the miserable conditions that the generation who had won the 'great patriotic war' had been reduced to. In Moscow, St Petersburg and car-producing Tolyatti thousands of old Soviets and young radicals took to the squares (conspicuously absent was Putin's 'generation emptiness') demanding less reform and more benefits. A disorganized rabble of twenty-something leftists, old communists and aggrieved pensioners even briefly blocked the road linking Moscow to Sheremetyevo Airport.

There was never a serious threat to the regime, but having seen how suddenly managed democracy unravelled in Kiev, it was paranoid. Nashi was created so that they would never be caught out in future. Nervously, the government immediately slowed the pace of economic reform, from then on attempting few structural changes that incurred social pain. 'We felt the troops were massing somewhere close,' recalled Pavlovsky. 'We needed something to fight against the ideology of colour revolutions, pro-Western anticorruption nationalism,' said Sergey Markov, his sidekick in Kiev. He was now also assigned to Nashi.

Yakemenko's army was ready by March 2005. Come 'Victory Day', when Russia decks itself out in red and remembers the more than 30 million who were devoured by Hitler's war, the self-styled 'Anti-Fascist Youth Group' was marching 60,000 strong on this emotive day, through the streets of Moscow.[64]

Across the country their $17 million budget was being spent building a new Komsomol that would feed recruits and rally the youth around the party of power. On the surface, a network of regional commissars were thrown up, teams of local agitators chucked together in all major cities, lecture tours and conferences kick-started with the old 'pioneer camps' being reborn as an annual 'Seliger' festival, named after the lake where it was held. In the shadows a 'battle-wing' was coming together to smash the 'Orange threat'. At first, these toughs had to live no further than a night bus away from the Kremlin, to be there by morning to lock arms around it. For all the fancy seminars, which looked at first glance like ambitious projects for a 'Putin Youth', the Nashi were on closer inspection a primitive financial dog-whistle there to get paid thugs into Moscow, hatched by men who clearly suspected they were not legitimate enough to rely on the army and the police if the 'Orange hour' ever struck. The campaign against the enemy within had begun.

The Fear of Empty Space

Russia had changed, darkened by Khodorkovsky, Beslan and Kiev. The Kasyanov government had been replaced by one of pliant cadres. Reform had slowed. Yet the former prime minister was holding out hopes to become Putin's choice for mayor of Moscow. As these dreams began to wither, he grew increasingly embittered at having been cut out of Russian politics – especially, he thought, since so much reform had been pushed through on his watch. Kasyanov began visiting his old mentor, the ageing and ill Yeltsin, in his retirement dacha. It was a 'golden cage', which Yeltsin was certain was bugged:

'He had a very high quality of life in the official state dacha, with official state cars. But he had bound himself not to criticize Putin. He was within a year extremely disappointed in him. He was completely against all the moves he was doing against the freedom of the press, to the parliament, to the governors, violating the constitution but pretending it had remained. This truly pained Yeltsin. He was extremely torn, morally and psychologically, by what Putin had become. And this inner torment I believe was one of the reasons that contributed to his death.'

It was not only clear to Yeltsin but much of the Moscow establishment that the regime was not quite the triumph it sold itself as on TV. In one way or another most agreed with the Khodorkovsky diagnosis – the state was inefficient. So why did Russia's elite continue to support Putin so passionately in his early years – despite the fact that the many shortcomings over terrorism, the rule of law and corruption were in plain sight? Khodorkovsky's sentence frightened the oligarchs, but it does not explain why there was a consensus, even passion, amongst the intelligentsia, the rank and file members of United Russia or the 'deep state' that had no fear of arrest.

Putinism is apocalyptic. The project is presented as nothing less than Russia's last chance to survive as a state: 'Russia will be a great power or she will not be at all.' The fear that should he fail, the country would fall into anarchy, pulled the establishment together. There was still widespread fear that Russia could collapse again. In private, many expressed their fears that Russia could within a few decades cease to exist. Demographics, China, Muslims, oil price crashes . . . there were many demons.

Nor was such an apocalyptic way of talking about Russia – an inevitable product of the fall of the Soviet Union and the 1990s collapse – restricted to Russians. The Western establishment used very similar language. The US National Intelligence Estimate 'World in 2015' and 'World in 2025' coolly predicted that Russia was at risk of dissolution, demographic imbalances and strategic irrelevance. As the pro-Kremlin intellectual Vyacheslav Glazychev once said of the Putin majority: 'Horror vacui – the fear of empty space – is most probably the important underlying reason for the unshakeable nature of this belief.'[65]

In the Kremlin itself they speak in the same apocalyptic tones about Putin, to the extent that you worry they believe it. 'You have to understand that Putin cannot let Russia go. Russia is his project. He has to hold on to it,' barked one wide-eyed government aide, leaning forward and touching my arm to stress his point: 'For the first time in a hundred years the country is developing like it should. For eighty years we were under a Marxist experiment and then ten years of total chaos. He brought order and stability. He saved us . . . Putin saved us . . . And only in twenty years will he be appreciated. Can you even imagine what Russia would have been without him?'

CHAPTER FOUR

THE VERTICAL OF POWER

THIS IS the view from his Kremlin office.

Under the pristine white of the Ivan bell tower is the world's largest bell, which was cracked and never rung. Under the golden domes of the Cathedral of the Dormition is the world's largest cannon, which was botched in the making so could never be fired. Behind the slender turrets of the palace of the Patriarch are the concrete pillars of the palace of the Soviets. Over the red walls are the peaks of Stalin's towers, but the eye seems to drift back to the five golden cupolas of the Dormition. There is a legend in Moscow that when the German armies reached its outskirts, during the blizzards of 1941, their forward units closer to these walls than Sheremetyevo Airport is today, these exhausted men from Munich and Dusseldorf swore they could see its gold-tipped towers, that in this cathedral Stalin ordered a secret service to be held. And the priests begged God to save the Soviet Union, which according to legend – they called 'Rossiya'.

This is the view from the office of the man known as the 'grey cardinal', the first deputy chief of staff in the Kremlin (1999–2011), the man charged with managing ('manipulating') domestic politics on Putin's behalf. His name is synonymous with the Putin system: Vladislav Surkov. For ten years this room was the nerve centre of Russia's managed democracy. Or, to be more precise, his secure-line telephones were. These six beige machines seem of a Soviet vintage and are a sign of apparatchik status. In January 2011 the speed-dial buttons on the largest phone bore several surnames in block capitals. Some, given their roles at the time, are of no surprise: RAPOTA – SVR, plenipotentiary to the Volga Federal District; KUDRIN – finance minister; ZORKIN – chair of the Constitutional Court; SHUVALOV – first deputy prime minister.

Others are to be expected, but depressing to see nonetheless, for a country that pretends to be a democracy with opposition parties in the

Duma: MIRONOV – leader of 'Fair Russia'; ZYUGANOV – leader of the 'Communist Party of the Russian Federation'; ZHIRINOVSKY – leader of the 'Liberal Democratic Party of Russia'.

This is not the strangest thing about Surkov's office, but what everyone always suspected. It was always well known that the Kremlin had a special department to deal with the 'tamed opposition' in the Duma. The unnerving oddities are the photographs that Surkov has chosen to frame. It is not his portrait of Putin in a knitted jumper, with a fatherly smile, nor is it surprising that there are portraits of Che Guevara, Jorge Luis Borges and Joseph Brodsky in the cabinet, beside a sign in Chinese characters that says 'Sovereign Democracy'. That a man who harangued politicians to vote the way he asked them to, dictated news broadcasts, created fake parties, instigated Nashi, oversaw ballot stuffing, directed election campaigns in contests without alternatives, was the boss of Gleb Pavlovsky and all Putin's political technologists: that he should consider himself a kindred spirit with a revolutionary, a writer and a poet tried in a Soviet kangaroo court – *that he should consider himself an artist* – is no surprise.[1]

Everyone of a certain creative disposition claims to identify with these people, or for that matter John Lennon, whose framed portrait is also in his cabinet. What is unnerving are the frames by the windowsill, next to his catalogues on modern architecture. They show an alarming degree of insight into the nature of celebrity and its relationship to power in tele-populism. They are the framed portraits of Werner Heisenberg, the Nazi physicist who failed to build Hitler an atomic bomb but developed the 'uncertainty principle'; the beaming Tupac Shakur in a hoodie, the 75 million record-selling hip-hop megastar of the 1990s; next to the quizzical stare of Barack Obama, pressing two fingers to his lips. Are we to presume that these are the inspiration for the 'Alpha Male'?

It would sicken all of them, no doubt, to know their portraits were placed as symbols of mocking self-awareness in the office of the man who created United Russia as a hegemonic party, announced 'Sovereign Democracy' as an ideology and injected into the country constant doses of propaganda, paranoia and fraud, by a man who excelled at ruling through patronage and corruption, whose name became synonymous in Putin's Russia with amorality and lies.

The pictures get to the heart of who Surkov is – and the insincerity at the heart of the Putin project. This is a man who is believed to have written a play under a pseudonym, the maiden name of his wife, which denounces the very system he had created and called it *Around Zero*. In the drama's introduction he wrote: 'this is the best book I have ever read'.[2] 'In Russia to be a gangster,' cries out its central character, 'is not to err but to conform.'[3]

The story of Vladislav Surkov, in his ten years as the 'grey cardinal' who managed democracy from this office, is not only the story of how the system was built – it is the story of how Russia is ruled.

The forces that had weakened Yeltsin's Kremlin had been raucous TV and a raucous Duma. To tame these for Putin, the 'grey cardinal' brought politicians onside in hundreds of little meetings in this office. 'He asked what I wanted from him materially in return for joining the party,' remembers Vladimir Ryzhkov, at the time the deputy speaker of parliament, 'When I told him that I wasn't in need of anything, Surkov was genuinely surprised.'[4]

Surkov created his clients by corrupting them. This office was one of the operations centres of a racket that a US Embassy cable source (his name deleted) described with 'officials going into the Kremlin with large suitcases and bodyguards', which the source speculated 'are full of money', and 'governors collect money based on bribes, almost resembling a tax system'.[5]

It was from this office that the Kremlin orchestrated the most important 'no-alternative elections'. Any genuinely dangerous opposition candidates were allowed no coverage on the national TV stations it oversaw, let alone allowed to register to compete directly in any votes. This meant that unless you read one of the liberal newspapers with a tiny circulation, or a few blogs – out in the provinces the opposition simply did not exist.

That was, of course, if there were any left – as so extensively were potential enemies, even former foes, brought onside with plum but powerless positions in the establishment. The opposition leaders left officially competing for the Kremlin, the ones on Surkov's speed dial, had been turned into Putin's clowns. They include: the buffoonish half-Jewish anti-Semitic nationalist Vladimir Zhirinovsky, whose 'policies' have included suggesting bringing polygamy into practice in Russia, reclaiming Alaska or a 2008 modest proposal to drop nuclear bombs in the Atlantic Ocean to flood Britain; also the perennial leader of the Russian Communist Party, Gennady Zyuganov, who called for the 're-Stalinization of Russia'. They secured in the mind of the majority of badly informed Russians an impression that anyone opposing Putin is a fool.

All of this created a system rigged for only one force to win, United Russia – the party of power.

Send in the Bears

It was another idea of the accidental father of Putin's Russia – Boris Berezovsky. It was 1999 and 'Operation Successor' was nearing conclusion, but the oligarch was not fit enough to celebrate. He had contracted hepatitis and with acute pains down his spine was lying in a hospital bed 'in delirium', tied up to a drip, fantasizing about a Kremlin party, a new party of power.[6] 'I had a temperature of 39°C, but at such moments the thinking process gets better. At first I began to think about the symbols of this movement . . . the Volga River came to me, then birch trees . . . but in the end I settled on a bear.'[7]

One of the men who came to visit Berezovsky was the new first deputy chief of staff, Vladislav Surkov. This young man was the big thing in Moscow PR and had been brought into the family by Voloshin, the chief of staff. They knew they needed the best 'political technologist' going and looked no further than who was working for the oligarchs. It was the 1990s and Surkov had 1990s dreams – 'I wanted to be like the hero in the movie *Pretty Woman*', as he put it.[8]

The young Vladislav Surkov hadn't always been called this. He was a natural at PR because he was used to half-truths. He was born as Aslambek Dudayev in the Chechen village of Duba-Yurt in 1964. His mother was a Russian schoolteacher, his father a Chechen who had gone off to military college and never came back. Once she realized they had been abandoned, his mother took him away from Chechnya, back to Ryazan in central Russia, where she changed his name to that of her own family – Surkov. He was then five years old.

They remember him as a brilliant young man, who was a hit with the girls. As Russia threw off communism, which he called 'an enormous parasite', he was experimenting with careers at a dizzying rate.[9] First metallurgy, then two years in the army (they say it was military intelligence) in socialist Hungary, then back to Moscow and drama school, from which he was expelled for fighting. At the age of twenty-three he was recommended as a bodyguard to Mikhail Khodorkovsky, who upgraded him almost immediately to the business team. 'He was a real hipster,' his colleagues remember, sometimes not pitching up to work before lunch.[10] But he was so brilliant that he managed to put the first advert on Soviet TV for Khodorkovsky's Bank Menatep. But he fell out with the young tycoon, who refused to make him a partner, winding up at the rival Alfa Group doing PR to further their bid for Russian domination. This is where the 'family' found him.

'There are no limits to a man's flexibility,' Surkov shrugged when asked about the arrest of Khodorkovsky, his former friend.[11] By then Surkov was famous in Moscow as an icon of post-modern cynicism, who smoked constantly, loved Allen Ginsberg and was always at the best gallery openings. Yet despite all this, he was the one who was building in the name of Putin the party that had been born in Berezovsky's delirious mind – United Russia.

The half-real, half-imagined Yukos threat had taught the Kremlin that it needed to make sure that it had a rock-solid control of the Duma. The half-real, half-imagined Orange threat had taught the Kremlin it needed propaganda and a huge support base to block what had happened in Kiev from ever happening in Moscow. Surkov had proved his loyalty to Putin when he did not resign – like his old patron Voloshin – during the Khodorkovsky affair. The consequences of the Yukos threat and the 'Orange menace' was that Putin came to see that the propaganda and political party projects Surkov was running were not just important but vital. They were upgraded and so was he, to the level of presidential aide in 2004.

He was now running the campaign against the 'Orange threat' and building the party. 'The bears', as United Russia was known, was no longer what it had been in 1999. In its first election that year (then known as Unity) it had only got seventy-three seats, just over 23 per cent of the vote and come second to the Communist Party. Now halfway through Putin's first presidency, Moscow was talking very differently. 'The aim for this party,' said the then leading United Russian deputy Sergey Markov, 'is to create a party that could rule Russia for fifty years like the Liberal Democratic Party in Japan or the Christian Democrats in Italy.' This was when Surkov's career really took off. Though never promoted to have an official role in the party, perhaps because the revelation of his Chechen heritage excluded him from high elected office, Surkov was by mid-decade seen as the party's official handler.

His project grew to gigantic proportions, with the Kremlin throwing all the energy into building up the membership base, the party infrastructure and the alliances it needed to 'rule for fifty years'. His political technologists and cadres distributed the party card far and wide, amassing 300,000 members a year and topping the 2 million mark in 2008.[12] The number of 'bears' kept on multiplying, as unofficially the authorities encouraged every official, policeman and ambitious businessman to sign on. The age when there was a 'correct' and 'incorrect' party membership had returned. 'Bear bureaus' were popping up everywhere – creating a vast network to campaign under slogans like 'Into the Future with Putin' or 'Putin – Strength'. They opened no less than 2,597 district and 53,740 local offices from coast to coast.[13]

Anything popular, they wanted to brand United Russia. So agreements were inked with seventy organizations, of all colours and causes, bringing even the potentially troublesome 'Association of Chechens' and the 'Union of Georgians in Russia', into Surkov's fold.[14] The most important of all recruits were the trade unions. Deals were signed first with the Oil, Gas and Construction Workers Union and then with the Federation of Independent Trade Unions of Russia.[15] In fact all forty-eight all-Russian workers' organizations and seventy-nine regional trade unions ended up branded and integrated into the United Russia network.[16]

To make Russia more generous, but a place where that generosity was synonymous with the party, United Russia started pouring money into more than sixty social projects and national charities it ran itself – with the 'bears' out campaigning for the 'Libraries of Russia', supporting 'Our Towns' or 'Our Parents'.[17] Pretty much any popular cause was soon also a United Russia cause. In this spirit, companies were encouraged to make donations to the party: fifty-seven in 2009 obliged, giving anything from $15,000 to over $1 million.[18] These donations were seen as a way of publicly declaring your loyalty, whilst also paying a political insurance premium in case they ever needed to ask officials – so many of them now 'bears' – for a favour.

This party construction effort sucked the elites into its orbit. By 2007, sixty-five of the eighty-three regional governments ruled under the party colours and, three years later, a whopping sixty of the *Forbes* top hundred powerful Russians were 'bears'.[19] But the party also had its eyes on the future. The youth groups that Surkov had sent Pavlovsky and Markov to found, Nashi and the party youth league, the Young Guard, were increasingly treated not as easily organized mobs but as a modernized Komsomol in which to groom the next generation. Several front men were 'kicked-upstairs' to the Duma to set a good example. Surkov wanted twentysomethings to have an orderly upbringing, not like his own, because: 'We almost completely lost the youth of the nineties.'[20]

All these efforts were rewarded. In 2008, Medvedev referred to it as the 'ruling party' and Putin – who had until this point thinly pretended to be 'above party politics' – promptly became its leader.[21] By the end of the decade 'Edro', as the party became known, was present in every corner of the federation. This slang name began as a joke, but slowly became more apt than funny – 'Edro' sounds like the word for atom, the building blocks for everything.

The party tried to pretend it had a greater purpose than just consolidating power for Putin – 'Putin's Plan'. When the party boss Boris Gryzlov, a grey and moustachioed gentleman from St Petersburg, was pressed by journalists in 2007 to explain exactly what this plan was, he snapped defensively: 'Putin's plan is simply the chosen course of the current president . . . Putin is the leader in charge of current strategy and this is why we have dubbed his ideas "Putin's plan".'[22]

In other words, the plan was whatever Putin wanted. Yet Mr Gryzlov was not hiding some shadowy agenda within the party, but the fact that 'the bears' were not really a party at all. The political technologist turned deputy, Sergei Markov, once admitted to me, in between hollering down the phone denouncing the opposition in a live radio interview: 'United Russia is not a party, or not yet anyway, it's just a mechanism for controlling people.'

He was telling the truth. The Kremlin had created United Russia as a tool. It was their appendage, not the other way round. The party had zero bureaucratic control over the Kremlin or Putin's inner circles. The organization, in and of itself, had next to zero policy influence. This meant that United Russia looked like a party, was organized like a party and campaigned like one but was actually more of a bureaucratic patronage network dressed in mass-party clothes. The leadership was powerless, because power was in Surkov's office. In other words, this was a recipe for corruption.

Once, I waited for Olga Krystanovskaya, an intellectual star within the party, in the lobby of Moscow's Hotel National. It is a horrible, expensive place opposite the Duma, replete with thick, unattractive ochre carpets, miserable grey moustached bellboys and function rooms where oil companies announce big deals – but a place to be seen.

As the leader of the liberal faction of United Russia and a sociologist who has authored acclaimed studies on the composition of the political elite, I expected Krystanovskaya to give me a more subtle, even positive understanding of the party than Markov. After yapping at the waitress for the hotel restaurant to 'cook it now', she rolled her eyes at questions about United Russia's internal debates.

'You don't understand, we are not a party like you have in the West, where the decision-making centre is inside the party. We have a decision-making centre outside the party, so when we get the order we move. When we have no orders we don't.'

When even its most senior members spoke of United Russia like this, it was only a matter of time before videos would start to leak, showing what the Duma now looked like. Managed democracy had rendered the chamber so lifeless that deputies increasingly could not even be bothered to turn up. In 2003 it was estimated that as many as fifty-seven of them had not attended more than three times, a figure that rose to ninety-seven two years later.[23] 'It is simply shameful to watch the empty seats', publicly cursed Medvedev in 2010, 'You must go to work!'[24] He had perhaps seen this infamous clip. In the near empty Duma, deputies could be seen clambering over empty chairs to press the 'yes' buzzers of those not present. Some of the few deputies there are sleeping through the vote, slumped like drunks asleep on the metro.

As the Kremlin built up United Russia as a patronage system and United Russia asphyxiated the Duma with its majority, the chamber quietly died as a meaningful institution. Most of its new members had little interest in being politicians at all, rarely giving interviews and spending as little time as possible in the debating chamber. The number of deputies that could be named even by keen observers seemed to decrease year after year, as less and less pretended to lead political lives. Even their own men were forced to admit that something was going awry.

'I know it is a rather paradoxical situation,' grudgingly noted the young Nashi lawmaker Robert Shlegel, one of Surkov's rising stars, 'that we have a lot of members of parliament who are . . . not public people.'

All this was not lost on the 'great puppet master' himself. At their closed meetings, Surkov lambasted the 'bears' as failures and profiteers:

> You cannot always be on life support! You need to be smart to survive . . . More importantly you need to enhance the thinking process. The intellectual life of this party is at zero. If only you could have come up with some interesting comments, like, 'We hoped for the best but it turned out like always' . . . but nothing. However, if you sleep colleagues, nothing terrible will happen. We will consider you a trailer and we will be the engine.[25]

Maybe Surkov was not so smart after all. A party built as a trailer cannot simultaneously be a car. He knew perfectly well why the party was incompetent, because he had not built it to be competent, but to be answerable to the Kremlin's commands.

Botching the Vertical

Amassing all this power was sold to the people like this. In the 1990s Russia had been in chaos. In the 2000s Putin was building what he called a 'vertical of power'. The bureaucracy would have iron down its spine and it would be answerable to him. Russia would become rigid. This vertical, he promised, would deliver what Russians so desperately wanted – a modern state.

Surkov, of course, never believed that Putin's vague vision of a vertical of power made much sense. He is far too clever for that. 'Our average bureaucrat has an archaic understanding of the technologies of power,' he commented in the safety of the German press in 2005, 'He imagines it as a vertical line with a telephone on top . . . and that's how the country is governed.'[26]

This is exactly what Putin wanted. His great ambition had not been to restore a party state. He had not been scarred by the loss of socialism, or even really the empire. What truly horrified Putin, when he first arrived in the Kremlin, was the near fiction of a Russian 'Federation'. One of his first jobs for Yeltsin was being his senior official charged with regional affairs. Putin knew, better than anyone, how weak Moscow's control over its own territories really was in 1999. It appeared to pain him. One opposition leader remembers coming to see the young hope to complain about the murder of one of his activists in the Buddhist republic of Kalmykia. In an outburst that seemed to be filled with anguish, even powerlessness, Putin snapped: 'What do you expect? Everyone in Kalmykia is completely corrupt! What can I do? The system is completely corrupt!'[27]

Putin systematically dismantled Russian federalism. This is because the traumatic experience of working as Yeltsin's eye on the regions never left him. This was a key part of his agenda from the start, unlike most of his political moves into authoritarianism, where he was reactively trying to crush any challenges that threatened to undermine him as they appeared.

Regardless of the rights and wrongs of his approach, the problems he was trying to deal with were real. Not only the 'siloviks' but also the free-market types in government agreed with him. 'Getting control over the governors again, who had been flirting with separatism and illegally funding themselves,' remembers Kasyanov; 'we always viewed this as one of our main tasks.' The former prime minister recalls that Russia was in a governance crisis as bad as its fiscal crisis:

> Then all these measures really seemed necessary, since after the 1998 crisis, there were big problems with the governors, who all 'swallowed' as much sovereignty as it was possible to digest, and in fact destroyed any common economic and legal space in Russia. The country was divided into fiefdoms, in which the governor was the king and god, who did not always obey the federal laws of the centre. The governors were delaying or preventing the exports from one region or the products of another, or conversely, prohibiting the import of agricultural products or alcohol themselves from other regions.[28]

Putin shared this diagnosis. It was in this initial mess that the slogan 'the vertical of power' was coined to fend off accusations of chaos inside the administration. This opaque slogan became the Putinist synonym for recentralization.

The greatest source of infuriation at the start of Putin's first term was that Moscow was making decrees and drafting laws, but they were not being enforced in the regions. This is why he created the Presidential 'envoys'. Their job descriptions were vague, their task simple. The men were dispatched to cajole the governors and make sure the local branches of the FSB, the interior ministry, regional TV, the prosecutor's office and the tax police knew who was boss.

The 'envoys' also surveyed whether regions were breaking federal law. This had become a chronic problem. Throughout the 1990s regional governments had been passing laws without so much as a fleeting thought for either Moscow or the constitution. This breakdown in the supremacy of central law reached such epic proportions that one 1997 government study showed that out of 44,000 laws passed by regional authorities, nearly half of them did not conform with federal law.[29] Moves were taken to correct such laws and amend local constitutions that violated the federal one. Grigory Rapota, whose name was on Surkov's speed dial, former envoy to both the Volga and the North Caucasus, explained the purpose of the vertical like this: 'We absolutely felt we had to bring this legal confusion under one pole of influence.'

Back in the capital, the Kremlin financially undercut the governors. The most important measure cancelled Article 48 of the constitution, which gave governors access to 50 per cent of national tax revenue. A new tax code and a new VAT law centralized payments, cutting the regions out of the spoils. Already by 2002 the era of financial parity was over, with Moscow gathering 62 per cent of all taxes.

Much the poorer, governors were confined to their regions by the law passed in 2000 that ended the role of the upper chamber, the Federation Council, as their power base in the capital. The governors were from then on legally disbarred from doubling as senators, which gave them access to legal immunity, but had to send representatives to the upper chamber instead. After Putin's decision in 2004 that from then on he would appoint governors, the transformation of the Federation Council into a rubber-stamping chamber and governors from Kremlin competitors to clients, was complete. None would now be elected and thus able to rally a mandate in his own right.

Finally, the Kremlin flushed out any remaining regional interests in the Duma by switching to a purely party lists system. The end of constituency MPs, coupled with a new 7 per cent threshold to enter the chamber, made it almost impossible for local leaders putting local concerns first to get elected, unless they were in the 'national parties', whose leaders were on Surkov's speed dial.

The name United Russia indicates the obvious – it too was to play a vital role in building the vertical of power. For three generations, the elite of this vast country had been organized in the Communist Party. This meant that Moscow used the party as a tool to control and discipline all politicians across the imperium. After its implosion the lack of a successful 'Kremlin party' during the Yeltsin years meant that regional politicians came in all shapes and sizes, representing all kinds of interests – and there were few ways that Moscow could corral them.

United Russia was the main tool to 'renationalize' all these politicians into a single structure that the Kremlin could use to control and discipline them. It was supposed to end an era when Moscow could do nothing to influence whoever was in the regional parliament in Siberian Krasnoyarsk, or who was governor in Arctic Chukotka. At the time of writing, United

Russia had a majority in 80 of the country's 83 regional parliaments, controlling 2,840 of the seats out of a total of 3,787, with 74 out of all 83 regional governors being 'bears'. Through conferences, manifestos and slogans – they were all reading Putin's script.

Regional politicians were now supposed to treat Moscow like the boss. Gleb Pavlovsky remembers orders starting to be given to them like they were bureaucrats, not elected officials in their own right. 'The directives from the top were like this: "don't elect that guy, elect this guy", "use X percentage for X party", and "carry it out with the means available to you on site".'[30]

The governors had tried to politically pickpocket Yeltsin. Now that they were being treated like apparatchiks again, it meant one thing – the vertical was complete. Putin's centralization and the rise of United Russia gutted these regional institutions of their meaning. Instead of a multi-nodal, autonomous and federal system able to react quickly in a high-speed post-modern world, the vertical had created a clunky imperial bureaucracy, incapable of acting on its own, utterly dependent on the Kremlin and essentially its patronage network.

They did not realize it at the time, but Putin and Surkov were building a device that would sap away their popularity. Erecting a clumsy, inefficient, vertical of power amidst rising corruption was not only creating a management nightmare for the future – it was laying claim and thus responsibility to all power and thus all problems in Russia. Boris Yeltsin had declined to join a party and used this 'distance' to dodge blame and deflect it onto governors, officials and even his own ministers from his perch as 'the father of the nation'. In encouraging all officials, be they corrupt tax officials in Udmurtia to the governor of Krasnodar, to join United Russia – he was making himself in the eyes of anyone who lived in the regions, not only linked but *also responsible* for the sins of that tax official or the crimes of that governor.

Building up the Bureaucrats

Strengthening the state was not just about reinstalling the Soviet chain of command. It was about massive recruitment. The bureaucracy ballooned, growing by more than two-thirds between 2000 and 2010, hitting nearly 1.7 million employees.[31] In particular, the agencies responsible for security, law and order expanded, the infamous 'siloviks'. Spending on them rose from \$2.8 billion in 2000 to \$36.5 billion in 2010.[32]

The FSB has not wielded great influence as an organization but has been rewarded for its loyalty. Yeltsin's break-up of the KGB was partially reversed. The FSB saw the responsibility for foreign electronic counter-surveillance, oversight over potential mutinies in the army, control over the border guard force and its own foreign intelligence bureau restored to 'the corporation'. FSB agents rose to prominence as the only trustworthy cadres who could coordinate the vertical of power being pulled together, as men from the 'corporation' were never suspected of any regional allegiances. Servicemen were now lauded by officials as nothing less than 'our new nobility'.[33]

Cuts were stopped with the FSB remaining a huge force. With over 350,000 employees, it is bigger than most Western European armies. It has been estimated that whilst in the USSR there was one KGB man for every 428 Soviets, the new regime had one FSB employee for every 297 Russians.[34] The ratio for policemen to population is similarly high. Russia had 611 police per 100,000 inhabitants, compared to 244 in the USA or 292 in Germany.[35] Overall there are over 3 million employees of the dozen 'silovik' ministries charged with security, ranging from the FSB to the police.[36]

Across Russia there was a low-key return to Soviet methods to tackle dissent. This took the form of closing down of papers, seizing 'dangerous' imported books, compounding print-runs, harassing dissenters, infiltrating opposition groups, threatening calls, detentions of unregistered protesters, violent break-ups of demonstrations, the sporadic use of mental asylums to imprison dissidents, and bogus charges of 'bad parenting' to scare them with the prospect of their children being put into care. In the North Caucasus there were extra-judicial executions.

The FSB started keeping a closer eye on the Russian population. By 2007 it had amassed over 70 million fingerprint dossiers for a country of only 142 million citizens.[37] The regular murders of journalists (it was never clear by whom) created a culture of intimidation and self-censorship. Since Putin came to power, the Committee to Protect Journalists estimates that at least twenty-six journalists have been murdered for practising their trade, whilst another fourteen have been killed for 'unconfirmed motives'.[38]

The country suffered higher death rates from terror attacks than Israel or Pakistan, whilst abroad it was unable to either foresee or prevent the coloured revolutions. One could be forgiven for asking if the Russian taxpayer was getting value for money for all its 'siloviks'. This underperformance was not lost on Surkov. 'Generally speaking,' he said, 'Our problem is that the political leadership needs to motivate the bureaucrats more.'[39]

Sovereign Democracy

In 2007, Sergey Ivanov, then the defence minister, felt that new times were in need of slogans. He called for a new ideological triad for Russia:

'sovereign democracy, strong economy and military might'.[40] His nod to the tsarist ideological triad of 'orthodoxy, autocracy and nationality' under Nicholas I was unmistakable – inviting ridicule by polite Moscow society who began mocking Ivanov with competitions for the wriest triad such as 'Oil, Censorship and Gas', or 'Putin, the Party and Petrol'.

The authorities were not deterred. Putinism had evolved far enough that by 2007 the Kremlin started to attempt to elaborate its own ideology. This was the inverse of the 1990s dreams of converging with the West. This new 'thinking' was first announced in a keynote speech by Surkov himself and called 'The View From Utopia'. There was little that was utopian about his eloquent but empty words. Russia was not going to develop into a Western democracy, nor did the West have the right to judge its political system. Beyond that, sovereign democracy was thin. The 'view from utopia' turned out to be as little as announcing that Russian political culture had some unique characteristics: 'Firstly, the desire for political integrity through the centralization of power. Secondly, the idealization of political struggle. Thirdly, the personification of political institutions.'[41]

In other words, continuity with tsarist-Soviet centralization, continuity with communist youth groups and propaganda, and the 'personification of political institutions' meaning the power of Putin himself. In 'The View from Utopia' the Kremlin had proclaimed it was like China setting its own 'sovereign' course. Just how far Moscow had swung away from hopes to build democratic Russia is captured in the memoir of one senior official, who published anonymously under a pseudonym. He recalled:

> So once again empire is on the agenda. The imperial project has beaten its competitors from our own times. The nation-building programme, 'the new Russia', has crumbled and been removed from the table . . . in their hands power is going to try and build a new empire, *presumably* one of the new type.[42]

The ideology Surkov had come up with was as insubstantial as it sounded. Putin's enormous popularity still meant that the regime neither needed nor was really able to craft a strong identity for itself beyond him. Yet what seemed like strength at the time was actually a weakness. One study of United Russia election material spelt this out brutally. A full 70 per cent of their statements were simply rhetoric, e.g. 'we want a modern economy'.[43] No wonder that polls revealed only 3 per cent of its members had joined for ideological reasons.[44] Little surprise, then, that in its own prospective members survey over 60 per cent said they had been motivated to join to solve their own material problems and half were motivated in order to make some money on the side.[45]

These numbers – and certainly far darker ones Surkov had access to – were doubtless running through his mind when he announced at a small political function: 'The biggest flaw prevailing in the political system is that it rests on the resources of one person, and as a consequence one party.' He then said: 'This makes the system unstable.'[46]

The Flaw in the Dictatorship of Law

At the end of his first presidency Putin could have been forgiven for telling Surkov not to worry. The bureaucrat plucked from obscurity to crisis-manage a crashed Russia had come out on top. Not only had he brought his rivals, the regional barons and the rebel insurgents, to heel but he had also amassed huge political resources in the most valuable of currencies. He now had power, popularity and petro-dollars in abundance. The gamble in arresting Khodorkovsky had paid off. The subsequent homage paid to him by the shaken oligarchs had secured the Putin consensus. Propaganda and paid state wages had built up a Putin majority. His propaganda and policies had made him not just popular, but with consistently over 60 per cent ratings he was one of the most popular leaders in Europe.

Putin's circumstances were not just favourable for state building. They were more favourable than the conditions in which China's Deng Xiaoping or Singapore's Lee Kuan Yew had begun their authoritarian moderniza-tions. Putin had the resources and the ambitions to rebuild the Russian state. Yet a decade later the state would not only remain inefficient, dysfunctional and venal – but was more corrupt than it had been a decade earlier. What went wrong?

Putin was no Lee Kuan Yew. His state-building programme was flawed, knotting the Russian state into a tangle of incompetent and inefficient institutions that bred corruption. Those powers 'renationalized' were not being embedded in federal structures but in the opaque circles around Putin and his 'friends'. The mechanics of power, rather than modernizing, were being turned into a court. The state was turning into a festering swamp of incapacity. This was a system not built with efficiency in mind, but built to be under Putin's control.

One of the first rules of management is that pouring vast amounts of money and drafting in large amounts of people will not make an organi-zation better at achieving results if its strategy is defunct and those in charge are incompetent or dysfunctional. Throwing money and more people at a problem may actually compound the problem by making an inefficient structure clumsier, with ever more dependents, without getting anywhere near increased efficiency. This is what started to happen to the Russian state.

Putin had made one huge promise when coming to power – 'democracy,' he said, 'is the dictatorship of law.' This slogan was repeated and repeated. The aim was to end the bureaucratic breakdown of the 1990s. Russian officials were supposed to become less corrupt, administration was supposed to become more successful, the FSB better at tracking down gangsters and the overall state less predatory on ordinary people. The justification for all the extra state capacity was supposed to be increased efficiency.

The Kremlin viewed this as synonymous with recentralization. It was not. 'Recentralization' under Putin did not see the strengthening of federal institutions at the expense of regional ones. It has meant the castration of all competing institutions to Putin. One by one, independent power centres that could restrain the executive were neutered. The power of the mass media, parliament, independent governors and meaningful elections to challenge the Kremlin and thus hold it to account for its inefficiencies was eliminated. Yet these institutions exist for a reason – they provide checks and balances not just to limit absolute power, but also to expose incompetence and curb gross inefficiencies.

Power was being personalized, in a defunct framework. Thus, the large amounts of money and cash invested by the Kremlin into building up the institutions that were supposed to make Russia less lawless did not deliver. The primary evidence of state inefficiency in Russia is corruption. The 'abuse of public office for private gain' continued to take place on every level of the state.

There is a difference between the kind of corruption that Putin might have wanted in order to increase his power, and the kind of corruption that Putin would not have wanted as it undermines his legitimacy. What he did not want was the continued bad behaviour of the petty bureaucracy, the police and the local security structures. They became increasingly predatory. This did not happen because Putin 'wanted it'. It happened as an accidental by-product of his flawed agenda.

What it created was the exact opposite of the 'dictatorship of law' he had promised. The fatal flaw was as follows. As Putin brought the loyalty of national and regional elites, he expanded the bureaucracy and the 'siloviks' as props of the regime. This was both rhetorical – honouring the FSB publicly and repeatedly – and practical as he encouraged all ambitious civil servants to join United Russia. As he relied on them and associated with them, this meant that they should not be challenged, humiliated or aggressively policed.

He did this, however, at the same time as closing down all institutions that could hold them to account. Those inside the petty bureaucracy who could have fought corruption on behalf of Moscow had been neutered.

The mass media, elections, local politicians and a national parliament de facto no longer existed as tools to fight abuses.

Putin created a system where he removed everyone capable of fighting corruption in the bureaucracy and made his image reliant on the bureaucracy. This gave officials impunity to behave in a predatory manner. Nor did he set an example. Putin believed that through his control of the national TV media he could hide Kremlin corruption from the public. He more or less did. His huge mistake was in encouraging the bureaucracy to join United Russia. Whilst they behaved in an increasingly predatory way, he began to associate himself in the minds of normal people with the policeman who wanted a bribe or the local official who wanted a cut.

Even United Russia's parliamentary leaders such as the slippery Vladimir Burmatov are well aware of this. We had a frank conversation over fruit juice in a dim cafe behind the Duma. 'The main problem in our country is the relationship between people and power. The people don't have a problem with Putin. They have a problem with the tax inspector, the traffic cop and with the local housing official. They then associate their misdeeds with Putin and United Russia. And this poisons everything.' Yet they had little to no idea what to do about it. As he left, the deputy threw down the equivalent of $30 to cover a bill worth less than $10. He was making the point that he was too rich to care about change.

Corrupt officials meant that Russian businessmen increasingly built in the 'rule of 30 per cent' into their budgets to cover bribes for the necessary officials. The statistics of millions doing so are shocking. Between 2001 and 2005 the think-tank INDEM estimated that the volume of bribes extorted by the authorities had increased nearly ten times to over $316 billion.[47] INDEM calculated that the average cost of a bribe had gone up over thirteen times in those years, from $10,000 to $136,000.[48] During Putin's first presidency Russia slid dramatically down the Corruptions Perceptions Index, compiled annually by the NGO Transparency International. In 2001 the country was in 79th place, alongside Pakistan.[49] By 2006 it was 121st in the index, with Rwanda.[50] This meant it was not getting any easier to run a 'clean' business, but harder to avoid living by the 'rule of 30 per cent'.

This made the 'dictatorship of law' sound like a bad joke. The predatory bureaucracy meant Russia remained a dangerous place for business. Surveys showed an increase in corruption on all levels of government. An anaemic rule of law meant businessmen could 'rent' courts to persecute their enemies. This is so pervasive that one study estimated one in six Russian businessmen had been prosecuted for 'economic crimes'. Most of these cases have no plaintiffs and a zero rate of acquittal, which goes some way to explaining why as many as 30 per cent of adult males have a criminal record.[51] This is not just continuity with the Yeltsin years, but a trickle down from the top. What the Kremlin did to its Khodorkovsky, countless bureaucrats did to *their* Khodorkovsky.

Putin had strengthened the FSB and bureaucracy. But corruption rose, as he had not answered one simple question. Who by the mid-2000s guarded the guardians? The answer in Russia was 'Putin', or nobody. As a result, the European Police Office (Europol) has estimated that 20 per cent of members of the Russian parliament, 40 per cent of decision makers in private enterprise, 50 per cent of bank directors, and 60 per cent of the directors and managers of state-owned companies had criminal ties.[52] The 'dictatorship of law' was, in reality, the dictatorship of a venal officialdom.

Soldiers of Surkov

There is always something diagnostic about a bestseller. In 2006 the novel *San'kia* started circulating online. After it was published, it consistently ranked in the top twenty lists for three years. There are rumours that Putin himself read it. This Russian book of the decade was written by an unlikely novelist, Zakhar Prilepin.

He had a shaved head and had been an OMON riot policeman who fought in both Chechen wars. When Putin came to power he was paid $26 a week and took extra shifts at checkpoints to make sure insurgents were not driving out of the Caucasus. 'They never had proper transit documents,' he recalled, 'I let them pass and they gave me bananas, apples and sometimes fifty Ruble bills – I was not ashamed.'[53]

His *San'kia* is set in the 'dictatorship of law', the story of Sacha, a blundering punk-nationalist whose father has drunk himself to death. He begins to 'run' with a group of pathetic revolutionaries, baby-faced thugs who can barely tie their own shoelaces, let alone fight the police. Sacha falls into their company not out of choice but because he is completely disorientated: a cipher for a fatherless generation. An avuncular professor, concerned by his brawls, invites him for a quick word. He knows full well how punks smash their heads open banging on the bars of the state. The professor raises his voice:

> You have nothing in common with the motherland. The same way the motherland has nothing in common with you. There is no more motherland. It's vanished, gone. There's no point playing these games – smashing windows, breaking necks and God knows what else. Do you really think that this people, half of whom are alcoholics and half of whom are pensioners need a purpose?[54]

As angry as he is ignorant, Sacha snorts back: 'What then – live here? In this country that will be dead in thirty years, over-run by Chechens and Chinese?'[55]

Surkov and Putin knew full well that there was already widespread anger at the bottom of society towards corruption, particularly acute amongst the young. It was not yet directed at Putin. This is why Surkov was keen to get them onside to avoid a repeat of the 'Orange scenario' in Russia, where a new generation exhausted by corruption had en masse deserted the Kremlin candidate. This is why to cover up the incompetence of the system, the government pushed ever harder to get the young to join Nashi, to give them a purpose in Putinism.

The people who read San'kia are the same people who joined Nashi. They are from what was then called 'Generation Elusive', those born between the last years of Brezhnev and the beginning of perestroika.[56] Those of this age in Russia, around twenty-five to thirty-five, are much too young to have ever had any illusions to shatter (communist, democratic) and end up in Putin and Surkov's 'Generation Emptiness'. They are a brutalized generation that entered the job market, right into the wreckage, where they found the cynical moral wasteland of the 1990s.

Their Russia has never known dreams; in the industrial cities they have taken to vicious, hooliganish behaviour. This generation thinks of itself as fatherless, without anyone to look up to – the death of the totalitarian state, which knocked the life out of the welfare state, emasculated tens of millions of fathers waiting for unpaid wages, sending them into alcoholism – all this left the young with only old burnt-out cynics, 'Soviets' or drunks to give them guidance.

As a result, a rainbow spectrum of cultish gangs, which promised blood brotherhood to the lost, flourished – from football fanatic attacks to neo-Nazis, even anti-Putin psychedelic punk fascism or art groups that stage public political orgies. Nobody in the Kremlin knew what 'Generation Elusive' believed in, other than that they felt cut off from power. None of this was surprising. The Soviet structures that reared both Khodorkovsky and Putin, the vilified KGB and Komsomol, bred loyalty despite all their brainwashing and oppression. This is because they really were real social lifts. The party turned Gorbachev and Yeltsin from peasants into masters of Moscow. But had they been born in post-Soviet Russia, they would have remained peasants, as the power elite itself was evolving into a removed aristocracy.

Surkov and Pavlovsky were convinced that at all costs they needed enough young out there celebrating the birthday of the 'national leader', young people who could get to Moscow overnight to camp out on Red Square and prevent this palpable resentment ever coalescing into an

'Orange Revolution'. Their secret ingredient to this 'purpose' was for Nashi to have all the camping, sex and rock stars of a romantic revolutionary movement.

In the mid-2000s I enjoyed watching the ambivalent, dismissive reaction of my friends at the elite MGIMO University to this paid-for 'mobilization' – people in exactly the age group Surkov was targeting. As one of Moscow's most prestigious institutes, a favourite dumping ground for the children of the minor oligarchy whose English wasn't up to scratch for abroad, its academic quality was corroding in proportion to the rise in chauffeured cars outside. Those studying here were not the grandchildren of the party elite but the sons and daughters of Khanty-Mansiysk oil bandits, FSB officers turned 'tax inspectors' or aluminium gangsters turned respectable United Russia MPs – a cross section of a coarse ruling class that had replaced the Soviet nomenklatura. Ashamed of such gruff parents, they loved nothing better than to pose as 'more European than thou', citing Jean Luc Godard movies or name-dropping Berlin galleries, knowing full well that their fathers (but not if they were girls) had plans for them in 'business'. But the idea of joining Nashi repulsed them. 'It's a Komsomol for churls and careerists from the darkest depths,' sniffed one daughter of a general turned entrepreneur. She was right – that was exactly what it was.

The crushing majority of young Russians, anyone not lucky enough to have fathers who struck oil in the 1990s, who could now bribe a place at MGIMO, or with well-dressed parents in the 10–20 per cent so proud (relieved) to be in 'the new bourgeoisie', are all what we would call in the West, the 'social excluded'. In the mid-2000s some 70 per cent of people were not middle class, living in a state where all the social elevators of the Soviet Union had rotted or snapped. Access to 'opportunity', to big sums and big resources, be they financial or political, was available only to a tiny, cobbled together Moscow power circle. If you went to school over the Urals in post-Soviet Russia, the idea of studying hard and becoming what you wanted was as laughable, as inaccessible as it is in the worst black American ghetto. Like there, the cult of 'gangster' thrived, likewise perceived as the only ways to riches and respect.

For such people, Nashi was a godsend. If you lived in a small town like Ivanovo, where 40 per cent of the population in 2005 lived below the Russian poverty line, it offered the promise to be suddenly lifted into a respectable structure that could get you to Moscow: conferences, a badge, events, even a career.[57] This is why over 120,000 rushed into an organization that celebrated Putin's birthday and marched along the boulevards round the Kremlin with hundreds of slightly comic drummers leading the way.

The crowning event in the annual calendar for a Nashist was camp 'Seliger'. There was cheering as Putin and other Kremlin hands did 'guest lectures', but crucially there was a good time with free booze, camping and encouragement to 'reproduce for Russia'. Pavlovsky was worried that those who turned up were really there for the beer and not battle, hectoring them that they lacked 'brutality'. But Nashi leader Yakemenko was on a high, spending the night with a teenager in her Seliger camp tent.[58]

The kind of girls who turned up at Seliger were poor, vulnerable people. One girl, Sveta Kuritsina, was cornered at an official conference and prodded to explain why she supported Vladimir Putin. This girl, dressed in fake white fur collar, mouthed such an astoundingly inarticulate response that she became an Internet sensation:

> Nashist: My name is Sveta and I am from Ivanovo city United Russia has made a lot of achievements. They lifted the economy, we became . . . more better dressed . . . and it ain't always been like it is now! And it was a very big achievement. And for the farmers' thing are going very well too.
> Reporter: What exactly have they done for the farmers?
> Nashist: Eurgh . . . There is like more land . . . eurghhh . . . Umm . . . I dunno what to say . . . I saw more land . . . Ummm . . . and more vegetables . . .[59]

This poor girl was universally mocked by the new middle class, by Moscow TV and by thousands of bloggers, as a symbol of 'the churls and careerists' that had joined Nashi. What she could not explain is that she lived in a 'hostel' with bare, damp walls and a faded poster of Angelina Jolie, in a town filled with alcoholics, heroin addicts and post-industrial decay. Coming to Moscow with five hundred people from Ivanovo to drum for Putin and Yakemenko was the highlight of her life. 'He is a great leader . . . The youth understands,' she told a reporter, 'and anyway I like older men.'[60]

These people would have shouted anything – and the 'political technologists' knew it. So the slogans that they encouraged this 'anti-fascist youth group' to chant were ones designed to reawaken as much viciousness out of historical pain as possible. To ward off the 'Orange menace' they chose to inject into the country a neurotic dose of hysteria and paranoia that Russia had been healing from – the Cold War atomic scares, the Nazi dimension, the foreign agents trying to break up the nation (like they had in 1991), the plotters waiting to attack Russia by surprise when she was sleeping (like they had in 1941). In other words: the enemy within. 'Drawing heavily from collective memory,' recalled Pavlovsky, 'was the stimulation of all past experiences of violence and insecurity – against which the authorities would be the only safeguard.'[61]

The enemy within was not readily available, so Nashi began to harass those who might be the sponsors of this shadowy presence – the ambassadors of state with which Moscow had imperfect ties. Nashi went into action waving placards such as 'Wanted the ambaSSador of eSStonia'. After the British ambassador Tony Brenton delivered what he calls 'a rather dull speech', they launched a campaign against him. 'You get a good insight into the psychology of paranoia,' he sighed, 'when something like that happens to you.' People like Sveta from Ivanovo were sent to stand outside his residence with posters that were either odd, 'ANTONY BRENTON: LOSER', or merely risible, 'SAVE RUSSIAN DEMOCRACY FROM TONY BRENTON'. More were sent to follow him around, jumping out at conferences, on planes, pretty much on any occasion, waving their fists and screaming things like, 'B-*rr*-enton! Apologise! B-*rr*-enton Apologise!' or 'B-*rr*-enton! Fascists Always Run First . . . B-*rr*-enton! Come back!'

Rubbing Salt into Russian Wounds

This whole campaign was not in actual fact designed to make Brenton feel paranoid and humiliated, but to be played endlessly on national television, to make Russians feel paranoid and humiliated. The months of the anti-Brenton campaign were shouting to those on the couch not to listen to 'the Orange siren song' as these were the voices of the enemy who had beaten Russia in the Cold War and then 'humiliated her' in the 1990s.

It did not take long to whip up residual neuroticism in a country fed such propaganda non-stop until the time of Gorbachev. Television again was the main instrument. 'Experts' invited to 'debate' issues started to come from anti-Western, nationalist or 'Eurasianist' think-tanks, whose purpose was not to think or write reports but to comment hysterically in every news source about shadowy villains. These 'intellectuals' pushed onto the talk shows were men such as Alexander Dugin: this 'thinker' frothed at the mouth calling for a restored empire, identified with the 'Eurasianist' architects of the Holocaust and shrieked what was needed was a Russian–Arab alliance to counter Washington. Flicking on the TV news one was bombarded by clips of officials making chauvinistic comments about Georgians, Estonians, Ukrainians and 'documentaries' about the 'attacks' on the ethnic Russian minorities in those countries. Broadcasts flagged up irritants such as human rights organizations as suspects of MI6 or CIA infestation, as a means of slandering them. They even accused mysterious foreign powers of financing the insurgency in the North Caucasus.

For Pavlovsky and the black PR artists, the Bush administration was a gift. To vilify an America that actually was invading third world countries, running a shadowy prison camp system for 'enemy combatants' caught in the 'Global War on Terror', which growled about bombing Iran as Dick Cheney pitched up 'promoting democracy' in Kiev and Tbilisi – was as easy as shooting fish in a barrel. They could not have invented a better cast of villains if they had tried.

The West, which Russia had craved contact with in totalitarian times, was vilified by Putin. Britain, he said, 'forgets it is not a colonial power', and whilst the PR campaign surrounding a law to limit the same kind of NGOs receiving foreign funding that had foxed the Kremlin in Kiev was pushed through, the 'national leader' snarled that they were 'behaving like jackals at foreign embassies'.[62] The fall of the USSR, said Putin, was nothing less than 'the greatest geopolitical catastrophe of the twentieth century'.[63] He publically lamented the authorities chose not to fight to save the Soviet Union.[64] This verse removed in 1956 reappeared in one of the busiest Moscow metro stations – 'Stalin reared us on loyalty to the people. He inspired us to labour and heroism.'

What Surkov was creating were people who, unlike him, did not understand that the totalitarian state – with its gigantic empire, hypocrisy and prison camps, which had incited Russians to make such sacrifices and given such little back – really had been something of a parasite. He was creating a cohesive cadre of future politicians around Yakemenko, who thought of it only as a vanished superpower.

Everyday Putinism

In places like Kaliningrad and Ivanovo the 'wild 1990s' were fading away. So had the shock of the Soviet implosion. The state, which had provided free education, free medicine, full employment and the feeling of fear, would never return. But something Soviet had – a pervasive feeling of pressure, that there were locked doors, low humming paranoia and the knowledge that there were things you shouldn't say in front of power.

This could be seen in a thousand small ways. Drunks on trains began threatening people by saying they were undercover FSB agents to intimidate them into handing over bottles of vodka. What it was acceptable to say in polite company inched more into chauvinism ('Estonia is an SS state'). Things that had been fringe comments became mainstream once Putin had said it ('NGOs are behaving like jackals at foreign embassies'). Ideas that belonged to cranks were discussed half-seriously ('Do you think there is an American–Georgian plot against Russia?').

When the politics of fear start to be used, normal people feel it first in schools. In Putin's Russia, one of Gorbachev's reforms to demilitarize normal life was overturned – in the classrooms. In came the old mandatory

Soviet military day. Most people found them comic, with old maps showing massed ranks of German and American tanks as the threat in the West, but the message was not lost on those present – Russia had enemies, Russia must be vigilant. From time to time, reports surfaced of children in particularly repressive regions being made to read poems in praise of Putin and United Russia. Across the board, textbooks were changed to mention that Stalin was an efficient manager and leading historians denounced them as 'culturally racist', but taking the sting out of it, Solzhenitsyn's *The Gulag Archipelago* was put on the reading list.[65] Yet, for the most part, this was just going through the motions.

Things became less of a laughing matter upon graduation. Russia craves for normal lives to be fully demilitarized and to have a professional army like a 'civilized country', but the post-Soviet army is still a conscript force. If you have any possible means of getting out of it – that is, even the slightest ability to pull strings or pay a bribe, get an 'unfit' certificate, or go to university – an eighteen-year-old boy will go to any length to do so. This is because a year in the army in Russia is a year that the teenage poor spend being brutalized into men. The really unfortunate have been sent to the 'internal abroad' in the Caucasus, but today it is not Chechens that kill the most ethnic Russian boys a year – but their 'elders'.

This is what they call 'Dedovschina', which means 'Grandpa's Terror'. This is an endemic hangover from the Soviet, even the tsar's army, where their officers and elders administer a vicious hazing on the recruits. It is every Russian mother's worst nightmare. It is not as universal as it once was but is still extremely common for boys to be beaten, humiliated and wounded in their own bases. There are many rapes and murders. The numbers are astounding. In the typical year of 2006 over 3,500 cases of violent abuse were reported and 292 conscripts killed or committed suicide.[66] Only thirty-six died fighting in Chechnya.[67] That is more deaths in one year than the entire losses of the French, German and Italian NATO troops in over a decade in Afghanistan. But of course most cases go unreported. Even if you are not beaten, a year in the army is still a year in an abusive institution where teenagers at their most impressionable get irradiated with its culture of heavy drinking, fighting and blood brothers against the world. It is little surprise that a lot of the poorest Russian young men are good with guns, prone to alcoholism and violently anti-Caucasian.

The lucky ones go to university – but they do not go to Moscow State University or to MGIMO. The institutes dotted between Smolensk and Kamchatka started to discourage anything 'Orange' on campus. How far they go in the name of 'stability' really depends on the dean. In one technical college in Moscow, thronged halls on the first day of term were bluntly told: 'There will be zero political activity here. Anyone who engages in political activity will be expelled.' In the elite establishments a few kilometres away, where the children of the elite park their Mercedes outside, date Western expats and look down at the scholarship kids from the sticks, hoping to enter the bureaucracy, the deans did little to harass opposition cliques. Yet the chances of a high-profile anti-Putinist speaker being invited, compared to say a senior figure in Putin's party, are slim.

Beyond Moscow regions, out in the provinces where 120 million Russians live, students involved in anti-Putin and ultra-nationalist cliques became nervous. If you weren't careful, this was something that could be used against you. In the Baltic city of Kaliningrad I spent an evening listening to a prototype set of fears whilst drinking with some twentysomething chemical engineering students and their girlfriends who were at teacher training college. Though they could not point to any concrete cases – or knew the names of anyone this had happened to – they knew the deans were members of United Russia and that if you crossed an invisible anti-Putin line you could get reprimanded for 'hooliganism', or lose your place in the subsidized dorms that they couldn't survive financially without. In other cities – Ufa, Vladivostok, Ekaterinburg – you hear the same thing.

Nobody knows where this line is, or many people who have crossed it, but it is there inside people's heads. It wasn't there before. 'What for? Lose my accommodation? Lose my chances for a good job? What for? I want to be a teacher, in a state school,' said Evgenia, aged twenty-four, that evening in the Kaliningrad basement bar. 'I don't want to risk this by protesting. Especially when protests don't work.'

The invisible line began to creep into your choice of work. Journalism, destroyed by the videocracy, came to be seen as a cheap PR hackery, a job for the insincere. 'Investigative journalism' was increasingly seen as dangerous and parents discouraged their children from going into it. What was on TV dropped a hint: Putin spoke dismissively after the star-reporter Anna Politkovskaya was murdered in 2006; after thugs tried to kill columnist Oleg Kashin in 2011, Yakemenko mocked 'the zombie' while he was in intensive care. The other side of the line grew in popularity: professors, polls and even (fatefully) Mikhail Khodorkovsky, noticed that the bureaucracy was becoming more and more popular as a career path. In remote areas the FSB academies enjoyed a boom in applicants.

One night in 2009 on the Trans-Siberian railway I sat in third class with a railway engineer from Omsk in Siberia, a schoolteacher from near Khabarovsk in the Far East and her fourteen-year-old daughter who was about to go to boarding school. 'When it was communism,' her pallid mother explained, 'I wouldn't have had to have paid so much . . .' But she was cut short. 'What's communism, Mummy?'

A wave of horror froze over the mother and momentarily paralyzed the man from Omsk. 'It's a country,' mumbled the engineer, 'where lots of things are free.' The mother snapped back – 'No it isn't! It's a country where . . . where . . .' For a split second I had the feeling that I was watching something profound, before I asked the girl a few questions about her boarding school. Bashful, she almost pouted – 'It's an FSB boarding school . . .' 'And does that make it a better boarding school?' I asked. 'Everybody knows that the FSB are the strongest,' replied the fourteen-year-old who did not know what communism was.

It was so easy for all Putin's PR men to bring that invisible line down in the heads of the old, who had been born in what Russians call 'the Stalin time'. It was very easy to encourage them into old Soviet patterns. One afternoon I sat with a friend in his *khrushchevka* housing block in south Moscow as his grandmother, called Ninel (Lenin spelt backwards) watched TV in the next room. Through the door she heard the names of politicians (Putin, Surkov, Nemtsov) and tried to tell her grandson to be careful. Don't speak to a foreigner like this about politics. 'Stalin was fifty years ago you silly old woman,' snapped my friend, a trainee diplomat, 'I can talk politics with a foreigner if I want.'

No, his grandmother was being silly, but not stupid. By 2005 the country had not returned to oppression, but it had switched back on the soundtrack of slogans against the enemy within that had once droned on alongside it. Khodorkovsky had gone to the Gulag alone. Yet he was also the only power broker who knew where Putin's invisible line was.

On a flight from the Siberian city of Barnaul to Moscow in 2005, with Khodorkovsky, Beslan and Kiev all behind him, the President invited his favourite journalist to dine with him. As the plane crossed the Russian continent the uneasy reporter, Andrei Kolesnikov, began to push Putin on the disturbing shapes he had begun to see in the system he was building:

'I don't like that sometime after you arrested Khodorkovsky, I lost the feeling that I lived in a free country. I have not started to feel fear . . .'

Putin interrupted: 'That is, the feeling of absolute freedom has gone, but the feeling of fear has not yet appeared?'

'Yes, the feeling that existed under your predecessor has gone,' said Kolesnikov.

'But the feeling of fear has not yet appeared,' asked Putin, as if mulling it over.

'Not yet,' said Kolesnikov.

To which Putin replied, 'And did you not think that *this was what I was aiming for*: that one feeling disappeared, but the other did not appear?'[68]

CHAPTER FIVE

PUTIN'S COURT

WHEN PUTIN inherited Yeltsin's office, he found himself alone in the castle. He had no reliable cadres in Moscow. He saw a parliament dominated by communists, was much too junior in the KGB to enjoy true authority in the FSB, found the regions run by barons and unlike the old man did not feel these were 'his oligarchs' sitting atop such huge financial flows. He had no court.

His evolution to tsar-like authority evolved through three stages. First, Putin brought in his clan. Gorbachev and Yeltsin had spent a long time in Moscow building up a power base and had no need to draft in people from Stavropol or Sverdlovsk. Putin had not had time, so he brought in his men from St Petersburg to be his clients. These were provincial officials, unready for national government, but they were the only people he felt he could trust.

Second, Putin made sure his was the only court. The oligarchs who controlled institutions that threatened his power – independent TV, or independent big oil – were exiled and their assets nationalized. Beginning with the exile of Berezovsky and Gusinsky, ending with the imprisonment of Khodorkovsky, the Kremlin eliminated all other politically threatening patronage systems in Russian politics.

Third, once these men had been eliminated and Putin re-elected, his friends evolved into tycoons. Through a combination of renationalization and awarding state contracts, Putin ensured that the largest financial flows from natural resources were in the hands of loyalists. It is exactly the same principle that led to 'loans for shares' – distributing the right to collect the rents from natural resources in exchange for political support. Ministers became millionaires, as they doubled as board members of state corporations. This made the Russian elite one of the richest ruling castes in the world. It cemented the Putin consensus with cash.

Sitting in a Kremlin office, Simon Kordonsky, now a leading sociologist with the looks of a drinker, was watching the consolidation of the monarchical presidency with horror and fascination. In the Soviet Union he had been an outsider, even briefly a tramp, but now he was at the heart of things as the head of 'expert control' in the presidential administration, then a senior consultant and speech-writer to Putin himself. There, Mr Kordonsky started to realize he was witnessing a historic regression in action. Convinced that tsarist Russia's reliance on exporting grain and the Soviet Union's reliance on exporting oil and gas had not only doomed them, but shaped them, he had come to believe that building a diversified market economy could free Russia from this political curse. By 2003, everything seemed to be slipping backwards. Kordonsky explains:

'Russia has always been a resource society. It is not a society structured like yours in the West. The state feeds itself off natural resources, which are then distributed, either as subsidies or as the rights to control rents by the Kremlin. The power of the state is the power to direct these flows, politics is competition to divert these flows – so what looks like corruption isn't corruption, in the sense of it being a defect in the system, it is the nature of the system itself.'

In 2005, Kordonsky left the government to work at the Higher School of Economics and write academic research on what he felt Russia had become. 'Essentially', he explained to me over green tea in a cafe frequented by the FSB, eating raw sugar from the pot with a spoon:

'The core of the economy is now no longer a market. The economy is based on raw materials and these are brought under the direct or indirect control of the state. So what looks like business is actually just a system of distribution . . . what this means is that upstairs there is a man, called the president, or the general secretary, or the monarch – the title is unimportant – who gets to decide what people or what classes of society benefit from the resource flows. All complaints are directed upwards, to him, the supreme arbiter. This all began with the Khodorkovsky affair and the transfer of control of all key resource flows under Putin's supervision.'

Russia's post-communist future turned out to be politically backward. 'It's so feudal,' sighed one assistant to the oligarchy, 'the way our tycoons relate to power.' The language used to talk about its leader was also turning not so much Soviet, as medieval. Surkov once said, in a sacral tone with a smile on his face, 'I honestly believe that Putin was the person who was sent to Russia by fate and by God in the country's difficult hour, for our greater, wider good.'[1]

The Embezzler's Palace

I am standing in front of a dribbling windowpane with Sergei Kolesnikov. The view over the city is grey and uninspiring. But he seems to like it. 'That's the Russian Orthodox Church, can you see?' The office is bare.

The only ever defector from Putin's inner circle of St Petersburg 'friends' tries to make me coffee from an instant machine that glows fluorescent colours. 'I'm sorry, I've never used this thing before.' This is his exile, in Tallinn, the capital of Estonia.

Over twenty years ago, in St Petersburg, both Kolesnikov and Putin were in a similar situation. Their old Soviet careers had reached a dead end. Kolesnikov was a biophysicist with a soft voice, sitting inside a doomed corner of the military–industrial complex. He woke up one morning and understood that the state was no longer interested in funding his research into mitigating the effects of biological warfare. 'I realized that there would be no more funding and in a few years it would all be rolled up.'

So he went into business selling medical equipment with a former KGB agent he knew well, Dmitry Gorelov, who knew another former KGB agent, Vladimir Putin, a guy from the mayor's office, who arranged for both of them to provide the city with their wares. This was a conventional 1990s business hook-up. Two decades later it had grown into a monstrous one. Playing every friend and connection you had was exactly how business was done all over Russia at the time – any contact, any old institutional tie in the USSR, was something someone was trying to turn into cash. Soldiers became bodyguards, mathematicians became financiers, biophysicists became pharmaceutical salesmen and KGB agents became democratic politicians. This is how a chunk of the nomenklatura became the capitalist elite. Because the state was barely functioning – nothing mattered more to people than their network or their ability to maintain them, manipulate them. When you ask Kolesnikov what Putin was like the first time they met and their business began, he pulls a strained face, as if not quite sure what happened. He claims he had not one hint of what doing business with this grey man would turn into:

'I first met Putin in 1991 . . . and he was an absolutely normal man. He was absolutely normal. His voice was normal . . . not tough, not high. He had a normal personality . . . normal intelligence, not especially high intelligence. You could go out the door and find thousands and thousands of people in Russia, all of them just like Putin . . . I was surprised when Putin became president. Of course I was surprised, everyone was surprised. At first I really wanted to support him and help him in any way I could. The 1990s had been a criminal, dangerous time. I hoped for something different.'

Soon after the inauguration, Kolesnikov claims he was approached by Nikolai Shamalov, one of Putin's 'friends' who had begun to grow fantastically rich. He asked him to do the new president a favour:

'Mr Shamalov explained that many oligarchs were coming to Putin offering to do something for him. "How can I help you Mr Putin?" "What do you need Mr Putin?" And he had decided it would be very nice for them to help some hospitals. And this was to be done through our medical equipment company Petromed. The first man to come to us was Roman Abramovich.'

But there was another, less noble side to Putin's request:

'Shamalov said to us – Putin wants us to put part of this money in an offshore account. So I asked: "For what? Personal needs?" To which he replied, "He wants to invest it in the Russian economy." So I thought, after he finishes his presidency, he just wants some money for himself, his family, his wife. And part of the money goes into the Russian economy, to help Russia . . . but of course I knew this was corruption. But it was *normal* corruption. It wasn't *stupid* or *bad* corruption.'

According to Kolesnikov, the scheme worked like this: Putin had stipulated that 35 per cent of the funds for urgently needed medical equipment would be held in offshore accounts. For example, of the $203 million that the original donor Roman Abramovich gave to help the hospitals, Petromed only spent $130 million, with the remainder ending up in a Swiss bank account. Kolesnikov says that Abramovich was blind to where the money went. By 2005, the fund had accumulated over $200 million and a firm called Rosinvest of which Putin held 94 per cent of the shares was created.[2]

Power and property in Russia are one and the same. As Putin consolidated his regime, his 'friends' financial consolidation followed. Mirroring his ascendancy, Kolesnikov alleges that Putin's 'friends' organized themselves as a business between 2002–3. However, only after the arrest of Khodorkovsky and the 2004 election did they 'go to the maximum' and their acquisitions 'explode':

'The change started after the arrest of Khodorkovsky. The words used to address Putin started to change. At first it was "boss" but then more and more would call him "tsar". It began as a joke. But then it became serious. This is because it was fast becoming true that nothing could be decided without him. You couldn't go to a governor anymore to get something started, because the governors would have to go straight to Putin to check it. But the 2004 election was the most important thing. They cemented everything.'

In 2005, he claims he was approached by Shamalov to do another favour for his 'tsar'. It began as a small house of 1,000 square metres on the Black Sea for $14 million dollars. Kolesnikov says that though he knew it was corruption from the start, the sums involved seemed small when many homes worth over $10 million or $20 million were being built along the Rublevka highway out of Moscow, the home of the elite:

'I understand that in the Western mentality this is not a good thing but, we thought, in three years his term will be up and it will be good for him.

When this began I was convinced I was building Putin's retirement home. I think . . . Shamalov thought like me. We thought it would be very nice for him.'

In wanting a palace in the south Putin was now following in the footsteps of the Soviet leadership. Russia's rulers have always summered on the Black Sea. Studded in the subtropical forests of Abkhazia are the 'dachas' of the general secretaries, each a tomb-like time capsule. The gates to Stalin's Lake Ritsa summerhouse are locked and the local militia pace outside. Inside it is wood-panelled and the furniture all low to fit his frame. The fittings are sparse. The bathrooms, simply tiled, are plain, cramped and unremarkable, like a provincial hotel. The bedroom is sparse and, into the dark wood panelling, the German prisoner of war who carved it, notched twists and cuts into the woodwork behind the bed, so at the flick of the light-switch, ghoulish shadows wrap round the room, like the swirling gloom in Eisenstein's *Ivan the Terrible*. There is no gold in sight; the dachas become more ornate as you move through time. The residence of Gorbachev is gaudy. It has the feel of a luxury hotel. Putin's domain further up the coast in Russia proper would surpass anything seen since the time of Nicholas II. Times were changing again, Kolesnikov remembers:

'By 2006 the impression started to emerge that Putin would rule forever. In 2006 the plan for the house on the Black Sea changed completely. Putin now wanted a palace. I think that it was in 2006 that Putin decided to stay and for that he wouldn't need a private home by the sea.'

Putin's power was expanding; the assets of his 'friends' were growing and so was his sense of self as a ruler. The project ballooned. Its size swelled from 1,000 square metres to 4,000 square metres. Modelled like a contemporary Peterhof, one of Peter the Great's most grandiose residences outside St Petersburg, it had evolved into an Italianate palace with everything the 'tsar' could need. They had built him a casino and a church, swimming pools and helipads, a summer amphitheatre and a winter theatre, and of course apartments for the staff and other servants.

'It's a fantastic place. The climate is wonderful. It's in a forest. It's so much nicer than Sochi,' said Kolesnikov. It was raining in Tallinn. 'Please, eat some of my sweets.' Throughout the period, Kolesnikov claims he was using the diverted funds not only to manage 'Project South' but also to invest in a host of other businesses across Russia, including factories and a port. These deals were what actually took up most of his time. 'At least some of the money was going back to Russia, and staying in Russia.' Kolesnikov then said: 'But you must understand Putin never really changed in this period . . . his voice became a little tougher, but he was still the same person. What happened was that the court created the "tsar". They created this very vulnerable system where all business and political connections went through him. The last time I talked to Putin about the palace was in 2008, at the beginning of autumn. We were having a meeting at a high-tech centre. And when the meeting was over Putin came over to me and said, quietly: "How is the situation coming together in the south?"'

Months later, the financial crisis tipped Russia into recession. Kolesnikov said he needed more money for the non-palace investments, the ones he enjoyed and which took up most of his time. But Putin said there would be no more money for the other projects and all the funds should now be spent on the palace. Kolesnikov admits that had Putin given him the money for the other projects, he might never have become a whistle-blower. 'Things might have turned out differently.'

Now working on the palace alone, the new situation was not to his liking at all. So in 2009, he alleges, he went to Shamalov and explained to him that he wasn't interested in doing things this way:

'What he said to me horrified me. "Do you not understand? He is the tsar and what are you? You are only . . . *his serf*!"'

Kolesnikov says he was profoundly shaken: 'After Shamalov told us who we really were, I started thinking. It is not just me who is a serf! I spent twenty years of my life in the Soviet Union. All my education has been about not being a serf . . . and I realized that if I am a serf, then everyone is a serf. I realized that Putin is not the "tsar". We had only called him that. Because a tsar has a dynasty, and cares for the country because it will one day belong to his son. A tsar cares for his people. I realized that Putin is a dictator. He cannot create a dynasty. And in the end all dictators end up the same way.'

By now Kolesnikov claims he was locked in a serious dispute with Shamalov: 'I thought I could just leave the system. But I couldn't. They wanted to make an example of me. They wanted to destroy me. So I fled to Turkey and then to the United States. I had heard from my friends in the system that they were planning to leave drugs in my car and have me arrested. I knew that if that happened . . . I would end up dead.'

Putin's spokesman and Mr Shamalov dismissed these claims. According to Kolesnikov, the palace cost as much as $1 billion. The authorities, of course, deny any connection with this Italianate property. Maybe, this could be because 'Project South' gets to the heart of who Putin really is. That he should have blurred the boundaries between profit and politics in 1990s St Petersburg is unsurprising. This simply made him a man of his time.

What the Kolesnikov documents seem to show us is that Putin never changed. Instead, as he has grown more powerful, he grew ever more corrupt. This means that Putin has never stopped behaving like a 1990s politician. He cannot change – and as long as he is in power, neither can

Russia. Nor can the incestuous relationship of power and corruption that spiralled out of control under Yeltsin ever end.

The Meaning of Friends

Putin is a family man. He may have come to power promising to 'liquidate the oligarchs as a class', but instead his rule has seen friends become oligarchs. Everybody who has worked with Putin mentions his incredible loyalty to those he trusts. Some say he has had this since childhood. His schoolteacher Vera Gurevich thinks this might even be the defining line of his personality:

'You see, at school he never betrayed his friends. He was the strongest at school and everyone was frightened of him. He was always the leader – but a secret, discreet one – who could organize people and rally them to do things. He wasn't ever crowing or shouting out like some of the boys.'

The Russian opposition alleges that those who knew him well in St Petersburg have prospered. Boris and Arkady Rottenberg used to work on their judo with Putin at the Yavara-Neva Judo club in the city, the sport he adores. Arkady Rottenberg was Putin's personal trainer and sparring partner. Now they are billionaires selling pipes to the government-controlled monopoly Gazprom. Gennady Timchenko used to be a member of the same club. Now he runs Gunvor, the third largest oil trader in the world. At one point it handled roughly one-third of Russia's sea-bound oil.[3] Timchenko denies that he has benefited from Putin's rise to power, that they are friends or that having sponsored the Yavara-Neva constitutes proximity.[4] Putin is the club's president. 'The relationship is one of casual acquaintanceship and not close friendship,' attests his spokesman.[5] However, when Gunvor was awarded rights to sell the oil that Rosneft had acquired from Yukos, at first no public tenders were held, to see if another company would offer a better price.[6] At great loss to the Russian taxpayer, Gunvor is based in Switzerland.

These men have done nothing illegal. Yet the Russian opposition points to the fact that many of the new oligarchs referred to as Putin's 'friends' made their money from state contracts, with state corporations, directly under the control of the president or the prime minister. The careers of the men with whom Putin founded the mysterious Ozero dacha cooperative in 1996, where the friends pooled utility bills, are even starker – of the original eight members all have become extraordinarily rich since Putin became president. Amongst the dacha friends, Vladimir Yakunin became head of Russian Railways, with its enormous annual turnover. Yury Kovalchuk is now a billionaire and major shareholder in Bank Rossiya, alongside fellow dacha owners Nikolai Shamalov and Viktor Myachin; their financial institution had built up its capital through a series of deals involving Gazprom. Meanwhile, Vladimir Smirnov has enjoyed roles managing lucrative posts, including overseeing export in the commercial arm of the Ministry of Atomic Energy. Sergey Fursensko has become a media magnate as head of the National Media Group, owned by Bank Rossiya, with key stakes in major channels NTV, Channel 1 and the newspaper *Izvestia*. His brother Andrei Fursenko has served in several ministerial capacities and is currently a Putin aide. The Russian opposition allege that Bank Rossiya is dominated by this 'gang', and that it is not really a bank, but an instrument used by Putin and friends for control and embezzlement.

If one adds up the assets of Putin's dacha associates, his acquaintances from the judo club with a few relatives, friends and former KGB agents, their wealth is in excess of $180 billion.[7] As a result, it is widely believed that Putin, through his friends, has established an immense personal fortune through their stakes in Russia's oil and gas industry. One speculative financial trail estimated he had become the richest man in Europe.

Those involved in Russian finance make investment decisions based on which companies are presumed to be 'Putin assets', which get preferential legal and political treatment. It is standard practice in the upper echelons of Moscow business to work out which ministers own what – and what Putin owns – and plot profit and loss accordingly. When being approached to join a corporate board, it is standard procedure to be told who the 'real owner' is.

Corruption in post-Soviet Russia is not just about theft, it is about power – used to consolidate both Yeltsin and Putin's regimes. The Russian opposition claims that the economy is now so distorted to the advantage of this group that they cannot only be accused of corruption – but state capture. In a pamphlet condemning Putin's embezzlement entitled 'Putin: Corruption', the opposition politicians Vladimir Milov and Boris Nemtsov lamented:

> The Putin system is remarkable for its ubiquitous and open merging of the civil services, and business, its use of relatives, friends and acquaintances to absorb budgetary expenditure and then take over state property, and the way it stays and sticks in power whilst functioning with near total opacity.[8]

His Courtiers

The Kremlin is a court more than an administration. Like any court, it is a venal and unideological place where personal ties and patronage, factions and feuding, are the arithmetic of power. Though most ministers are courtiers, not all courtiers are ministers. Putin's court is a place where influence is played for between the oil oligarchs and mining magnates, coveted by his 'friends' and craved by the 'families' of his favourites. It is a society of palatial estates in the woods over the Moscow ring road, dynastic marriages, grey cardinals, pillaged fortunes and nepotism shrouded in paranoia – against a backdrop of assassinations, exiled intriguers and the imprisoned oligarch.

This court is a far cry from Russia's democratic or socialist dreams. We see an opulent rococo palace built from funds skimmed from donations for urgently needed medical equipment. A coterie of 'liberal modernizers' with crooked embezzlement trails. A clan of anti-Western 'siloviks' whose pastimes include luxurious holidays on the Côte d'Azur and buying up the mansions of Mayfair. An ideologist who smiles on television one day that Putin was 'sent by God', only the next to fail to deny he is in fact author of a theatre piece where a 'vulgar Hamlet' decries his country's corrosive corruption. A cabinet where a former furniture salesman can be a defence minister, where ministers are married to one another and most of its former KGB agents had mere walk-on roles in the Cold War. This is a court stuffed by more men from St Petersburg, almost all associates of the man they sometimes dub the 'tsar', than at any point since the Romanovs. This is Putin's court, a place where any major decision requires his stamp of approval or signal of acquiescence.

The true courts of our imagination, those of Tudor England, only reached their theatrical pinnacle once the crown had subjugated all competing feudal sources of power and loyalty. By the reign of Elizabeth I the court had become the sine qua non of political advancement. Access was the currency of influence. The devolution towards a new form of court politics in Russia began with Yeltsin's destruction of the party, the side-lining of the 'organs' and his 1993 neutering of parliament, and was in all senses complete by 2003 after the elimination of Khodorkovsky's competing patronage system.

Russia's neo-courtly politics has seen Western analysis lazily lapse into the techniques of Kremlinology devised during the Cold War to pick up ideological tremors within the Politburo. Typically, such neo-Kremlinology divides Putin's entourage into 'liberals' and 'siloviks' with the embassies and think-tanks projecting onto their scuffles and appoint-ments a half-imagined idealistic struggle over policy between conservative Chekists and economically liberal 'reformers'. This is unhelpful. So unhelpful, that a conversation about 'clans' usually reflects merely the hopes and prejudices of the analyst. Those who are pessimistic have a tendency to see a stranglehold of a menacing 'silovik' clan headed by Igor Sechin, whilst optimists tend to see a 'liberal' grouping that the West needs to support, headed by, at times Dmitry Medvedev, Alexey Kudrin or lately Igor Shuvalov.

Kremlinology is unhelpful, as Putin's Kremlin has more in common with the court of Elizabeth I than the Politburo during 'stagnation'. In that Moscow, a catfight primarily between different ideological tendencies culminated in Gorbachev's election as general secretary of the Communist Party of the Soviet Union. Power and corrupt practices were part of a Politburo politician's calculations, but their divisions were overwhelmingly on principle. Not so Putin's Kremlin. At the court of Elizabeth I, politics was a constant jostling between 'factions' and favourites. These factions had some idealistic tints but cannot be compared to twentieth-century 'believers'. Elizabethan factions were loose and informal groupings, friends and networks, competing above all for patronage and power for its own sake. Their tussles had ideological tints but were for the sake of spoils not causes. Putinist 'liberals' and 'siloviks' have more in common with renaissance factions than the 'hardliners' and 'democrats' of perestroika. They are not parties. 'We are a team,' smiled one Kremlin aide, 'We stick together . . . But you should see how we fight!'

The best way to map the Russian elite is to look at the oligarchs on the *Forbes* rich list of Russia's wealthiest, then superimpose a list of ministers, senior officials and directors of state corporations, then mind-map out a list of Putin's personal friends, before visualizing a spider-diagram spreading off to include the family members and network of all of the above. Background does not neatly translate into clear-cut political camps.

For all Putin's bravado about 'liquidating' the oligarchs, they are still powerful. Amongst them are several major species. On the one hand there are the 1990s oligarchs who do not owe him their wealth, and the new Putin oligarchs who became billionaires under and thanks to his rule. After the Khodorkovsky trial, the oligarchs positioned themselves around Putin – treating him as the arbiter and supreme adjudicator. Though they retreated from daily policy-making, they did not disappear. The number of Russian billionaires exploded from zero in 2000 to eighty-seven in 2008.[9]

Amongst them distinct strategies emerged in trying to deal with Putin. The first was that deployed most successfully by Roman Abramovich – who did everything to help him, in order to protect himself. The second strategy is those of oligarchs who tried to stay out of Putin's way, ingratiate themselves with him personally whilst consolidating their own empires, with their own clear opinions on where Putinism should develop. The leading practitioners of this group are the ALFA group oligarchs, such as Mikhail Friedman and Viktor Vekselberg. The final oligarch strategy was actually Putin's own – the success of his friends.

Putin imposed a consensus on the oligarchs between when he turned on Berezovsky and destroyed Khodorkovsky. He then made himself indispensable to them. Putin became the arbiter, the dealmaker and the fixer. If you were on his right side, he was also the facilitator. This meant that these men actually came to want him. Most of them at first enjoyed this stability. Despite making millions and billions, the oligarchs had felt hunted throughout the 1990s. One whisper in Yeltsin's ear, or one sharp power play could cancel out fortunes. There was something comforting to know that Vladimir Vladimirovich was always there. Some came to think, even in the 1990s, that they had always needed him. Knowing who was all-powerful, actually made them feel safe.

The Road to Rublevka

Under Putin the Russian ruling caste has become one of the richest in the world. Putin rewarded his ministers in the late 2000s with the right to serve as board members of state corporations. The Russian opposition claims Putin has ensnared their loyalty through a web of corruption. This wealth has become synonymous with a stretch of estates and exquisite mansions along the Rublevka highway heading west through woodlands from Moscow. This traffic-clogged road has a sense of history. Here, Ivan the Terrible would immerse himself in falconry and along its path tsars would make pilgrimages to a holy monastery, amongst them Peter and Catherine the Great. And it was here, far from the factories that pollute the rivers that run to the east of the city, that Stalin and his henchman lived in comfortable – but compared to what would ensue – quite plain dachas. Come the Cold War and the 1950s, the Rublevka was closed to the public, now the preserve of the general secretaries' residences. Brezhnev and Andropov would live here. In 1989, at the juncture of history, Yeltsin would claim that an unknown gang tried to throw him off the Rublevka bridge. In reality, he was just drunk.

Under his reign and that of his successor the stretch has transformed into a Russian Beverly Hills. The gated communities first built for the Soviet upper castes are now the homes of the wealthiest; sealed communities of veritable palaces with armed guards and CCTV surveillance. On the Rublevka, where Putin and Medvedev live, the highway is closed to traffic twice a day as they commute to the Kremlin or the White House. The Rublevka is also a social world: of elite schools, where dynastic marriages such as those between the daughter of Igor Sechin to the son of current plenipotentiary envoy to the Southern Federal District are practised, a place where the reality of Moscow is half-removed.

Driven home by chauffeurs, the financially unlimited children of the elite ride home most nights in a drunken stupor, and have little clue what it is to live in creaking Soviet housing or wait in line for bread. 'My real fear for Russia is the kids,' the aide to one of the nation's most powerful tycoons once confided. 'Unlike their parents who are really sharp men who fought their way to the top, they are foolish, easily seduced by foreigners, drunken, drug-addled with more money than sense. Yet their parents want them to have an inheritance.' Accordingly, Putin's courtiers have rewarded their sons with well-paid jobs in state corporations. 'If these children inherit it all then it will be a true disaster,' said one of the oligarch's men.

Rublevka is not just a place but a way of life. Courtiers are said to have a love for Italian Brioni suits and are rarely seen without their finery. Rublevka shines on their wrists. A few snapshots from 2009 caught the senior central banker Alexey Ulyukayev wearing a $78,000 watch, the then deputy head of the Kremlin administration Sergei Naryshkin a $29,500 watch, the then minister of finance Alexey Kudrin a $14,900 watch and the then first deputy mayor of Moscow Vladimir Resin a $1 million watch.[10] Putin wears such watches, but is also generous with them. Twice that year he gave away watches worth $10,500 to a Siberian shepherd and a provincial Russian joiner.[11] The next year, for good luck he tossed a $10,500 watch into the freshly laid cement foundations of a new hydroelectric plant.[12] These were, of course, not Putin's best watches. He was seen in 2009 wearing a gold watch worth $60,000, on other occasions craft-pieces worth a mere $20,000 and all together a sum of some $160,000.[13] Nothing wrong with that, but then why was Putin's official income declaration that year just shy of $170,000?[14]

Putin really has been living like a tsar. By 2011 the value of his eleven sighted wristwatches had risen to $687,000 and the presidential estate had swollen to more than twenty residences, fifteen helicopters and four yachts.[15] His forty-three Kremlin aircraft alone are worth over $1 billion.[16] Nor is he the only one living like this. There is great comfort and gold off the Rublevka. Moscow has more billionaires than any other city in the world, its seventy-eight billionaires leaving New York's mere fifty-seven far behind.[17] The 'average' member of the power elite isn't doing too badly either. In 2010 the average board member of Gazprom earned $2.9 million, whilst those at Sberbank received $2.4 million.[18] These wages are respectively 400 and 325 times the national average.[19] Putin has always been open: he is no egalitarian. Even when he was running for president he made his thoughts clear:

> Our society must understand that a minority – a certain category of people – must be paid very well by the state, so they can secure the standards of living for the majority. When will we finally understand

this? Our people aren't stupid. It just hasn't been explained the right way.[20]

But under all this is a huge free-floating, cavernous anxiety. Unlike the 'new nobility' they purport to be, none were born to wealth but scrabbled, sometimes shot their way into it. Everything they have, no matter how much of it, remains unsecured. For some, without Putin it could disappear; others to anger Putin, could make it disappear. All are frightened of a better-connected criminal asset-stripping scheme backed up by the bureaucracy. The wealthier you are in Russia, the more vulnerable you actually are. 'It occurred to him after some particularly great hash, that in post-Soviet economies the primitive accumulation of capital was also final', is how the writer Victor Pelevin once put it, but it is how elites behave.

For a while, I got to know a petrol-princess who was driven about by a thuggish driver back and forth to Rublevka. Money had made her financially weightless. Free from most things, apart from that huge doubt. I had three long conversations with this girl on a bench in Paris. And then a few more in Moscow in some bar with a stupid piano modelled on 'an intelligentsia apartment in the 1930s', which never exactly made me feel at ease. She always drank and smoked so much more than me, but I very rarely saw her eat. So she told me her whole short story. We became friends, of a sort.

A quarter of her life had been spent like this. Several kids and no money in Siberian Surgut during the collapse. She told me about Chinese traders swapping passports of men who had died in the Chechen war, a lack of food, how cramped their apartment had been, with lots of children. Once she said she had a Chinese grandparent, then changed her mind and told me she was lying. I think she just didn't know why she had a slightly Asian face. What she was more certain of is that she had moved to Moscow when her father had made it out of Surgut into the stratosphere of post-Soviet wealth. The company is rumoured to be one of Putin's alleged 'personal oil companies'.

She was not coy about showing that off. Ambitious provincials would hang off her like a micro-court of greedy middle-class twentysomethings with Moleskines and schemes to seduce her for money. To them she liked to show off how much she knew about 'culture', about almost everything really. But, she didn't like talking about her parent's politics. Or inviting people back to her family home. Maybe she also felt a bit embarrassed that her mother had built it to look like a wooden gingerbread house for her children. 'She's so stupid. She thinks that Putin is great and all this is because of Putin. But my father . . . when I ask him, he tells me that it's all a disaster and because of Putin none of this is safe.

'The worst thing about growing up in Rublevka was after the Khodorkovsky arrest my classmates started to disappear. I'd come in to school and there would be the empty seats . . . the teachers would say, "Don't worry, he went to Israel . . . he went to London . . . he went to New York . . . he went somewhere else . . . but don't worry, he's safe." '

Shallow Chekists and Faint Liberals

Coming together in Rublevka is a social world that pulls in even opposition leaders. We should understand Kremlin factions as many faces of the same court – where some are used to seduce, others to intimidate, some that are masks and others that can only be seen in the mirror. Those in the loose 'liberal' faction like to season their speeches with sprinkles of fiscally neoliberal terms, noises about improving human rights and puff about technological innovation. A taste of this talk was on offer at Davos in 2012. Arkady Dvorkovich, a chess-playing and tweeting minister, lamented the 'oversized and constant pressure from the state', whilst the influential first deputy prime minister Igor Shuvalov noted that the government must 'heed clear and tough warnings that the situation must be changed'.[21] Yet this liberalism is thin. Their ideal has been the authoritarian modernization practised in Singapore, not the democratic transition in Poland. They want a slow and gradual liberalization on the regime's own terms, as practised in Taiwan, not a sudden and threatening break.

Yet a closer look at Mr Shuvalov shows him to be more of a courtier than a reformer. Within the entourage Shuvalov has become the court 'chamberlain', who has excelled in paperwork and is responsible for managing disputes. One US Embassy cable even reported that Putin had delegated so much everyday administration to him that he was 'the actual prime minister'.[22] Like any member of Putin's government he walks tall and can fail even to acknowledge those he thinks are his inferiors. At the FIFA award ceremony, handing the right to host the World Cup 2018 to Russia, a balding young man from the England team walked up to congratulate him. Shuvalov shook hands with him so dismissively, failing even to make eye contact, that he had to issue an apology. This man was Prince William.

A quick glance at his 2010 official income statement shows an official living in as much luxury as a prince. His family in the two preceding years earned in excess of $48 million.[23] They own two plots of land of 40 acres, an apartment of 175 square metres, a rented apartment of 643 square metres, a residential property of 1,479 square metres in Austria and an apartment of 424 square metres in London.[24] They also possess a fine selection of cars, amongst them a Jaguar, three Mercedes, a ZIL limousine and other luxury vehicles.[25] Funnily enough, the earner in the family is not the politician but his wife, who earns thanks to 'securities'.[26] And despite embassy gossip that he is a reformer, documents have revealed that he has amassed a fortune by co-investing over $200 million with the oligarchs Suleiman Kerimov and Roman Abramovich.[27] The opposition suggest this is either cronyism or bribery.[28] With fortunes like these it comes as no surprise that men like Shuvalov have not struggled harder for reform. In an ideological feud, beliefs tend to override faction's material interests. This is not the case in Shuvalov's Kremlin. The two most prominent 'liberals', the 2000 to 2011 finance minister Alexey Kudrin, and Dmitry Medvedev, who have both called for reform, are said to detest each other. Kudrin eventually resigned, partly because he refused to serve under Medvedev as prime minister after the 2012 elections.

Putin's court is a provincial place. The most powerful ministers and magnates are old colleagues and friends of Putin from St Petersburg. Many of those characterized as liberals are rather St Petersburg 'civilians', whilst those seen as 'hardliners' are mostly St Petersburg 'siloviks'. They are two sides of a local political mafia that grew up around Anatoly Sobchak whilst he was mayor. The two 'civilians' who had the biggest mark on economic policy as veritable 'chancellors' to Putin were German Gref, the moustachioed ethnic German, and Alexey Kudrin, the fiscally conservative economist who used to share an office with Putin when they worked for Sobchak. Always slightly outspoken, Gref served in the government until 2007 and Kudrin until 2011. Both can claim credit for the policies that brought macro-economic stability such as balancing the budget, bringing in the flat tax and liberalizing legislation.

Yet their liberalism had limits. They enjoy a lavish lifestyle, with Gref marrying like a tsarist aristocrat in one of St Petersburg's most gilded palaces. Kudrin approved of the 'state champions' in the energy sector, including Yukos assets, being brought under control of the state oil giant Rosneft. There are allegations that he was unable or unwilling to control corruption in the finance ministry. Groups of officials from the Federal Tax Service in hock with criminals appear to have stolen hundreds of millions of dollars in the late 2000s, usually under the guise of 'tax refunds'. One of these raids included an attack on the Hermitage Capital fund, then the biggest foreign investor in Russia. This shocking case saw a foreign investor who had investigated corruption in state companies chased out of Russia and the $230 million in taxes it had paid given as a rebate to the raiders by the finance ministry. They were a gang of officials and criminals. The affair eventually resulted in the death of Sergei Magnitsky, who was working on the case defending Hermitage. Kudrin, when asked as to why he had done little to stamp out the practice, has claimed unconvincingly that he 'did not have the authority' to investigate thefts.[29]

On the other side of the court stand the St Petersburg 'siloviks', former security men, of whom Igor Sechin, the 'standard bearer' of the faction, is believed to jostle for influence against the 'liberals'. Sechin is a man from St Petersburg town hall, just like Kudrin and Medvedev. At the time, he was so close to Putin's family that when his wife had a car crash during one of his foreign trips, she only needed to say 'call Sechin'. He is currently head of Rosneft, having served as a minister and in the Kremlin. Sechin is not a good-looking man. His grin is almost monstrous with his pointy ears adding a comic touch to his unsettling background. Before returning to St Petersburg, he is said to have been a military intelligence, even KGB, agent serving as an 'interpreter' in Mozambique, amid allegations of arms trading. He was intimately involved in the carve-up of Yukos. He was, of course, Khodorkovsky's nemesis, and the Yukos assets were swallowed by the state oil-giant Rosneft, of which he was then a board member.

Today his name is something of a myth. Since the Yukos affair Sechin has been accorded (in neo-Kremlinology) the role of leading the 'hard-liner' faction. He is believed to have championed authoritarian moderni-zation, state capitalism, mega-projects and an anti-Western foreign policy. Drawn from the lowly ranks of Soviet security 'organs', Sechin and those like him within the court regret the fall of Soviet power but not the planned economy, and share a fascination with China's political system. They are less prone to speechifying than the liberals, but occasionally their views do trickle out. Vladimir Yakunin, the head of Russian Railways and an orig-inal member of Putin's Ozero dacha cooperative, wrote a 2010 letter to *The Economist* in which he declared, 'state capitalism simply works better'.[30]

But it would it would be a mistake to think of Sechin as a 'hardliner', in the ideological sense as can be found in Tehran. The CVs of the St Petersburg 'siloviks' are unimpressive. None of them had been placed in highly impor-tant posts in the late Cold War. Igor Sechin had been stationed in hardly central theatre Mozambique; the former defence minister Sergey Ivanov's work in East Africa is alleged to have ended badly; the former head of the FSB and current secretary of the Security Council Nikolai Patrushev was security service chief in provincial Karelia. The 2007–12 defence minister Anatoly Sverdyukov was the director of a St Petersburg furniture store as recently as 2000. He rose to ministerial rank in a government headed by Viktor Zubkov, who was then his father-in-law. Boris Gryzlov, the long-serving speaker of parliament, is a co-inventor of a quack 'radiation filter' deemed unsafe for human use by the Russian Academy of Sciences.

Russia is thus not run by the successors of Andropov's KGB. This would be the equivalent of calling a British government colonized by a gang of MI5 agents and police constables from Birmingham an MI5–MI6 state. Consequently, both their state capitalist and anti-Western agenda is thin. They have never seriously proposed genuine mass-militarization and patriotic-mobilization of the population. There is no noticeable difference along the Rublevka in their lifestyle from that of the 'liberals'. What has happened is that the old bureaucratic influence of the KGB and the 'power ministries' has become bound up in these men's personal access to Putin through their appointments to head them.

Putin's men are courtiers, not committed agents. It would be wrong to think of the 'siloviks' in government as sharing the same ethos as the KGB 'corporation'. They may be comparable in their methods but not in their sense of duty. The KGB was murderous and repressive, but by and large, not obscenely corrupt. Lenin's original Cheka disdained materialism and the West. One proudly self-confessed believer in Chekism, Viktor Cherkesov, a senior security official, wrote in 2007 a stinging denouncement of what he saw as the shallow Chekism of the Putin court:

> The country survived a full scale catastrophe in the early 1990s . . . some Chekists quickly fell away and parted from the professional community. Some became traitors. Some became sweepingly depraved. But a core of our professional community nevertheless stayed . . . Falling into the abyss post-Soviet society was saved on the Chekist hook . . . Yet this caste will be destroyed from within when warriors start to become businessmen.[31]

Cherkesov was retired in 2008. Yet whatever his internal motives for his denouncement, he is correct. The Chekists of the Putin court are more businessmen than anti-Western warriors. Whistle-blowers have come out of the establishment alleging that hostile takeovers of profitable enterprises have been undertaken under the supervision of Igor Sechin and the 'siloviks'. Their business interests and contacts with foreign capital temper their anti-Westernism. Sechin, according to one US Embassy cable was considered by many of their sources to have come to realize the importance of working with Western funds and technology in the oil and gas industry. Nor are members of the 'siloviks' disdainful of Western lifestyles in the way that the original Chekists were or like the hardliners of Tehran. They are also believed to have vast assets spread across the EU – from bank accounts, properties, companies and a noted preference for educating their children in Swiss finishing schools and British universities.

Emblematic of this is the case of Yury Luzhkov, who as mayor of Moscow used to engage in nationalist tub-thumbing calling for Crimea to be returned to Russia and sponsored home building in contested South

Ossetia. When forced from his job in 2010 he chose to spend most of his time in his palatial London residence on Hampstead Heath, one of the most expensive properties in Britain. This attitude does not make them less unnerving than the ideologues of varying sorts who ran Russia in the twentieth century. The twenty-first-century Kremlin seeks personal power for the sake of power, and money for the sake of money. Reflecting on Putin's court, the influential analyst Vladislav Inozemtsev caustically wrote: 'Russia is not under KGB rule. Russia would be so lucky!'[32]

In Tudor England, the Crown tended to adopt either a 'distant' or an 'engaged' approach to its courtiers. An engaged Crown would see a quick turnover of favourites and ministers, sharp U-turns and policy reflecting to a large extent the foibles of the monarch. Yeltsin had such a court. The strategy of Elizabeth I was a 'distant crown'. This was marked by ministerial stability, long tenures and delicate management of factions, designed for all, feeling their turn could come and an isolated ruler without clear favourites or successors. This is Putin's strategy. He has been forced to engage in faction management. Like Elizabeth I and unlike a twentieth-century dictator, he may have the power to destroy or humble a faction leader but can do little to remove the faction or tendency itself. Putin's faction management is reflected in the way he tends to stay above the fray of political disputes. His point of view on policy tends to be heard only as the arbiter's final voice. 'The genius of Putin', said one aide to the oligarchy, 'is his faction management. He keeps perpetual uncertainty. No enemy is an enemy forever, no friend is a friend forever. Thus we have a sort of stability.'

As a result the Russian cabinet has been marked by an almost extreme continuity. There were virtually no changes in personnel of the two cabinets put together after 2004 within electoral cycles. His attempt to make factions feel they will eventually 'get their turn', can be reflected in his encouragement of both Medvedev and the 'silovik' defence minister Sergey Ivanov to think they could be his 2008 presidential candidates. Ivanov was so convinced he was Putin's choice that he had a full wardrobe makeover in anticipation. Yet to distract attention from these intrigues, the Kremlin has drafted politicians with the charisma to distract preying eyes.

Like any court Putin's has had its jesters, chief amongst them the cherub-cheeked Dmitry Rogozin, the ranting nationalist currently serving as minister for the military–industrial complex. He is what the English would call a 'character', prone to flamboyant outbursts. In person, he seems unable to miss a pun and smiles broadly at his own witticisms, as if surprised by them. Just like Putin, he slips into criminal slang when it suits him. His university classmates remember him not as a fool but as a clever 'careerist'. Rogozin is the son of a prominent military historian – and like many of those steeped in the past, he has positioned himself as a nationalist. Rogozin is a proud handball master and a politician, whose party trick has been to throw out politically incorrect comments, pounding a point with passionate intensity and a populist touch. He made his name in right-wing nationalist circles, from his first attempt in 1992 to contest the legality of the Soviet dissolution to his demands that the 'garbage', by which he meant migrants, be cleaned up in Moscow. His willingness to chase the xenophobes' vote eventually turned him into one of Russia's most popular politicians.

This is when the Kremlin found a use for him. Keen to ensure such voters' loyalty to the court, Rogozin was invited in and promptly sent to Brussels as ambassador to NATO, a great stage for regular TV interviews to fill the evening news, with even his pop-star wife providing news copy, serenading him in a YouTube video: 'I know what you want and I know what you think, making love to me is like having a good drink.'[33] Catapulted higher still to oversee one of the biggest financial flows of all – the military–industrial complex – in 2012 Rogozin's nationalist quips and turns were seen as essential to have onside, to shore up government popularity. Like any jester, Rogozin's job is to distract from and not determine politics. Seen as a populist project, his former classmates say Rogozin has been left an embittered cynic after years as Putin's jester. Diplomats attest that the 'great nationalist' often travels on the private jet of a Caucasian billionaire.

Within the courtyards of the Kremlin, Putin cuts a lonely figure, ever alone. Unlike his courtiers who, like their Western counterparts, try to be seen as often as they can, smiling with their wives, Putin's spouse is an absence, practically never seen. It is widely believed in political circles that he no longer enjoys the refuge of a warm family. This makes Putin's life oddly closer to Elizabeth I than the loving father Nicholas II. Whilst Obama, Medvedev or Cameron regularly attend conferences, rallies or hospital openings holding their wives hands, using them as electoral assets and simple support, Putin works in solitude. At his rallies, he is alone. At summits, he is alone. At the banquets, too.

There have been increasingly rare sightings of Putin with his wife Lyudmila. These included them filling out the 2010 census form together. She fidgets uncomfortably throughout, as if distressed by his presence. Many in Moscow believe she has been sent to live in a monastery. Rumours circulate that she has suffered a nervous breakdown. Putin's daughters are absent from Moscow and their whereabouts guarded like a state secret. Journalists are too frightened to ask him at press conferences. Once, whilst answering questions with Silvio Berlusconi, a reporter from *Moskovsky Korrespondent* dared ask Putin if he had really left his wife to marry a twenty-four-year-old gymnast. His pleasure was not pronounced and

Berlusconi started to make a machine-gunning gesture with his hands.[34] *Moskovsky Korrespondent* was quickly closed down by its publisher. There are those who claim that Putin's alleged relationship with the gymnast has resulted in a baby boy. With the mention that Putin may have a son, a shudder comes to anyone who thinks of the future.

Dead Souls

The face of Putinism that stares out of mass corruption is neither one of liberal or state-capitalist authoritarian modernization. The allegations that the Russian elite could consider it acceptable to divert funds for medical equipment in order to build a palace – in a country with a health care catastrophe where, on average, male life expectancy is at the same level as impoverished Papua New Guinea or Pakistan – is truly outstanding. They show that though the Putin regime may have ideological tendencies, and stated ambitions towards modernization and state strengthening, its politics is dampened by its avarice.

The face of the regime seen in the mirror of such allegations is one that is neither wholeheartedly interested in building an authoritarian 'China' nor modernizing into 'Europe', as its political ambitions are knotted into financial interests. It is a regime whose insiders would never truly confront the West, for risk of losing their assets, nor which would appear capable of improving the state to Western standards, for risk of undermining their hold on them. Worse still, having directed such a massive transfer of assets, Putin is vulnerable that should he leave power they could be redistributed again.

'Let the dead bury their dead and mourn them,' wrote the young Marx, 'for our fate will be to become the first living people to enter the new life.'[35] This was the spirit of Yeltsin's court and Putin's Moscow, the stage for Surkov's 'puppet shows'. This was the capital of a country where the oligarchs and the power brokers – with the most unlikely of CVs – had not inherited, but seized huge pieces of the Soviet raw materials complex. They felt they had won out where everyone else had lost; they felt they had understood how to live in a country where everyone else was drowning – because they were geniuses. The Putin court, those that had survived, those that triumphed, felt not only incredible self-worth, but also the right to incredible privilege. To quote Surkov:

> We must all agree with the following proposition, genius is always in the minority, but their doings make the majority richer. And the majority must understand, that there are privileges, which we give to talented people . . .[36]

CHAPTER SIX

DIZZY WITH SUCCESS

By 2006 Russian fiction had taken a darker turn. The writer Vladimir Sorokin was so appalled by what he saw as the political drift towards a dictatorship that he wrote *Day of the Oprichnik*. The year is 2028 and the monarchy has at last been restored. The nation has burnt its passports on Red Square. Russia is walled off behind a great wall and the Oprichniks – as the dedicated servants of the sovereign are known – roam Moscow raping the wives of their enemies, constantly taking bribes and guzzling imported narcotics, before repenting fervently before the Lord. But proud, imperial, holy Russia is just an illusion. The entire country is economically dependent on China. Asiatic settlers are everywhere in Siberia and dominate commerce even in Moscow. The ruler's own children are brought up speaking Mandarin. On instructions from the Kremlin, one Oprichnik is ordered to take banned classics to be burnt by a Siberian witch. He begs her for a sight of the future, as she tosses *Anna Karenina* into the fire, but she just snarls, 'The country will be alright.'[1] This is a thin satire on Putin's state. Yet the idea of a country dominated by an arrogant, at times criminal, elite was not just a flight of fancy. Sorokin had been harassed and sued by the Kremlin's youth groups for 'pornography' and his works had been thrown into a giant papier-mâché toilet before being dynamited. But outside the cramped and dimly lit offices of a tiny, ageing and ignored circle of human rights activists – nobody seemed to care. Why?

The short answer as to why Russians shrugged off creeping authoritarianism is – supermarkets. The long answer is that during the 2000s Russia enjoyed the first period of macro-economic stabilization since the mid-1980s, finally bringing dividends to the masses from de-Sovietization. Macro-economic stabilization brought about a social transformation. Between the 1998 default and the outbreak of financial crisis in 2008 Russia ceased to be a shortage economy and became a consumer society. This meant that the 2000s for everyday people was not just a decade of weak institutions and creeping authoritarianism – but globalization. The same trends of opening up to the world, mass foreign travel and foreign investment that were changing China and Brazil, were remaking Russia. This boom helped build an emerging middle class, which now armed with cheap mobiles and computers, was making the leap into the consumer life-styles that Russians had craved since the USSR began falling short of rising expectations in the 1960s. The people loved it and associated it with Putin. In the Moscow suburb of Zuzino, one housewife once bluntly told me, 'I lost interest in politics when I stopped having to shop in the market and started to shop in the hypermarket.' She spoke for millions.

The material hardship that Russians endured during the shortage economy of the late Soviet Union and the Yeltsin depression was endlessly contrasted with the consumer society that has come to Russia during Putinism. For instance, in the 1980s condoms disappeared from Moscow for months; shortages saw toilet paper also disappear. Economic collapse in the late Soviet era meant that by 1989 the average person spent 40–68 hours a month standing in line.[2] By April 1991 fewer than one in eight of those polled said they had seen meat recently in state stores, whilst fewer than one in twelve had seen butter.[3] In the 1990s millions of state employees were often not paid at all. Others were regularly given their pay cheques in vodka or meat, if they were lucky. There were bread shortages comparable to those last seen in Western Europe immediately after the Second World War. The economy was in such a dire mess in 1998 that large enterprises were doing 73 per cent of their business in barter.[4]

In those first few years of Putin, the Moscow that I got to know was a dirty place in a poor state of repair. It felt like a wrecked satellite of Europe, whose people constantly asked you to bring the unobtainable from the West, before apologizing over and over for 'our Russian poverty'. Its sense of style was summed up in leopard-skin print and leather jackets. The streets were full of the corporations of the dying – whimpering street children by the railway stations, staggering babushkas by the metro gates, shivering prostitutes on the boulevards. Twice, both in winter months, I saw collapsed old women in the metro tunnels. The drab, darkly dressed crowds stepped over them. I was certain they were dead, but I too stepped over them.

This was nothing surprising. The metro was where the homeless usually went to die in winter, to die where it was warm. This Moscow, the one I first criss-crossed, was a city so full of countless disfigured homeless alcoholics, in their thick, stinking, putrid uniforms of dirty, dark clothes, sweating and staggering between the monuments of the defeated and drawn to the bustle of the imperial train terminuses (Belarus, Kazan, Kiev, Kursk, Leningrad, Yaroslavl . . .), that it was as if a race of zombies lived side by side with the Muscovites. These, the 'bamjee', were the victims of the Yeltsin depression and the abandonment of Gorbachev's anti-alcohol campaign. They had always been many, but as I was told again and again, as I asked about this dying underclass, no one could quite explain how it had undone so many.

In the winter, when the temperature can fall as low as –30°C, when car headlamps and the street lights make the snow as bright as the night moon, they would gather around vents, trying to keep going all night so not to stop, not to fall into the exhaustion that turns into frozen death. In the day they would try to sleep in the metro, especially on the carriages of the circle line, in the cavernous marble Stalinist halls, by the baroque mosaics, under austere colonnades, in the dingy light, by the roar of the trains on platforms designed by the red architect Alexey Dushkin after examining drawings of ancient Egyptian tombs. This is where many, in this underground populated by thousands of russet-coloured wild dogs, gave up, especially in February, and died.

This is still the case, but I find I saw it much less, heard it talked about much less, towards the decade's end. Then it was common, it was unsurprising, to see the elderly, with their forlorn medals, selling their possessions at little hard-scrabble sales within the glint of the red ruby stars of the Kremlin towers. The desperate sold these insignia; the utterly desperate sold everything. Under weak February light I turned the pages of a black-and-white Soviet family photo album that a deeply wrinkled, grey-faced woman in a peasant's kerchief was selling on the steps of the Lenin Library. The story the pictures told: a burly man smiling at various Soviet civil ceremonies, with a new baby girl, getting married, an earlier shot of young men in uniform in front of a tank: 'That's my husband.' They cost $1 each. As I passed her a note, I saw her gloves were threadbare, her fingers blue.

Putin's Boom

In 1996 a former *Economist* Moscow correspondent along with a professor at the London School of Economics co-authored a book called *The Coming Russian Boom*. Two years later Russia went bankrupt, the book disappeared, the authors were humiliated and foreign investors rushed for the airport. Then the boom happened anyway – remaking Russia's economy and society, transforming even its ethnicity.

Russia, in 2000, was the world's tenth largest economy by average value of GDP measured by purchasing power parity, smaller than Brazil, but surged back along with living standards under Putin.[5] By 2005 it was bigger than Brazil and Italy, as the eighth largest.[6] In 2010 it was sixth, having overtaken Britain. Restoring it to its 1990 position of fourth, ahead of France, seemed likely.[7]

The upward cycle during Putin's first presidency was dramatic even by the standards of Russian history. Everything that could have gone right for Putin had done just that. Thanks to the efficiency gains pioneered by Khodorkovsky, by 2008 oil production had jumped by two-thirds since the 1998 crash.[8] More was being produced and it was also worth more as the oil price had risen thirteen times over.[9] In 2007 annual oil export earnings were over $173 billion, up from $36 billion in 2000.[10] Having eliminated Khodorkovsky, the government had been able to increase oil taxes tenfold to feed the state.[11]

The Kremlin was taking its handsome cut. The consumer boom meant a tax boom; the oil boom meant a direct revenue boom. The result was a better-fed state, as oil and gas account for almost two-thirds of Russia's export revenue and almost half of federal budget revenues. The state was also a market player in its own right. The crown jewels of the hydrocarbons industry were in the hands of the state monopoly Gazprom and the expanded Rosneft, the devourer of Yukos.

The critical oligarch Alexander Lebedev was half right when he described what had happened with this gigantic windfall: 'One third was pocketed by 200 individuals. One third was spent on improving wages and salaries in the budget sector but they were eaten up by rising prices, and one third was thrown out the window for, say, the [2014] Olympics.'[12] Yet the boom was so huge that most tycoons, investors and citizens looked the other way as this happened.

The boom was not restricted to hydrocarbons – the value of other Siberian treasures soared. Gold was up 225 per cent, nickel rose by 69 per cent and aluminium by over 30 per cent.[13] Because the Russian economy is dependent on the success of these key exports, the commodities 'super-cycle' hiked up overall GDP, kick-started industrial expansion and trickled down to the consumer. Economically, this was one of the biggest strokes of luck the country had ever experienced and allowed Russia to achieve what in 2007 the World Bank heralded as 'unprecedented macro-economic stability'.[14]

Quickened by the surge in oil prices the government policy of paying off foreign debts, lowering sovereign debt, balancing the budget, building up reserves and liberalizing the economy paid off for ordinary people. For the country as a whole, the economy grew at an average of 7 per cent a year during Putin's presidency, and government debt was reduced to just 9 per cent of GDP by 2010.[15] Foreign investment flooded in, the stock market boomed from just $74 billion in 2000 to over $1 trillion by 2006.[16]

For normal Russians, the raw materials boom fuelled a consumer revolution. Real incomes rose 140 per cent and unemployment slumped.[17] GDP per capita in PPP terms, which had stood at $5,951 in 1999, jumped to $20,276 by 2008.[18] Russians living below the poverty line fell from around 30 per cent in 1999 to about 13 per cent in 2008.[19] The stock of private housing increased by over one-third.[20] Mobile phones and personal computers went from being unknown to ubiquitous. New car registrations increased by two-thirds.[21] Globalization brought foreign companies into every (legally permitted) Russian sector and major city, whilst Russian companies entered the markets of almost every foreign country. These facts suggest that it would be surprising if Putin had not been so popular; any politician in his place would have been as popular – indeed one who had built up democratic institutions and fought corruption might have been unimaginably so.

Russians were well positioned to enjoy a strong rise in consumer power. To this day, most have low debt and many own their own homes without mortgages, having 'inherited' them from the Soviet state. The jump in real incomes was thus immediately available for shopping. The first major foreign supermarket chains arrived in Russia in 1997, but it was only in the mid-2000s that they proliferated. European giants such as Auchan and IKEA threw themselves into the market earning record profits. Russia's one IKEA store in 2000 had spawned fourteen by 2011.[22] Modern malls were soon present in almost all major cities from Krasnodar in the south to Yakutsk in outer Siberia. The average spend was so much in many of these that foreign investors quickly realized that Russia's GDP per capita was surely a heavy *underestimate* with perhaps as much as one-third of the economy still in the shadows. This is without even calculating what Russia's value might be if money that was being stolen or smuggled out of the country could be counted.

The boom returned Russia into a solvent actor on the world stage. To Moscow's enormous satisfaction, on 31 January 2005 the government paid off its entire balance of IMF debts, three and a half years ahead of schedule. In summer 2006 the remaining $23 billion debt it owed to its 'Paris club' of creditors was paid off. As pro-government commentators crowed from every federal TV channel, the state – which had effectively been in receivership when Yeltsin defaulted in 1998 – was 'independent' once again. However, it was not lost on the smartest observers, including Surkov, that this upswing was precariously reliant on commodity prices:

We are not like Kuwait. We are a very big country with a large population. We have stretched wide and we have a very big and costly infrastructure. Besides, we should also bear in mind that we are a northern country. Our expenses are too high. We will be unable to be a prosperous small emirate; we are a great big country, which oil will be unable to feed. We should learn to earn money with our brains.[23]

The 'grey cardinal' failed to mention that it was during the first ten Putin years that Russia, the world's largest oil producer, had seen its budget dependence on hydrocarbons remain firmly closer to the profile of the world's second largest oil producer, Saudi Arabia, than that of the diversified economy of the then third, the United States. In 2001 oil accounted for only 34 per cent of export revenue, but it had grown to 52 per cent by 2011.[24] In the same ten years, oil and gas exploded from just 20 per cent of government revenue to 49 per cent.[25]

This was not entirely the fault of Putin's economic planners. This is the pattern they inherited – and is as it has always been. The cycles of Russian history turn in accordance with commodity prices. Under the tsars, the government lurched from repression to reform in line with the price of its lifeline export – grain. In 1929 it was the collapse of the grain price that shattered the precarious balance of Lenin's New Economic Policy and pushed Stalin towards collectivization, terror and totalitarianism. The Soviet superpower invaded Afghanistan when the price of oil was at historic highs in 1979–80 and collapsed as it tumbled, creating first a fiscal crisis, then a balance of payment crisis, then a food crisis as the state was forced to beg the West for credits to feed its cities. Such is the fate of a state that raises its revenues as a raw material exporter.

As always at the head of these historical cycles, the regime grew hubristic. The change that had taken shape could be seen in the capital's skyline. The buildings thrown up in Moscow in the 1990s were glassy, forward looking and derivative in their design. They were built like they did not belong in this city – like the first forward units of a Western reconstruction army. Yet without anybody taking much notice at first, throughout the 2000s the style morphed. Russian petro-rubles began to throw up a fashion all of its own. Bullying towers sprouted round the ring roads, with gothic turrets over dark-tinted glass fronts, topped by sinister spires, their curves and points mimicking the Stalinist skyscrapers of the centre in their domineering presence, and their utter disregard for the old Moscow they overshadowed of crooked lanes, white churches and flecked pale paint.

The boom was not just dramatically changing Moscow but Russia. It was driving four megatrends below the surface. The boom was building up a middle class, bringing millions online and sucking in millions of mostly Muslim migrants. The surprise cultural winner of the boom years was not one of Putin's projects – but a resurgent Orthodox Church. It also changed the way in which the Moscow political class behaved. As the price of oil soared, it was growing ever more ambitious, but its foreign-travelling children shunned Nashi and were in love with glamour magazines, blogging and being hipsters.

The Rise of the Middle Class

They were neither 'new Russians' nor 'old Soviets'. These were people who dismissed as sad throwbacks both the old men that still pinned 'hero of labor' to their lapels and the leather-jacketed bandits they crossed in the streets. They read the Russian version of *Elle*, bought their furniture from IKEA, wanted iPhones and went on holiday in Turkey. This was the kind of Russian which flourished under Putin – those in a new rapidly growing, educated and globalized consumer class whose emergence is the best thing to have ever happened to this country.

The biggest myth that the Moscow elite and Western analysts held in the 2000s about Russia was that this 'new middle class' was a thin crust sitting on top of a huge retrograde mass of drunken urban peasants who would vote for Putin, Zhirinovsky and probably even Hitler if given half a chance. This elitist point of view – which was implicitly Putin's and the purpose of managed democracy – did not recognize how deep, fast and thick social changes had taken place. The emerging middle class ballooned during this period, expanding to at least a quarter of the population, one-third of the adult population and became a majority in Russia's major cities.[26] Yet at first it confused people – meaning a dispute about what to call this class raged through the late 2000s. Was it really a middle class when it was a minority? Or should it be called the 'independent class' or 'people who can live by themselves?' Or the 'creative classes' as its more artistically inclined members insisted? No two analysts agreed, other than on that a vague, but tangible new way of being Russian was right in front of them.

The blogger Dmitry Drobnitsky spent the 2000s arguing with his friend Boris Mezhuev, a senior lecturer in philosophy at Moscow State University, about the new middle, creative or independent class. He insisted that it existed and that there was also a new 'identity' that it encompassed, that was much bigger and more important than the 'middle class' in terms of an income bracket. Working in management, in packaging and graphic production, Drobnitsky spent his days coming into contact with these people. His friend didn't. Both op-ed columnists in the fiercely pro-government newspaper *Izvestia*, owned by Gazprom, a Putin ally, their confusion mirrored a broader confusion in Putinism. They met in Kofe Khaus, the smoke-filled knock-off Russian Starbucks, where they would hash out this dispute. One afternoon I dropped in on them and listened to Drobnitsky outline to Mezhuev his new not-quite-post-Soviet everywoman.

'Who is this person? Who is the new middle class? Imagine her like this? She is thirty-eight and she came to Moscow from a provincial city with her friend. They lived together at first and things were pretty difficult. Her friend didn't make it and went back to the sticks. They don't talk so much anymore. She is working as an accountant in one small private firm, she works hard, rents her apartment, and does some freelance accounting on the side for another firm.

'The thing that's rather difficult for her is that she has a son, but she's single. This means there's a lot of stress. She uses social networks in the evening to relax. But there are some things to look forward to in her life. Last year she went to Turkey with her friend from the office. Next year, she plans to go Israel. There was a Jew from her school, who emigrated in the 1990s, and she says life is good there with little crime. Now there are no visas she'd like to see for herself.

'Then one last thing about her – when things started to get better in the early 2000s she made a lot of big plans for her son and what they would do when Russia finally "made it". She's become a little tense recently that it won't. Another thing has changed too . . . She used to always pay bribes to policemen. But she thinks that's not 'cute' anymore and stopped doing it. Oh, and she looks immaculate. Being neat and not scruffy and Soviet is very important to her.

'No, she's not interested in politics. But she likes VKontakte, the Russian equivalent of Facebook. Her friends post links there and she likes them, usually as a "cute" way of saying "Hi". Well . . . occasionally, she does stumbles across funny pictures that mock the police . . . and occasionally Putin.'

Towns like the once sleepy Moscow satellite of Khimki – exactly the kind of place where we can imagine this Russian everywoman renting her apartment, in a new 'evro-remont' ('euro-refit' apartment) – were transformed. Dozens of giant steely complexes were thrown up, selling everything from imported cheese in chilled cabinets to soft furniture. Those who lived there were able to buy high-quality Western clothes, imported technology and Western medicine in abundance. A Russia of post-industrial consumer cities like Khimki had emerged, encompassing over one-fifth of the population.[27] For those lucky enough to live in them, the Putin years were the years that their lives were finally modernized.

Just as Putin started to pull back from the West, Russians themselves began to globalize. There was an explosion in air-travel routes linking provincial Russian cities to the outside world. The formerly closed city of Ekaterinburg in the Urals, of grim vodka-racketeering fame in the late 1990s, was now linked by dozens of direct flights a week to booming tourist resorts in Turkey, Egypt, Israel, Thailand and across the EU. Tourist companies even started operating in the former Gulag town of Magadan on the north Pacific coast.

There were now so many tourists from the 'depths' that it became a national joke. In a Russian copy of the hit British TV show *Little Britain*, called *Nasha Russia*, one sketch involved Gena and Vovan, two workers from the polluted tank-factory city of Nizhny Tagil in the Urals. 'Tagiiiiil', they shout during drunken scenes while on holiday in Turkey, where the pair defecate in swimming pools, 'Tagiiiiil'. A cruel joke, yes, but a sign of progress. The very idea of a tourist from Nizhny Tagil in the twentieth century would have been preposterous.

This was an incredible turnaround. In 1999 the Russians who were travelling abroad often did so on old Soviet passports. By the end of the decade almost 10 million Russians were travelling abroad annually, a more than 50 per cent increase from the start of Putin's term.[28] For a nation where the Iron Curtain had left normal people with minimal exposure to East Asia and the West, the excitement felt by regular tourists is hard to convey. For centuries Russia was a country with the saying 'See Paris and die'. Millions had now seen it and returned to tell the tale in Omsk, Tomsk and Krasnoyarsk. Russian women began to joke that they had stood out (the few who could get out) during the twentieth century when they travelled in European cities, because they were so badly dressed, but now they stood out – to the chagrin of Europeans – for always being overdressed. It was no longer true that Russia knew less about the world than the world knew about Russia.

Not everyone was living like this. This 'new middle class' was a minority. The majority of Russians remained poor or socially excluded. Roughly 25 per cent were living in the blue-collar industrial cities and over 38 per cent were rural or semi-rural, still struggling with the collapse of collective farming.[29] Yet poverty was not as crushing as it had been. The number living on less than $15 a day fell from 64.4 per cent in 1999 to 30.6 per cent in 2010.[30] Amongst the Russian poor, 15 per cent now owned a plasma TV and over 35 per cent a refrigerator.[31] This may not have been a gigantic leap to European living standards, but it was still an improvement.

As Russia grew wealthier, it grew steadily healthier. Official estimates of male life expectancy soared between 2005 and 2012 from 59 to 64. Russia's demographic crisis was brought under control as young people felt secure enough to have ever so slightly more children, whilst those older lived slightly longer. According to official estimates in 2005 the population fell by more than 700,000, but by 2012 it had at last stopped shrinking.

The growth of prosperity for around 20–30 per cent of the country in the new middle class was also the growth of class differences, regional disparities – but before the financial crisis not resentment. The irony was that for the new middle class, Putinism was popular as it was experienced as a revolution in their way of life, but it was also popular amongst the poorer bulk of society, precisely because it was not revolutionary.

The opposition and the liberal intelligentsia almost disdained this new class – as they accused them of thinking only as consumers, not citizens.

This is because these people's lives were marked by a complete rejection of politics. Pessimists pointed to the fact that in 2008, as much as 50 per cent of the new middle class were working for the state.[32] But this attitude was more to do with the way people thought. This was half flight, from the misery of the 1980s and the troubles of the 1990s, into the overflowing supermarkets Yeltsin had promised them; but also half satisfaction with a leader who had delivered in his promises to them, seeing them dismiss as irrelevant his trampling on the rights of 'others'. In long evenings I spent with friends in this new middle class Moscow, hanging out on their new sofas, in their tasteful new apartments – asking about Putin's authoritarianism, I felt like we were discussing something distant and not relevant to them, like a conversation in New York as to whether American forces had committed war crimes in Iraq. The new middle class was not looking at the Kremlin – but somewhere between apathy and IKEA.

Putin's Missed Opportunity

Prosperity strengthened the Putin consensus and the Putin majority. The apathy of the new middle class became the bedrock of his 'stability'. Yet was the boom cementing all this 'luck' or 'Putin'? In fact there was more government intervention to create a boom than many think. One study calculated that no more than 50 per cent of GDP growth in the period was due to the rise in oil prices.[33] Policy choices accounted for some of the rest. Studies have shown that the flat tax, which increased labour supply and lowered tax evasion, boosted growth. The decision to create a 'one-stop shop' for business registration, taking no longer than a week, also helped. A key reform was ensuring inspecting agencies only had the right to do so no more than once every two years. Making licences valid for five years improved the climate for small and medium businesses. The choice to exempt about 90 per cent of businesses that had previously required licences also boosted growth.[34] The Kremlin's choice of a conservative macro-economic policy, financial-sector reform and the decision to build up reserves calmed investors and interests rates, whilst creating enough market confidence to support an investment boom. This helped the stabilization of financial services and their strong link-up with the property and consumer sectors, further fuelling growth. All this strengthened the middle class.

Not everyone, of course, agreed. The influential economist Sergei Aleksashenko, deputy governor of the national bank when Russia defaulted, looks back miserably at the boom as a gigantic missed opportunity: 'None of those reforms you listed can really be counted as major reforms . . . is a reformed tax code really a major reform? Looking back on it I feel saddened that Putin wasted the best decade in Russian economic history on his corrosive agenda.'

Studies backed this up. A report by the prestigious Centre for Strategic Research headed by a former deputy finance minister estimated that in 2010 only 36 per cent of the reforms envisaged in the government's 'Strategy 2010' a decade earlier had been achieved.[35]

Much more could have been done, but Russia was still leaving poverty behind. The Putin government saw the consumer revolution as its finest achievement. However, it was going to be one of its biggest problems. The old politics of the Putin majority was based on there being one huge, form-less mass on the verge of poverty that could be rallied round the standard of 'stability'. Russian society was now becoming more diverse – but the 'United Russia' straightjacket would soon leave this new middle class feeling suffocated and impotent. The Kremlin did not grasp this until it was much too late.

The Rise of the Runet

That Russia would become an Internet success story in the first decade of the new century would have seemed utopian to those who knew the Soviet Union in its final years. The technological lag in personal computing was enormous. The joke, 'the USSR makes the most advanced micro-chips in the world, they are the biggest' reflected reality. Computers in regular offices were virtually absent in the late 1980s.

The situation had been stood on its head by 2010. Russia was now the largest Internet market in Europe, with the greatest online penetration rate amongst the BRICs (Brazil, Russia, India and China), with the most engaged social networking on earth and a huge and sophisticated blogo-sphere with more interlinking between different political poles than in the USA.[36] This 'Runet' was mostly being trafficked through Russian search engines, Russian email giants and Russian-owned blogging platforms. Partially this is because the state allowed the Internet to develop without government interference. Mostly, it was driven by the innovation that made the Internet and computers cheap enough around the world for vast numbers of people to have them at home. These technologies – unlike upgrading whole industries or bureaucracies – could be implanted into Russia by any individual who wanted to.

As Putin's videocracy was created he chose not to follow China and erect a 'great firewall', despite suggestions from the security services. Attempts by the FSB to have a surveillance role in the Internet were not followed up. At the time, mobile phone and Internet penetration rates were minimal – as were the capacities of the Russian state to monitor them.

With almost all the population getting their news from national TV stations, which the Kremlin had brought under its control, the existence of an online discussion world did not seem harmful but useful. Authoritarian regimes usually struggle to deal with the paradox of needing to censor information about their country's problems whilst needing reliable information about those same problems. The Internet was seen as something that could help policymakers to know how bad things really were. The Kremlin also felt that a small world commenting freely on the problems of Putinism could be useful as an echo chamber, for dissenters to let off steam. Keen to promote science and technology as part of 'catching up with the West', these ideas came together – around the time that Putin made the fateful decision to leave the Internet open.

The Russian Internet developed around three defining features. The first was that, unlike in other Eastern European countries, the platforms that hosted it were largely indigenous because of the Cyrillic script, allowing it to become a 'pole' in the emerging online world, like China, which also uses home-grown platforms. The largest search engine, Yandex, was Russian, as were the largest social-networking sites, VKontakte and Odnoklassniki, and the largest email provider, Mail.ru. Moscow was keen to encourage national champions and let them get on with their business. In an area unconnected to the Putin state, many online companies became islands of decent corporate governance. According to Anton Nossik, one of the fathers and leading blogger-managers of the Runet, this was the very secret of its success:

> The Internet in Russia evolved into a kind of alternate reality to the rest of the economy. As it began to boom there were no FSB raids, no hostile takeovers, no state monopolies and no ministries that needed bribes. The Internet grew in Russia in a kind of utopia – where there was no state. This was the only part of the economy where to be a player and to be a winner you needed no political connections, no United Russia membership card and no visits to the Kremlin. Its triumph was possible as this was the only bit of Russia without bureaucrats.

The second defining trait of the Runet was the incredible success of social media. By fortunate coincidence VKontakte lured students online at the same time, between 2006–7 that the site Odnoklassniki pulled online all those with very little reason to be there – those in their fifties and sixties. By promising to reconnect them to their old classmates, and thus the Soviet Union, this site brilliantly brought online the demographic that no one expected to see in social networking. There was one popular foreign exception amongst the dominant platforms – Livejournal. Originally a US blogging portal that was somewhat popular in the early 2000s, the site took off in Russia. It allowed blogs to have 'friends' or followers, blending blogging with social networks. Initially, it was also invite only. This appealed to the original community of Russian bloggers, who were mostly exclusive, well-to-do Moscow journalists and writers who knew each other offline. This platform became the heart of the Russian blogosphere.

Over the course of the decade the opposition – be they nationalists, liberals or ecologists – migrated into blogging. As censored TV news declined, losing 40 per cent of its audience between 2000 and 2006, the online world thrived and social networking flourished. By 2010 the country had the most engaged social networking community in the world – whose users were increasingly following and linking to blogs. Russian political blogging, due to its elitist and 'Moscow community' feel, was more convivial than the American blogging scene – where partisan bloggers simply linked to each other. In Russia, one Harvard study showed that bloggers from different political 'poles' were more inclined to link one to another. The same study also picked up that there was a 'nationalist' and a 'liberal' cluster online – but in an interesting indication of the next generations' politics, there was no 'Putin' cluster.[37]

The third feature of the Runet was that it went mainstream in the second half of the 2000s, exploding just at the start of the credit crunch, unlike in Western Europe where it had taken place a decade before. This meant that the web's cultural imprint was defined by the financial crisis. Yet few were optimistic in the late 2000s about the possibility for the Internet to affect change. The title of the publication *The Web that Failed* summed up expert opinion on its political potential.[38]

The Kremlin did not begin to comprehend that they had set themselves an online trap. In 1999 it would have been possible to censor the Internet without major protests – users were only 1 per cent of the population. By 2005 this was already impossible, with users at 15 per cent. By 2010 a majority of Russian households had a personal computer and an estimated 43 per cent were users.[39] The Putin videocracy that managed democracy depended on only worked when the crushing majority got their news from state-controlled TV. With more and more of them switching online – it was being hollowed out by millions of bloggers.

The Rise of Migrant Russia

Russia in the 2000s was not just becoming richer – it was becoming less Russian. The boom was sucking in so much cheap labour that Caucasian and Central Asian migrants could now be found literally anywhere, even on a third-class train ride to Siberian Omsk. That was where I met Hamid, the only man on the night-train who wasn't drinking. He still had a long way to go. Hamid drove a clapped-out Soviet bus in a Russian mining colony beyond the Arctic Circle, where temperatures regularly plunge below –40°C. Yet this native of desert Uzbekistan had few regrets about migrating to Russia. 'In my country there are more men than jobs – in Russia there are more jobs than men,' he explained.

Hamid was no strange oddity but one of at least sixty Uzbeks in the carriages. He is a staple of today's Russia, because in the 2000s Russia became a migrant country. This influx was at odds with the conventional Western narrative, where demographic collapse is endlessly cited as driving Russian decline. Whilst true that the native Russian population fell dramatically during the 1990s, there was also a huge, and under-recorded, influx of people like Hamid. Russia is now the second most popular country for migrants in the world after the United States.

Starting in the early 2000s Moscow and other major cities were transformed. Migrants flooded in from the former Soviet republics of Central Asia, the Caucasus and Eastern Europe to do the work that natives turned down. It created a racially distinct underclass out of the old 'little brother nations' of the imperium. Today, Tajiks sweep the streets, Azeris wait tables and Uzbeks work on construction sites. They are treated as something between invisible inferiors, children and slaves.

Nothing catches this better than walking home in Moscow in the snow late at night, at the darkest hour when everyone who is still awake is Asian – gangs of shivering Kyrgyz migrants, pausing to share cigarettes, shovelling snow under the orange street lamp glow in order to make room for the morning's traffic. Many of them live in squalid basements sharing fetid mattresses, wooden barracks outside the city, or huddled in cramped apartments with dozens of men sleeping on the floor. They are everywhere, even beneath the piecrust architecture of the tsarist centre, where Kyrgyz squat whole basements, Uzbeks cram twenty men into leaking attics and Tajiks stuff as many as they can into suffocating dormitories.

Visa-free regimes between Russia and most of its former colonies, plus the corruption of officialdom, means that few people bother immigrating formally. Nobody knows precisely how many migrants there are in Russia, but officials admit there are over 10 million with the true figure (if one accounts for illegals) as high as 15 million and rising fast.[40] Between 1992 and 2008, Russia officially lost over 7 million people, despite the immigration of ethnic Russians and others with Russian citizenship from other former Soviet republics.[41] But if you add these new migrants to the calculations, it now has more people than it lost. In short, though the ethnic

Russian population has fallen, Russia does not have a demographic crisis – but an ethnic crisis.

Ethnically the country was undergoing a seismic shift. Experts estimated that Russia was on its way to becoming 20 per cent Muslim by 2020, with Islam's demographic share having exploded 40 per cent since 1989.[42] The emigration over two decades of millions of Jews, Volga Germans and the Balts was interpreted as 'de-Europeanization', whilst the migrant wave swung the racial balance in Russia back towards Turkic groups for the first time since the eighteenth century. Projections by the nation's leading demographer Anatoly Vishnevsky estimate that if current trends hold, by 2025 as much as 15 per cent of the population will be recent immigrants, rising to 35 per cent by 2050.[43] Most of them will be Muslim. More and more apartments for rent qualified their adverts as 'Slavs Only'. I emailed one once: 'Does it matter if I am a non-Slavic Jew for renting the one-bedroom apartment with the shared bathroom on the eighth floor?' The reply – 'This may be negotiable' – was revealing. After two centuries of being fixated by Jews, the cosmology of Russian hate was fixating more and more on Muslim migrants.

The Kremlin found itself in a strange bind by the decade's end. It had been appealing to nationalism, but it had no choice but to admit over 10 million migrants in order to keep the economic boom afloat. Demographers estimate Russia now needs to admit at least 700,000 more in order to sustain growth.[44] Nor could it really police its borders with ex-Soviet states. This meant it was forced to present an anti-chauvinist position, in defence of a huge mostly Muslim migrant wave. Putin began trying to discreetly fashion a more multicultural society. He has announced that for those who wanted to tie their future to Russia 'the door will always be open'. The head of the Federal Migration Service admitted that migrants are key to improving the demographic situation.

But capitalizing on immigration involves more than just letting people in. Life for migrants became increasingly tough; most lived in penury often harassed by skinheads. Across Russia, cases of near slavery have been reported, with Uzbeks, Kyrgyz and Tajiks tricked or otherwise forced into working in agriculture or on construction sites for little or no pay.[45] Even in Moscow, dozens of the sullen Central Asians behind the tills in corner shops – who people see every day – have been found to be beaten slaves.[46] Unprotected by the (ignored) labour code, Putinism has created a huge racially distinct underclass that risks not only driving down workers' wages and rights, but also undermining the case for innovation or basic efficiency gains with plentiful cheap labour. Able to import near-slave labour at minimal costs, employers had no need to modernize or protect workers' rights. This was not appreciated at the time, but due to the weakness of the rule of law, migrants may have been contributing to growth but they were stalling Russia's modernization – and further devaluing what it meant to be a 'Russian citizen'.

This problem, like so many other governance failures, was obscured in the boom years. Putin had not realized it but, by allowing the import of millions of Caucasian and Central Asian migrants, he was cracking the Putin consensus. At the beginning of the decade he could be seen as a nationalist hero, fighting for Russia in the Caucasus. Now he was seen as a man who would flood Russia with Muslims for the sake of cheap labour. As the nationalists lost interest in Jews, only to discover Islam as the enemy, Putin lost them.

The boom had created a new Russia of bloggers, consumers and migrants. It was a place dizzy from change, which was trying to hold on to something. The hand it clasped was not that of Putin's creations – be they Nashi or United Russia – but the Russian Orthodox Church. To the chagrin of its liberals, the most conservative force in the country would emerge as one of the biggest winners of a period of rapid change. As the country became less Russian ethnically, it was becoming more so culturally.

The Rise of Holy Russia

The revolutionaries who came to power during the collapse, hoping to overturn 'Actually Existing Socialism', failed to see their wishes for Russia come true. Except one – Patriarch Alexy II of Moscow. Yeltsin and Gaidar certainly died with regrets. Russia had not become democratic. The economy had not decoupled from a state-driven oil and gas complex. Yet as the Patriarch passed away in December 2008, he could have looked back at his revolutionary aims when he was anointed in 1989 – to bring the Russian Orthodox Church back from the margins of society into its driving force – with a feeling that he had triumphed where the democrats had failed.

In the course of his reign the Church had exploded not only in terms of adherents, but also in terms of power, wealth and infrastructure. The year before Alexy took over in 1988 there were only 22 monasteries and 6,893 priests and deacons in the country. Two years after his death there were 804 monasteries and a veritable army of 30,670 priests and deacons in Russia.[47] Across the country, over a hundred Orthodox 'brotherhoods' had been founded. Amongst the people, over two-thirds now identified as Orthodox believers, up from less than half in the mid-nineties.[48] All in all, Holy Russia was resurgent, an astonishing turnaround for a religion viciously persecuted under the Soviets.

The wealth of the Church exploded, with one tentative 2001 estimate (believed to be a vast underestimate) putting its worth at over half a billion dollars.[49] Its budget is now a secret, but the Orthodox Church's fortune is estimated at being several billion dollars at least. Since then, its property portfolio has exploded, with a 2010 law pledging to restore to the Church all lands expropriated during Lenin's revolution. This could make it Russia's single largest landowner.[50] Its power and prestige skyrocketed, with the Patriarch living in the Kremlin, blessing the President after each inauguration, regularly broadcast alongside Putin and his ministers, with his priests integrated into the army and the religion de facto that of party and state.

The Church succeeded both by default, because Russian liberal and nationalist projects failed, but also because it knew its way politically. Alexy II and his inner circle had played the politics of the Yeltsin and Putin court perfectly. Many commented that the suspected former KGB role of Alexy II and the alleged involvement in espionage of his successor Kirill I had equipped them with the tools to co-opt and infiltrate the Kremlin into a religious agenda. Upon assuming the Patriarchy in 1989, Alexy II had done his best to support Yeltsin during the 1991 coup, urging Russians not to spill blood to force the democrats from the White House. He had offered the government support, thus legitimacy, at critical moments, endorsing Yeltsin in the 1996 election.

The Church went out of its way to infiltrate the beaten Russian Army into its sphere of influence. They began by signing treaties on cooperation with the army, the border troops and the emergency ministry to play a role promoting the faith amongst the rank and file. The military felt deeply embattled by the attacks on it from the media during the first Chechen war and embraced the Church, which was on their side of the culture war promoting Russian warrior saints. The result was that under Putin, Alexy II achieved his dream – with chapels re-established in military bases in 2005, whilst calls began to return military chaplains.

Alexy II knew how to cash in his support for Yeltsin for political favours. No sooner had he backed the ailing leader's 1996 re-election, did the government begin drafting a new law curtailing what the Church described as 'the invasion of the sects'. The law elevated Orthodoxy, Islam, Judaism and Buddhism to higher levels of rights and benefits, with the implicit hint that Orthodoxy was more equal than the others.

Alexy II had known how to make money for the Church in the 1990s. With the bandit economy as the way of life, he secured the right to trade duty-free cigarettes, with the Church becoming the trader of 10 per cent of the country's tobacco.[51] When the tide turned towards nationalized conglomerates, he successfully positioned the Church as something akin to a 'state corporation', a spiritual version of Rosneft or the bank VTB.

Nominally, it would be independent but Alexy encouraged Putin to 'invest' in it and think of himself as its major political and economic shareholder. Gazprom and Rosneft are believed to have made huge donations to the Church. Putin's close St Petersburg allies Sergey Ivanov, the defence minister (2000–8), and Vladimir Yakunin, head of the Russian railways, both came out as strong supporters of this religious revival.

The Church also thrived because, guided by prejudice alone, one survey saw 37 per cent of bishops deem democracy 'not for Russia'; it worked out what the Putin project was and how to work with it quickly.[52] By turning itself into a 'state corporation' of sorts it managed to amass the funds for its massive construction campaign. Yet buildings were not the only infrastructure it erected: the Patriarchy built its own mass media. By the end of 2010 it was publishing twenty journals, broadcasting on six radio stations and operating two satellite TV channels.[53] Online priests formed a cluster of popular Orthodox blogs heavily linked into the large 'nationalist cluster' of the Runet. The Church sponsored its own talking heads, with the Patriarch's press service constantly commenting on major talk shows.

Orthodoxy resurgent could be felt even in liberal Moscow. Gay pride demonstrations were banned. Then, over the Soviet baroque skyline, rose the gigantic gold cupola of the Cathedral of Christ the Saviour. The cathedral had been destroyed by Stalin in order to create space for his dreamed of Palace of the Soviets, which would have towered above Moscow topped by a statue of Lenin, whose shadow would have fallen over the capital of socialism. The act of destroying the cathedral – imagine Mussolini dynamiting the Florentine Duomo, imagine Napoleon wrecking Notre Dame de Paris – symbolized the ultimate horrific assault on Orthodoxy in the eyes of Russian conservatives. The site also came to symbolize the failure of Stalin's utopia. The marshlands underneath proved unable to sustain the foundations of the tower he dreamed of, which kept collapsing back. After the war, construction was abandoned and a gigantic open-air swimming pool opened, heated so that in the winter a tower of steam, like a ghost of a dream, hovered above Moscow.

To the faithful, the restoration of the Cathedral of Christ the Saviour, built by the tsars to celebrate their victory over Napoleon, symbolized victory over Stalin. It was a political more than a sacred place. Believers seemed to sense this, never praying in distress or coming for solace. It attracted mostly protesters in a culture war for or against holy Russia, such as the infamous 'Pussy Riot'. This symbol of the Church's political victory also symbolized how it had embraced Putin too closely. With less than 7 per cent of the site said to be used for religious purposes, with an underground car park and the conference halls rented out for money, the unlovely half-a-billion dollar building stood for a byzantine symbiosis between the Patriarch and the Kremlin.[54]

In Moscow, the new Patriarch Kirill, escorted by bodyguards and the owner of a $30,000 gold Breguet wristwatch, drove around the capital in luxury cars with a blue-bucket alarm to break traffic.[55] The fringe beards of perestroika were now national politicians. Yet for normal Russians, the flamboyance of restored power was not their daily experience of the Church. In every provincial city, from Abakan to Yuzhno-Sakhalinsk, locals puffed with pride at the new golden-domed church built as their post-Soviet landmark. In a country in disarray, sickened by the breakdown of the welfare state and the rule of law, a new army of priests and monks offered a compass, charity and a helping hand to those desperately needing someone to fight off the moral vacuum that underlay the epidemic of heroin, alcoholism, murder, corruption and prostitution. The Church set up drugs clinics, soup kitchens and orphanages – and the people in Siberia and the Urals felt that the Patriarch's men were doing something for them.

The Moscow intelligentsia first mocked the Church as something medieval, then denounced it as something medieval: yet in contrast to the historic failure of Russian liberalism, it was running the most successful social project in the whole country. In a hundred small ways, the country was culturally being rewired. By the end of Putin's first presidency, the vast majority of Russian homes had icons again, the majority of Russian cars had icons on the dashboard: tiny gold baptismal crosses, rare in the USSR, were now so common they no longer stood out, with regular church attendance (if still below 10 per cent of the population) higher than it had been in almost eighty years.[56]

The infiltration of the Church into the political routine of the country had become so common that it was no longer noticed. Endless TV clips would show the Patriarch inviting Putin, or Medvedev, to attend a mass, with the President graciously accepting. Invented traditions, such as the President after his inauguration being blessed by the Patriarch in the Kremlin Cathedral of the Annunciation, in an act eerily reminiscent of the enthronement of the tsar, were shrugged off as the new normal. The triumph of the Church was visible in the size of the crowds it could draw. In 2011 – outdoing the numbers present at any of the protests surrounding contested elections – over 285,000 gathered to kiss a relic of the Virgin Mary's belt as it was paraded through Moscow.[57] In its journey across Russia, over 2 million had pushed their way to touch its holiness.[58]

The rise of the Russian Orthodox Church both aided Putin and eventually subtly undermined him. It blew into society a sense that Russia needed to be Russian, not a 'reproduction of the Western model', to quote Patriarch Kirill.[59] It reinforced in its sermons that Russia was the centre of an Orthodox-Slavic civilization that sooner or later would be not just the third Rome but the 'second Brussels' reuniting the lost lands. All of this was helpful to Surkov and 'Sovereign Democracy'. Yet the Church was also injecting into the national bloodstream an overwhelming sense that all was not morally right, that Russia was disorientated, that Russia was sick, that it needed to cleanse itself, to be less corrupt and above all to be holy.

Putin undoubtedly thought that by allying himself to the Patriarch he was allying himself to a politician. This was true. But he was also giving free range to a cultural project that was raising questions he had no answer to: only 'stability' – is Russia for Russians? Why is the state not fighting drugs or helping orphans? How can Russia live without lies? The Church was preparing for a culture war against liberal Russia – meaning sooner or later that Putin would have to abandon consensus politics and take sides.

Kudrin Succeeds, Surkov Fails

The government was not fretting about the growing number of consumers, bloggers, believers and migrants. In Putin's 2007 state of the nation address he declared that, 'Not only has Russia fully overcome a long period of production decline, but it now ranks among the top ten economies in the world.' The same year he boasted to Europe:

> Historians will be the judges of what my people and I achieved in eight years. We re-established Russia's territorial integrity, strength-ened the state, moved in the direction of a multi-party system and re-established the potential of our armed forces.[60]

Boastful, self-deceptive propaganda from a corrupt regime? Or a heady but still broadly fair assessment of a Russian government that had achieved macro-economic stability for the first time in a generation? The truth is that it was both. Much of the work led by finance minister Alexey Kudrin was a success. Though macro-economic stabilization and the development of a consumer society is something, it did not add up to comprehensive modernization. The Putin regime's success at financial stabilization reflected the fact that it was at its best when dealing with technical tasks that could be done from offices in the capital with the minimum of stake-holders, and thus conflicts with vested interests. They did well at stabi-lizing the ruble but not at guiding corporations to diversify the economy; success was found in reducing inflation and cutting red-tape but they fared poorly at weaning policemen out of organized crime, or pushing corporate boards to stop behaving like 'politburos', without any respect for minority shareholders. The narrower the task, such as paying off debts and building up reserves, the better the regime did.

Their success in tuning big macro-economic indicators was exactly because these tasks were not dependent on Russian specifics at all, but were the same all over the world. Putin and Kudrin could get the rates right in the central bank whilst failing to infringe on the fusion of property and power, the massive corruption in public procurement, chronic theft from road-building budgets, the poor organization of public services and the personalization of power itself around Putin. Not surprisingly given that the regime was corrupt, objectives that required a substantial change in political behaviour and people management failed, despite its success in macro-economic stabilization.

The biggest contradiction of all was that as Kudrin and Gref's plans bore fruit, the projects steered by Surkov failed. 'Sovereign democracy' was never taken seriously as an ideology and neither United Russia nor Nashi ever developed into a factory for quality cadres. None of these initiatives supposed to improve Russia's poor-quality governance achieved this. They merely added new sinecures and extended patronage networks that obstructed this goal. By creating institutions like these merely as Kremlin tools, without any autonomy, Putin and Surkov could not fill the holes left by the silencing of parliament, national TV and regional governors: they had put the Kremlin back in control but left it no better at governing.

This meant that the 2000s boom in the Russian economy covered up serious structural weaknesses that posed a long-term threat to the country's development. But most politicians in the Kremlin did not see how vulnerable these deficiencies made them, as by the late 2000s they felt they were running the most successful Russian government since the 1961 Soviet triumph that had made Yuri Gagarin the first man in space. Polls concurred. This boom in living standards had become bound up in Russian minds with Putin. Gleb Pavlovsky reminisces how at the time:

> It was significant that he was the insurer, the guarantor of slow but definitively rising living standards. Broadly in Putin's system, precisely because it turned out to be more financial, than administrative or political (the administration here is pretty bad) – this insurance guarantee was crucial.[61]

However, the contradiction between the economic successes and bureaucratic failure – one side expressed in Kudrin and the other in Surkov – could not be postponed forever. The poverty and national disintegration of the 1990s had stopped, whilst the corruption and the monarchical presidency born in the 1990s had reached grotesque and exaggerated proportions. This made the Putin consensus and the Putin majority inherently vulnerable. Surkov had failed to create tools that could control the way society was evolving. It was now going its own way, driven by megatrends that Surkov could only try to steer – a growing consumerist middle class, the expanding Internet, uncontrolled mass migration and religious resurgence. Russia was being reshaped but not by the state.

However, the government was not so worried. As the economy boomed in the run-up to the 2008 crash, both the new middle class and the political elite were willing to look the other way. In Russia, as in China, consumerism had turned out to be far more complementary to authoritarianism than ration cards. In fact, Putin seemed so successful that at some moments during the decade there may have been more unrest in the hinterland of Beijing than in provincial Russia.[62] 'Putin – Stability', as the posters he smiled from said.

Delirious Moscow

Tastes change. The most popular Russian novels of the decade were not ones about heroic masses, but dashing tsarist agents. Known as the *Fadorin Series* these were pulp detective thrillers set under Nicholas II. They sold over 20 million copies, because they indulged a country dreaming of a gilded age, without any of the pressures of the 'collective'. The empire that the author Boris Akunin had chosen to set his adventures in was that of the 1880s, one that Russians could recognize, a place where power was both autocratic and fragile, the country both optimistic and paranoid. In the most popular book in the series, *The State Counsellor*, the hero-detective resigns from state service having saved the tsar, unable to put up with its dirty methods to ensnare terrorists. Akunin wanted to make a point out of this – think of yourself as an individual.

This reflected the ways in which the boom was changing Russian minds. The 2000s saw a rejection of the tradition of 'togetherness'. Those in the new middle class were not saving Russia from communism, but putting themselves first. These new consumers were engaged in escapism and flight. Whilst showing minimal concern for their fellow countrymen, or interest in the state, Russian families were quietly renovating their apartments, buying modern cars and installing new televisions. For the young this was cool, not wasting time handing out pamphlets about political crimes at mass gatherings like their parents had done. Little wonder that these tsarist fantasies appealed.

Moscow changed as a social world. Paranoia about Balkanization died as a conversation topic. Travelling, getting up to speed with and ideally owning current London and Manhattan trends was cool. These were the years of 'glamour'. The gangster chic of the 1990s was replaced by a fashion for velvet jackets and opulent clubs with aggressive 'face control'. There were dreams of Italian fashion, sophistication and glasses of Cristal. The highest compliment you could pay someone was to say he was 'successful', whilst to call someone 'political' was practically an insult.

Out in the provinces, copying what was happening in the capital was cool. The websites of small opposition factions were generally quiet as vast numbers of fan pages for London or Paris sprang up. In Moscow 'the theory of small deeds', a tsarist-era philosophy that urged Russians to concentrate on small civic acts and forget political overhaul, was popularized by Vasily Esmanov, the founder of a fashion portal with a name that rang with the age: lookatme.ru. The twentysomethings who were addicted to this website felt they had left the 1990s behind: 'We are different,' said Esmanov, 'we are the first Russian generation raised on global culture.'

Moscow lost the 1990s feeling of free fall and zero gravity. One could be forgiven for believing that the city was deliriously passing through three time-historical zones at once: Berlin in the early 1930s, Chicago in the mid-1930s and Paris in the mid-1960s – the marching of boots, the ever-presence of crime and the dreamy, mocking rejection of a post-imperial regime by an experimental new generation.

One young man who captured the post-post-Soviet groove was Filip Dzyadko. In 2007, at the height of the boom, fortune handed him the editorship of the Moscow free-sheet *Bolshoi Gorod* ('Big City'). It had been going for a while but never quite found its voice. Dzyadko did. The magazine began trying to build a new aesthetic and was left to collect in the 'free cafes' of the city. He wanted to fight Putin's 'greyness' and the messed-up, ugly symbolism of his regime that mixed up banal, dated Soviet icons and practices – from the saucer-like hats worn by the police, the hammer and sickle flag of the army, to the advertising hoardings exhorting people to have more children, right down to the hydroelectric plant on the 100 ruble note. To do this *Bolshoi Gorod* exploded into colour, restyled Cyrillic and glorified social activism.

A new fashion was sweeping Moscow. 'Glamour' was giving way to hipster chic and the cult of 'creativity'. This began in the 'free cafes'. These were a new 'underground'. It was centred on the fake French bistro Jan-Jak, the 1930s 'intelligentsia' themed Mayak and Materskaya. 'It's like we created our spaces,' said Esmanov from lookatme.ru, 'but we wished we could teleport between them, not have to go through dirty and badly maintained streets that we feel don't belong to us.' Here *Bolshoi Gorod* became a crucial identity marker for young Muscovites to show they were not 'grey' people like those in the Kremlin; it was left in these places as an alternative marker. Its whole aim was for Dzyadko to fight what he called 'a time without ideology, a grey time without ideas'.

An archipelago was emerging in Moscow of 'free places', but without politics. Dzyadko explains: 'It was not political. The whole thing can be summed up in the popular photographs of the time – for example, a woman looking into the distance with sad eyes, let's say in Tokyo – and people would look at it and go, oh, how sad, how beautiful . . . but it was absolutely without meaning. But there was longing in it.' Dzyadko thinks the boom in foreign travel was crucial. 'People started going to Europe and seeing how things were there, and they came back with the desire to create their own nice spaces, attractive spaces inside Moscow. The boom was enabling young Muscovites to globalize and modernize themselves, in spite of the regime's incompetent institutions.'

It seemed Putin had nothing to worry about. These people were a ridiculous small minority and their new fashion didn't have political edge. 'There was nothing rock and roll about this,' remembers Dzyadko. 'This was not about standing up and announcing things, but saying them softly. There was no "loudness" – it was about dancing, quietly.'

But a whole network of new media was growing in Moscow, linked into this new beauty-seeking youth culture. These publications – not Nashi – were the winners of the 2000s that defined a generation. They were materialistic, stylish, inward-looking and anti-political – the self-portrait of a new middle class that wanted to be 'successful'. *Afisha* magazine became increasingly popular when its owner took a bet on a talented twenty-one-year-old editor in 2008, reaching a circulation of over 183,000.[63] A Russian version of *Esquire* was founded in 2005. The crowning 'hipster media' achievement was Dozhd the online, independent TV channel, launched in 2010. With its funky studios it looked like it was broadcast from Shoreditch in London, even Williamsburg in New York, but not Moscow.

This was derided by the controlled media as 'dem-shiza' or democratic schizophrenia. Prior to the outbreak of financial turmoil in 2008, it seemed like the Kremlin propagandists were wasting their time. The 'free cafes' were vacuous places, where talking about either Putin or Khodorkovsky was looked down on as 'not cool'. This attitude was more useful to the Kremlin than any censor. Even one of their most fashionable and politically minded frequenters, the celebrity journalist Leonid Parfyonov, was saying things like, 'I am a professional journalist, not a professional revolutionary. My job is to report and not climb the barricades.'[64] It was a sign of how far Muscovite culture was to change that both Parfyonov and the writer Boris Akunin became powerful orators of the December 2011 protest movement.

The keenest observers of society were getting agitated. Gleb Pavlovsky began to show signs of this, telling me, 'The hipsters are very interesting

. . . there is a new "youth" way of behaving . . . I think Moscow is changing.'
But those in universities, such as Vyacheslav Glazychev, who had written
widely on the 'unshakable nature' of the 'Putin majority', felt a change
under way in the world of the 'golden youth' that ran so close to the world
of power in Moscow. But he wasn't sure what it was. In his 'den' of weird
objects under a picture of Dubrovnik he sighed:

'The generation that became adults under Gorbachev and Yeltsin are
burnt out completely. Nobody knows what's coming with the new generation, for the moment, they are just babes in the wood. But it will be very
different. It always is.'

He was right. It was in the 'free bars' of Moscow that the first seeds of
a new opposition began to germinate but had not yet sprung to life. One
evening I sat on a cracked balcony with a friend, smoking cigarettes with
the names of Soviet space missions. 'I'm fed up of Moscow,' she complained,
flicking our *Apollo-Soyuz* butts off the dusty ledge, 'I can't stand this social
scene anymore. It's all glamour and no substance. It'll never amount to
anything.' And for the remains of the decade, she was right.

Dreaming with BRICs

As Moscow changed socially, it changed politically. By the late 2000s feelings of vulnerability had evaporated. A hubristic mood had settled over the
barons of the city – stability had been secured. Now Russia was resurgent.
Fired up by surging oil prices, a booming middle class and high growth
rates, the elite felt that Russia was rising with China. Taking at face value
the 2001 Goldman Sachs pamphlet that classed Russia together with
Brazil, India and China as the world's four largest emerging economies –
the BRICs – the establishment came to believe that the country would
continue to grow rapidly until it had caught up with the West.[65] The high-
brow magazine *Ekspert* even predicted that the ruble would join the US
dollar and the euro as a global reserve currency, whilst Putin predicted that
Russia would 'overtake Britain and France' in GDP terms in 2009.[66]

Russian intellectuals and politicians felt they were fireproof, with think-
tankers devoting panels to the idea that Russia's commodity-driven
economy had 'decoupled' from the West. This optimism in global growth
prospects was not uniquely Russian. Prior to the crash in 2008, most
analysts had a rosy view of future GDP potential. Western analysts shared
this enthusiasm for the Russian market – from the creators of the BRIC
brand at Goldman Sachs to the director of Deutsche Bank in Moscow,
who believed Russia had made 'a macro-economic breakthrough'.[67]

The intensity of this mood was understandable. It was not at all unique,
but fostered by a fast connecting new global superclass for whom Davos

had replaced the United Nations General Assembly as the true gathering of power-brokers. In Brussels, elites felt sure of themselves as an emerging 'normative superpower', and in Washington the 'project for a new American century' seemed realistic. There was a widespread belief propounded by the US economist Ben Bernanke that the global economy had entered a 'great moderation', and some analysts argued that economist Milton Friedman had been right to argue it was 'depression proof'.[68]

What marked out Moscow was that this was the first time since the late 1970s that the Russian elite had tasted success, rising influence and an economic boom. In this pre-crash world that treated GDP as a synonym for power, and saw Western banks as the pinnacle of efficiency and good forecasting, the delirious excitement of the Kremlin courtiers could be forgiven. They were presented with data that suggested that by growing at merely 3.9 per cent a year, in nominal GDP terms Russia would overtake Italy in 2018, France in 2024, Britain in 2027 and Germany in 2028.[69]

Economic self-confidence dovetailed with a change in self-perception as a foreign policy actor. Moscow identified with the BRIC countries and began to see itself as a rising power. In Europe it became increasingly revisionist. The foreign policy debate in Moscow started to dwell on a supposed long-term decline of the West, and how to restore Russian influence in former Soviet states. Russian diplomats like to talk about how they felt like poor cousins or unwanted guests with Western counterparts under Yeltsin or during Putin's first few years. Their behaviour changed markedly during his second term.

Russia was no longer intent on 'joining the West on its own terms', but striking out as an 'independent', 'sovereign' player in international affairs. The establishment spoke increasingly about the coming end of the American 'unipolar' world. Sergei Lavrov, the Russian foreign minister, began to let slip that he felt the West had seen its day. In 2007, at the Munich Security Conference, Putin felt strong enough to start openly challenging it. He accused the US of having 'overstepped its national borders in every way'.[70] Dry and confident, Putin's demeanour unnerved American officials. After the 'Munich speech', the normally sanguine Defense Secretary Robert Gates exclaimed, 'One Cold War was quite enough.'[71]

As Putin's reputation rose domestically he ceased to be treated like a conventional politician. Influential players called on him to 'follow Roosevelt' and alter the constitution to run for a third term, whilst commentators discussed whether he should be considered a great man of history.[72] Behind the Kremlin walls, the idea began to circulate that he might rule forever. Even Moscow's democratic aristocrats such as Mikhail Gorbachev publicly credited Putin with having 'pulled Russia out of chaos and earned a place in history', which had enabled Russia to enjoy 'a resurgence'.[73]

Inevitably, Putin began to change. His Western guests first picked up on this shift. Jonathan Powell, the chief of staff to Tony Blair, recalls how both he and the prime minister were touched on their first visit to Russia when Putin pointed out the shabby block of flats he had grown up in as a child, whilst driving away from a state function at a tsarist palace in St Petersburg. As Powell wrote in his memoirs:

Each time Tony visited him in his dacha he had acquired more grooms for his horse and lived in greater luxury. Angela Merkel described a joint German–Russian cabinet meeting in Siberia in 2006. She said that she had found it difficult to convince Putin that cabinet ministers should be treated with respect rather than contempt. For Putin hubris resulted partly from the trappings of office and partly from the price of oil.[74]

Power loves to build, because rulers die but architecture remains. Putin's Moscow began the biggest construction project since Brezhnev's 1980 Olympic games – Moscow City. These gigantic skyscrapers, the tallest in Europe, with names such as 'Imperia', 'City of Capitals', 'Federation', 'Russia' or 'Eurasia' were launched in quick succession between 2003 and 2007 with the intention of creating a 'global financial centre' for over 200,000 people to work in or visit at any one time. These sub-utopian glass fragments of a BRIC dream were seductive to Muscovites. They call them the teeth, or the claws, pushing up like fangs at the city's edge. To the drunken financiers in rooftop bars, they smiled like a Cheshire Cat over the Kremlin. Yet the new mood did not calm everyone. A popular political joke in Moscow in 2007 had Putin discussing with Medvedev the issues of the day.

'We have won the right to host the 2014 winter Olympics, the economy is booming, the oil price is rising, the poverty rate amongst your subjects has fallen from 30 per cent to 13 per cent and we have even won the Eurovision song contest in your honour,' says Medvedev. Putin nods approvingly thinking of tasks left for the government to accomplish, before announcing, 'This means it is now time to win World War Three.'

The Short Cold War

The coloured revolutions in Ukraine, Georgia and Kyrgyzstan coincided with the oil boom and Russia paying off its international debts. This gave the Kremlin the confidence and resources to strike back. Russian foreign policy became increasingly aggressive. Kremlin ideologues began to argue for an 'Eastern European Union' to counterbalance a 'declining European Union'.[75] The Kremlin began to support 'counter-Orange revolutionaries' in Ukraine, Georgia and Kyrgyzstan and set up a network of think-tanks to promote its policies.

Russian-backed political agitation rose throughout the region. Moscow even launched cyber-attacks on Estonia and used gas cut-offs on Ukraine to force its agenda. In Europe, Russia courted a special relationship with Germany and Italy to undermine a common Western front and played divide and rule inside the EU. Globally, there were attempts to derail Western projects at the UN Security Council; investment in closer partnerships with China to counter America; demands that the US withdraw from Central Asia, including attempts to bribe Kyrgyz leaders to remove an American base and increased ties with US foes in Venezuela, Iran and Syria.

Many began to fear a new Cold War. They say that history repeats itself, first as tragedy then as farce. This observation applies to what happened between Russia and the West in 2007–8 during the 'short Cold War'. The Cold War itself was a global struggle played out on almost every possible level – from culture, industry, space races, to proxy-wars and the arms race. The short Cold War was a much-reduced affair. Between 2007–8 the Russian establishment came to believe it was a strategic imperative to prevent NATO membership for Georgia and Ukraine. More importantly, it thought it now had the resources to defeat NATO expansion, where under Yeltsin and in Putin's first term it had been forced to swallow it.

On these two fronts were played out a limited confrontation, which in the Caucasus ended in war. For Russians, Ukraine is not really abroad. The language, history and culture is so close and shared, and families so mixed up, that a trip there 'does not count as being abroad'. This translates into a belief by swathes of the establishment that Ukraine is not a 'true' state and cannot be permitted to be 'severed from Russia'. This goes as far as the hope of eventual reunion. As one former Russian official, who published under a pseudonym, wrote in his memoir:

> Russian bureaucrats know the Soviet Union is dead. They do not know that it cannot be recreated. Indeed a re-union around a core of Russia, Ukraine and Belarus seems rather likely.[76]

Stopping Ukrainian NATO membership is essential to Russian hopes for maintaining a sphere of influence or reintegrating with the two Slavic ex-Soviet states. And without a sphere of influence, Russian intellectuals lament, 'we are just a big state'. In practice this sees Russian diplomats give various arguments from 'having Ukraine in NATO is as intolerable as Britain seeing Ireland join the Warsaw Pact', or, as the pro-Kremlin analyst Dmitry Suslov bluntly explained, 'This is impossible for us as Ukraine to Russia is not Austria to Germany, but Bavaria to Germany.' Feelings were particularly intense as huge numbers within the Russian establishment had been born in Ukraine or studied there, or have Ukrainian parents. The other side of the coin was that a successful pro-Western democracy in Ukraine would undermine Putinism by example. This is why at the NATO Bucharest Summit in 2008 Putin threatened the US and said 'Ukraine is not really a state', as he sought to dissuade NATO from giving it – together with Georgia – a Membership Action Plan, an agreement that starts a country's nuts and bolts integration into the alliance.

In a different way, Georgia was a challenge. Mikhail Saakashvili, the 'rose revolutionary' president, pioneered a 'Georgian model' for post-Soviet states. Ideologically it was a fusion of reformist economic liberalism and pro-Western nationalism. It was also a threat to the Putin model because it was hugely successful in eliminating petty corruption and gangsterism. Contrary to Russia, on indicators that measure corruption, property rights and ease of doing business Tbilisi's score rose rapidly. After the overthrows in Ukraine and Kyrgyzstan, the Georgian model was held up as a way forward. Opposition groups across post-Soviet states admired it as a successful model to exit trapped post-Soviet transitions – not Russia.

The short Cold War turned hot in Georgia in August 2008. On the night of the opening ceremony of the Beijing Olympic Games a decision was taken in Tbilisi to attack and occupy South Ossetia. Saakashvili believed that reuniting – if necessary by force – with this rebel region of Georgia that had broken away in the early 1990s was his destiny and a national imperative. However, South Ossetians' ethnic kin were mostly living next door in Russian North Ossetia. Most had with the encouragement of Moscow, acquired Russian citizenship during the 2000s. Russian officials say that the 'Georgian Hitler' attacked Russian peacekeepers and sought 'genocide'.[77] Most Russians, including opposition activists such as the then little-known Alexey Navalny, shared this view.

The then Georgian National Security Council chairman Alexander Lomaia said that Russian provocations and troop movements to reinforce their position in South Ossetia had placed them in what he called, 'a Zugzwang, the chess move where you are compelled to move'. Tbilisi argued that Russian forces had moved into South Ossetia as violence in and shelling of the ethnic Georgian controlled areas round the breakaway enclave threatened the collapse of their government unless they reacted. Compelled to or not, the Georgians moved and the Georgians lost. Claims during the war of a 'Russian invasion' cost the Saakashvili government something more valuable than territory – its perceived integrity in international affairs.

In essence the war was the collision of three hubristic projects. The first was the Georgian hubris that it could crush two Russian mini-client states without consequences. The second was the American hubris that it could build client states out of core ex-Soviet states and integrate them into NATO without consequences. The third was the Russian hubris that it had a veto on the foreign policy choices of Georgia and Ukraine and could crush, invade and depose the leadership of an American client state without consequences. At the time, few outside 'situations rooms' in Russia and the West realized how close to a broader war the rivalries of the short Cold War had actually reached. If the Ukrainian 'Orange' president had decided to enforce his threat that the Russian fleet might not be allowed to return to its Crimean base that served as a support base during the war, the prospect of Russian troops entering Donetsk in Ukraine as well as Gori in Georgia was a real possibility.

In the bar of the Tbilisi Hotel Marriott on the night that the French President Nicholas Sarkozy flew in from Moscow with the terms of the ceasefire, one European diplomat mused, 'power like water will find its level', and of all three hubristic projects the Russian one was closest to the real power level. Giant posters in support of the South Ossetians were thrown up in Moscow emblazoned with the war's start date '08.08.08' and 'Tskhinvali we are with you'. Though they claimed not to have goaded the Georgians into the war, Kremlin intellectuals began to talk, behind closed doors, of 'Putin's historical defeat of NATO expansion by force of arms', or 'the first ever direct Russian defeat of an American client state'. Weeks after the war, in a forest in eastern Siberia, Putin shot and tagged a tiger. Moving towards the beast knocked unconscious with a tranquilizer dart, he smirked, 'She won't forget us.' Putin's popularity rating had reached 83 per cent.[78] The message was clear. Russia was back. This marked the peak of Putin's popularity.

After the ceasefire I travelled over the front lines into South Ossetia on the back of a Russian military truck. There were burnt-out villages, ransacked post offices and shredded farmhouses. In the undergrowth there was a deep rot – the smell of death.

In the village cum capital, Tskhinvali, freshly pasted posters demanded: 'Recognize the union with Russia'. Nothing had escaped the tears, chips and blast of this short, nasty war. Men in ill-fitting, unmatched camouflage outfits circled around in stolen cars from the southern villages. In the hills were roars and rumbles as the Russian Army cleared the last ordinance. Further back, shouts and the occasional crackle fired gleefully into the air. The militia pushed itself forward: 'We gave it to them. They'll never come again.'

Under the poplars, through the dusk on Stalin Street, militias drifted towards the megaphones; a ring of Russian tanks formed a semicircle around a Soviet town hall. It was a wreck, like everything else in Tskhinvali. Until a few weeks earlier this had been the government building of the unrecognized mini-state. Soon it would be the headquarters of a 'government' recognized by Moscow. This meant effective annexation. Behind the tanks, floodlights clacked on over the throng. Dignitaries in bad suits took their seats in front of the armour. 'Is Putin coming?' hissed the rumour. There was a rush to light the memorial candles spread over the steps of the ruined offices. Russian soldiers tied wrist ribbons – the Russian and Ossetia tricolour, as one. I climbed onto a tank to stand next to a young Russian trooper. 'How do you feel?' I asked. 'Tired,' he laughed.

I did not realize it at the time but I was watching the peak of Putinism. The camera crews of federal TV pushed and angled for the widest frame with the perfect pitch: a memorial concert that is also a victory concert. The marching, mournful chords of the Shostakovich's Leningrad symphony began to play under the conductor Valery Gergiev, then director of the London Philharmonic. A friend of the Kremlin with a private jet, he pulled the orchestra and the crowd into the message: Russia respects her dead. Russia is back. Russia has won. Troops quivered with emotion and exhaustion. The young man dressed in camouflage standing next to me on the tank turned to me and whispered; 'I feel like my grandfather must have felt.'

A winner in a patriotic war. For the first time since General Alexander Gromov had crossed the bridge over the Amu-Daria river out of Afghanistan in February 1989, Russia was no longer in retreat. For weeks, news channels had been playing footage of tank columns threatening a European capital. In Russia and the West – there was political hysteria. Diplomats cabled from Moscow on Russian intentions in the Crimea. Newspapers published maps with troop numbers, once again in red and blue solider-shaped icons.

Over the phone, I rowed with Russian friends. 'NATO is wrong.' 'Russia is right.' 'No, NATO is right.' 'Russia is wrong.'

For a few weeks the war seemed extremely meaningful to Russia's development. Yet it was nothing of the sort. What seemed to be a sideshow in the 2000s – migrants and supermarkets, consumerism and tourism, tacky churches and hipsters – would all turn out to be hugely significant, the sociological remaking of Russia. The foreign-policy posturing of the late 2000s turned out to be incidental to the country's eventual course.

As Western diplomats nervously debated whether Russian forces would next invade Crimea, alarm signals began to go off in world financial markets. In the offices of the Georgian National Security Council I watched as officials at first began to argue that the sudden collapse of the Russian stock market was 'because they invaded us', but by the time they realized that it was not just the Russian economy that was in free fall but the entire global financial system that was seizing up, it had become apparent that Western politicians had all but forgotten about them. Suddenly, unexpectedly, the crash was about to bring European, American and Russian hubris abruptly down to earth. At the moment of his greatest victory, forces that would tear apart the Putin consensus and expose the weakness of Russia's claim to be rising with China were already at work.

PART TWO

Watch the Throne

CHAPTER SEVEN

SERVANT MEDVEDEV

PUTIN IS said to spend much of his time reading tomes on the lives of the tsars. Maybe he has let their shadows slip into the making of his choices. Many have an eerie echo of the past. When Russia was young, Ivan the Terrible, somewhat like Putin, chose to formally abdicate from the throne in 1574. He demanded that his boyars kneel before a converted Tatar noble called Simeon Bekbulatovich. Ivan insisted he was but a simple nobleman. Bekbulatovich was now their lord. After eleven months Ivan returned to the throne, proving for all to see that power was Ivan and there was no power without him even in the institution or robes of the tsar. When Putin ignored appeals from the elite to change the constitution and run for a third term in 2007, he anointed his most skilled courtier Dmitry Medvedev as his candidate, whom he would serve loyally as a mere prime minister. With this choice, the legend of servant Bekbulatovich began to haunt Moscow until Putin, like Ivan, returned to the Kremlin in 2012.

Soon known as 'the tandem', these two cooperated so smoothly in governing Russia, because they had already worked together for years. Like most leading Kremlin politicians they had got to know each other when Putin was in St Petersburg town hall. His young charge was the quintessential insider. He was the most junior member of the gang. Medvedev had proved his loyalty early – running Anatoly Sobchak's election campaign to the Congress of People's Deputies back in 1988. Nor had he ever flaked off into the anti-Sobchak opposition. Serving the 'great democrat' was his first real job after university, where he was taught by none other than Sobchak, who sent him to work for Putin straightaway, as a legal consultant for the city's foreign relations committee. This is a man whose entire adult life has been spent working in one way or another for the St Petersburg family. Unlike older members of the Putin elite who before coming to work with Putin had lived Soviet lives – sometimes several, either in the KGB, the military, or even just managing furniture stores – Medvedev had no other politically meaningful professional experience. He could be trusted. After all since his early twenties in the early 1990s, he had been spending weekends with the Putins at their dacha in the Ozero cooperative.

'Medvedev seems to enjoy working on our team, but I am not sure how we are going to use him yet,' said Putin pensively in 2000 of the younger man he had brought with him to Moscow.[1] A job was found for him, first as his 2000 election campaign manager, then as chairman of the Gazprom board of directors, before becoming the Kremlin chief of staff. These are all roles in which Medvedev excelled as a courtier – not a politician or administrator – earning him the sobriquet 'the vizier'. He was as secretive as any other insider. Amongst his first acts on becoming chief of staff – a promotion after Alexander Voloshin, the previous office holder, resigned in protest at Khodorkovsky's arrest – was to ban free contacts between Kremlin staff and the press. He made it clear that when push came to shove you were either with Putin or against him. After Andrei Illiaronov, the neoliberal economics advisor to Putin, made a show of attending Khodorkovsky's trial he was told by Medvedev that he had crossed the line. He was informed, 'You've made your choice about whom you are going to meet with.'[2] Four days later he was fired.

Few expected Medvedev to be the choice. His technocratic manners, fluency in English and management consultancy jargon, sprinkled with the Davos patois of the super-elite stood out in the Kremlin. His working life had not been spent in Soviet Russia. Putin's choice was greeted with enthusiasm by government economic liberals, embassies and many oligarchs. It seemed a victory for a certain tone – smiling and relaxed after stern KGB stares, at ease with video blogging where Putin does not even use the Internet, and more importantly not post-Soviet in personality but almost, tantalizingly, un-Soviet.

Medvedev was the first Russian leader since Nicholas II not to have been a member of the Communist Party or a KGB agent. He did not come from a peasant family persecuted by Stalinism, like Yeltsin or Gorbachev, or a rat-infested post-war *komunalka* like Putin, but one of the drab but decent blocks of flats and scientific families that the USSR was producing in the last decades of its existence. He was an only child. He had a very happy childhood. In a photo that Medvedev likes to place prominently on his website, it would be hard to imagine a baby with a broader smile. He had grown up in a different era in St Petersburg from Putin. Nobody wanted to watch spy thrillers. People wanted to listen to rock music. And Medvedev wanted to listen too: he loved Black Sabbath and Deep Purple. But he studied hard. The story he tells of himself is very different from that of the working-class brawling of little Putin. It's that of a diligent, hard-working, not particularly creative but intelligent young man from a good family, with a slightly clunky way of thinking and speaking, with none of the Putin or Khodorkovsky mystique. This is how he remembers falling in love:

> In the second and the third grade I was very interested in dinosaurs. We studied them, drew them, discussed them. I learned all the periods of the earth's development, starting with the Archaean and ending with the Cenozoic era . . . In the fourth and fifth grades, I was taken by chemistry . . . I did experiments. Then it was sports. We would practice three or four times a week. And then all of that ended in a single moment. A new life began.[3]

He met Svetlana when he was seven years old. He began dating her at high school, and this he claims, was the only year his grades suffered. They married when he was twenty-four.

Today in the drab but functional school where Medvedev had studied and met Svetlana, at the edge of St Petersburg, where the suburbs of Soviet grey blocks make it indistinguishable from anywhere else in Russia, his old maths teacher Irina Grigorovskaya thinks about him every day. 'Svetlana was a very popular girl and she liked many boys. We could all see how this made Dima nervous, even dismal, at times,' she told me, in a quivering tone of defensiveness towards 'Dima', as I asked if he had ever seemed weak as a boy. 'He seems so soft, but there is something hard inside him.' On the far wall behind her, a framed picture of Putin and Medvedev in tandem stares past her. 'There used to be a lovely picture of Dima and his wife there,' she remarked, as if piqued, as it drew my attention. She continued, timidly:

'He was moving a lot and was very lively. But it was enough to only give him one glance, or even one word, and he would stop it and do what he had to do . . . but he was very goal driven. He would always think what his plans were and how to achieve them. He wasn't the smartest boy in the class . . . There was one who was even brighter, but he was lazy and amounted to nothing.'

She chooses her words carefully. 'Yes . . . Dima did always do as he was told. But he always had his own ideas. He was reliable.'

It is easy to imagine this lovely young man having taken one different turn and not having wound up immediately after university in St Petersburg town hall. He would have been an exemplary lawyer, maybe working for an American law firm. In another life he might have been a man like Sergei Magnitsky, the attorney at a Western law firm, who died in jail, having been tortured and denied medical care, a victim of the Hermitage Capital affair. He wasn't, because from the age of twenty-three he was working for Sobchak, then directly with Putin. He was a part-time consultant for the city Foreign Relations Committee, run by Putin. He dropped by every week, sometimes more than once, to do one-on-one legal work with Putin. Ever since he was twenty-four Medvedev has always worked with Putin, with only one short interruption after 1996 as Putin made his transition to Moscow. When the 'Tsar' decided he wanted Medvedev in the Kremlin, it was none other than the 'silovik' Igor Sechin who made the call telling him to start packing. Perhaps the essential thing you need to understand about this man is not that he could have been a very normal person, this is obvious – but that Medvedev was raised by wolves.

The Tandem

After Putin announced Medvedev would run for president in 2008, the muzzled parts of the Russian media spent an inordinate amount of time reporting on his cat – Dorofei, a Neva Masquerade. In a pathetic premonition of his owner's career, Dorofei overestimated his strength and was savaged by a cat belonging to Mikhail Gorbachev, their neighbour at the time. He recovered from his injuries on a course of antibiotics but in the end had to be castrated.

Medvedev himself was introduced to the people on billboards, walking side by side with Putin. Younger Russians groaned at the clumsy imagery recalling the 'great friendship' of Lenin and Stalin. The image was simple: power was not being handed over but split. It was instantly dubbed 'the tandem'.

From the beginning Medvedev was never viewed as fully independent or fully in power. Once Putin was no longer president, this is when he truly became the leader – the one upon whom everything depends. 'There is personal chemistry, I trust him, I just trust him,' said Putin, 'we are people of the same blood.'[4] Medvedev came across as the perfect son-in-law; the kind of clever and unthreatening man who possessive mothers suggest their daughters should marry. This was a man, after all, with an aquarium in his office. And he even cared for the fish himself. He was a hit with the West's men in Moscow. Unlike Putin, diplomats cooed that he was always polite at dinner.

Putin and Medvedev were more similar in policy content than presentation. Medvedev picked up the same themes of modernization and improvement, but more earnestly discussed government lapses and mistakes. He stressed technology, legal reform and anticorruption where Putin spoke more of power, enemies and state strengthening. Many, including one source in military intelligence, saw Medvedev as more a de facto vice-president, spokesman or foreign minister: 'Putin knows that he [Putin] is personally unacceptable in the West. This is why he created Medvedev. He says the things Putin cannot himself say convincingly.' The Putin consensus had seen the boss deliver mostly cocksure presentations on the state of Russia. In his final state of the nation speech he boasted of Russia's return to the top ten global economies, whilst in Medvedev's inauguration speech he lamented 'legal nihilism'.[5] Medvedev encouraged and excited chunks of the intelligentsia. He spoke like a political liberal, if a rather rhetorically inept one: 'freedom is better than un-freedom. This principle should be set at the core of our politics. I mean freedom in all its manifestations, personal freedom and economic freedom and finally, freedom of expression.'[6]

The pessimists argued that the regime, in spite of being corrupt – or rather because it was so corrupt – was striving for the appearance of legality. Many analysts saw in Medvedev, the man who denounced how 'no other European country can boast of such a level of disregard for the law', a ridiculous tribune for the elite's insecurities, overcompensating with words for what was being stolen by the barrel.[7] The pessimists said it felt satisfying for the elite to wave the anticorruption flag, lest it fall into others' hands, and that to feel legitimate it would say almost anything. This was a policy charade, they said, uttered by the president of charades – who took his orders from Putin in the prime minister's office.

The optimists argued that through Medvedev, Putin would transcend himself and be able to fade safely and politically away. They set the Moscow tone. Despite what had happened to Khodorkovsky, then after Beslan and Kiev, choosing Medvedev calmed the chattering classes. It seemed to say, Russia was not turning into a dictatorship after all. The new president seemed so unthreatening – after all, he was almost obsessively posting criminally bland pictures he had taken himself on his website: of snowmen, sea views, sunsets. One young diplomat who had accompanied him sightseeing after a major international summit summed up the President this way. 'He's not stupid . . . he's pretentious, that's the word for him, and obsessed by his camera, constantly rather comically taking pictures with it . . . But he's still the worst photographer ever.' There was very little aggression in Medvedev, something almost childlike about him, which everyone could pick up on, and which had doubtless allowed him to glide so inconspicuously to the top. In his own words:

I do not feel that I have become a person who is addicted to publicity like a drug. I do not feel a physical need to always be in the limelight. At the same time I have changed in certain ways. Otherwise I wouldn't be able to do what I'm doing now. Such are the rules of politics; the nation must know about the actions of those in power – we did not come up with the rules, it is not up to us to change them, and that's probably for the best.[8]

In fact, this marionette presidency both underlined and undermined the power of Putin. The most dangerous moment for any authoritarian regime is always when it tries to reform itself. Medvedev built up the constituency, intellectual infrastructure and anticipation for reform only to have them bitterly disappointed when he failed to deliver, announcing he and Putin had decided 'years before' that he would return in 2012. After years of insisting he was 'president', that he wanted to run for that office again, this comment implied Russia had been duped and insulted by the very people who had wanted him over Putin. This was after years of bad news. It was under Medvedev that the financial crisis exposed Russia's governance crisis. One after the other Putin's claims to have 'pacified' Chechnya, established the 'dictatorship of law', 'liquidated' the oligarchs, turned Russia into a fast-growth BRIC economy and the state into the vertical of power, were exposed as boastful illusions.

Waves of Confusion

Putin had so successfully branded Russia as a BRIC economy and GDP growth had been so impressive – second only to China in this quartet in the 2000s – that the Russian elite seemed to have forgotten the inherent frailties of an emerging economy dependent on commodities. At the first Davos meeting, focusing on mounting economic problems in 2008, the Russian elite came across as hubristic. Participating in a panel discussion entitled 'If America sneezes does the world still catch a cold?' the normally sober then finance minister Alexey Kudrin boasted that Russia would be 'an island of stability' and that 'interest in Russia would grow'.[9] Putin as late as December 2008, almost three months after the collapse of Lehman Brothers had triggered financial meltdown, in his first broadcast as prime minister suggested the crisis would never impact Russia. He said the country would experience only 'minimal costs for the economy, and more importantly our people'. Behind closed doors, the elite almost welcomed the crisis, believing it would harm the West whilst leaving a 'decoupled' Russia stronger still.

A year later, none other than Surkov was now warning of the 'waves of poverty and confusion rolling from the West'. Instead of minimal losses Russia suffered the worst recession of the G-20 countries in 2009. The economy contracted by 8.9 per cent, a deeper slump than insolvent Greece in 2009 or 2010.[10] Russia's Central Bank spent one-third of its then $600 billion reserves in an attempt to ward off the collapse of the ruble.[11] From peak to trough the Russian stock exchange lost over 80 per cent of its value and the oil price temporarily collapsed by 70 per cent.[12] The government was facing a budget deficit and private companies hit a credit-crunch as Western banks restricted lending. Bubbles were exposed in property and retail as their dependency on now-restricted foreign lending hit hard. Unemployment jumped and capital flight increased, hitting an enormous $131 billion in the third quarter of 2008 alone, or roughly equivalent to one-third of the government's hydrocarbon revenue that year.[13]

The crash had poured cold water on Russia's overconfidence. It was no longer clear that Russia was really a peer to the other BRIC economies. The mood swing was so sudden, that Medvedev himself admitted in front of a high powered American audience at the influential Brookings Institution, a Washington-based think-tank, that he was 'astounded' when the crisis exposed Russia's systemic vulnerabilities.[14] Nothing captures the elite's panic more than reports that a programme had been installed on Medvedev's computer, along with those of Surkov and the powerful Kremlin aide Sergei Naryshkin, mapping Russia's crisis regions in a danger index composed of sixty indicators, including Putin's local popularity.[15] As one government-affiliated analyst put it, 'We thought we were rising with China, now we know we are declining with Europe.' Capturing the new disquiet amongst the oligarchs, the billionaire Peter Aven publicly warned (but discreetly in a think-tank publication): 'The last Russian government to face such momentous questions was Mikhail Gorbachev. The fall in oil prices in the autumn of 1985 resembles what happened in Russia in 2008.'[16]

This worried crisis talk about systemic volatility was not a uniquely Russian thing – the *Financial Times* itself would run a series on 'Capitalism in Crisis' during the Medvedev presidency – but it had shaken the confidence of Putin's own ministers in his 'stability'.[17] The first cracks appeared in the Putin consensus. Parts of the government had started to sound like opposition critics.

As the urbane communications minister Igor Shchegolev once explained in conversation: 'The economic structure maintains tremendous risks. As soon as the markets tremble, the oil price falls and all our social problems come out as a threat.' For him this had come as a shock: 'What changed during the crisis was that Russia realized that it had been globalized, that a market move in the US could actually hurt normal Russians and make them vulnerable.' The return to Moscow of fears of economic volatility had convinced certain ministers of the need to change course. As Shchegolev explained to me on the sidelines of an international confer- ence: 'We saw that the economy was too reliant on raw materials. We realized we needed to develop scientific, commercial skills. This is the key idea – we are simply far too reliant on raw materials.'

It was in this climate that Medvedev began to undermine Putinism by promising to reform it. As president he promised, but broadly failed, to modernize what he called the four 'I's: institutions, investment, innovation and infrastructure. But he did greatly develop a fifth 'I': ideas. Medvedev was powerful enough to define Russia's problems, but not powerful enough to do much to solve them. His defining moment was the launch of his modernization campaign with his essay 'Forward Russia', in September 2009. In those pages he rhetorically asked, 'Could a primitive economy based on raw materials and endemic corruption take us into the future?'[18] Sounding almost like an opposition activist, Medvedev lamented how 'the global economic crisis has shown that our affairs are far from being in the best state. Twenty years of tumultuous change has not spared our economy its humiliating dependency on raw materials. Our current economy still reflects the major flaws of the Soviet system: it largely ignores individual needs.'[19] He bemoaned a 'half Soviet social-sphere', crumbling infrastructure and weak democracy.[20] Medvedev argued that Russia's political institutions were too weak to support the development needed to catch up with the West.

In short, he suddenly catapulted all the major failings of Putinism previously only analysed by elite newspapers such as *Kommersant*, the think-tank INSOR or in the series of opposition pamphlets called 'Putin: The Results' into the heart of the national debate. 'Forward Russia' started a political campaign to build up a reformist pole in the elite. Medvedev continued to denounce 'legal nihilism', corruption and the 'signs of stagnation'. As president he fostered new thinking in the establishment by patronizing INSOR and the Skolkovo research centre. The offices of INSOR or the 'Centre for Contemporary Development' are set in a small park inside a huge tsarist nobleman's house in the chic and expensive Mayakovskaya district. As a statement it was not really a mere think-tank – the echoing entry hall is larger than the offices of any typical European research centre. The largesse of this establishment reflected that none other than Medvedev was chairman of the board.

Then head of INSOR, the economist Igor Yurgens, an elegant man, always in rimless glasses, his face distinguished by jet black eyebrows and snow white hair, explained how Medvedev got in touch: 'He called us – he wanted our party of liberals to be part of something. But he never promised us we would be the *only* party feeding into his thinking. So we published thirty books on how liberalism can be put to good use. They used some parts of it, but not others.'

The centre served unofficially as Medvedev's research department with its analysts writing private briefings, policy programmes and agendas for him, whilst presenting his point of view to Western diplomats. Meanwhile, at the Skolkovo science park his stated ambition was to create a Russian 'Silicon Valley'. The minister responsible called it a 'growth spot' for the economy, pioneering a low-tax, high-tech future with foreign partners. Skolkovo stood for an alternative to the state capitalism of mega-corporations like Rosneft and Gazprom.

Medvedev also tried to endorse emerging Russian media trends. He opened a blog and started to tweet, even visiting the hip online TV station Dozhd; he denounced the beating of the famous journalist Oleg Kashin. He is believed to have given signs behind the scenes that the anticorruption activist Alexey Navalny, who would later emerge as the pre-eminent opposition leader, was not to be harmed. In fact Navalny's later work exposing corruption by crowd-sourcing the investigation of government contracts would have been impossible without Medvedev. It was he who had ordered that all government contracts become publicly available. This reform immediately saw suspicious deals discussed in the press and enabled Navalny and his army of volunteers to start investigating suspicious orders and tenders for corruption – from orders for furs placed by the government of St Petersburg's education department to requests for an antique bed from the ministry of interior.

Medvedev's reformist campaign boomeranged and damaged the Putin consensus. Medvedev highlighted the structural problems of Putinism and built up a constituency wanting and expecting change. When he failed to deliver, he discredited the Kremlin's abilities to pursue modernization. After Medvedev began his forward-looking speeches Moscow fizzed with talk of a Putinist 'perestroika' but this gave way to talk of 'Brezhnevization'. The political buzzword soon became 'stagnation', in Russian a synonym for the Brezhnev era that preceded Soviet collapse.

This debate was not happening in a vacuum but in a tense period nationally. The economic crisis revealed Russia's chronic governance crisis. The government had made good policy choices in the 2000s that had contributed to growth, but after a decade in power they had failed to improve Russia's very weak institutions. By 2010 indicators showed that Russia was as corrupt as Papua New Guinea, with the property rights of Kenya, as competitive as Sri Lanka, with the police reliability of Mauretania.[21] Fast growth and confidence meant this weakness was overlooked in the 2000s and seen as on its way out. By 2009 it looked as if it was here to stay.

What these abysmal rankings reflected at the street level was a society where everything has a price tag. The magazine *Bolshoi Gorod* playfully estimated that the bribes for being stopped by the police on street corners could cost $30 to have them drop the charges for 'hooliganism', or for drug use as much as $340; to ignore draft dodging could cost $680. The bribes in courtrooms could ruin a business: reclassifying a criminal case could cost $34,000; having an investigator reclassify or drop a criminal case between $3,000 and $1 million; getting various 'services' from the prosecutor could set you back from $5,000 to $5 million, whilst the cost of an appeal to the court of arbitration could set you back $20,000 or $25,000; and a favourable verdict could cost $100,000.[22] Even the Ministry of the Interior admitted the average bribe had soared from the equivalent of $292 in 2008 to over $7,670 by 2011.[23]

Intellectually, what the Russian debate in the media meant by the 'new stagnation' boiled down to three fears. The first was that power had become so personalized around Putin that the system could no longer change. It was frequently repeated that there was not pervasive corruption infecting the system, but rather that the system *was* corruption itself. This fear was best captured in a cartoon of Brezhnev's face moulded to an ageing Putin in 2024, when, if elected as president in 2012, Putin would have to stand down. This fear also had an economic face. Like the Soviet Union, the Russian economy and national budget was again hooked to natural resources and dependent on a high price of oil. The concern began to circulate that Russia was under a 'resource curse', in which, thanks to huge oil profits, the elite had no incentive and interest in reforming. The third fear was that in terms of everyday life, nothing would ever change. Policemen would continue to demand bribes, the threat of 'raiders' or a tax inspection would still hang over businesses, the prospect of decent health care and roads, let alone courts, seemed to be becoming ever more distant.

The Putin consensus and the Putin majority had started to decay as its economic 'winners' had started to feel like losers. Without any of these things their gains were not substantive but sandcastles. In Moscow, the bourgeoisie found a new favourite topic – emigration. Polls showed that more people wanted to emigrate than had during the collapse of the USSR. Estimates put the soaring Russian population of London, a favourite destination, at over 50,000.[24] But the fear of stagnation was only rammed home to me when I had a fight with a friend over her obsession with emigration and disinterest in the opposition. Not a provincial, but precisely the kind of well-educated, multilingual Muscovite upon whom modernization depends. 'You just don't get it,' she shrieked. 'You just don't get it at all – what it really feels like to come from a country where everything, anything, can be stolen from you by a policeman with a smile on his face, with one knock on the door. Where everything has already been stolen and every single ceiling is made of glass. You just don't get it.' I think that afterwards, she cried.

1 Troops loyal to Boris Yeltsin storm the rebellious Russian parliament in October 1993. There was hysteria the country might collapse completely.

2 The aftermath of a murder in a St Petersburg stairwell, late 1998. In the 1990s over 150,000 people were murdered in Russia. Even national politicians like Galina Starovoytova were gunned down in their stairwells.

3 Yeltsin weeps at Putin's May 2000 inauguration. His abrupt December 1999 resignation speech implored Russia for 'forgiveness'.

4 The oligarchs: Boris Berezovsky (left) and Vladimir Gusinsky (right) mistook the new president for a weakling. Aiming to manipulate Putin, within a year they had both fled into exile.

5 Putin was both shadow and deputy to Anatoly Sobchak (left), the flamboyant mayor of St. Petersburg from 1991 to 1996.

6 The billionaire Mikhail Khodorkovsky was arrested in October 2003 and sentenced to eight years in prison. His clash with Putin determined who was sovereign over oil – big business or the state.

7 The 'national leader' was remade by television into an 'alpha male' in ever-changing costumes. The aim was a Putin for every Russian.

8 Political technologists: Vyacheslav Volodin (left) holds the tract *His Ideology*, whilst the spin-doctor Gleb Pavlovsky smiles (centre) next to the 'grey cardinal' Vladislav Surkov (right).

9 Putin exults at an ice-hockey win. In autumn 2008 it seemed he had delivered the impossible: a decade of BRIC economic growth, a 140 per cent hike in incomes and the defeat of an American ally in Georgia.

10 The tandem: Dmitry Medvedev, president 2008–12, insisted he was not a puppet, until he shuffled aside for Putin, his prime minister, at the next election.

11 Russian Patriarch Kirill I (centre right) hailed the Putin era as 'a miracle of God'. The resurgent Orthodox Church and the Kremlin are increasingly allies.

12 Alexey Navalny led the 2011–12 protest movement. An internet politician, a liberal and an Islamophobe in trendy clothes, Navalny captured all the promise and flaws of the new opposition.

13 Detested by many Moscow liberals, Evgeny Roizman is the most popular politician in his Ekaterinburg hometown and across the Urals. He is a vigilante, opposition activist and icon-collector who runs a private network of heroin 'clinics'.

14 Over 100,000 gathered to call for the dismantling of Putinism on Moscow's Prospect Sakharova, on 24 December 2011. The movement subsequently disintegrated.

15 There is a battalion of OMON ('Special Purpose Mobile Unit') in every region. These riot police are used to break up anti-Putin rallies, peaceful or otherwise.

16 Putin is accused of paying the Chechen leader Ramzan Kadyrov (centre) 'tribute' in the form of lavish subsidies in exchange for peace. 'Stop Feeding the Caucasus' has become an opposition slogan.

17 The Primorsky Partisans tried in 2010 to start a guerrilla war against the police in Russia's Far East. Accusing the authorities of being predatory drug pushers, their final makeshift video electrified Russia.

The Spectre of Stagnation and Manual Control

For middle-aged Russians this fear of stagnation was becoming acute. This generation had all watched the humiliating archive footage of Brezhnev's 1979 New Year's address. Stagnation is personified in the infamous video, which shows the General Secretary hulked over a small desk in front of dark green curtains. He appears deeply confused, coarsely clears his throat and seems not to fully understand the instructions coming from the clearly pitched voice – the tone one uses to address somebody senile – of a younger aide. After changing two identical pairs of glasses Brezhnev mumbles, 'that's better now', before trying to read a pre-recorded speech scrolling down the screen before him. He slurs, asking for help, losing his flow before groaning, 'Where's me boy?' making the aide quickly return to the ailing leader festooned with medals, the incarnation of an ailing state. The popularity of this footage on YouTube rose throughout the crisis; the debates underneath it became increasingly about the present: 'Just imagine Putin in ten years,' snarled one of the commenters.

For those who remembered the Brezhnev years, by 2010 there was something in the air of history repeating itself. Like Putin, Brezhnev was not always a synonym for stagnation but in his earlier years was seen as a dynamic young man delivering impressive growth in real incomes and industrial development. This switch to the regime being perceived as politically and intellectually fossilized began in 1972. That year, under a media blackout in the paranoid years of the Cold War, a pall of smoke covered Moscow as the surrounding forests burned. The Soviet authorities struggled to respond to the fires – even having to resort to extensive bulldozing and hurriedly laid concrete firebreaks as flames lapped at the city's suburbs. That summer, a cholera epidemic broke out in the south. Quarantine regimes were frantically imposed on the Crimea, Kazan and Astrakhan. The Kremlin seemed incapable of protecting its own citizens and Moscow's silence only left them aggrieved and confused. Just like Brezhnev, Putin's reputation was stained by his inability to respond effectively to natural disasters and infrastructure breakdowns during the Medvedev presidency. As in the late USSR, these shocks framed the government as dysfunctional, amateurish and ill-prepared.

The 2010 forest fires were a turning point for Putin's reputation. The blazes streaking across the whole Russian continent even smothered the capital in thick poisonous smog for several days, reeking of the surrounding burning peat bogs. It was thick enough to obscure St. Basil's from one end of Red Square. Officials refused to disclose the scale of the disaster to an angered public, but estimates are that as many as 56,000 died from the heatwaves, smog and fires that summer.[25] Officials seemed incompetent, as military installations were engulfed by flames, despite their protestations that all was under control. Nationwide the fire service proved so inadequate that vigilante groups were formed to save dachas and villages, whilst young people set up support groups and hotlines to make up for insufficient public services. A vague panic gripped the wealthiest Muscovites. Flights abroad were snapped up and the elite began to curse the Putin team; 'this time they cannot even protect us', became a refrain. Others groaned, 'We now have Asiatic smog thanks to our Asiatic system.' To this background Putin's intense telepopulism, which involved flying a fire-fighting plane personally, 'calling' Medvedev from the 'scene' to compensate those made destitute, came across for the first time as misleading propaganda.

It was becoming clear to the public that the vertical of power did not really exist. Unlike overmanaged Soviet Russia, problems echoed those of the weak tsarist state. During the Medvedev presidency the 'tandem' was exposed as having to use 'manual control' to micro-manage industrial disputes, forest fires and anti-terror drills. Whereas Putin was widely mocked in the Western media for dumping water on the forest fires himself, Kremlin insiders did not see it as a laughing matter. In fact the bureaucracy was so appallingly ineffective that Putin is said to have been forced to take personal command of the fire-fighting operation himself, in order for things to get done. So deep was his suspicion that without his personal monitoring of local officials and construction workers, they would not rebuild the incinerated homes, he went as far as to install a video-link to the ground on his desk. As during the sinking of the Kursk, or the siege in Beslan, Putin believed he had been misled by officials assuring him that the situation was under control when it was not.

The difference between this crisis and previous ones was that this was the first taking place in a Russia with a near majority online. This huge potential was waiting to be unlocked. It soon was, but not by Medvedev. On the other side of the world, Grigory Asmolov, the twentysomething son of a former education minister to Yeltsin, now an Israeli, was sitting in Harvard watching his country of birth go up in flames:

> They were saying that everything is under control, but the wild fires were everywhere. The evidence was all over the Internet . . . videos, pictures, blogs and all over YouTube . . . and some of these were becoming very famous, like these shots of people in cars shooting away from the flames, getting away from the inferno only just in time. There was even smoke in Moscow. There was clearly a gap in the services the government was able to provide to its citizens, and what was needed to help them. All this information was spreading all over the blogosphere . . . There were all these requests for help, offers to

help, guys saying they need food, or they could offer blankets . . . you could call it spontaneous mass communication . . . I had this idea. Let's put all this on one map.

Asmolov approached a friend with 'technical capacity' with the idea of using a platform that had been used to coordinate volunteers in Haiti and Chile after quakes. Emailing back and forth they found two or three programmers. In Moscow a 'situations room' was thrown up in a flat. At first there were around five to seven volunteers, eventually growing to between ten and fifteen. The site www.russian-fires.ru was soon a crowdsourcing hub for help.

I didn't need help. Sitting in a friend's apartment with the fire-smog outside, I remember just staring at the flame icons on this site. We sat there drinking something disgusting in the heat, horrified at how all Russia was on fire as if attacked, but amazed that somebody had made this map. I remember my friend clicking on various fires, mumbling: 'Before I saw these maps I felt I was living in the Moscow apocalypse . . . there's just no proper information anywhere about what's going on . . . the TV telling us that Putin says it's all fine . . . it's such a joke.'

From the apartment window you couldn't see the ground or the other side of the street. The migrant workers from Central Asia seemed particularly nervous. That night we ended up dancing. The smog had seeped into the club. We were all laughing. But in the morning it hadn't cleared up. By then everyone was walking around with hastily grabbed surgical masks on to filter the foul air. Asmolov recalls:

The Russian fires were a clear example that the state was unable to provide basic services to people . . . I just felt that I wanted to help. We had the capacity to do it. And we did it. But you have to understand, the degree of creativity developed by Russian Internet users is a testament to the scale of the problems they are forced to deal with, first and foremost.

As part of Medvedev's attempts at a more open government, Asmolov was invited to meet him for a frank conversation in a small group. This kind of thing never happened under Putin, and when such 'experts' did meet him, they were quiet, waiting for their turn to speak. Asmolov says: 'Personally, he was a very nice person to talk to . . . He was very informal, very "cool" you could say . . . very friendly. He didn't say anything stupid. He really looked very interested.'

Medvedev promised the group a number of things. These included an investigation into the Internet attacks on anti-government websites, widely believed to have sponsors inside the Kremlin and Nashi. Asmolov smiled: 'Nothing happened on Internet attacks of course . . . and no, I wasn't disappointed. I have no expectations of Russia, so how could I be disappointed?'

The forest fires were merely the worst incident in the increasingly visible weakness of the vertical of power. Putin was forced to step up his 'manual control' with the beginning of the financial crisis. An outbreak of industrial unrest in the single-industry town of Pikalyovo saw him rush to the scene. This was not just telepopulism but micro-management betraying a nervousness that if the matter was not fixed fast it could escalate. Manual control went as far as workers receiving text messages informing them their salaries had been paid. US diplomats were scathing in their cables about what the incident revealed:

> That the impasse required the involvement of Prime Minister Putin – the man 'responsible for everything' in Russia – illustrated the weakness of the federal system . . . none of the institutions designed to protect citizen interests functioned; labour unions, political parties, or even state institutions like the Federal Anti-Monopoly Service could not bring about a solution (even after President Medvedev reportedly told the Leningrad Oblast Governor Serdyukov to fix the problem in March).[26]

Nor was Pikalyovo the only such incident. After a deadly explosion killed forty-six people at the Sayano-Shushenskaya mega-dam in Siberia, Putin again flew to the scene. His speech exhorting the oligarchs to invest more in infrastructure may come across as strongman behaviour at first look, but is actually that of a sign of weakness as he was forced to cajole them through telepopulism.

The need for 'manual control' and the absence of the vertical of power was because a corrupt system was neither capable, nor willing, to implement Kremlin orders. At the height of Putin's power in 2006 one US Embassy cable reported, 'It was rumoured within the presidential administration that as many as 60 per cent of his orders are not being followed.'[27] Half a decade later Putin conceded that as many as 80 per cent of Kremlin orders to the regions were routinely ignored or obstructed.[28] Even Gleb Pavlovsky has written that within Putin's state, 'everyone has an interest in the current system and everyone is disloyal to it! Everyone works as provocateurs of conflicts which are settled by bonuses from other players.'[29]

Neither could Medvedev pull the levers of power to greater effect. He repeatedly called meetings to express his exasperation at orders going unfulfilled, achieving nothing or having to be reissued. In a revealing attempt to ease Medvedev's concerns, one minister remarked in 2010 that in fact the amount of presidential orders completed on time had risen by 68 per cent, with now 20 per cent of orders implemented on schedule.[30] During his time as president, Medvedev was forced to also practise 'manual control', as varied as inspecting train stations and airports personally to ensure anti-terror measures were in place. He was even reduced to angrily demanding 'who owns this place?' outside dilapidated provincial factories. He bemoaned:

> What is not coordinated by the president is not coordinated by anyone. This is bad and it means that we have an absolutely out-dated, inadequate management system, which should be changed. Because when all signals come from the Kremlin, it shows that the system itself is not viable and must be adjusted.[31]

'Manual control' has in fact forced Putin and Medvedev into a gruelling travelling schedule within Russia, significantly more intense than most European leaders. The practice is not restricted to the highest level. Senior officials are also forced to control their own departments, through 'manual control'. Russia's chief investigator regularly has to travel to the scene of any major incident, once leading to him being injured in a secondary blast after a terrorist attack. Amongst the many governance failures that have chipped away at the myth of the vertical of power, the most decisive in turning public opinion was the 2010 mass murder described in the introduction to this book, in Kushchevskaya. The murder trail revealed that a criminal gang had infiltrated the local authorities and repeatedly bribed officials to be able to operate. The gang leader, a local council member, had even boasted he was a guest at Medvedev's inauguration. Putin himself admitted that in Kushchevskaya 'all the organs of power have failed'.[32]

Many in the Russian establishment shivered at the implications of Kushchevskaya. It was a case that clearly showed that despite Putin's claims to have ended the 'chaos of the 1990s' there was as much continuity as change in much of the country. In sharp contradiction to Putin's talk of the 'dictatorship of law', the chief justice of the constitutional court Valery Zorkin decided to speak out in a state newspaper. Zorkin argued that such cases had happened time and time again, with the intertwining of the mafia and the state now posing an existential threat to Russia. 'One has to admit, honestly, that the disease of organized crime has too deeply infected our country,' he wrote.[33] 'Crime is undermining the fabric of our legal system . . . corroding the fabric of our still immature civil society.'[34] Zorkin asserted that a 'fusion of authorities and criminals' had already taken place in many parts of the country and it was growing impossible to distinguish between state and mafia operations.[35] Implicitly arguing that the Putin regime had failed, Zorkin ended with a stark warning: 'If the mafia isn't pushed back it will raise the question of whether Russia can survive beyond the next ten years.'[36]

This awareness of the chronic weakness of the vertical was by now so strong that even the government officials charged with manual control barely bothered to disguise its weakness, including Grigory Rapota, the former deputy chief of foreign intelligence. He had done well under Putin. After a stint as a minister he had been appointed to be the presidential envoy first to the Volga region and then to the Southern region, containing the North Caucasus. He argued: 'Everyone understands that manual control is not the way to run a country. But everyone also understands this is the only way to deal with our crisis.' He then tried to shift the blame away from the state onto the Russian people themselves: 'The Russian mentality is not only used to this kind of administration, but also used to the government regulation of all aspects of life. Not just bureaucrats, but the people, of whom bureaucrats are a part. Only, when we have a new generation – who are now about fifteen to twenty years old – in power will we be able to run Russia in a different way.' Rapota may not have been watching the clock. By the time of our conversation, in 2012, any Russian of working age in the last year of the USSR would have to be aged thirty-nine or older.

Behind closed doors, the elite sounded very different. 'We are an ocean of inefficiencies', in the words of one government advisor, repeated around the most expensive tables of Moscow. The incompetence of the vertical was not just a matter of governors and officials lining their pockets and forgetting about Kremlin decrees, as forests burned outside. This feckless governance was translating into incalculable waste in the very public services the country needed to work properly if it was ever to modernize. A look out of any window, even in bijoux central Moscow, looked onto bits of backwardness – tangled webs of electrical wires are strung across the streets, in a way that had long vanished in most of the rest of Europe. Not to mention the smoke stacks belching steam next to the main government building.

The most shameful and important 'ocean of inefficiency' was public health care, constitutionally mandated to be free of charge in the Russian Federation, but so corrosively corrupt and clownishly run that 30–40 per cent of costs come out of people's own pockets and 50–70 per cent forgo medical care as they cannot afford it.[37] The 'vertical of health', the IMF calculated, was achieving results similar to countries that spent 30–40

per cent less on their health care systems.[38] All this in a country with a
health care system that was actually huge – Russia has twice as many
doctors and three times as many hospital beds per capita than the United
States, but because it cannot deploy them effectively it has infant mortality
that is 40 per cent higher and African-level male life expectancies.[39] All this
in a country with 18 million veterans and 39 million pensioners, which
somehow felt it more important to invest over $50 billion into the Sochi
2014 Winter Olympics instead. 'We are an ocean of inefficiency,' as the
elite like to say.[40]

Why the Vertical Failed

The reason that the vertical of power failed was not due to the 'mentality'
of the ruled, but the fact it became a 'vertical of loyalty' intertwined with a
'vertical of corruption'. The crooked apex of the pyramid only sent distor-
tions down through to the base of the structure. By prizing loyalty above
all and being willing to permit embezzlement to be able to sustain it, the
Kremlin gradually removed incentives to be efficient. Thus the vertical
created a situation in the late 2000s where governors were no longer afraid
of being 'sacked' from below as they were no longer elected, and not
frightened of being 'sacked' from above providing they were loyal. The
castration of TV news and the intimidation of investigative journalists
further reduced pressure to provide efficient governance. Also, by never
allowing United Russia or Nashi to develop into real political institutions,
never ceding any policy control over to them, the Kremlin effectively
ensured they ended up as patronage networks. These factors all worked
against institutionalizing the Putinist vertical of power.

Most of the failures of Russian policy implementation occur when laws
and projects have to be turned into reality beyond Moscow. This would
not be a problem if the Kremlin had turned governors and bureaucrats
into professional managers. The vertical of power is partially based on
China's hardwiring between Beijing and its provinces. Yet it missed out a
key function of the Chinese system. Communist Party functionaries are
working within a simple incentive structure that encourages them to grow
their economies and over-fulfil the five-year plan. Successful functionaries
will be promoted to higher office whilst poor-quality officials risk demotion. Not so in Russia. One study found there to be no link at all between
governors' reappointment and economic growth. In fact it showed a slight
negative correlation.[41]

For Pavlovsky the system's initial weakness stemmed partially from the
compromises the Kremlin elite had to make with local elites in 1999 in
order to gather enough support to run the country: 'The recruitment of

regional and federal governments was done in clear terms; play by the rules, but play Moscow football. The agenda is set in the centre but this does not interfere with your local political technology.' However, in 2012, over a decade of centralizing measures later, he would bemoan the fact 'there is no vertical of power in Russia, only a vertical of loyalty. Even in Ukraine they have a more effective bureaucratic vertical that gets things done.'

The key problem with the vertical of power is that grabbing power back for the centre does not translate into improved governance. Putin's orders overcentralized authority, broke up potentially threatening agencies and limited the power of regional elites. This led to a situation where only the Kremlin was in command and authorities beneath them had been constricted in their ability and autonomy to carry out its orders. Thus, unwittingly, the vertical of power created 'manual control' by refusing to delegate. The overcentralized 'vertical' had stunted necessary 'horizontal' bureaucratic ties: inter-agency links are weak, inter-regional contacts limited, individual initiatives stunted, all of which fuel bureaucratic turf wars. Overcentralization also saw local governors become disconnected from the sources of industrial and financial power in the Moscow conglomerates. Their reduced tax-raising powers meant they had less money to get things done. By the late 2010s the inverse problem of the late Yeltsin period was emerging; too much decentralization meant the regions were taking matters into their own hands, presently overcentralization means nothing can be coordinated or implemented without constant Kremlin micro-management.

Further distorting Russian governance is Putin's return to the Soviet–Imperial system of 'rotation'. Under Yeltsin, local elites had become self-contained with the exception of the FSB, which still followed the Stalinist system of 'rotation', with security chiefs being moved around Russia like pro-consuls to prevent them 'going native'. Putin first imposed rotation on regional prosecutors, then police chiefs, then judges, before making governors appointees. By 2011 none of the six most senior officials in the typical Krasnodar or Irkutsk regions were locals.[42] This increased Moscow's control over the provinces but it did not improve governance. Those 'serving time' in the provinces often failed to build proper links to manage their bureaucracies, and had a tendency to behave like a quasi-foreign presence, treating their stations as temporary jobs before going to bigger things in the capital. These are fertile conditions for corruption. A trend has also emerged of those in rotation 'commuting' back to Moscow at weekends, where their families live. Across Russia this system has increased loyalty at the cost of efficiency.

Undermining the prospect of a genuine vertical of power was the institutionalization of a new pattern of behaviour amongst the Putinist elite across Russia. A Putinist political culture had emerged of national, bureaucratic, regional and even village elites monopolizing state resources, turning their political power into business influence, entrenching nepotism and accumulating privileges with impunity. On the one hand this reflects the still quasi-nomenklatural existence of the Russian bureaucracy. As in Soviet times they often enjoy the right to special hunting lodges, holiday resorts, tax exemptions and agency membership cards that they can wave through traffic jams, or even sometimes to get them out of arrest. On the other hand, this reflected the fact that Russia now had a quasi-Soviet system of bureaucracy but without any of its checks and balances. The Communist Party and the KGB had previously held each other in check. Under Putin's system internal monitoring devices no longer apply, but neither do external ones, as Moscow has systematically removed democratic checks and balances from below.

By Medvedev's presidency this trend had deepened to a point where a joke that reflected elite monopolization of resources became popular: 'Russia needs more successful entrepreneurs – therefore Russia needs ministers to have more children.' A clear illustration of how far this witticism had come to reflect reality was Medvedev's attempt to end 'double-hatting' of ministers simultaneously serving as board members of state corporations, leading to conflicts of interest. In an illustration of how limited the vertical actually was, the replacement put forward for minister Viktor Zubkov, retiring from the post of chairman of the Russian Agricultural Bank, was the son of his political ally, Sergey Ivanov – Sergey junior.[43] The same pattern can be observed elsewhere. For example, the son of the president of the Security Council found work advising Igor Sechin at Rosneft and was awarded the order of merit by Putin for 'years of conscientious work' despite having been in the job less than a year.[44] The son of the head of Rosneft first found work within the corporation and then at Gennady Timchenko's company Novatek, whilst the sons of both the chairman of the Federation Council and the former head of the FSB found jobs at state banks.[45]

Across the country the process of defederalization and building the vertical had by the early 2010s not produced state efficiency. Instead they had entrenched elite corruption, oligarchic behaviour and the monopolization of resources, which were undermining the quality of governance in Russia. Discretion given to local chiefs has given Russia a distinctly variable geometry of liberalization and policy implementation. The Kremlin's overlooking of regional 'political technologies' was most evident in the 2000s in the Volga Muslim republics of Tatarstan and Bashkortostan where 'small Putins' were allowed to consolidate control over the governing apparatus and oil interests.

Medvedev's presidency saw a large number of governors replaced. However, closer inspection of the anticorruption logic behind replacement of his biggest scalp – the long-standing Mayor of Moscow, Yury Luzhkov, does not show a diminishing of 'local political technology'. The current mayor, Sergey Sobyanin, has shown little restraint from policies that look distinctly like that of his predecessor. Luzhkov was widely denounced as his wife had grown into Russia's richest woman on the back of a Moscow-based construction company. Soon after Sobyanin's odd choice to replace the capital's asphalt pavements with slabs was taken, it was discovered his wife owned a factory producing pavement tiles. Regional governors have also displayed the same knack for finding their children good employment. In April 2010 the broadsheet *Vedomosti* published an investigation into the flourishing business activities of the children of the governors of Kaliningrad, Kalmykia, Voronezh and Sverdlovsk. The story was published under the satirical headline, 'They are just plain lucky.'[46]

Losing the Narrative

The paint peels on the walls of the Russian State University for the Humanities as Kremlin intellectuals pull up their chairs for a meeting of the John Locke Club, for thinkers supporting United Russia. Bored students and pale blondes, bathed in iPad glows, ignore the discussion. Yellow lighting. The smells of institutional Russia: wet clothes, wafts of canteen boiled meats and cheap cleaning fluids. The professors wait for their turn to speak, while texting under the table, then lecture lacklusterly on the theme of the day: 'How to make United Russia a real political actor.' Boris Mezhuev, a prominent conservative philosopher, takes the floor, though scant attention is paid: 'But of course United Russia can't be a real political actor. There is only one political actor in this country and we all know his name.' A ripple of surprise, then nervous laughter turns to murmurs of quiet agreement.

'The trouble with this regime – despite being here for so long – is they have not managed to institutionalize anything of their system,' confides Mezhuev afterwards. 'The parties are plastic. Politics has no meaning here anymore.'

The financial crisis, and the chronic governance issues it had revealed, had made such tiny gestures of dissent and contempt for the ruling clique commonplace in Moscow by the summer of 2010. It seems hard to imagine now – but that summer the increasing decline in the quality of Putin's personal PR and the rising talk of stagnation was standing to benefit Medvedev. At a think-tank dinner, one popular radio host I like too much to embarrass announced: 'He is in a great position. Either he can become president again or the first leader of the Russian opposition.' The think-tankers nodded, knowingly.

He became neither. This merely reflected the fact the 'tandem' was the last propaganda coup of the Surkov years. Since 2008 it brilliantly deflected attention from the regime's failings and avoided comparisons between them and the opposition by focusing all media eyes on Kremlinology. Would Medvedev assert himself? Was Medvedev incapable of fulfilling his rhetoric or being tied down? As 2011 wore on, the issue of the succession became so consuming that Russian journalists and Western diplomats would joke about 'the question'.

'A person who thinks he can stay in power indefinitely is a danger to society,' warned Medvedev, observing that, 'excessive concentration of power is a dangerous thing.'[17] His commitment to what appeared from his speeches to be an ambitious modernization agenda was cited by financial analysts as evidence of blocked reformism. As the volume rose on the debate around stagnation it simultaneously focused attention on the modernization agenda. INSOR released what was clearly an ambitious election manifesto and Medvedev was alleged to have lobbied for support from industrialists and the military–industrial complex. However, by summer 2011, the gap between rhetoric and fact had started to widen. Moscow chatter about Medvedev had turned from the cautiously optimistic to the concerned. From my notebook a few quotes:

- 'Medvedev is strong enough to say what is wrong with Russia but not strong enough to change Russia.'
- 'Medvedev means well but is being held back by Putin.'
- 'Medvedev needs a second term to become Medvedev.'
- 'Medvedev is weak, but a weak Khrushchev beat Beria.'

Though they will now deny it, a majority of observers and investors expected Medvedev to return to the presidency in 2012. Not just because one-term presidencies are euphemisms for failures, but because Medvedev controlled the political narrative. It went like this – the only response to stagnation was modernization, and in the Asian century what was needed was authoritarian modernization, not the chaos of democratization.

In authoritarian states, slight differences matter. Even the most marginal appointment in its upper hierarchy can eventually lead to political freeze or thaw. For the intelligentsia, Putin and Medvedev, almost by accident, had come to symbolize two possible futures. Medvedev: weak leadership with authoritarian modernization. Putin: strong leadership with authoritarian stagnation. But editors were still scared of

Medvedev – the following poem was pulled from the online TV channel
Dozhd. It was deemed too insulting, or close to the bone:

> He may at times cast glares of ire,
> And huff and puff and strain to look like a Tsar,
> The shadow lies as I request,
> And we'll be friends as in the past.[48]

Putinist telepopulism that had seemed so effective in the 2000s had started
to turn crass, as within the Kremlin a classic intrigue was taking place.
Whilst Putin and Medvedev were not in conflict, their insecure factions
started to compete. Pavlovsky was fired for publicly supporting a Medvedev
return to the presidency and he claims that Surkov's eventual demotion
was because he also wanted this to happen. In sidelining them the Kremlin
lost its finest 'political technologists'. Online advertising was appearing,
urging girls to 'rip' their shirts for Putin as half-naked female twentysomethings from 'Putin's Army' scrubbed cars for the cameras. The leading
Putin campaigner Sergey Markov tried to explain these stunts to me: 'You
see we are trying to combine a strong sexual message with a strong political message.' This might have worked, but there was no clear Putin policy
platform. Younger Russians had started to see right through this game. It
became increasingly popular to trade satirical poems, this one a children's
poem from 1956. It needs no explanation, other than in Russia 'Medved'
means bear and 'Vova' is a diminutive for Vladimir:

> We're going to the circus today!
> In the arena once again, with the trained bears,
> And Uncle Vova the tamer,
> From delight the circus goes numb,
> Laughing, holding onto Daddy,
> The growling bear does not dare,
> Only comically sucks his paw,
> Takes himself by the collar,
> What fun it is in the circus with Vova and the Bear!

The regime was not just losing the narrative. It was making others lose
their script. Medvedev's mixed message – both seeming weak and encouraging others to take a stand for modernization – began to encourage unin-
tended dissent. It had taken almost ten years for a public figure to denounce
the strangling of TV in the presence of the powerful and not in the columns
of a fringe opposition newspaper. Ironically, it took place where the
Kremlin's agents felt the safest – the podium of the 2010 Russian annual

television award ceremony overlooking a dozen tables of black-tie executives, their female acolytes and the editors of state TV – the wealthy
winners of Putinism, the rewarded, each with a multi-entry Schengen visa
in his pocket and a Star-Alliance card in his wallet.

It came from the supercelebrity Leonid Parfyonov, the most famous
journalist in Moscow. He had been asked by the organizers to make a
speech about the issue he considered to be the most urgent. Why be
worried of Parfyonov? His TV show had been taken away from him in
2004 and he had moved quietly on to other things. As he mounted the
podium, he gulped with a shaking hand in the glitz and the violet tint of
the studio. The celebrity jerked his shoulders. He lifted his hand to his
mouth and looked at the floor. He did not lift his eyes from the paper as he
began to speak:

> After the real and imagined sins of the 1990s national television
> broadcasting has been put under state control at the beginning of
> the new millennium. This happened in two steps, first the media
> oligarchs were removed and then media made to join the ranks of
> the war on terror. News and life in general was categorised as suitable
> or unsuitable subjects for TV broadcasting. One could get an idea
> of the authorities' goals and objectives, their moods and attitudes,
> their friends and enemies, just by watching any significant TV
> programme. Legally speaking this isn't news but rather government
> PR, or anti-PR . . .[49]

After a few moments his pitch seemed to falter:

> Federal channel reporters don't see officials as newsmakers but rather
> as bosses of their boss. Legally speaking in this case a reporter is no
> longer a journalist, but rather a state employee that worships submis-
> sion and service. Thus you can't interview the boss of your boss: it's
> like an attempt to uncover somebody who doesn't want to be uncov-
> ered. . . . National broadcasters don't dare throw critical, sceptical or
> ironic remarks to them. . . . Supreme power seems to be the dead of
> whom we never speak.[50]

Time to Switch to the Sports Channel

Supporters of a Medvedev policy agenda had by September 2011 started to
become increasingly shrill. Members of the factions answering directly to
Putin and Medvedev appeared to be clashing, as did those trying to curry
their favours. 'If stabilisation goes on forever, it will lead to stagnation,'

warned Igor Yurgens, the head of INSOR.[51] However, it was becoming abundantly clear by the annual Yaroslavl conference, which Medvedev hosted in September 2011, that he was not going to fight for his job. In his headline speech at the event Medvedev gave the speech of a bureaucrat and not a campaigning politician. Humiliating him further, echoing Russia's poor state of repairs, a plane carrying Lokomotiv, one of the nation's premier league hockey teams, had crashed in the city's airport days before the conference, killing all but one of its forty-five passengers.

The 'tandem announcement' did not tarry. It came at the annual United Russia party conference on 24 September 2011. 'There is nothing that can stop us . . . I have not lost my commander's voice,' rang out the call of Vladimir Putin from a triangular podium before an electronically shimmering Russian flag, where minutes before a haggard Dmitry Medvedev had announced he was backing the once and future President for a mandate that could see him rule until 2024.[52] The audience of United Russia delegates applauded like a Soviet Party Congress, rapturously. This moment will be remembered as the highest peak of Putin's power over the Russian establishment.

Minutes later, government advisor Arkady Dvorkovich let out two anguished tweets. 'This is not a time for happiness.' 'Time to switch to the sports channel.'[53]

In St Petersburg somebody winced. 'I feel towards him like a son,' said his schoolteacher Irina Grigorovskaya, still so fond of him, not wanting to dwell on her feelings that afternoon. She watched him that day like so many million others, but unlike them she felt sorry for the child who had once drawn dinosaurs and loved chemistry experiments:

'There have been some moments when I felt sorry for Dima . . . because he was being treated too roughly by Putin. I felt like this watching the United Russia congress when he had to announce that Putin would be the president after all . . . I was a bit disappointed, but I expected before the presidency that it would be just a rest for Putin . . . I know how hard this must have been, I feel sorry for Dima in an almost physical way.'

She was still preparing to vote for United Russia in the parliamentary elections and, of course, for Putin. 'Who else is there to vote for?' she sighed, looking at me like somebody very worried. It was a genuine question.

Putin had said that it had been 'decided between us several years ago' – as if letting slip that all the uncertainty of the tandem had been a lie.[54] It was a mistake, insulting those taken in by it. Medvedev's presidency had built up the intellectual infrastructure, constituency and anticipation for change. Medvedev's term had seen the political and economic claims of

Putinism exposed as lacking and the 'economic winners' of Putinism come to fear stagnation. Putin would soon realize he had miscalculated the mood of the prosperous. By returning without a clear narrative, by sidelining Medvedev, the 'modernization' candidate, Putin entered the electoral cycle perceived as the 'stagnation' candidate.

Why Putin chose to return is both self-evident and yet unclear. He has hinted the financial crisis influenced his decision – yet for Russia the worst was over by late 2011.[55] There are those who believe that the drift of segments of the elite over to Medvedev frightened him during the crisis, or that he was concerned that he might lose control of his assets or ability to protect his friends. An unshaven Pavlovsky told me as he stuffed his face full of *pelmeni* dumplings in a cheap self-service joint that in the summer of 2010 a 'physiological deformation' overcame Putin and his working relationship with Medvedev soured. 'It was natural, like when you work with someone, to start to feel ill at ease with them.' But he admitted he didn't know. 'It was something with Medvedev, I think, but it's not clear. We'll have to wait for his biography.' It is likely that Putin grew suspicious of his courtier, who had made feeble last-minute attempts to gather support for a second term. But it is unlikely Putin was motivated by material interests: these would have been just as well protected in the position of prime minister.

One Kremlin aide claimed that his boss, a leading minister, had been informed the 'agreement reached years before' had been that whoever had the highest rating would run for president. This would explain why there were competing stunts, even cadres, but no actual struggle. Yet the same official admits that he and his boss only learnt the news at the United Russia conference as well. 'I have no idea why Putin did this,' he said, slowly, trying to find the right words, 'but you have to realize he isn't really a politician. He won't let Russia go.'

As for Medvedev, he was despised from the minute he did not run, by the same liberal elites he had once charmed. That autumn I went to see Igor Yurgens. The establishment liberal sounded dark and paranoid:

'I felt depressed. It was not a shock. We all knew how difficult it was behind the scenes. Like Kosygin's change in the 1960s in the USSR that didn't happen, Medvedev's change – these are both historical mistakes – geopolitically characteristic of our Russian reality and part of our paradigm.'

As we talked, cloud cover had filled his office with gloom. He did not switch on the light: 'The political system is not capable of fitting with post-modern forces already at work inside Russia. The political system is feudalizing whilst the productive forces, or at least the best part of them, are in the post-industrial epoch. We are awaiting a shock like something out of Hegel. This shock – it can be an event, it can be a person – it's synonymous.

'The change failed because the new forces of consolidation of the middle class, within the intelligentsia, the new generation – were not ready and not strong enough. The old forces – the individuals, the Church, the military industrial complex, the siloviks, the conservatives – they were all strong enough. It was a generational change that did not occur. If you go back to Turgenev you find the same thing – this is *Fathers and Sons* – the fathers don't want to let go, whilst the sons are too cowardly and not strong enough to make it happen.'

Putin succeeded because others failed. His opponents up until this point were all too rash, weak, corrupted or unpopular to expose him. Medvedev never really was one. Under him the opposition within the elite had failed, but across town from its intrigues a new generation of opposition leaders had started to be heard on blogs and in anti-Putin bars. They were not going to shuffle back so limply at the sound of Putin's 'commander's voice'.

CHAPTER EIGHT

NAVALNY AND THE EVOLUTION OF THE OPPOSITION

THE EVENING'S political discussion was passing off calmly, even convivially, at the bohemian bar Gogol. Just off a chic Moscow alley lined with luxury boutiques, a small gathering of 'oppositionists' were on stage debating the usual topics: Putin, politics and protests. Maybe half the audience knew each other already – in October 2007 the opposition was still a small micro-society of its own, an exclusive set by virtue of being short on recruits. The pretty, political Masha Gaidar, daughter of Yeltsin's radical prime minister, was talking with a rising anti-Putin star with a nationalist twist. Then from the back somebody started to make some noise. Hecklers, who had been downing vodka all evening (one of their gang having just vomited in the toilet) began to disrupt the panel. The yobs screamed that Gaidar is screwing her handsome debating partner. They then yell more obscenities at her. An outraged activist pours lager on the heckler's head. Then a beer bottle gets hurled at an opposition activist. Once the talk is over Gaidar's co-panellist slips off the stage. He is on edge. Things degenerate. He begins to scuffle with the obscenity hollerer. They take it outside. Shots ring out. The man is wounded. Alexey Navalny has blood on his face. Plastic pellets have flown through the air. He has shot the heckler four times with what Russians call a 'traumatic pistol.'

'Yeah . . . Yeah, this happened,' is how he recounted it to me. 'The Kremlin had sent these thugs to disrupt our show and at the end of it most of them left. These kinds of guys only work for money. So they just left. One guy was still there shouting at me to come and fight with him. I had three hundred people looking at me right then – I had to do it – so I went out to have a fight with him. I shot him with the traumatic pistol. But like all Russian traumatic guns it was absolutely useless . . . and so this turned right away into a normal Russian fight.'

This man who fired the plastic rounds is the same opposition rabble-rouser who within a few years would emerge as Putin's first real challenger.

His return crowned Navalny the leader of the other Russia. He answered
the opposition's cry for a leader. It was his slogans that led the protest
movement and he was its driving force. He has built the new opposition
and his anticorruption efforts have done more to expose the bankruptcy of
the 'dictatorship of law' than any other.

The fact that the opposition has turned this troubling man into a hero
is testament to their desperation at Putin's return. A showman with a quick
temper, Navalny is a pure product of Putinism. His looks as if made to
order for TV: chiselled, blond and blue-eyed, definite and charismatic like
a younger, finer Putin. In his instinctive paranoia, nationalism and
Caucasophobia, he is a man of his time. They have called him an 'expert at
manipulating the Internet mob'.[1] This is true, because he is one of Europe's
first Internet politicians. There is no irony that repressive Russia and not
tech-savvy Britain should have given birth to an Internet-populist. Putin's
castration of television and de facto ban on potential rivals enjoying screen
time on major channels has steadily turned the blogosphere from a fringe
activity to an alternative mass media. Just as the blind develop an acute
sense of smell, so Navalny has turned this hyper-developed Russian media
organ into his support base.

As Putin was a decade ago to all Russia – Navalny is everything to all
people in the opposition. The liberal treasurer of the December 2011
protest movement Olga Romanova saw him as a 'future president'; the
nationalist leader Vladimir Tor says he is 'a man I can do business with'.
Nationalist, liberal, blogger, democrat – many opposition activists see
themselves in him. In a more sinister way Navalny sometimes speaks like
Putin. A decade ago Putin promised to 'liquidate the oligarchs as a class';
now the blogger-challenger lashes out at the London-based Russian-
Jewish oligarchs, Boris Berezovsky and Roman Abramovich, hollering that
'we must exterminate these thieves who are drinking our blood and
chewing our livers'.[2] Once Putin promised a 'dictatorship of law', now
Navalny bellows, 'there is no vertical of power – only chaos'. Where the
president promised to 'waste them in their outhouses', the Internet activist
has said, 'I suggest a pistol', to make meat of Islamic gunmen. Putin said he
would restore 'constitutional order' in the Caucasus, now Navalny
demands the region not get preferential treatment, that the government
'stop feeding the Caucasus'. One by one Navalny has picked up these
Putinist themes and inverted them into an anti-Putin opposition agenda.
The crisis of Putinism has, ironically, left Putin vulnerable to a 'real Putin'.

Navalny commands a stern, glaring presence in person. Unlike the
shuffling and grey Putin in St Petersburg, he is a natural politician.
Whereas Putin needed Surkov, Pavlovsky and their whole team to cut an
'alpha-male' image in his early years, without them coming across as shifty

and nervous (such as after the sinking of the Kursk), Navalny is capable of pulling charisma on any smartphone clip, mocking post or wry tweet. He has no need for Botox.

Where Putin understood TV, but claims never to use the Internet, Navalny has understood online potential. He has been tweeting his slogans, running anti-Putin YouTube song competitions (prizes include a bottle of whisky) and using crowdsourcing to build activist hubs to fight corruption, utilities fraud and bad roads. In the winter of 2011–12 Moscow bars such as Gogol went silent as he entered; at meetings of opposition committees he mastered the room like the showman he is. He is the first of a new wave of post-Putin politicians, not creations of the 1990s, who have been thrown into prominence by public disgruntlement at Putin's 2012 return. Navalny's rise to fame is intertwined with the story of the rise of the Russian opposition from a fringe, elite affair meeting at bars like Gogol, drawing only a crowd of liberal elite, and *Novaya Gazeta*-reading familiar faces, into a force capable of sustained protests that exposed the end of the Putin consensus and the Putin majority.

Political Childhood

Navalny has a theory about his generation being on the cusp: they received a full dose of Soviet 'irradiation' in childhood but lived their adult lives in another country. They have no professional experience of socialism, contrary to Putin's generation who grew up in the 1960s and 1970s in the shadow of successful space-station launches and a craze for World War Two spy-thrillers; the party drilling into them authoritarian work-habits during the 'era of the three funerals', as Brezhnev, Andropov and Chernenko passed away. Unlike their cohort, Navalny's generation have no fond memories of Soviet power. He once remarked, 'My generation caught the Soviet Union when it had become an absolute game of acting and deceit.'[3] This is how he remembers the USSR:

In my main childhood memory I'm standing for milk. The whole time standing in line for milk. When I was seven, my brother was born and he needed a lot of milk. So at the very back the whole time, I had to stand in line [. . .] When people now start telling me stories, especially young ones, which the Soviet Union did not catch, how great it was, I do not need them to tell me, I was in line for milk. My mother and father still remember at five a.m., having to take turns to line up for meat. And this was a military town with a good supply. I do not believe the Soviet Union is indiscriminately to blame for everything. But now we live better than we did then and I have no nostalgia for it whatsoever. There was nothing to eat in the Soviet Union.[4]

This feeling might come from the fact that young Navalny was one of the first Russians who knew the 1991 coup d'état that finally destabilized the system was under way, as the tanks that surrounded the White House were manned by the men from the military base he then called home, near Obninsk 100km from the Soviet capital. That they refused to shoot on KGB orders was a legend for the community.

Unlike the flip side of Putin's generation who turned into Yeltsin's 'liberals' – those dissidents and economists who were professionally incubated in research centres and universities, feeling their creativity suffocated by oppressive thought control – Navalny feels remorse looking at what happened in the 1990s. As a boy during the 1993 shelling of parliament, he dashed into Moscow with a friend to catch the fun of the fair, to hear the shootings and see the snipers. They crept over the fence into the city zoo to be as close to the White House as they could; 'all around was shooting, and in its cage rushed a terrified tiger. That's when I understood they would drive us out, repress us and shoot. All this laid the foundations for what is happening now. This Putin did not do.'[5] He has said that he understands now: 'I share responsibility with what happened then, with a lot of people, because I was also standing behind that position.'[6]

Navalny entered one of the lesser of Moscow's elite academies, Patrice Lumumba University of People's Friendship, a slightly run-down establishment founded to educate the Third World in Russian. This dream, like so many others, had failed. By the 1990s the university was a place where nervous Africans dared not come out of their dormitories for fear of skinhead attacks. A failed experiment in multiculturalism made of chipped concrete and declining education standards, it was also the alma mater of another symbol of the Putin era, the tawdry spy Anna Chapman, a 'honey-trap' agent deployed in London and New York by Russian foreign intelligence. Maybe they met.

But unlike Chapman who had youthful fantasies of marrying a foreigner and living in the West, Navalny had 1990s dreams that did not come true. 'To market fundamentalists like me, it seemed like they would all become millionaires. Everybody thought if we were smart, we would soon become rich [. . .] but then it suddenly became apparent that the rich are those that are somehow connected to the government.'[7] He graduated a frustrated young man with a law degree and a specialist diploma in finance, something which had turned out to be a piece of paper whose value he had somewhat overvalued. Success was not forthcoming. Bored by his office job as a legal clerk for a property firm, Navalny began to drift into politics.

At the turn of the century the Russian 'opposition' hardly existed. The Russian Communist Party had the largest following in the country but had developed into a monstrous political centaur, neither one thing nor another. Whilst holding onto the flags and symbolism of the Left it had abandoned a meaningful leftist agenda. The party had ditched the call for 'workers of the world to unite' as the slogan no longer reflected 'a real preparedness on the part of the international workers' and communist movement'.[8] Instead it was campaigning on a red-brown mix of Russian nationalism against the 'worldwide behind the scenes forces', their descriptions of which smelled strongly anti-Semitic.[9] Under the leadership of Gennady Zyuganov, who had been implicated in anti-Gorbachev plots with the KGB in the last years of the USSR, all alternatives within the party for a different kind of leftism, from the democratic socialists to the syndicalists who had flourished during perestroika, were suffocated and destroyed. Whilst lauding Stalin as a 'great statesman', Zyuganov also seemed to denounce the revolution of 1917 as caused by 'in equal degree the errors of the Russian government in its domestic politics and the external, corrupting influence of Western civilization.'[10] Obsessed by the Romanovs, the leader of the zombie carcass of the Communist Party cited his influences as the author of *The Decline of the West*, Oswald Spengler, and the anti-communist 'Eurasianist' Lev Gumilev, espousing a foul-smelling bureaucratic-nationalist intellectual ratatouille.[11]

This incoherent mix, drawing support from mainly pensioners, old scientific single industry towns and the lowly ranks of the bureaucracy was not some strange aberration but a reflection of millions of Russians' own disorientation, personally and intellectually. Navalny considered the party – with its offices across the country, its own governors and large membership base – but dismissed it as 'ideologically unacceptable'.[12] To the Right the clownish Vladimir Zhirinovsky, a half-Jewish anti-Semite whose xenophobic rants mesmerized swathes of the rural and the miserable to vote for him as a protest party, was also deemed unacceptable by Navalny, as it was clearly not 'serious'.[13] Neither of these parties he believed seemed seriously interested in fighting for power. They had accepted their place in the Yeltsin–Putin system as purely parliamentary and regional organizations without a chance of entering the Kremlin. This left only one choice: Yabloko. 'I joined this party,' Navalny explained to me, 'because I was outraged at the plan to raise the threshold for the Duma to 7 per cent to keep out the liberals. It was my personal choice. My act of defiance.'

In 2000 Navalny knocked on the door of the one pro-democracy and pro-market party that had always opposed Yeltsin's excesses. It was the year of the *Kursk*. He says he was greeted by suspicion and a lack of understanding as to why on earth he was even trying to join in the first place:

'This was the beginning of Putin's time and nobody joined a party out of conviction.'[14] Yabloko was one of the last pieces of perestroika left. It was headed by Grigory Yavlinsky, one of Gorbachev's ministers and author of the never-implemented 1990 plan to turn the Soviet Union into a market economy. On almost every issue in the 1990s Yavlinsky had seen which way the wind was blowing and gone against it. He paid for this stance. Though he has never said who was behind it, his piano-playing son was once abducted and had his fingers chopped off. He received them by post. This did not stop him opposing shock therapy, trying to mediate in the 1993 clash between the Kremlin and the rebellious Congress, opposing military action in Chechnya and running against Yeltsin in 1996. He is the best president that post-Soviet Russia never had.

This stance had turned his party by the time Navalny signed up into a liberal, intelligentsia equivalent of Zhirinovsky's 'Liberal Democrats': a machine behind a talking head nobody expected to ever win, but who you could cast a protest vote for. He was just like Zyuganov and Zhirinovsky in another way too. All three have been turned into the authoritarian mini-Putins of their own parties, refusing to let other candidates stand for the presidential election or rise up through the ranks. In exactly the same way this personalization of power stunted the Kremlin, it stunted these politicians from creating real political organizations, resulting instead in small nomenklaturas either out in the few regions they controlled in the case of Zhirinovsky and Zyuganov or merely in a Moscow-based organization for Yavlinsky. There was little aimed at real action. 'The trouble with these guys,' Navalny moaned, 'is that they decide one day "I am the coolest" and they just stop listening to anybody. They turn away all outside advice.'

In the first few years of Putinism, before the 2003 Duma elections, these parties put up little committed and even less effective resistance to his policies. The communists were withering as a genuine party as they accepted funds from Khodorkovsky, letting their 'socialist' deputies vote repeatedly against tax increases on oil, which would harm the oligarch's profits. But Putinism did not yet feel fully authoritarian. For the misfits and political obsessives such as Navalny, leafleting for Yabloko, they never expected Yavlinsky to become president but, as he puts it, that they could 'build a big democratic coalition that could capture a big chunk of power'.[15] The constant stream of mishandled terrorist attacks that were the backdrop to Khodorkovsky's swagger and ambitions made this seem a distinct possibility. Instead the 2003 election came and horrified the opposition parties. Yabloko failed to make it to parliament for the first time. They claimed they were the victims of electoral fraud and accused the Kremlin of foul play. Navalny was having none of it. He was convinced the party had failed to make it into the Duma because it had lost touch.

At the time, Navalny spent long hours campaigning with Ilya Yashin, the leader of 'Youth Yabloko'. He is terribly fond of him – 'He is a great guy, he really thinks outside the box.' A persistent campaigner with a taste for fashion brands, Yashin summed up the opposition for a lot of people in the mid-2000s. He once did an illegal bungee jump off a Moscow bridge shouting 'bring back the elections you bastards', only to be left hanging there for hours. Another time he donned special fireproof clothing, doused himself in gasoline and set himself alight with a placard 'No successor or burn in hell'. He ended up hospitalized from inhaling the smoke, with mild but painful burns. To young Muscovites studying at top universities this kind of opposition seemed attention-seeking, silly and unable to answer any question that touched on real politics, let alone the economy. For all their stunts and campaigning, neither Yashin nor Navalny were particularly well liked or effective in Yabloko. Looking back on what went wrong, Yashin says, 'The thing is that opposition was previously just failed 1990s politicians and celebrities . . . too many officers and not enough foot soldiers. We may not have been populist enough in the past.' As nothing they did seem to make a dent in the Putin consensus, Navalny and Yashin began to realize that the 'systemic' opposition of registered parties competing for the Duma would never bring them to power.

This is because Putin and Surkov were systematically destroying the Duma. First the 'bears' from United Russia were brought in as a parliamentary majority, then with the destruction of Yukos major alternative revenue streams for parties other than the Kremlin disappeared. Following Beslan, the Duma laws were modified to effectively remove any chance of an independent being elected to the chamber. Finally, after the Orange Revolution in Ukraine, the state shifted from denouncing 'international terrorism' as its main public enemy to the 'Orange threat', or the enemy within. This transformed the opposition. This left the old 'systemic' opposition such as Zyuganov, Zhirinovsky and Yavlinksy with their deputies in the Duma too constrained and passed-by to be meaningful politicians. These measures began to unnerve many of those who had given Putin the benefit of the doubt. It was only as late as 2004 that Yeltsin's former protégé Boris Nemtsov began warning of a dictatorship, and only after Beslan the same year that chess champion Garry Kasparov finally decided to go into politics. Away from the cameras, a process of radicalization was under way amongst the ranks of the discontented. Just as Tsar Nicholas II's refusal to work with the original Duma in the lead-up to the First World War had seen the nature of his foes morph into increasingly radical and conspiratorial factions, a new 'anti-systemic' opposition of marches, punks, movements and protests was emerging. Navalny followed the wind.

The Dissenters

By the year 2006, the dissenters' marches had begun. They were the baby steps of anti-Putin protest politics. In St Petersburg over three thousand protesters marched down Nevsky Prospect towards the Winter Palace shouting 'shame', 'down with Putin', 'out with corrupt power'. Over three thousand OMON riot police met them, in tundra camouflage and crash helmets. As always, the Kremlin had picked the provincial OMON to beat up and arrest some demonstrators, knowing full well that guys from the sticks were particularly eager to truncheon liberal urbanites. Those demonstrating were a different kind of people. Under the common cry of 'we want another Russia', a coalition was forming called the Other Russia, bringing together psychedelic punk fascists, liberals, nationalists and democrats all interested in direct action. The authorities' response only radicalized them further. Warnings were placed on the metro urging people not to join the dissenters. State TV warned about 'extremists'. Navalny and other 'systemic' activists joined them.

At an opposition conference entitled 'A new agenda for liberal Russian forces', held in a hotel in St Petersburg, I had a chance to talk to Garry Kasparov in the lobby. In the build-up to further dissenters' marches, he cut a sad figure. Crowds were gathering outside but not to overthrow Putin. The electronics giant Samsung was distributing exciting balloons. Kasparov's manner was an instant turn-off. An American beside him was gushing, 'Garry, Garry-y.' He snorted at suggestions that the opposition was going nowhere, 'I wouldn't be so pessimistic. The window of opportunity is open and though time is slowly running out, more and more people are coming round to our point of view.' He glared at suggestions that his 'Other Russia' coalition with cultish extremists like the National Bolsheviks was a turn-off for liberals, insisting, 'Though we have received criticism for bringing in groups such as the National Bolshevik party we have strongly moderated their position. We do this because we need another Russia.'

Kasparov was not as successful as he made out. By mid-decade the punk-poet Eduard Limonov and his National Bolsheviks were in the front line of the opposition, egging officials, occupying government buildings, plotting a coup in Kazakhstan and waving their cartoon flag blending Nazi and Soviet imagery: a black hammer and sickle in a white circle on crimson. To meet Limonov you had to call special numbers, which were often changed, and wait at meeting points for his lieutenants to take you to his 'secret location'. I was told to wait outside a Moscow McDonalds on a bright summer's day for one of his goons. He arrived in a long black leather coat of the kind seen in *The Matrix*, an orange fleece and black sunglasses. I was told to close my eyes as we entered a Stalinist baroque block of flats, and forbidden to open them until we were inside the apartments. The leather men smoked in the kitchen and tippled as I talked with the man they called 'father'. I sat down. He explained some of his policies:

- moving the capital to a new purpose-built city in Siberia safe from NATO attack;
- creating large quantities of martyrs;
- re-creating a totalitarian USSR.

Limonov rubbed and stroked his arms as we talked. He spoke softly, sometimes in a hiss. His eyes never seemed to stay still. He croaked from time to time and insisted we spent the afternoon speaking in his impeccable French, which only made him seem stranger still. He had been a dissident and a writer, who escaped the USSR on an Israel exit visa gained by pretending to be Jewish, and famous for his autobiographical novel about gay sex with black drug pushers while living as a down-and-out exile in Manhattan. In the novel, he asks his black lovers to call him 'Eddie'.

'It's a novel . . . it is . . . a fantasy . . . a fantasy,' Limonov groaned, massaging the muscle in his left arm as the swallows swirled in a faint blue sky.

Returning from exile, his newly formed National Bolsheviks had campaigned for totalitarian restoration under the slogan: 'Stalin, Beria, Gulag!' Announcing in the 1990s, 'enough walks in the park with red-cheeked girls, it is time to walk with loyal comrades underneath a red flag', Limonov had casually paid a visit to Serb forces shelling Sarajevo and fired a sympathy round into the city with them.[16] The fact that in the mid-2000s this man could have attracted a dedicated following of hundreds of young Russians alienated by the regime and been considered a leading opposition politician is a testament to two things: the sickness of politics and the utter failure of the establishment democrats. Limonov raised his voice:

'You know why I went into politics? Because politics is the greatest of the arts . . . Politics combines rhetoric, theatre, literature and cinema. When you stand and address a crowd of 200,000 people screaming your name – Limonov! Limonov! – It feels just like a drug. It washes right through you like a drug.'

The fact that hundreds of alienated kids joined the National Bolsheviks was a damning verdict on all the country's politicians. Limonov in alliance with Garry Kasparov was a key driver behind the mid-2000s 'Other Russia' coalition. Yet these underground psychedelic-fascist pseudo-revolutionary communes of the National Bolsheviks impressed none other than the murdered journalist Anna Politkovskaya. She saw them as the first faction that dared take direct action. But theirs was a strange punk world, as much a rejection of the conformity of Putin-worshipping Nashi as the lawyer-economist dreams of Navalny and his generation. Navalny's good friend and ally, Zakhar Prilepin, reminisced in his blockbuster novel about the National Bolsheviks:

> The atmosphere in the bunker was always joyful and noisy. It was like a boarding school for delinquents, the studio of a crazy painter, or the military encampment of some barbarians that had decided to go to war God knows where. And there were girls – their faces jarringly mixing both disgust for the world and the noblest of ambitions for this same planet. This may seem strange – but that was the essence of who they were.[17]

They were the first rebels against post-Soviet cynicism. In Zakhar Prilepin's novel *San'kia*, a book close to the hearts of a generation of lost, angry young Russians, repression begins to brutalize the likes of them. The gang of 'unionists', a thinly disguised National Bolshevik cell, gets beaten up and their faces bloodied at protests, then arrested and eventually, mentally scarred. As the pages turn, the rather sweet – if stupid – boys brawling with men from the Caucasus at market stalls after a few shots of vodka are planning murders, becoming terrorists with a plot to shoot their way into the governor's office. Along the way a caricature of a Russian Jew tries to dissuade them as they move to smash their heads in on the bars of the state. In the novel, the punk-fascist is a failed, tragic hero. And it was with his good friend Zakhar Prilepin, whose first name he gave to his first-born son – that Navalny began a journey into nationalism.

Context is everything and in the mid-2000s Putinist anti-terror nationalism was beginning to boomerang. As war and poverty drove ever greater numbers of gun-wielding young men north out of the Caucasus into ethnic Russia in search of enough money to eat, the same generation of young, heavy-drinking and conscripted guys sent to fight them began to brawl with them in their home towns. The regime was starting to feel blowback as fragments of their wars came home. As in Prilepin's novel, town after town saw the vertical of power and 'the dictatorship of law' collapse.

The first implosion of order was in Yandikh on the Caspian Sea, on the fringes of Europe, in 2005. Natives brawled with local Chechens in ethnic clashes that eventually needed the OMON to restore a semblance of peace. The following year in the far northern city of Kondopoga, near the Finnish and EU border, the same thing happened. For several days the town was gripped by mass ethnic clashes after a gang member from the Caucasus shot a Slavic Russian. Nationalist leaders descended on the town to demand 'expulsion', as Chechen leader Ramzan Kadyrov threatened the region if his people were harmed. It was the following year that Navalny and Prilepin, who fought in an OMON squad in Chechnya, together with other 'democratic-nationalists' launched NAROD, a Russian word close to the German 'Volk', or a blood-tied nation. Their manifesto bombastically began: 'Russia is facing a national catastrophe' and announced the state's mission was to stop 'the degradation of Russian civilization and create the preconditions and development of the Russian people, their cultural, language and historic territory.'[18] Alongside a demand for free elections and free TV their policies included a wholesome range of proposals including:

- Restoring the 'organic unity of Russia's past', from Kievan Rus to the USSR.
- Recognition of the breakaway statelets Transnistria, Abkhazia and South Ossetia.
- Refusal to accept the various amnesties offered by Putin to Chechen fighters in his first term.
- Tax exemptions for small businesses.[19]

The breakdown of order in these towns were the crucible for a new Russian nationalism. NAROD and other movements are products of Putinism, blending a literalist understanding of its propaganda against 'terrorists' and 'oligarchs', frustration with an increasingly muzzled TV and parliament with a seething rage at Putinism's perceived non-nationalist hypocrisy – allowing mass migration from Muslim ex-Soviet states and paying generous subsidies to Kadyrov. As the flame-haired opposition commentator Yulia Latynina once explained to me, 'What is happening here is what happened in the Arab states. The Sheiks ruled, saying "We are the real Muslims", whilst they stole, drank oil and shopped in the West. When they failed to deliver development, the extremists came to the street shouting, "No, we are the real Muslims!" Putin said he was a nationalist, but now the real nationalists are starting to come out onto the streets.'

NAROD were busy making videos. One shows Navalny as a 'dentist' extracting teeth, the kind of 'extraction' that he cheerfully recommends should happen to illegal immigrants; in another video Navalny in front of a green screen is explaining how to kill roaches with a fly swatter. A video-screen jumps from a picture of roaches and flies to one of a North Caucasian insurgent – with 'Homo Lawless-icus' written underneath. One erupts into the studio and Navalny flies into action. The smoke clears. He has shot the rebel, 'I suggest a pistol.'[20] He smiles. When his friend Masha Gaidar (whose heckler Navalny had shot four times in bar Gogol) saw the video, she said: 'This is fascism.'[21] Even his mother refused to speak about politics with him.

Navalny was expelled from Yabloko in 2007. He stormed out shouting 'Slava Rossii', which signalling 'Glory to Russia' – a very ethnic understanding of the word – is a taboo for well-to-do Russian liberals. He began warning of the dangers of the 'Islamification' of Russia.[22] Nor did Navalny stop at words or videos. He was loudly agitating for Russian gun rights.

Soon Navalny was invited by far-right nationalist leaders to co-organize their annual flagship event, the 'Russian March'. As the culture of street protests (though still fringe) was growing, Russian nationalists were staging an annual jamboree in Moscow. Navalny was proudly marching side by side with chanting nationalists: skinheaded holocaust deniers, men howling 'stop feeding the Caucasus', calls of 'Russians, onwards', football hooligans, anti-immigrant organizers, all waving the Romanov flag, with the black, yellow and white they had made their colours. Navalny not only organized these rallies, but spoke at them every year. He could frequently be heard saying that Russia and Ukraine could become one country again, and started to use the aggressive football hooligan's slogan: 'don't forget, don't forgive'. Trying to explain himself as still being a democrat after all that, he rather goofily held up a placard in front of a camera:

I'm going:

> Dissenters' March
> The March: Moscow is a Russian Town!
> Green March

GLORY TO RUSSIA!

P.S.: I basically love Marches![23]

We talked about this – his nationalism – in a Vietnamese cafe near his small office in Taganskaya, a run-down district on the edge of central Moscow. 'Do you think Russia is for Russians?' Navalny raised his head and waves his hand:

'No, not like that . . . I think Russia is for Russian citizens . . . that's a totally stupid, totally old-fashioned way of thinking. I don't want that. I want a visa regime with Central Asia to stop uncontrolled mass immigration. France has visas with North Africa. Britain has visas with India. Does that make me a nationalist?'

Then he went still and looked me in the eye: 'I have some conservative views, but I joined Yabloko for a reason . . . I'm more or less a liberal kind of guy. I believe in law and order and getting things done. Not this ideological mumbo-jumbo.'

We are left to presume either that NAROD and all the rest was positioning, or that Navalny changes his mind.

'You know, what my real dream is?' asked Navalny quietly, putting down his fork. It was not nationalism. Like Putin had promised, he wanted a gigantic transfer of assets out of illegitimate hands. 'My dream is that somehow . . . all the money that left Russia, that was taken away by the crooks and thieves and stashed in London or Switzerland can be brought back.'

He then started to talk about who, in a perfect world, he would like to see tried in court for robbing the Russian people. 'All Putin's friends in the Ozero gang and the oligarchs Abramovich and Usmanov.'

'That could mean redistributing over 40 per cent of the Russian economy,' I said, slightly thrown at what economic disruption post-Putinism might entail.

'So what? There are plenty of minority shareholders, plenty of windfall taxes and ways to make this happen. We could also have lustration against anyone who was in United Russia down to the regional leader level . . . But only if we come to power with over 70 per cent of the people behind us.'

It struck me while talking to Navalny in the dingy cafe that his anger about corruption, towards the 'thieves', was not just a turn of phrase aimed at Putin. It was a new form of old rage, close to the anger at unjust privatization, the 1990s fury at the oligarchs who robbed Russia – but where Putin had eclipsed Berezovsky in the cosmology of bloodsuckers as the 'Tsar of Thieves'. To restore ownership to the nation, to take it out of the hands of a cabal, had been the very promise of Putinism. But then what? When Russia had woken up from this nightmare, what did Navalny want to breathe and see? 'I want Russia to be a big, irrational, metaphysical Canada.'

I left Navalny baffled, both drawn to him, but unsure if I even liked him.

The Underground

Navalny has come to sneer at 'mumbo-jumbo' politics because nothing he was involved with in 2007 made any impact. Medvedev became president and even more governors and deputies turned into 'bears'. Yet the opposition was evolving away from being old perestroika personalities on talk shows. But like the 'systemic opposition' before it, the movement failed to make any impact on the 2007 parliamentary and 2008 presidential elections. The dissenters' marches made no difference. The Russian March made no difference. Neither, unsurprisingly, did the Green March, or any of the marches Navalny attended. Soon Limonov saw more and more of his activists jailed and their 'cool' factor wavered. Instead another tsarist throwback was developing – a cultural underground.

As his commitment to Yabloko flagged and the dissenters were dispersed and dismissed as crazy during the boom years by the Putin majority, Navalny became a king of the 'Stray Dog Cafés' of the new century. Under Nicholas II, the artists of the imperial city gathered at the 'Stray Dog Café', named because unlike the hounds that ran with the regime, they were strays without owners or leashes. As Russian politics suffocated under Stolypin, it was in these fashionable bars – or rather salons, or small theatres – where Blok sat with Akhmatova and Gumilev and other cultural luminaries, during the pre-revolutionary 'silver age'. It was an intensely creative world. In the late 2000s a Putinist descendant began to emerge in Moscow. Salons such as Masterskaya near the secret service's Lubyanka headquarters, or Gogol near the Moscow mayoralty, began to host constant political debates, poetry readings and discussions. Navalny together with Masha Gaidar turned himself into a showman and host of these underground talk shows. They invited liberals, journalists, Putinists, all and sundry, to have the debates that would never have appeared on television. Everybody shouted, argued about where Russia was going, drank fancy wines, imported beers and smoked heavily. The underground was fun, but known to almost no one outside of the chattering classes. Yet Russia is a bit like France, where Parisian elites have a stranglehold on influence – and this was enough to worry the authorities. They wanted to be the only political show in town.

This is where Navalny attracted his first 'fan' in the Kremlin. In his office Vladislav Surkov, a trained theatre director, was said to be fuming at the smash hit of the debates. At the time, the power of this half-Chechen consigliere was mythical. He was the 'grey cardinal'. At a private briefing two Russian journalists once saw a cockroach scurry between his papers.[24] The girls screamed, but what unnerved the reporters was that as Surkov flicked the red roach with the back of his hand off his desk, it occurred to them that he could do the same to any United Russia deputy. The opposition was also living with the same impression of Surkov's power. Accusations and counter-accusations swirled of FSB plants and moles. Any disruption was seen as 'Surkovian puppetry'. Navalny grins: 'I heard that Surkov had been really impressed by me. You have to understand. The online space at that point was really limited. We had no TV space at all. It was so important for us to have these debates. And they sent guys to break up even this.'

This brings us back to the shooting. When hecklers tried to disrupt Navalny's debate with Masha Gaidar, he claimed the yobs were football hooligans, that they mentioned Surkov's name, and were sent to the Gogol bar by Surkov himself. On the photos blogged from the scene they don't exactly look like football fans. One of those present said that Navalny did not fire in self-defence. Navalny then effectively argued it was all right as he wasn't trying to kill him and did not fire at his head, adding that it was acceptable as he shot him: 'a) outside the debate hall; b) not to the head; c) from an acceptable distance.'[25] The Gogol shooting captures the ambiguities of both Putinism and the opposition: in his instinctual aggression and paranoia Navalny was behaving like a product of Putinism. Answering a xenophobic question on his blog demanding the right for Russians to carry guns, he posted: 'All the rest are hiding behind the defences of the "Holocaust" fund. It's stronger than any pistol.'[26] The case against him was dropped. In opposition circles it was debated whether this was a sign of the authorities' complicity or Navalny's political ties. Both options are two sides of the same coin – a society without proper gun legislation, easy on the trigger, without proper rule of law.

Surkov may or may not have been behind the heckles, but the opposition still failed to be heard outside the Garden Ring, the name for the ring road that encircles Moscow's wealthy heart. The 2007 parliamentary elections and the 2008 presidential elections swept more 'bears' into the Duma and placed Medvedev in the Kremlin. The dissenters' marches had died down. The National Bolsheviks' bunkers were no longer thronged. Opposition leaders were still unattractive and uninspiring to normal Russians: mostly ex-ministers, sprinkled with ex-dissidents.

The Democratic Aristocrats

During the Medvedev years the pre-eminent face of the opposition was Boris Nemtsov. Once Yeltsin's favourite, once keen to 'kick the oligarchs out of the Kremlin', he was broadly seen by normal Russians as only wanting to claw his way back into power. He is easy to caricature because he has the charms of a pro athlete. 'I'm so famous in this country,' he announced when we met after a small rally. 'I can't go anywhere. They all know who I am.'

The vocal opposition leader had picked a plush coffee shop to sound off, to the distinct displeasure of several paying customers. Suspiciously tanned and jarringly arrogant, this fanatical surfer and tennis player had slowly outplayed the moody chessmaster Garry Kasparov to seize the underwhelming title of pre-eminent leader of the Russian opposition. He ordered a few cognacs, then blasted out, 'I am indeed Boris Nemtsov' to a curious couple to our left. He then began showing off his latest acquisition: a delicate, finely crafted watch.

'This is a present from Gorbachev. Look, it's got "Gorbachev Forever" inscribed inside.' He laughed a little. Nemtsov's exorbitantly priced tuna sandwich then arrived. With the food on the table, he began to outline how the opposition had reformed itself since Medvedev's arrival in power, whilst chomping on the oily dish. Nemtsov has been awarded a plaque by *Novaya Gazeta*. He had brought it with him to the cafe. He picked it up, grinned, then placed it delicately next to his sandwich. Though much disliked as a man, his commitment had helped found Solidarity. Unlike Other Russia, the new organization brought together most liberals opposed to Putin in a common front with a small but dedicated regional network. Without much attention being paid to it at first, Solidarity slowly created a situation where a small but persistently engaged 'anti-systemic' opposition infrastructure now existed. It was a sad little world of tiny, badly lit offices and old computers – but it was there.

Sitting next to Nemtsov was an early aficionado of the iPhone in Moscow, the smart, expensively dressed former deputy oil minister Vladimir Milov. With a sharp brain Milov was in some ways exactly what the opposition needed – and exactly what it could do without in the same person. Together with Nemtsov he brought the brainpower to bear so they could slowly begin to churn out a series of reports – *Putin: The Results*; *Luzhkov: The Results*; *Putin: Corruption*; and *Putin: Corruption II*. The general public didn't hear of them, but these documents were corrosive on the Putin consensus. They were universally read and quoted in the policy community and by journalists. Soon, Medvedev's own think-tank INSOR would be using facts and arguments that had surfaced in Nemtsov and Milov's pamphlets.

But at the same time Milov incarnated some of the worst characteristics of the opposition: his suave manner and urbane intellectualism made him seem out of touch and easy to caricature to factory workers in provincial cities such as Nizhny Tagil or Tolyatti – as someone only interested in recouping his former oil ministry. Between him and Nemtsov the relationship was also strained, one of the micro-rivalries that the opposition seemed to spend more time focusing on than fighting the authorities. Once, with Nemtsov not present, Milov told me he felt there was 'political hazing' in the opposition, with older politicians dominating and blocking younger leaders rising up. Though Navalny would soon harvest a lot of the work Nemtsov and Milov had put in over the years – intellectually and in terms of infrastructure – he caricatured this elitist world as the ineffective 'court of Nemtsov and Milov'.

Impetuously I asked both 'democratic aristocrats' if they felt they were not quite proletarian enough to compete with Putin's persona; one that smacks of a lower–middle-class fitness fanatic. 'No. They have chosen us because we are articulating their demands,' Milov retorted on behalf Russia's masses. But for all their bravado in the plush cafe that afternoon in late 2009, the 'court' knew they were making little impact in the hinterland. After finishing his sandwich and downing his cognac Nemtsov lamented: 'The reason the opposition has been so ineffective is that the vast majority of Russians live out in the regions. They only have state TV out there . . . and we are strictly banned from being featured on it.' Milov nodded thoughtfully.

Navalny had realized that Nemtsov and Milov's personas and 1990s party structures were never going to break through in the aftermath of the 2007 parliamentary elections. Frustrated and wound up with what he saw as a lack of power lust and creativity in the opposition, he provocatively presented a paper entitled 'The death of the Russian opposition and how it can be renewed'.[27] To the disgruntlement of many of those present he held up NAROD as a 'network' bringing together liberals and nationalists as an example for the future: 'The victory of this opposition is only possible with a political consolidation and synthesis of the ideas of democracy, social justice and nationalism. That is – forming a large united front of leftists and national democratic forces.'[28] In what may have been a coded reference to Yavlinksy he lamented the continued hold of 'the political culture of the Soviet era of stagnation' over the opposition.[29] Navalny then dared them to understand: 'The model of the opposition parties has exhausted itself, as the officially registered parties are fully dependent on the Kremlin's dishonest "rules of the game" set by President Putin's administration. Success in the struggle against the regime can only be with a network structure, bringing together representatives of the overwhelming majority of parties and ideologies.'[30]

Not everyone in the opposition liked to be told they needed to become one and the same with the nationalists and stop fighting for a particular vision of Russia. Lev Ponomarev, a scruffy perestroika-era perpetual dissident, banned Navalny from attending one of his conferences. He shot back in a rather Putinist fashion, 'What a cruel world and how cruel of Lev Ponomarev! Now we can't take part in filming the next instalment in that soap opera "Opposition United", which they make especially for CNN.'[31]

Whatever Navalny's posturing, by 2009–10 the opposition was generally moving towards regular and sustained direct action. Their next instalment was more dramatic and had a catchy name, Strategy-31. The new regular protests were named after Article 31 in the Russian constitution that guarantees freedom of assembly. Every month ending on the 31st opposition activists, dissenters, students, 1980s die-hard dissidents and truckloads of crash-helmeted OMON, police and police dogs would gather at Triumphalnaya Square in central Moscow beneath the statue of Vladimir Mayakovsky. The Soviet poet had killed himself in 1930 after writing how 'the love boat smashed up on the dreary routine', before being immortalized in a bullying bronze statue he would have detested. Around his plinth monthly scuffles took place.

The routine went like this: the opposition were denied a permit, they came anyway for an 'illegal demonstration' and militarized goons were already in wait with truckloads of back-up down the side alleys. Around one hundred to two hundred people on average would glide towards Mayakovsky. As they approached many would start shouting 'shame', 'Russia will be free', and would wave A4 printouts emblazoned simply with the digits '31'. Then the OMON would smash up the gathering. Nemtsov and usually Limonov would be handcuffed (as if they had tried to rob a bank) and driven off to a police station for a cursory detention and fine.

Navalny may have sneered that Lev Ponomarev was making a TV show for CNN, but it was certainly painful to make. Once, at an illegal protest, I was standing next to him when a bruiser in a black T-shirt popped up in the middle of the crowd, quickly said something on his mobile, then in the blink of an eye brutally attacked the seventy-one-year-old man half his size. As the opposition 'protest-boat' smashed itself up every odd month in a dreary routine under the Mayakovsky statue, the authorities got increasingly nervous. First, the square started to host special events. One month the square was clogged by a high-speed car demonstration. As opposition activists with A4 paper bearing '31' were being smashed up by OMON, a man and his five-year-old son crossed the road. An OMON with truncheon screamed: 'Get the hell out of here!'

'But my son just wants to watch the cars.'

'Get out now!'

Beyond Dissent

Navalny was not the first political blogger, he was not the first online politician, or even the first opposition leader to understand that Putin's decision not to implement FSB demands for Chinese-style Internet censors left the online heights waiting to be seized. He was simply the first blogger-politician to do it really effectively. This is because Navalny correctly understood there was a fundamental contradiction at the heart of Putinism. As the state became increasingly authoritarian, society was moving in the other direction. As the regime restored the Soviet anthem and neutered parliament, the economic boom saw computers and mobile phones flood Russia, giving normal citizens the action-tools to participate in an increasingly dense ecosystem of civil society.

The 2000s, not the 1990s, was the decade that Russian civil society really took off. The irony was that even though the country had been more liberal in the 1990s, the economic turmoil of the period wrought havoc on

NGO finances, undercut their influence and sapped the spirits of the generous. Scandalous 'charities' discredited private giving and the mass slump into poverty hollowed the means to give. Russia had exited the Soviet Union with a fragile NGO ecosystem that simply couldn't cope with the depression that followed. In 1986 the country only had twenty NGOs.[32] In 1991 this had ballooned to over 10,000, each one of them vulnerable.[33] Once the Yeltsin decade closed and the economy stabilized, the clusters and dots of social activism began to consolidate. Despite Putinist laws making NGOs vulnerable to state closure in the mid-2000s and his propaganda against them, the decade saw a boom. By 2007 there were well over 100,000 NGOs in Russia.[34] This was paralleled in a surge in private giving with over forty well-financed private foundations and $2.5 billion in corporate donations in place by the decade's end.[35] The authoritarian clampdown on access to the Duma or the mysterious murders of journalists did not affect this trend.

It was in these thousands of little initiatives that Putin lost his monopoly to shape society. There were groups that hunted for lost children in Moscow, or priests that gathered to feed the hungry in Siberia; there were anti-heroin vigilantes in the Urals and environmentalists on lake Baikal. They were small in number, often hounded, and lived in resentment of incompetent United Russia officials who they thought were not doing their jobs – but they were everywhere. The new opposition was not going to be rallied by old 1990s politician-outcasts but would grow out of this thickening, crystalizing society. Some called it 'the civil archipelago'.[36]

Bringing all this to a wider audience was the rise of the Internet and mobile phones. When Putin came to power only 1.03 per cent of Russians were online. By 2010 this had risen to 43.37 per cent.[37] The same explosive story goes for mobile phone use, which went from virtually nothing in 1999 to almost everyone by 2007.[38] As more and more of the mobiles became smartphones, the opposition now had a whole new dimension for activism. The barriers to entry were collapsing and Navalny got caught up in this trend early. He started his own blog in April 2006. He chose to write on his 'about me' page that he was 'a Democrat, who is not delighted with the Liberals'.[39]

Yet it was neither a democrat nor a liberal who was the greenest shoot of anti-government activism but a suburban mother of two in her early thirties with an unfashionable fringe haircut living on the edge of Moscow. Evgenia Chirikova lives in a run-down Soviet apartment block in Khimki. That a new form of politics should come from here is no surprise. The town's fortunes have followed Russia's since Stalin.

Thrown together by Soviet shock-workers on the eve of the Second World War, it was the furthest point of the German advance, the closest front line to the Kremlin. After the war it became a hub of the space industry and, after the fall of the USSR, a hub for supermarket mega-halls. Under Putin, Khimki saw the best of times and the worst of times. A construction boom saw good-quality apartments flung up in all corners, a huge cluster of metallic malls with an IKEA and Auchan settled on the outskirts like nesting UFOs. Real incomes soared. Yet so did corruption, the beatings of journalists and disregard for the average citizen. In Khimki normal families were not concerned by arcane debates over nationalism or democracy, which obsessed the pseudo-political peacocks in the under-ground debating halls. They cared about practical problems and the very simple feeling that something was being stolen. Or that they were being trampled on.

Chirikova was walking in Khimki forest with her husband. She had moved to Khimki so their daughters could breathe clean air. In Moscow, if you stand on a balcony, overlooking some of the worst traffic on earth, and face the horizon on a clear evening you see a thick black band of pollution rimming the metropolis. She wanted to live on the other side of that, next to one of the capital's last forests. Walking one afternoon between the trees with her husband she saw they had been daubed in red paint. They were slated to be chopped down to make way for a new highway that neither she nor the people of Khimki knew anything about. Until that moment she had been commercial and not political. Her anger at the destruction of the forest close to where she had chosen to make a home revealed she was not just a small-time businesswoman but had a civic leader inside her. Sitting with her in her kitchen as she gave her very young daughter a big mug of coffee and insisted I eat some breakfast cheese, I was suddenly struck by something. There was something so different about her from any of the Russian politicians I had ever met. She was normal. Sitting in her kitchen, she was coasting on genuine outrage at the 'murder of the forest'. She was not a posturing nationalist waving a microphone on a stage, or showing off a 'Gorbachev Forever' craft-piece watch whilst downing overpriced cognacs:

'At first what did I think of Putin? Oh . . . well I thought he was a young, handsome, sporty man who was doing lots of things for the country, of course. I only became active in the last few years. Before that I was just an ordinary woman . . . I was a simple businesswoman, and I had abso-lutely no interest in politics . . . After the Yeltsin period, when Putin was around at first, I thought he was good . . . OK, maybe years ago I thought nothing . . . I didn't know about corruption . . . so I just thought Putin was an intelligent man doing something for the country.'

This illusion evaporated for Chirikova when the news of the planned motorway cutting right through the forest suddenly exposed her to the authoritarian, corrupt and violent intrigues the regime was willing to go through to protect its business interests against civil society. Putinism in Khimki was not just consumerism after all. The local authorities and the foreign companies who would be doing most of the work refused to engage with the small protest movement she started to rally. They tweeted, blogged and appeared on TV saying they wanted to keep their trees, but to no avail. This sudden eruption of civil activism electrified the Russian intelligentsia. Right up until 2010 the US Embassy was cabling back to Washington that the country had a 'third world middle class', which was now 'largely risk averse' and 'had absorbed the bureaucratic thinking of the majority'.[40] Navalny was particularly captivated by Chirikova, especially by her practical-politics-first approach, which he argued had achieved more on a local level than the establishment parties were capable of. As Chirikova and the 'Khimki Forest Defenders' grew, they started to symbolize something in Russia: a sudden coming together of improved living standards, the spread of civil society into a new kind of politics. And it was then that the authorities tried to make her stop:

'They started to pressure us. They pressured my business – we have a small engineering firm, you see – they came to our bank and asked for all our bank details . . . but worst of all was what they did to our clients . . . they went around telling them that we were involved in extremism! So the bank gave us no more credit . . . and as you can imagine, this was a huge blow.'

As she explains what happened, her child begins to looks worried:

'The worst was when they tried to take my children away. They sent round here a woman from the government with this computer typed-out sheet without a signature on it . . . it was an anonymous denouncement. I was terrified. Anonymous denouncements . . . as if straight from the time of Stalin! It said that I was not a fit mother . . . that I was not looking after them, not feeding them! But they didn't get them and this made me deeply determined to keep being socially active.'

This was not yet the moment that brought home the true gangsterism of the authorities. Journalists started to be detained after covering the forest protests. The editor of the local paper, Mikhail Beketov, started writing about corruption and embezzlement in connection with the motorway project. So, someone blew up his car. Then he was beaten up so savagely that he lost three fingers, a leg and fell into a coma. Another reporter was later attacked with an iron bar. Chirikova sighs:

'It was only after what happened to Mikhail Beketov that I really understood the depth of corruption in this country. I'm not afraid of what they will do. I'm not afraid of tomorrow. I was born in a communist country. And I just look at how everything changed . . . fifty years can change in a single day. And though I see a really, really depressing situation I remember the 1990s. I remember many, many tramps in the street . . . many, many pornographic magazines being sold in the street . . . I remember my teacher leaving . . . I remember lack of money for food . . . I remember we had to grow food and eat it with water. And my father was a scientist! A physicist! Growing his own vegetables to eat! My father has a PhD! So I am not afraid of turmoil after this . . . I am afraid that Russia has no future.'

Not all these groups were so sweet – but many were shaped by the problems and prejudices of Putinism itself. One evening near the gritty roundabout under the squat tsarist turrets of Belorusskaya Station, where the rails lead to Minsk and the west, I met up with a small vigilante group called 'Svetlaya Rus'', or 'Bright Russia'. Their name alludes to the memory of a purer, whiter time. Some were reformed skinheads in metal-tipped boots. Others were pimply nationalists who had found the group through blogging, not fighting. 'We are an NGO,' they said as we walked towards some apartment blocks, 'dedicated to cleaning the filth out of the basements.' We came to one locked door. A heavy smashed it open. We ran through the dank, urine-smelling cellars until we found the 'vermin'. A group of Uzbek migrants living there illegally. The boys frogmarched them outside and made them throw their meagre possessions into a skip.

Humiliated and silent with furious, brown eyes, the migrants glared as they were forced to sit on the pavement. I could not bring myself to meet that gaze. The 'civic activists' laughed: 'We need a little Russian Buchenwald we do.' The migrants were then told to scarper, homeless into the night. The boys did three or so raids a week – sometimes turfing out hundreds of Central Asians. 'We are kind of "whatever" about Putin,' said one, a school history teacher, who compared contemporary nationalist leaders unfavourable to the Nazi pantheon, 'but we hate United Russia, it's a party of crooks. The local housing officials are the ones filling basements with migrant filth.' Groups like these were incredibly popular – the ones that blended a love for vigilante policing born out of Putin's weakness, with the same talk about beatings and strength that his telepopulism is made of.

One evening I went for a walk with a friend of this vigilante group. Andrei Mironov was an old, small man. It turned out that he thought the vigilante group were fascists, but was pleased on some level that someone was fighting off the illegal squatters that filled every basement in the neighbourhood with health hazards. Mironov is one of the last Soviet dissidents to have been imprisoned for his political beliefs, with the signature of Gorbachev himself. We walked around one of Moscow's nicest districts, the Patriarch's Ponds. It is leafy and quiet, with elegant tsarist houses. This is where in Mikhail Bulgakov's *The Master and Margerita* the Devil and his cat are first sighted on a park bench, offering cigarettes in whatever brand you can imagine. But this area is being destroyed. One by one, corrupt developers with fake papers are pulling down these discreet buildings and replacing them with nasty, cheap high-rises that make them more money. 'They will rip the whole of Moscow down,' says Mironov as we stand by the latest wreck. Yet after twenty years he sees something by way of hope. 'I call it the Chirikova generation. I remember that day in 1991 when the coup d'état to impose Stalinism again was foiled. I saw this twelve-year-old girl. She was so proud, so happy, that she had won her dignity. And I thought – they will never be able to take that away from her. This is what is happening now. That girl and that generation have grown up.'

Navalny.ru

Navalny was amazed by the Khimki 'forest defenders'. Their protests had forced Medvedev himself to postpone the construction work. True, the forest had been smashed through to make way for the motorway. True, their leading lady came across as ill-informed and at times a bit kooky on screen. But it was indisputable that these suburban eco-warriors had done something stunning. Unlike any of the projects Yabloko or NAROD had peddled, the Khimki front had grabbed the front pages and mobilized an entire town against the authorities. It promised a new kind of social politics. Its message to the opposition was clear. Practical politics not principles was the way forward. Once again Navalny got the message and went with the flow. Long discussions on 'Russianness' and 'democratic-nationalism' were out. He was reinventing himself as a corruption-busting blogger. He was convinced that you could mobilize people with the very simple idea that something had been stolen. He was right.

Navalny's webpage announced that its mission was to win the 'final battle between good and neutrality'. Each post was aimed at undermining cynicism and apathy by concrete action. Slowly these pages were turning into the front page for his politics. The site tried to come across as everything that Putinism was not: funny, forward-looking and morally upstanding. He made people laugh, announcing his pride at a new son so that 'pink would no longer be dominant' at home, typing excitedly that he was looking forward to the toy guns.[41] His tweets were irreverent – from re-tweeting a 'dubstep cat' to shouting out how much he loved CAP LOCKS.[42] But he could also make people angry at the authorities by posting his anger at wasted funds and dilapidated infrastructure. Navalny made Putin seem old. This was an online island of wit and wisecracks in an ocean of state TV propaganda.

As Navalny's following steadily built up, he was not only gathering readers just to entertain them. He was building up followers for his forthcoming announcements. In the same way that Chirikova had gathered support to save her forest, Navalny decided to put his financial–legal training to use and become a minority shareholder. Russians sympathized with Khimki being trampled on and losing its beloved forest. They were riveted by a shareholder fighting under a simple slogan – that something was being stolen.

'My corruption fighting projects began as a complete accident.' He was tipped off about what looked like a flagrantly corrupt contract at the ministry of health. The ministry wanted to design a new $2 million website to connect doctors and patients but any developers only had sixteen days to submit a design – surely, they already knew who had won. Navalny mobilized his readers. 'I appealed to them to write letters to the ministry saying this was corruption. And we won. It was a successful campaign and they cancelled the contract and the corrupt official resigned.' From that point his inbox went into overload. 'I started getting two, three times more emails than usual, saying "I have a case of corruption", or asking "Can you denounce this corruption?" So I decided I had to organize myself and my anticorruption activities.'

Navalny also decided he would get his hands on what all Russians wanted – shares in big state-controlled companies – and show that he and by consequence all Russians, were being taken for a ride and robbed by corruption inside the national champions. The guise of the 'minority shareholder' hit a chord with Russians in a big way. The philosopher Boris Mezhuev believes that it resonated as all Russians felt like frustrated minority shareholders in Putin's oligarchic–bureaucratic fusion.

'Navalny was perfect. He, as a minority shareholder, was the perfect hero for the country. A guy who could be the director of the company but who is being denied his chance as the system is unfair. He cast himself as a victim of social stagnation, which most people also felt they were too.'

Navalny began filing lawsuits on companies arguing that because they were corrupt the value of his shares was being undermined. This was perfectly legal and had been pioneered as a technique by foreign hedge funds. Those close to him say that it was none other than Bill Browder's raided Hermitage Capital that was one inspiration. Navalny's first big call was accusing the state bank VTB of massive embezzlement. Soon his blog was regularly posting documents and flagging up tell-tale signs of corruption across the country. As the financial crisis hit and the middle classes began to have second thoughts about Putinism, his blogging activity started to pay off – Navalny won his first election. Admittedly, only the October 2010 online poll for an 'Alternative Mayor of Moscow', a gimmick run by Kremlin critical news sources, but by trouncing Boris Nemtsov he had won a symbolic victory. Together with Evgenia Chirikova, Navalny was now the face of the new opposition. Nemtsov and

Milov were being overtaken – left behind in their exquisite clothes and cafes.

Like any clever investor gunning for a piece of the oil boom, Navalny bought some shares in the national pipeline monopoly Transneft. Little did the government know that the company was so endemically and flagrantly corrupt that some poking around by a blogger could expose it to the millions. The month after becoming 'online Mayor', Navalny became a household name when his minority shareholder strategy hit a bull's eye. It would be hard to think of a project more symbolic of the bloated ambitions and dysfunctions of Putinism than the Eastern-Siberia Pacific Ocean (ESPO) pipeline. Its goal (originally planned by Khodorkovsky) was to build the first pipeline to the Pacific and turn Russia into a global energy exporter, not one only supplying the EU. Officials dreamed that with a pipeline to China they could get the Europeans begging for energy-mercy by threatening to turn off the taps to the West. Russian diplomats liked to tease EU leaders with such a possibility. Yet despite its realization being a first rank geopolitical goal for the Kremlin, it had been chronically delayed, disrupted and gone disastrously over budget. It was none other than the ESPO about which Navalny had managed to get hold of documents that showed a spectacular $4 billion fraud conducted by the company.[43] As the country emerged from the deepest recession in the G-20 in 2009, these accusations riled the reading public. In the late years of the Medvedev presidency it was becoming received wisdom that something, and something big, was being stolen – and Navalny was the man trying to stop the thieves.

Navalny was not quite the solo warrior. He was becoming an influential politician in a country where everything is about connections. Any Russian politician, even in the opposition, has to be playing games and building bridges to the establishment. Nemtsov is a good friend of many oligarchs. Milov, as a former deputy oil minister, is a man about town. And Navalny was no exception. Throughout his career he had built up friends in the establishment – from Nikita Belykh, the liberal governor of Kirov, for whom he worked as an advisor, to Stanislav Belkovsky, the 'political technologist' who had accused Yukos of planning a coup but 'worked' with Navalny on NAROD. Nor had he miraculously become a successful minority shareholder activist overnight without some advice from its most skilled practitioners. The expelled head of Hermitage Capital, Bill Browder, knows Navalny well. His company had pioneered a strategy of becoming a minority shareholder in state companies, revealing corrupt goings on that triggered investigations, leading to a stock-price rally as investors assumed the problem would be fixed. The strategy ended with him being expelled as a 'national security threat'. Browder is not coy about ties to the opposition:

'Yeah, Navalny, I've known him for years. I taught him the ropes and introduced him to some people back in 2006–7. He's a man after my own heart. He's genuine in his absolute disgust for the criminals doing all this stealing. When he started out we spoke to him a few times. He said that he was directly inspired by our work, but whatever he's developed, he mostly achieved it himself . . . modelled on things we've done. But I make a point of not speaking to him anymore, so not to disrupt his meteoric rise.'

Navalny began to accrue a lot more contacts as his fame rose. In 2009, one of the board members of Alfa Bank, one of the country's largest financial holdings, decided to email Navalny. He had been watching him for a while and was very impressed. He could mobilize people. He was charismatic. He seemed the man for his times. 'I wrote to Navalny to say, "I'm working at one of the country's biggest financial holdings, focusing on corporate governance and anticorruption, I'm impressed by what you are doing and have a few suggestions to make,"' explains the same man who is now his closest advisor, the sharp and intense Vladimir Ashurkov. 'All my life I've been interested in politics, but not until I met Alexey did I see someone whom I thought could make a breakthrough. I had a very well paying, comfortable job, but I felt that the things that were happening to my country were getting out of control.'

Ashurkov was told by the country's then fourth richest man and his boss – Mikhail Friedman – to keep his activities secret. Together Navalny and Ashurkov began to design a new generation of online campaigning tools to mobilize Russia against corruption. His presence calmed people. Flanked by highly intelligent liberals, he looked less like a demagogue. 'Look, nobody was more surprised than I was that this rich guy is coming to my office, sitting in my office and working with me,' says Navalny. 'Nobody believes me but I have never met any oligarchs or any Kremlin people. Ever.' But nobody of course, did believe him.

As 2009 gave way to 2010, a team was beginning to form around Navalny. The country's most famous editor, Evgenia Albats, saw leadership potential in him. The country's most famous economist, Sergei Guriev, formerly close to Medvedev, started to advise him and arranged for him to do a World Fellowship at Yale University. One economist closely affiliated to the government even began boldly announcing to visiting foreign investors and analysts that he could be the post-Putin president. Their drift to such a troubling figure – 'a democrat who is not delighted by the liberals' – was an expression of the liberal establishment's desperation as it became clear that Medvedev was unable, or unwilling to fight for Medvedevism. Navalny was their danger and their rabble-rouser, who gave them tingles as he ranted so charismatically. And they loved him for it.

Their fascination with Navalny was influenced by the Moscow intelligentsia's belief that democracy had been a success in Eastern Europe as it was given a boost with a healthy dose of anti-Russian nationalism. It was widely believed that a shot of nationalism could reinvigorate the Russian democratic movement. In private the doyens that were becoming Navalny's elite supporters spoke disturbingly as if they thought they could 'control' him. Many saw his charisma as a vehicle they could direct. There was even a rumour that he could be a Kremlin project. Whatever his eventual ties to the authorities, his growing number of friends in high places showed how unhappy and amphibious – living official and opposition lives – a segment of the elite had become. One well-placed source claims it was Medvedev himself who decreed inside the Kremlin that Navalny could not be harmed.

Medvedev helped Navalny in other ways too. The Kremlin stand-in had his own anticorruption ambitions. Chief amongst them was his zeal to rid the bureaucracy of its traditional backward practice of non-public disclosures of its expenses. Medvedev's ambition to reform the system started creating loopholes for Navalny to humiliate it on a daily basis. This is how the opposition leader's 'Rospil' was born. The name is a pun on the Russian word for 'sawing off', as in 'sawing' a chunk out of a budget. Its technique was decidedly early 2010s. Rospil tied together three big trends: the rise in philanthropy, the boom in the Internet and growing civil activism. It worked like this: volunteers across the country would pore over officials' expenses, forced online by Medvedev, and alerted Rospil to suspected corruption. Donations would fund a small team of young Rospil lawyers who would then investigate them. This was a new kind of corruption fighting NGO – and a smash hit. Donations poured in – reaching over $270,000 and saving the Russian budget $1.3 billion.[44]

With Rospil going online in October 2010 there was now a small team working for Navalny. Rospil was an incredibly fashionable, though difficult job. This is because, for all Medvedev's fighting talk, corruption was rife. In 2010, the huge bribes in the education sector alone were biting into household budgets. It was estimated that a place at a good Moscow nursery school would demand between $500 and $5,000.[45] Entrance to a decent school could set you back between $1,000 and $50,000, whilst a place at a prestigious university between $5,000 and $20,000.[46] This was not the end of it. Good grades in your final exams cost a backhander of $20 to $500.[47] 'I'd just had enough, I couldn't take it anymore,' explained Lubov Sobol, a young lawyer working for Rospil. Yet his team had noticed something unnerving in the way Navalny was increasingly being deified. Just as Surkov in his tract 'the view from Utopia' had said that the 'idealization of the leader' would always be the case in the country, so something of a 'leader-saviour' cult was developing around Navalny.

Two team members told me: 'We get poems sent to us about Alexey, we get letters of joy, we got an invite for us all to come and live in a dacha for free all summer and of course lots of stuff that has nothing to do with corruption. For example it's very common for us to get letters like – "Help! My roof is leaking, I suspect corruption," – to be addressed to us.' His staff venerated him but also found him a character. 'Navalny is . . . an anger man,' confided Rospil's coordinator, but his colleague Lubov Sobol gushed: 'Alexey is the best boss in the world. He is the most democratic man in the world. He is the perfect boss.'

As the last days of doubt before Putin's announcement that he would be returning in 2012 drew near, Navalny was going viral. Within twelve months his blog started to hit over 100,000 readers, soaring to over 1.2 million monthly views and 200,000 followers on Twitter. Rospil was joined by Rosyama – a crowdsourced project that targeted bad roads, which picked up 30,000 online activists.[48] Focusing on these projects, eschewing arcane debates on whether Russia needed a parliamentary or a presidential republic, a constitutional preamble with or without mention of ethnic Russian rights, or any of the other abstractions that obsessed the opposition, demonstrated that Navalny had understood why his entire political career up to this point, along with that of the entire Russian opposition, had been such a flop. In his rush for concrete projects, he was stealing from Surkov the very slogan he had invented for United Russia – 'The Party of Real Deeds'.

A Hero of Our Time

But sometimes a phrase can be more powerful than an organization. All of this activism was crowned by one slogan: 'United Russia is the party of crooks and thieves'. There is an element of genius in this catchphrase. It has a ring to it, an irony to it. It is both funny and furious. It was an instant way of expressing Russia's frustration with the rent-seeking, oligarchic, oppressive system, without having to use those same clumsy words. To a certain extent the slogan had to have been evocative – because it went viral. Accidentally, it found the Achilles heel of Surkov's propaganda. They could successfully hide embezzlement in the Kremlin from the public, but not the fact that petty provincial officials were corrupt – whom they had all encouraged to join United Russia, thus associating their greed with Putin even in the remotest Russian village.

This is why by the eve of the Russian parliamentary elections in 2011 over ten times more people knew the slogan – 'the party of crooks and thieves' – than knew who Navalny was. Pollsters estimated that a majority of Russians had heard the phrase used. And so it was that the tag 'the party of crooks and thieves' stuck like glue to United Russia. These words by themselves – freely circulating, viral words – were one of the most powerful grenades thrown at the Putin consensus, the first words that ever wounded the Putin party.

Navalny had broken two Russian barriers – the sound barrier and the trust barrier. In a decade, which had begun with Putin imposing a 'videocracy', he had found a way to circumvent it and reach the Russians who were not supposed to know about him. In a decade, which had been marked by a bottomless cynicism and distrust of all politicians ('PR-shiks') he was taken at his word. No opposition politician had been trusted on his claims about accountings like this before. By April 2011 independent polls showed that 68 per cent considered Navalny's allegations about corruption reliable, rising to 88 per cent amongst Muscovites, 79 per cent amongst the wealthy and 76 per cent of young people. Navalny was becoming more than an opposition leader.[49] He was leaving Nemtsov, Milov and Chirikova behind – he was fast becoming a Russian hero.

Navalny became a hero because he was the young man in whom young Russians saw themselves. He was a hero of his time. He has depicted his enemies – corrupt officials – as the enemies of Russia whilst presenting himself as the defender of Russia against these 'bloodsuckers'. Navalny brought together in one personality all the virtues and vices of the genera tion that had become men under Putin. Navalny is his generation in his instinctive Caucasophobia, rumbling nationalism and aggressive streak that fired plastic pellets at a heckler outside a bar. Navalny is his generation in his selfless activism, witty blogging and anti-authoritarian willingness to debate an issue and lose a vote.

He summed up the paradoxical consequences of Putinism. The propaganda that the Kremlin's relentless PR machine had been feeding Russia had left it a much angrier and more Islamophobic country than Yeltsin left it. Yet that same Kremlin's overarching projects to build a 'United Russia state' with a tame television system had left the country far more anti-authoritarian and sure of its commitment to free speech and a fair vote than it had been in the 1990s. All of this comes together in Alexey Navalny, the democrat who breathed the independence of the Internet, but marched with fascists every year screaming 'stop feeding the Caucasus'. Playing to his Aryan looks he cuts the part of a leader and smiles in this self-mocking way that would have been such a hit in the Central Committee or Hollywood. But his is a weak, cold, handshake.

'Are you ever worried they are going to kill you?' I asked as we picked at a disappointing lunch deal at the Vietnamese cafe near his office.

'Look . . . I really, really hate this regime,' he replied, menacingly. The way he said it made me suddenly try to hold his gaze, but his eyes tipped slightly downwards, as if talking to someone other than just me.

'They are leading this country into a catastrophe. It is not the opposition that will make the country collapse. Putin will make the country fall
apart. But it's not like they will kill me tomorrow. There is a risk of course
. . . There is a risk they could do . . . but it's completely ridiculous to
compare me to those guys that were fighting apartheid. There is a constant
routine . . . they raided my flat, they hack my account, there are people
who follow me . . . you're speaking English . . . so "you're a spy". But . . .
here I am sitting in this cafe.'

Navalny's wife Yulia was not quite so calm. After he had given a presentation to a crowd of adoring and, thanks to him, worked-up students at the
New Economic School, one of them asked him that same question. And
she burst into inconsolable tears.[50] He was not going to stop:

'By coming back Putin has decided to turn Russia into an authoritarian
state like Belarus. He is pushing, a bit here, a bit there, to find out how far
he can go. And there is only one thing that can stop him. A gigantic protest,
or the West.'

CHAPTER NINE

THE DECEMBRISTS

THE KGB always thought Putin was flawed. Personnel training for Soviet foreign intelligence was onerous, pursued with a rigor and exactitude second only to that given to its cosmonauts. Agents were subjected to months of psychological tests, pulse measurements, head scans, role-plays and 'Western' life-simulations in its sealed academies, between bouts of form-filling and hours of language classes, broken up only by over-boiled institutional meals in its canteens, which sometimes were more or less the high point of the day. The agents would chatter about where they would all wind up – would it be London, Tokyo or West Berlin? Everyone wanted to be in a 'real foreign country' with blue-jeans and cassette-players, not in the empty-shelved Warsaw Pact or anywhere near 'socialist' consumer goods, which were of such pitiable quality during Putin's education that over 2,000 Soviet colour TVs were self-combusting in Moscow every year.[1]

But the agency, for now, just wanted to catalogue their weaknesses, because identifying flaws in others is the same as knowing exactly where you can make your incisions. Putin admits the KGB evaluated him as a stunted man. The instructors concluded he was at risk, but not in the slightest to succumbing to the temptations of women or drink, but due to a pervasive 'lowered sense of danger'.[2] He was also classified as a man unhelpfully unsocial, quite closed-off. This may explain why the KGB chose to place him in a second-tier East German city, not over the front line in the West, where a TV self-combusting was simply unheard of and a Soviet agent needed to be on his guard. A posting to Dresden can only have been a disappointment. Years later, Putin still only grudgingly half admits the agency's character assessment. 'I don't think that I had a lowered sense of danger, but the psychologists came to this conclusion having followed my behaviour for a long time.'[3]

But they were right. This same stunted sense of danger saw Putin misjudge the public mood and hostility present in Russia to his 2012 return to the Kremlin. No sooner had the announcement been made but disgruntlement, with a shadow of defiance, seemed to have seeped through the capital, to hang in the smoke-trailed air of the bars that Moscow's intelligentsia and moneyed elite had made their hang-outs. In these shallow places, where politics had been waved away during the boom years, snatches of political conversations began to be overheard, muffled by talk of emigration, London and frustration. For the denizens of Moscow's trendiest haunts, like the fashionable fake French bistro Jan-Jak, a different kind of blog was becoming more popular – the easy materialism of *Look At Me* was out and Navalny's page that said he was waging the 'final battle between good and neutrality' was in.[4]

'This repoliticization happened slowly, the way everyone used to wear Levis, but now everyone wants Diesel jeans. I think I was always talking about politics, but maybe even I wasn't,' pauses a friend and magazine editor in a Georgian restaurant with Dubai prices and a slick feel, such that even to call it a Georgian restaurant, the Russian equivalent of an Indian takeaway, seems somewhat misleading. 'But then it started to get stronger. It started with the financial crisis, which shook us up. At first a few at the table wanted to talk politics. Then more did. And without really noticing we were all talking about politics again.'

Celebrities, for whom guessing the public mood was necessary to stay in the public eye, began to flirt with a shallow, smirking, anti-Putinism. At one end, the beaten journalist and former sailor Oleg Kashin found himself turning into a celebrity. With a terrible spittle lisp, f-ing his way through his analysis, Kashin's line had once been as fringe as him. 'Whenever you get the hell out of Moscow, you know what they tell you? They say: "We are just a bloody Moscow colony." This whole place could just collapse in ten years or so,' mouthed off Kashin, at the same table, in the same Georgian restaurant. 'Russia could collapse all over again.' But Kashin was now being invited to give speeches, more or less like this, at the nightclub Bright Night, belonging to the grumpy oligarch Mikhail Friedman. They hit a nerve. Kashin had once been a nobody, and a reporter for a pro-Putin newspaper. The sourer the political chatter got, the more famous he became. At the other end of the spectrum, celebrities who wanted to stay the centre of attention began to snigger publicly at the Putinists.

Ksenia Sobchak was rightly called the 'Russian Paris Hilton'. She had posed topless for *Playboy*, she had worn big pink bows and been the daily bread of the editors of the city's celebrity press, but in a country whose superpowers include female looks, she was startlingly plain for an 'It girl'. Through the 2000s, she was one of those pointless half-loathed characters, famous for being famous. And in a Russia where connections count for everything, she had one of the best sets of all. She was the daughter of

Anatoly Sobchak – the first mayor of St Petersburg and former boss to Putin, thus former boss to a big chunk of the Putinist political elite. To see a video with Sobchak giggling was not a surprise, but to see one of her taking her camera phone towards the Nashi leader Vasily Yakemenko dining in a restaurant where champagne costs $46 a glass was. 'I'm an "It girl", but how can he afford that with a civil servant's salary?'[5] The Nashi commander squirms angrily. The video went viral. It meant only one thing – being vapid was no longer fashionable.

Like Sobchak, other celebrities and establishment figures began groaning at the sight of Putin after his announcement. The editorial line at the main financial daily *Vedomosti* (co-owned by the *Financial Times*) began to denounce 'stagnation'; the former Medvedev-inclined economist Sergei Guriev started to bemoan the government in its op-ed pages; formerly pliant TV anchors started complaining about censorship; even gallery owners, whose fortunes were amassed doing 'political technology' for United Russia, turned to tweeting snide remarks about the creatures in the Kremlin. All of it was very self-consciously elitist, neither expecting nor really requesting an echo from beyond the 'Garden' ring road that splits the Moscow of Dolce Gabbana bags from the Moscow of endless Soviet housing estates, Azeris hawking watermelons on street corners in the summer, and alleys smelling of alcoholic urine.

Russians took to calling the Putin–Medvedev swap the 'rokirovka' – or castling – a defensive chess manoeuvre where the king is swapped with the rook. If anything it was the inverse, a move that instead of switching the king into a secure corner of the board left him as an exposed centrepiece, visibly the fulcrum of the game. The 'castling' laid bare Russia's personalized power, its presidential tsarism. Putin's decision to close down Medvedev's 'modernization' candidacy without much explanation, or even why he had chosen to return to the Kremlin, stunned wealthier Muscovites. Lacking an explanation, the 'castling' seemed to be both gratuitous power-hunger, whilst also confirming the creeping chatter about stagnation or 'Brezhnevization' within the establishment and the emerging middle class. It demonstrated in one manoeuvre that politics, despite all the talk, despite the 1990s and the 2000s, was still a matter for a tiny power circle. By 'castling', Putin underlined that his KGB instructors had been prescient as well as accurate. The move revealed not only a lowered sense of danger, but a lowered sense of awareness of the extent to which the country had changed since Yeltsin asked him to 'take care of Russia'.[6]

Putin – like a Soviet secretary general – seemed set to rule at least until his constitutional term expired in 2024. This would make the rule of this lieutenant colonel the longest since that of Stalin. 'I'll remember the day

Putin announced his return for the rest of my life – 24 September 2011 –
because all my friends and I calculated how old we would be in 2024,' said
Leonid Volkov, an ambitious city councillor in Ekaterinburg, capital of the
Urals. He was not alone. Capturing the horror many felt at this prospect,
already living in a reality where in political conversations 'he' often did not
need to be named, for the listeners to cotton on who 'he' was, the poet
Dmitry Bykov wrote a pastiche on Mayakovsky's utopian ode 'Here will be
a Garden City', in which the ubiquity of Putin, 'a meek colonel from the
swamps of St Petersburg', is as oppressive as it is inescapable.

> As agile as a lover, he got himself inside our skulls.
> I am looking at the Lieutenant Colonel and I see that he is us,
> All we can do is drink ourselves blind,
> That is the only garden city we will find.[7]

The same dim resentment, the same extremely weak but pervasive sense of
dread could be felt in the outer tiers of the ruling elite. The day of the
tandem announcement, I exchanged a few emails with a friend in the
diplomatic service. He wrote back in one-liners – 'Chaadaev was right' –
referencing the pessimistic cultural critic that had exchanged letters on
Russian identity with Pushkin, coming to the terrible conclusion, 'alone in
the world, we have given nothing to the world' and 'that we exist only to
teach the world some terrible lesson'. I emailed back, asking what he
meant, but this time the reply was terser still: '1991'.

To some people this was no surprise. 'It was never a secret, this was the
plan from 2008,' said Sergey Kolesnikov, Putin's self-exiled former business partner in Tallinn. 'In 2008, every day I was talking to Kovalchuk and
Shamalov, and we discussed politics and this plan. And this is what was
known behind closed doors. In some parts of the state this was always
common knowledge.'

Though many claimed they had seen it coming, it was still a shock,
however much anticipated. Previously pliant members of the tamed
Kremlin parties, which, bereft of power and lost for content, had fallen
into patronage systems, were likewise unenthused by Putin's return. 'It was
when the castling happened that I realized I could no longer support the
regime,' says Ilya Ponomarev, the young MP with a complicated back-
story and friends in very high places, holding court in a pastry-specializing
grand cafe round the back of the Duma. Akademiya is the cafe of plotters,
Nashi-deputies, stooges and opposition activists alike – because for the
establishment, Moscow is a small place. 'Make sure you take the Napoleon
cake . . . this is their signature,' says Ilya Ponomarev. This deputy should
not be challenging the system – his mother works for Abramovich and is

the senator for the territory of Chukotka on the Bering Straits. Whilst we take down the Napoleon cake he gets in a fluster as he has forgotten his credit card, but this turns out to have been in the pocket of his plush sky-jacket all along. 'I'm often in London,' he grins. As the chairman of the Duma subcommittee on Innovations and Venture Capital and involved in representing Medvedev's science park Skolkovo abroad for lucrative busi-ness deals, he was nothing if not a winner. 'But when it was announced that Putin was returning I realized that there was not going to be any reform, that there was going to be stagnation, which is potentially catastrophic for the country. Before the "castling" I had not thought this way. The move closed off the prospect of the system genuinely evolving.'

A Change in Pressure

This frustration within the establishment at first appears hard to under-stand. In the abstract it touched on a fear of social ossification, personified by Putin. 'It's not a frustration with economic stagnation, for now the economy is quite all right,' explains the conservative thinker Boris Mezhuev:

'It's a specific kind of social stagnation. It's frustration with the sense that we live in a society where everything is treated as a resource – you become dean of philosophy just to exploit it for money, you become editor of a major newspaper just to exploit it for money – it's a frustration with a society where the only thing that counts is connections and resources and has nothing to do with merit. It is a fear that Russia is turning into an anti-meritocracy: a place where elite oligarchic monopolization represses those that have the capacity to rise.'

For young politicians like Ilya Ponomarev, FSB officers and aspiring oligarchs, this fear was very real. Putin had surrounded himself with people of a similar age and background. Putin's return meant that they would be staying in the same positions – perhaps until 2024. Those who knew them well said that in the security services this fear was particularly acute. Whether you were a young Duma deputy or a security officer, the 'vertical of loyalty' was whispered to mean you would remain middle-rank forever. A similar resentment at the very real gerontocracy of the Brezhnev era had pushed talented apparatchiks around Gorbachev.

In the weeks that dragged through a boring autumn leading into the campaign for the parliamentary elections, Russian journalists began twitching, as if smelling a gas that no one could see. Things had started to go amiss. It began with the mocking jokes – 'the man referred to as President Medvedev', or quips about Putin's seemingly strangely adjusted features: 'Mr Botox'. And then a flutter of seeming malfunctions in the social order:

an audience stood up to clap at a foreign movie screening about jailed Khodorkovsky, cars had begun honking at the long motorcades blocking traffic in the most congested major city in the world as Russia's leaders belted in black limousines back to their estates on the Rublevka; to the intense distress of a police officer, one man refused to move his car even though he was told 'Putin is passing'.[8] The glamour magazine *Afisha* was running increasingly political and biting front covers, while across town, United Russia posters were occasionally torn off the walls of housing estates.

Perhaps it was unsurprising as to why people were so disengaged. The party's leafleting – showing space rockets, fighter jets in formation, combine harvesters and overproducing factories – looked both eerily and irksomely Soviet. The bland slogans on leaflets pushed through letterboxes in Moscow, 'The Future For Us', made such little attempt to persuade voters, they reminded elderly residents of Soviet 'elections' – where only one candidate had been on the ballot. The corrosive effects of a lack of narrative began to undermine Putinist telepopulism. The Kremlin's main asset, the popularity of its front man, was no longer what it had been. Opinion polls began to tell a story of flagging enthusiasm. The number of people who trust Putin had fallen to 47 per cent in November 2011 from 69 per cent in 2009.[9] His personal approval ratings had slumped from 83 per cent after the Georgian war in 2008, to 61 per cent in November 2011.[10] They fell seven points after the announcement of his return that September. In a further poll breakdown only 26 per cent believed that Putin had adequately or successfully coped with Russia's problems and 50 per cent disapproved of the Russian government.[11] The discrepancy between 'trust' and 'approval' suggested that many were supporting Putin as they saw no alternative.

They say that all outbreaks of unrest take place to a backdrop of exhaustion, and are an unleashing of repressed agitation. It always begins with one event, one unpredictable twist that takes even those who wished for it by surprise. At the end of November 2011 it happened. They booed Putin. It was a mixed martial arts contest – 'struggle without rules' in Russian – and the beery crowd, swaying slightly, were the kind of people Putin thought were 'his people': lower middle class and interested in fights, the meat of the Putin majority. Stepping onto the stage he moved to congratulate the Russian wrestler who had slammed an American, whose tattoos in Russian Cyrillic for 'Freedom' seemed to have earned him little sympathy. 'A true Russian warrior,' Putin told the victor, as a whistle comes, then a brave, tentative boo from the safety of the dark stands under spinning spotlights, before an ascending orchestra of booing, first nervous, then a loud and gratuitous: 'Get out of here.'[12] Locked in a moment that to describe as 'awkward' would be more than an understatement, the 'warrior' with a dropping lower lip looks aghast at the once and future President.

The video went viral. In offices and on Facebook pages from Kaliningrad to Sakhalin, people were asking: 'Have you seen this yet?'

The martial arts fans had achieved something that opposition politicians had long failed to do: to make Putin look weak. The political atmospheric pressure was changing. Occasionally, in bars the perestroika anthem 'Changes' by the iconic Soviet rock band Kino was being played. It invoked what Russians refer to as the 'kitchen period', when collapse was only muttered about in private for risk of looking unhinged or somebody listening in. The lyrics go: 'In the kitchen like a blue flower, gas burns, cigarettes in our hands, tea on the table, so there this scheme is easy, there is nothing more left, it's all up to us.'

The song is about realizing you can revolt, but struggling to make it real. Though the 1980s and 1990s had been a chaotic and hungry time, there had been a sense of hope and not one of pervasive cynicism. Despite material gains, the despondency of the intelligentsia was asphyxiating in the run-up to the 2011 Duma elections. A kitchen period of a sort had emerged in Russia, but in a country awash with consumerism it was far trickier to exit from, a bit of booing none withstanding. Yet even fierce loyalists in United Russia, like the lawmaker Vladimir Burmatov, recognized that something had gone very much awry.

> The people simply did not understand the place of Putin in politics after his return. The people did not understand why the swap with Medvedev had happened. And as a party we felt we were the strongest, incontestable and we stopped speaking to certain sectors of society. In the elections that followed we lost them completely: the intelligentsia, the middle class and the young. Especially in Moscow.

The Electoral Detonation

They say it is always the authorities that provoke unrest, although they never do it consciously. When managed democracy had begun, it was done in the name of the elite and the middle class, whipped up into fearing the 'Bolshevik menace' of 1996, for people who craved stability in Putin, who wanted modernization in Medvedev. The winter 2011–12 election cycle was seen merely as parliamentary and presidential plebiscites to validate Putin's decision to return. This was not an 'engineered' outcome but an autocratic choice. It was not made in the name of elites and the middle class – like in 1996 – but in spite of them and against them. It was a decision that said Putin had become like a tsar, accountable to no one.

The December 2011 parliamentary election was supposed to have delivered a resounding victory for United Russia in order to pave the way for Putin's return in the March 2012 presidential vote. It was rigged in the following way. To begin with, parties that might have proved popular were not allowed to register and thus participate. Government-controlled TV relentlessly covered the activities of Putin as 'prime minister', giving him in his other capacity as chairman of United Russia a vast air-time bias in favour of the governing party. On the ground, several tactics were promoted to boost Kremlin votes. Many students in state dormitories across the country were informed that if they did not vote for United Russia they risked losing their accommodation. Similar encouragements were made to many state employees. At polling stations themselves a technique known as the 'carousel' was in full swing. Paid to vote for United Russia – usually cited at around $15 – crowds were shoved onto buses and then delivered from one polling station to another around their locality, voting for Putin's party again and again.

The team leaders of this fraud were usually state employees, especially teachers, who were offered 'bonuses' larger than several months' wages for this work. Anyone handing out leaflets for the party was paid to do so. Typically in Putin's 'elections' the 'Citizens Initiative', headed by none other than his former finance minister Alexey Kudrin, estimated that in big cities 5–10 per cent of votes were cast by 'controlled voters' and 5–10 per cent by 'payroll voters', or from manipulated lists of 'dead souls'.[13] Their research suggested that with 20–25 per cent of the population as 'controlled voters' a low turnaround could easily give the regime the 45–50 per cent it needed to claim victory.[14] The orchestrators of this were almost always in the governor's office, in which the occupants all knew that when United Russia had got only 35 per cent in the 2010 Tver regional elections, the regional chief 'responsible' had been fired. It was a warning shot to the rest.

There was no real alternative on the ballot paper itself. Voters found only parties that the Kremlin had permitted to register – tamed parties whose leadership was riddled with collaborators and whose chiefs were on Surkov's speed dial. The largest, Zyuganov's KPRF, Zhirinovsky's LDPR and Just Russia, chaired by Putin's St Petersburg ally Sergey Mironov, were all essentially state-sanctioned private nomenklaturas, not 'parties' in any meaningful sense of the word. However, those who only got their news from controlled national TV were supposed to have been duped into thinking they were the 'opposition'.

Inside the polling stations vote counts were then sent to the Central Election Commission, where they were often inflated, sometimes by two to three times. An indication of ballot-stuffing on an industrial scale was the statistical spread of the votes – whereas the other parties recorded a normal distribution of some low returns to some high returns in certain constituencies – Putin's party disproportionally scored high results.[15] Voter turnout also displayed a linear correlation to United Russia voting, pointing to massive ballot stuffing.[16] The results for voter turnout are studded with precincts reporting exact round numbers – from 80 per cent to 100 per cent, benefiting the Kremlin's deputies.[17] Voters in the military, asylums and prisons, or any other closed-off institution were all suspiciously fervent United Russia supporters. Shamelessly, one Moscow psychiatric hospital reported 99.5 per cent support for Putin's party.[18] On the ground this translated into a ridiculous situation where some neighbouring precincts – well documented from Moscow to Ural Magnitogorsk – would return United Russia votes at around 30 per cent and others at 80 per cent.[19] There were none in the middle. Out in the regions, especially in the non-Russian North Caucasus, the numbers had more in common with elections in a Middle Eastern dictatorship, with results of over 90 per cent for the party of power being returned.[20] It has been estimated by statisticians that as many as 14 million votes could have been stolen.[21]

A feeling of impunity had overtaken the vote-riggers. We can impose any result. We can decide on any number, regardless of what polling may say. The results came in at 49.3 per cent of the vote and 238 of 450 seats.[22] Yet analysts have estimated they could not have got more than 35 per cent of the vote.[23] And it is always when a feeling of impunity overtakes the elite that it enters into grave danger.

Under Putinism the elections were supposed to have been fully converted into 'plebiscites', ratifying a decision already taken, and richer Muscovites transformed into an 'offshore elite', frightened of the masses and living increasingly well, but in various forms of exile: virtual exile as Internet use boomed, internal exile in the small clubs for the 'dem-shiza', or democratic schizophrenics, or in physical exile in London or the Côte d'Azur. In the run-up to the December 2011 parliamentary elections, nobody expected mass protests or that their detonator would be the Russian constitution and an Anglophone dandy working at a management consultancy.

Ilya Faybisovich is exactly the kind of person Putin expected to shut up. Wearing carefully selected tweeds and thick-rimmed glasses popular in Dalston, formerly in London for seven years and working for a global American consultancy, he blends into a generational style of Muscovites in their twenties and early thirties usually labelled 'the hipsters'. This is the kind of person who may be what is dubbed 'an office plankton', but yet dresses immaculately as if for a night out in Shoreditch rather than commuting on the crammed Moscow underground. The city's 'hipsters' come across as self-consciously globalized and at ease with the West, so different from the post-Soviet wounded in much of the country. With a kind of avidity and intensity in fashion that makes up a youth culture, which their 'Soviet' parents cannot understand, the 'hipsters' were not expected to have a sense of politics. And if they did it was late-night bar chat. Mr Faybisovich, more or less, had shut up. He had been blogging 'all about London'. He remembers: 'There is no clear explanation about why what was about to happen, actually happened, but there was real rage at the election results as they came in.'

And the numbers that came in were painful to the ear. In Moscow one exit poll, later withdrawn for 'inaccuracy', gave United Russia 27 per cent of the vote but this had jumped to 46.5 per cent of the vote when the Central Elections Commission made its announcement.[24] Faybisovich explains:

'I had registered to be an election observer and gone to my local precinct. I'm not a communist at all, but had registered to observe the vote counting as one of them. So . . . I turned up at the polling station and they denied me access. They were nervous, scared and clearly implicated. I was accused of "bias", shown the door – thus ending my short career as an election monitor.'

Faybisovich, angered at being chucked out and with United Russia's 'obviously fake poll results' ringing in his ears, grumpily went to the Moscow non-fiction book fair. 'It was then I realized that I had to do something. I started sending out a message, a stream of consciousness really to around 120 friends, saying we had to do something.' It was then that he stumbled upon the fact that one of the fringe opposition parties, that had long struggled to make an impact, was holding on to a protest permit in central Moscow. 'They are a bit older than us, the kind of guys that though they knew Facebook exists, they didn't really know it exists because they didn't know how to really use it to promote things. Their page had hardly anybody going to it. I said, "Let me do some PR for it," and I became admin for the protest page.' The next day RSVPs had gone from 180 to 2,700. Calling friends, sending personal messages, writing on walls, the rally that could have been yet another empty occasion was gathering traction. They managed to secure the independent radio station Ekho Moskvy into pitching in some support too – and over 5,000 people turned out.

'When I saw how many people had turned up at Clean Ponds for the rally' – the small pool where in the 1990s the police turned a blind eye to the boozers, punk-rockers, skinheads and all-day outdoor drinkers – 'I just felt relieved,' recalls Faybisovich. Two days of online activism had turned a non-event into a protest. But not quite a political protest. With make-shift placards against the 'party of crooks and thieves', printed with the

United Russia bear angrily lugging a giant sack of money out of the map of Russia, those present were making a moral point, not supporting a particular person. Spontaneous, slightly shocked at its own attendance, the gathering at Clean Ponds was as fascinated by itself than those on stage.

The protest needed a hero and it found it in Navalny. His slogans were the ones they chanted, his ideas were the ones they talked about. It was a spontaneous protest: these were not his people, but they looked to him with fascination, as something just short of their leader. The rise in discontent, the exasperation with the old opposition, had turned his into a household name in Moscow in 2011. They called him a phenomenon. Shouting into the snow, he was yelling, 'They call us "micro-bloggers" and "network hamsters" – I am a hamster and I will gnaw through the throats of this cattle.'

That somebody unknown could organize this rally, said two things. First, there was a huge desire for somebody, anybody, to do something. Second, that yet again, the old establishment opposition of Nemtsov, Milov and Yavlinsky were missing in action. Faybisovich, the unlikely Facebook spark, thinks that three things brought people together that evening:

'It's a simple thing really. Before there were not enough people who had enough to eat to care about where the country was going, but now there are enough people who have enough to eat to care about what kind of country their children will live in. You throw in the fact during the 2007 elections that we had no smartphones, now all kinds of electoral violations are recorded and spread over the Internet and then finally the slogan – the campaign from Navalny branding United Russia the "party of crooks and thieves".'

Clean Ponds was instantly dubbed the 'rally of the ruined shoes' because under 5,000 pairs of feet, the snow had given way into liquid mud. But the name also said something about the kind of shoes these people were wearing. It was rather the 'rally of the ruined expensive shoes'. Those there were pleased to see that it was a rally of the 'right sort'. Over 80 per cent had some sort of post-secondary-school education, compared to just 30 per cent of Russians at large.[25] There was also a faint echo of the Decembrists, the failed 1825 elite uprising of St Petersburg's finest aristocratic officers who, having experienced the West during the Napoleonic wars, wanted a constitution. That night in December was a demonstration from inside the Schengen visa-holding Moscow elite, but unlike the tsar's officers they were far from the point of picking up their muskets. This was a protest to say 'we exist', not 'we want power'.

Then it seemed it had all gone wrong – with arrests and the Moscow riot police wielding batons, grabbing Navalny into custody as he pulled back shouting, 'all for one, and one for all'.

The police had not quite jumped the protests. Navalny and his friend, the opposition activist Ilya Yashin, well-known for stunts including anti-Putin bungee jumps off Moscow bridges, decided to walk to the Lubyanka, the KGB turned FSB headquarters. 'Why?' groans one organizer, 'Because they wanted to feel shivers run down their spines.' This was not in the permit and the organs reacted clumsily, arresting over 1,000 people, not realizing they were scoring an own goal. 'It helped us massively, but I do not feel guilty about this as their police brutality is what they have been doing every day for years,' grins Faybisovich. Police, brutality ignited a protest movement out of the Facebook-fuelled gathering. The mood combusted out of a mix of elation and surprise in Moscow's small world of 'the right sort', overjoyed to have found itself on the streets, sparked by their outrage at the castling and industrial ballot stuffing.

'Looking back I don't think we made any mistakes in the winter wave. It was so spontaneous. It was completely grassroots, totally chaotic and spontaneous, it was real . . .' smiles Navalny. 'But I am certain I did one thing right. It was absolutely the right thing to go and be so aggressive that night with my speech about the "killer hamster".' He smiles to himself, as if about to giggle at the words 'killer hamster'. 'It was absolutely the right thing to do to go on the illegal march.' Navalny says that thrown into custody and cut off, he had no idea what was happening outside. 'In prison we heard that things were getting exciting outside. And we were thinking, 'Oh, it would be so cool if 10,000 people came to the next protests. Oh, we thought it would be incredibly cool if 15,000 people came to the next protest. We were sitting in prison and just had no idea.'

Over the next few weeks a wave of elation tore up the Putin consensus in the Moscow bourgeoisie. There was a raw gas in the air of the cafes – that left those who breathed it in dizzy, then giddy, with the sensation that their energy was mounting, that it would simply prevail, that they were winning. The activists who had thrown together the rally at Clean Ponds threw themselves into a Facebook feed about further protests. By one big stroke of luck, the hard-left skinhead activist Sergey Udaltsov was holding on to a permit for a protest on 10 December. All they needed now was permission from the authorities to carry it off and enough people to turn up. What became known as the 'Orgkomitet' began to take shape. Senior editors at the glamour magazine *Afisha* came on board, joined by celebrity reporter Oleg Kashin and the well-known publisher Sergey Parkhomenko, who is Faybisovich's stepfather, and other bloggers and 'men-about-town'. Together with the activists from the old, 'political', opposition they began negotiating with Moscow city hall and publicizing the gathering. With RSVPs hitting over 20,000, big-name celebrities started to come on board:

from the singer Yury Sevchuk to the TV personality Leonid Parfyonov and the writer Boris Akunin. Parfyonov says he felt he had no choice: 'I decided I had to be there, when Akunin phoned me. He said, "We just have to go. The people who are protesting are our audiences, our auditorium. We have to be there for them."'

All those writers, hipsters and TV presenters previously uninvolved in politics were rushing to make suggestions to the 'Orgkomitet', urging people to come out to shout Navalny's slogans because they felt sure the 'old opposition' was feckless enough to let the moment slip with its ugly 1990s faces who would inspire no one to show up. The tense, last-minute negotiations with the Town Hall and the deputy Kremlin chief of staff to get the final go-ahead for the rally, and the Facebook groups to get people out, were not only about clean elections. It was a revolt against the old opposition – and with it the birth of a new opposition.

Across town Boris Nemtsov had been taken by surprise by the lead-up to 'Clean Ponds', but he was sure that a generational change was under way. The former deputy prime minister who most Russians associate with the liberal cabinet during the 1998 default, told me he was sure that the younger generation were now immune to Putin's endless refrain – 'Without us we'll be back in the 1990s'. As he said this, he turned to the blonde beside him: 'My girlfriend is born in 1990 . . . she does not know what is Yeltsin . . . she thinks that Yeltsin – is me!'

We Went to the Swamp

Despite announcements from the police they would be 'looking for draft dodgers' at any protests, official health warnings that the mass gathering could trigger a SARS outbreak, sudden orders that the planned protest day was a compulsory school test for all city students, and cries for Internet censorship inside the 'organs', the authorities relented – the rally could go ahead at 'Bolotnaya', or 'the swamp', a thin strip of land between the Moscow river consisting of a walkway and a small park, home to thirteen ghoulish bronze statues called 'Children are the Victims of Adult Vices: sadism, theft, ignorance, violence . . .'

Over 60,000 people went to 'the swamp' that day. An appalling sound-system meant that no one could hear the stage, but that hardly mattered. Mikhail Fishman, a prominent anti-Kremlin journalist, who had once been filmed in a compromising situation in what was believed to be a government sting, waved away suggestions that the emerging protest movement was badly organized: 'the organization, the politics the programme didn't matter that day, what mattered was the crowds who were looking into each others' eyes, and seeing they were there.'

There was mild euphoria, with shouts of 'clean elections', 're-elections' or 'down with Surkovian Propaganda'. The Kremlin control of TV was suddenly relaxed and the rally was allowed to be covered, impartially, on national TV. Some claim that the costs of the rally were covered by dissenting MPs from the formerly tightly Kremlin-controlled Just Russia party, others pointed to the complete incoherence of those on the stage – from one man shouting for the restoration of 'Soviet power', to an angry nationalist being heckled – but it was the TV superstar Leonid Parfyonov who stole the show.

'I was shaking,' Parfyonov told me. 'I had been waiting ages and I was incredibly cold. I had never given this kind of speech before, to a rally and I certainly had never spoken in the street before. I climbed onto the podium and I suddenly saw hands raise – each with an iPhone, each hand with hundreds and hundreds of dollars in their fists – and I instantly saw exactly what kind of people had come to the swamp.'

His nerves did not show. With a clear, rising tone, instantly recognizable and trustworthy to any Russian TV viewer, he told 'the swamp':

'I've spent roughly half my life in my motherland, in the Vologda region, and half my life living in Moscow, and I can quite easily imagine the moods of these two regions. In the Vologda region United Russia received 33 per cent of the vote. Although this place is quite conservative and reliable, "Vologda guards do not like to joke", and so on, this figure in general does not surprise me: one-third of the country boys for Soviet power, not more. And the governor of Vologda Pozgalev, yesterday, after a meeting with Vladislav Surkov, could honestly tell the press, "We had an honest election." What could I do? But 50 per cent for United Russia in Moscow, this is utterly hard to believe. Vologda region is now for the first time more liberal than Moscow? It is not unlikely, it is just ridiculous.'[26]

This sense of the insult to Moscow, the insult to intelligent, liberal, clear-thinking people who cared about their votes as well as their cars, resonated out across 'the swamp'. The official presidential twitter feed had re-tweeted the following: 'It has become clear that if a person writes the expression "party of crooks and thieves" in their blog then they are a stupid sheep getting fucked in the mouth :).'[27] On television Putin himself sneered at 'the swamp'. Asked what he was doing during the protests he replied, 'I was learning how to play ice-hockey,' adding that he thought the white-ribbons the crowds had starting pinning to their clothes as their symbol reminded him of 'contraceptives' – pale limp condoms.[28]

As activists threw themselves into a new round of protest planning it was becoming clear that Putin, with such comments, was not in control of events. It was also very clear which personalities he had lost. The glamorous elite of journalists and personalities like Parfyonov – who a few years ago had said, 'my job is to report, not climb the barricades' – had turned on Putin. The new dominant pole in the Russian chattering classes was now what you could call 'champagne anti-Putinism'.

It was far harder to pin down who exactly were the 'masses in the swamp'. Moscow struggled to put a name to them – 'creative classes' was too exclusive and classist and 'new middle class' was too narrow a term that didn't capture the ranks of students, state employees, elderly or just simply 'lower middle class' that turned up. A large but broadly aspirational section of the population had broken off from the Putin majority. One poll suggested 70 per cent considered themselves 'well off', reading the news online, in a city where only half feel 'well off' and in a country where around a quarter do.[29] This was the 'insulted minority'.

In Moscow, their semi-revolutionary sentiment that winter may have, at times, even been dominant. What was so frightening about the rallies was constant chants of the slogan: 'Russia has no future.' The protests were the beginning of the rejection of the 'Stability First' national ethos driving politics since the default. 'Stability' had come for the Moscow middle class to mean stagnation – and the eclipse of the future.

In the bohemian club Masterskaya, with its stage, wooden tables and old-fashioned lampshades, I have watched an open mike and photo-slideshow on 'tell us about your Soviet childhood', overheard dull conversations about Moleskines and apps, listened to the Israeli novelist Etgar Keret describe Moscow as a 'sexy kind of hell', but before the protest movement I had never seen politics there. Not the stage filled with girls exhorting you to join their 'anti-Putin metro flash-mob', opposition activists explaining that '@wakeupru' was their twitter feed and explaining the entry and exit points to the planned mass demonstration on 24 December. Everyone was so excited, even sharp minds such as Maxim Trudolyubov, the opinion-page editor of *Vedomosti*, Russia's leading broadsheet. 'It was,' he said, 'like in 1991 when the atmosphere . . . was the *exultation* of the nation. December 2011 was that . . . in miniature.'

This was mania. Bound up with a sudden sense of release after years of Putin and the delirious lives these young activists and opposition leaders were leading – mixing in all the alcohol, the late nights, the snow and the adrenaline rush of new technology. Later, I learnt that this behaviour was not real political enthusiasm, but similar to the '1968 revolution', that everyone was 'enjoying so much', rejecting De Gaulle and his stuffy slightly authoritarian leadership in France over forty years ago. Once the Moscow 'spring' was all over, I told the '68 student leader Daniel Cohn-Bendit about this buoyant atmosphere. He smiled: 'Revolutions where people seize the Winter Palace are now impossible, an illusion . . . the only kind of revolution possible now has to be a moment that changes values.'

On the metro – with the girls in the flash mob – as the North Caucasians pushed by in their uniform black leather jackets and the police in crash helmets looked on, we boarded the metro carriage. Stations may be marble, with colonnades, chandeliers of Siberian crystals or bronze-works of Socialist workers but the carriages are always the inverse, yellow lighting, cramped, Soviet 1970s, careering down tunnels with an aircraft-like roar that obscures the tinned woman's voice asking you to 'mind the closing doors'. Between the central stations the flash mob covered their mouths in stickers – 'They stole our voice', which is the same word as for 'vote' in Russian – and stickered the windows with exhortations to come to the mass protest on Sakharova – leaflets showing Putin's face in a crossed-through red circle. Moving from one carriage to the next, with police coming after us in their tundra-blue uniforms, a friend said: 'I now realize how absurd this is, that you can be arrested for anything, and that they are chasing stupid anti-Putin kids when they should be doing something about criminals.' We got on another train, but for a while we were too nervous, without the flash mob, or for that matter of the police, to slap up the stickers. My friend croaks: 'OK, yes I will slap it up then, I don't want to be afraid.'

Less than three metro stops from the bohemian idealism of Masterskaya, where the previous day an overexcited radio host had told me he could be the 'next' foreign minister, the city was neither completely free, nor completely afraid. Most people were deeply uncertain. It was unclear in the arguments I had with friends that lived at stations beyond the Garden Ring, but also in most Russians minds, what was more frightening – stagnation or a revolution. Long-suppressed arguments had come to the surface. About the Soviet collapse, about the Americans, about the Chechens, about whether Russia was even worth saving. People began discussing if the regime might actually fall.

Prospect Sakharova – an auspicious name for a venue hosting a mass rally on 24 December 2011 – is so called after the nuclear physicist, who had watched Soviet hydrogen bombs explode like giant red balloons on the steppes of Kazakhstan, then mutated into a dissident and moral sage whom the intelligentsia rallied around during perestroika. Prospect Sakharova – the place where Nashi came to trample, rally, shout out 'Putin, Putin' and drum their trademark drums. Those who came out of the metro station came out with a gulp in their throats. The enormity of the crowd, its fur coats, ski jackets, craning its neck to see the stage, wide-eyed and legs sunk on the sidewalk into the dirty, pollution-singed piles of snow they call 'porridge', seemed frightened of its own size. A crowd large enough to lose mobile coverage in, to lose friends in, or children. Right ahead were anarchists putting on balaclavas, a gang waving a banner inscribed with 'all power to the Soviets', some girls in pink lipstick with a cardboard placard 'Yes We Can Too', racist football hooligans waving the Romanov flag, the yellow-black-white of the nationalists, a small cluster shouting 'Bring back the tsar'.

'Oh my God,' winced a nuclear technician, 'I have come to a rally with, 'Bring back the tsar? Bring back Soviet power? So what is it – after Putin – the deluge? This is too populist . . .'

Maybe not quite: over 100,000 people came to stand on Prospect Sakharova that day, the temperature a few degrees below zero.[30] Many more came to take a look, then left. Out came those who had broken off the Putin majority. Countless thousands had meandered in and out during the long afternoon rally. Though the flags of the nationalists, the communists, the hard-leftists and the other parties of cranks and fools together were about even with the orange and green banners of the democrats, most of those who came were ordinary Muscovites who had come to make a moral point. A lot of interest was being paid to the 'make your own poster' tent and the 'free protesters tea' stand. The politicians were wooing them, not the other way round. It was a carnival of political naivety. Faybisovich, worried about nationalists at the front, put it this way: 'This is what happens when you don't have politics for ten years.'

Those clusters of flag-wavers and leafleteers were a parade of the politicized, upon whom the sleeping pills named 'Zyuganov' and 'Zhirinovsky' had worn off. This agitation was a sign that the hegemony of the Kremlin's two tame parties, the KPRF and the LDPR, was slowly wearing off on the Left and the Right. The most popular leftists were the 'Left Front', who scrawled '1917–2017 COMING SOON' on the side of railway tracks, wore leather jackets and flew the red star. They worshipped their leader, Sergey Udaltsov, the skinhead great-grandson of a Bolshevik general, who in shades and leather had the punk look, they crowed, 'of a guy who really knows what its like inside prison.'

Their guys mostly came from the industrial towns around Moscow and in the Urals, gang-like brotherhoods that held 'study sessions' with Marxist thinkers and staged rallies, where they rattled chains at policemen, started fights and on the ground were indistinguishable from the KRPF youth, whom in Ekaterinburg I found completely out of control and dreaming of the day Udaltsov would seize the party – 'So we can smash OMON!' Their policies included shutting down the stock exchange and their banners read '1991 – Never Again.' This was their protest too.

The Romanov flag was flying, the shouts of 'Russians, onwards' as they marched holding it before them, waving it above them, announced the nationalists. These were men shouting 'Russia for Russians', young men whose fathers could have been tempted into voting for Zhirinovsky the populist – 'because he tells the truth'. These were men led by the likes of Vladimir Tor, who believes all illegal immigrants should be deported, that Chechnya should lose its autonomy and be subject to direct rule and that the 'Russian state should work for the Russian ethnos'. As he told me all of this he snapped – 'I love the mosaics of Samarkand, but in Samarkand . . . we cannot have these 15 million migrants in the country that belongs to *my* children. I love my children!' Those shouting 'Russia, Russia' on the square were those that Putin could no longer fool with patriotic tough-talk: for all his nationalist posturing, it was hard to argue with Tor when he said, 'this clique rules not in the interest of Russians, but in its own inter-ests' or that 'they have done nothing to stop this tidal wave of Muslim immigrants, because we don't even have a visa regime with Central Asia.'

That day there were protests of over a thousand people in St Petersburg, Perm, Samara, Kazan, Ekaterinburg and Novosibirsk – but Moscow to Russia is like Paris to France, and this was the only protest that mattered. From the back of the stage, watching as first Boris Nemtsov spoke and was booed, waiting for his turn to speak Navalny could have been forgiven for feeling vindicated – the idea he had tried and failed with NAROD – was coming together right in front of his eyes. There was indeed a huge constituency out there against Putin, but it was heavily made up of nation-alist and leftists that the democrats needed to compromise and unite with. Only 60 per cent of the protesters considered themselves 'liberal'.[31] These were the slogans on Sakharova that day:

> 'Down with the party of crooks and thieves'.
> 'Don't forgive, don't forget'.
> 'Russia has no future'.
> 'Russia will be free'.
> 'All for one, one for all'.
> 'Putin – Thief!'

There was no euphoria in this crowd, but a serious sentiment, mixed with concerns and resignations. It was then that Navalny came to the stage. His performance, mesmerizing and at times shrieking, for a moment held the crowd. Everyone but him had been booed by some of those present. This was the moment he became beyond doubt, the opposition's pre-eminent leader. But on stage Navalny himself was in a huge panic. 'I climbed onto the stage and I . . . it was really cool actually, there were so many people, I had never seen so many people in my whole life. And then as I grabbed the microphone I realized that I had forgotten everything I was going to say . . . there were no words there . . .' He sighs and looks at his shoes. 'Out came these strange words':

'I read a thin little book. It's called the *Constitution of the Russian Federation*. And it is clear that the only source of power is the people of Russia. So that is why I do not want to listen to people who say we should now appeal to the government. Who is power? We are the power here.'[32]

Navalny, pulling himself back slightly, moves into a softer cadence before shouting out:

'Do we want their blue-bucket lights on our cars? Do we want their privileges? Do we want to drink oil? I see enough people to take the Kremlin and the White House right now. But we are peaceful people – we do not do this. But if these crooks and thieves continue to deceive us, continue to lie and steal from us, we will take back what is rightly ours.'[33]

As Navalny spoke, 100,000 people wondered if they were watching a revolution in Russia and asked themselves, their breath turning to a vapour in the cold air, if Putin's career could be measured in years or months. But with the right pair of eyes, looking over the crowds and the Romanov flags, to Navalny clutching the microphone with bulging pupils, you could see his speech was the point where the wave broke and began to roll back. It hit a wall inside Russians minds, because this is still a cautious country. The meaning of Sakharova was not revolutionary – because most Russians did not want a revolution, they wanted change but not at any price. The protests reflected both how much Russia had changed under Putinism but also how it was still a scarred country, not at ease with itself. After the rally Navalny clicked play on the video: 'Afterwards I watched that speech online and I thought . . . "Oh my God what a bullshit."'

Anti-Orange

Three days later Vladislav Surkov found himself demoted. 'Stabilization had devoured its children,' he snarled on the radio, before letting out a sudden laugh. 'I am too odious for this brave new world.'[34] Surkov was reassigned to a ministerial portfolio. 'We are already in the future,' he remarked, 'and the future is not calm.' He said he would no longer play domestic politics. Out amongst the protesters his new brief as minister for modernization projects was mockingly referred to as the 'minister for nothing'.

Cutting the cords from the puppet master was not the end of the show. It set the stage for a huge and hateful firework display of political ventriloquism to keep Putin in power and jump the hurdle of the March 2012 presidential election. The first act was designed to distract the opposition and give the illusion of concessions to those out on the streets. The lead role was taken by Dmitry Medvedev who, in tones of concern and aghast expressions, proposed a package of reforms that at first glance appeared to be concessions: the return of gubernatorial elections, easing party registration, meetings with senior editors and selected protest leaders. But not Navalny. Medvedev began parroting protest slogans and encouraging his subordinates to do the same. At first these declarations were greeted excitedly, until it transpired that a 'presidential filter' would apply to gubernatorial elections and the eased party registration had seen a rush of obvious Kremlin clones like the Party of Beer Lovers.

This was a distracting flare from the main propaganda effort; the main stage would be the most emotive high point in Moscow, the Poklonnaya Hill. The name means loosely 'the kneeling hill', the place of submission, where Napoleon had waited in vain after the battle of Borodino for the Kremlin keys to be handed to him. It is today home to the gigantic dome of the victory park, the memorial to the 1941–5 war, the site of the eternal flame and the tomb of the Unknown Soldier. It is not a place to desecrate, this is a place emotively visited by that now frail generation in their final years.

Here the 'anti-Orange' protest took place. To demonstrate to those in the swamp that whatever they could muster, they could muster more, an estimated 125,000 people were brought to Poklonnaya on 4 February 2012. From a stage emblazoned with the slogans 'Meeting of Patriotic Strength', and 'Russia Forever', the crowd was told that the opposition would hand the keys of Russia's nuclear weapons to the United States. The agitators bellowed and frothed at the mouth. The speakers of the 'anti-Orange committee' tried to scratch every Russian scar in the crowd until it drew blood. The 'Anti-Orange Appeal' announced:

'When I look at the leaders of the Orange zone, I find in them the demons and the devils of the 1990s that ruined my country and plagued the great productive power of the Soviet Union, brought the Americans to our secret centres and allowed them to make off with piles of secret documents . . .

'Another of its features – this blatant social arrogance. In fact – we can call it the social racism of the current leaders of the street. This is the revolution of the rich, the revolution of mink-wearing revolutionaries in dialogue with the mink-wearing liberal revolutionaries inside the Kremlin over the heads of the people, in total disregard for the people [. . .]

'The third feature of the Orange street, that has appeared in all Orange revolutions – is the willingness to be led. These Orange revolutionaries are not national leaders. The people may think they are real revolutionaries, not Orange – but the master of their minds is the West – the United States and NATO.'[35]

This kind of visceral state-sanctioned anti-Western propaganda was more reminiscent of Tehran than Moscow, a decade earlier. Yet this crowd was mostly made up of men and women forced to be there. Many were state employees who had been given 'bonuses' to head out there, many were migrant workers who could not speak Russian, many were bused in from factories in the provinces to make up the numbers.

To fake the imminent March 2012 presidential elections, the Kremlin needed to fake a protest movement. To fake legitimacy, the $12 billion oligarch Mikhail Prokhorov was encouraged by the Kremlin as a liberal 'vote catcher'. His policies, as Greece teetered on the edge of default, included 'joining the Eurozone'.[36] This is because his purpose was not liberalism, but to look daft enough to enable Putin to win.

They had also stopped pretending everything was all right. There was no more dreaming with BRICs. One afternoon I went to see the Nashi MP Robert Shlegel for coffee. He was tense:

'This country is not turning into a dictatorship! I was born in Turkmenistan; I know perfectly know what a dictatorship is ... And I know better than anyone how dysfunctional, how incapable, how appallingly badly run this system is, which is why I am fighting every day inside the party to make it better ... I never believed the 'Orange threat' when I joined Nashi in the first place ... but now, it's real. Those people – Navalny and his friends – they are real revolutionaries, who will wreck this country.'

Putinism had become tautological, its means and ends had become identical. Unable to offer any positive vision for the country, any project to justify Putin to 2018, the propaganda had fallen back on 'stability'. Russia needed to vote for 'stability' to preserve 'stability'. Unable to conjure up an imagined future, it fell back on invoking half-imagined horrors from the past. It cast support for Putin not as something positive, in the name of an agenda, but as something negative, against 'chaos', 'the Orange Revolution' or 'NATO'.

Russia is a wounded nation. From the moment Navalny had shouted out at the crowd 'there are enough of us here to seize the Kremlin and the White House right now', the protests began to get smaller and smaller and Putin gathered greater and greater numbers of 'protesters' to his own 'rallies'. Playing on fears and trying to rub wounds with salty fingers, whilst pretending to bandage them, the Kremlin's propaganda went into overdrive. Videos circulated warning that without Putin the country would simply collapse.[37] The Chinese would take Siberia, NATO would enter Kaliningrad, the Internet would be cut off, Navalny would be awarded the Nobel peace prize and hyperinflation would return in a 1990s redux.[38] State TV incessantly suggested that the Americans were funding the rallies, Putin said Hillary Clinton was paying for them – 'the Orange Revolution' was coming. Those close to the Kremlin felt satisfied by

February. 'The protest wave has peaked,' said Gleb Pavlovsky, attending one inconspicuously in a thick hat.

A revolution scare went through the population. Little-known voices on the blogosphere put it better than any politician. From Kazan one young woman, a United Russia activist, if a surprisingly eloquent one, wrote about her horrible feelings of history repeating itself. It was hardly a tone of hope:

> Of course the collapse of the Soviet Union was a complete shock to them. A large family in which the cities of Minsk, Riga, Kerch, Frunze and Moscow were suddenly divided by international borders and suddenly the phrase 'rights of the Russian speaking population' entered into their lexicon. Then the research institutes, where mom and dad worked, stopped paying wages. That's all, but mom and dad still went to work every day, hoping that their salary was about to be paid. I was small and I did not understand. Then I grew up and I thought this would never be permitted to happen to me and that we had found our place in the new reality. I had not become a millionaire – but I had not slipped into poverty. But more importantly, in contrast to the generation of my parents, who were dissatisfied, who watched in silence during the looting and destruction of the country, I thought my generation would never allow it – never. I was 13, 15 and 17 and I thought I knew everything, but actually I didn't understand. Now I'm 27, almost 30. And I was horrified to realize that I cannot do anything. And my generation, pushing its completely valid claims, printing out slogans on A4 pieces of paper – without any irony – means my country is getting closer to the abyss. Now, at the rally for 'Clean Elections' in Kazan, my Russian friends have come face to face again with those weird-looking guys, shouting separatist slogans on the stage and speaking about the special status of the Tatar language . . . I am taking the most valuable thing and trying to escape – just like my relatives when Soviet Frunze became Kyrgyz Bishkek.[39]

Andrei Zorin, an eminent Russian cultural historian from the University of Oxford, avoided the protests. That December he came to Moscow and felt ill at ease looking at the leaders of the opposition movement and the young anti-Putin journalists organizing the protests, the talented circle behind *Bolshoi Gorod*, Dozhd and *Afisha*. He personally taught half of them before he emigrated:

> I didn't go to Bolotnaya. I have this feeling that the situation is actually extremely grave. I don't think this pleasant joking manner

with everyone going to the protests to enjoy them is right. There need to be specific political goals. There need to be specific measurements of the risks, evaluated against those goals. I don't think that any of them properly realize that this may end in blood sooner or later. One can even argue – it will be OK, that it would be revolution – but I do not sincerely think this is what they believe in. If you ask any of them if Putin's Russia is really worth giving your life for just to get rid of it – I am not sure any of them would say 'yes'. It's like a game and it's one that is separating them from the fears of the rest of the country . . . But I am an old man, and I should not say that the creative, modern youth are flawed.

The newborn protest movement was unable to answer these questions. It was not ready to run into the Kremlin, as it could barely walk. Without structure, without a policy platform, it was not resistance ready to break through the OMON to force a recount – it was the very beginning of resistance to Putin. In Moscow, around 50,000 people showed themselves ready to come out every few weeks until summer 2012. Yet even if the protest leaders kept the pressure up with street parades, human chains and escalating Internet activism it could not really answer six simple questions:

1 Who appointed you as the opposition?
2 What have you got to say to people who are not Muscovites?
3 What would you do if you took power?
4 Who exactly is your leader?
5 What exactly do you believe in?
6 What policies to do you have to fix a broken state?

Without a clear answer to these questions, in a country where the oldest voters were born under Stalin and the youngest under Yeltsin, even the protesters themselves did not want a revolution. They did not want to seize the Kremlin; they wanted managed democracy to evolve into democracy. Even those on the streets were frightened at what mass violence or confrontations with the police might bring. At many protests, right at the back of the crowds, sometimes wearing a hat just to make sure he was fully disguised, was Dmitry Polikanov, the chubby-cheeked deputy head of the Central Committee of United Russia. 'I went as an observer, to see what was happening,' he told me, 'but I was calmed, when I observed that the crowds did not treat those on the stage as their leaders.'

He was right. Fears like this kept Putin in power and stopped the protest movement turning into a full-blown revolution. But the protest movement illustrated just how unstable Putinism really is. It illustrated that the Putin consensus was over and that the Putin majority had dissolved. The regime, for all its attempts to build a vertical of power and enthusiastic support with youth groups like Nashi, was forced to pay people to attend its rallies and to use the most fearmongering rhetoric to clinch victory in the 'plebiscite-election', despite Putin's only permitted opponents being ones who could not seriously challenge him.

The official results of the March 2012 election came in at 64 per cent, but independent experts placed his true share of the vote somewhere between 45 and 50 per cent.[40] This would include all those state employees paid or compelled to vote for him. Almost all the votes used to make up the difference had been shifted from the oligarch Mikhail Prokhorov, who according to one independent estimate saw his vote-share shrink from over 21 per cent to 7 per cent.[41] In an open contest these votes would have been cast for a liberal anti-Putin candidate. Perhaps this is why – standing in front of a crowd of 110,000 – as the exit polls came in that he had, after all, 'won' the election, Putin had to wipe tears from his eyes. Imitating Navalny he shouted over the crowd bused in from the sticks and given free vodka, 'We won,' and the 'enemies of Russia that only want to bring chaos to our country' had been defeated. 'Glory to Russia,' he finished, with tears in his eyes. Tears of exhaustion?[42] Or realization at how fragile his 'stability' was after all? Russia had changed, but the regime had not.

Over the weeks that followed, the blogosphere seemed to drown in elegies, but not for Putin. One bitter blogger posted a few days later the reasons that the movement failed to stop Putin's return:

> The answer is very simple: the 'swamp' was not really directed against the political regime, but against the country with the name of Russia, as it has existentially been for centuries. On the 'swamp' people came out to say that they are tired of living in the novels of Gogol and Shchedrin's stories, in this darkness, in this filth with the heads of fools. It was a real testament (paradoxically) to the success of Putin's modernization: the political class had emerged capable of forming the demands of civilization, including the rules of civilized politics. On the 'swamp' was born a new country, but it was not this pained baby that won on 4 March. Putin raised up the old Russia in its boots and galoshes, wife-beating and vodka-tippling. They came and destroyed our iPhones.[43]

The winter protests were not an earthquake on a Richter scale strong enough to bring down the Kremlin walls, but tremors unsettling enough to make cracks appear in the rooms of the palace, exposing the fault lines under the regime. They were the birth pangs of a new opposition, of a new Moscow – the first malfunction at the beginning of the unravelling of managed democracy. The demonstrations ended the Putin consensus and the Putin majority. They exposed that all was not well, in a system with no 'the dictatorship of law' and an incompetent 'vertical'.

The protest movement showed that it was no longer possible in Russia, if it ever had been, to speak of 'the masses' or the 'people'. The contradictions of Putinism had created different countries on different trajectories for whom the winter's rallies and marches were a Russian clash of civilizations. In neither was Putin loved or feared, but rather what he represented – stability or stagnation of the state. In a sense, the dividing line in this clash was a question of what period in history frightened you the most: the 1980s stagnation or the 1990s chaos? But in the months that followed, even Navalny had begun to feel he had hit a far bigger problem than the OMON – a brick wall in people's minds. Something profound had changed in Russia – but far from everyone in it. Navalny sighed:

'Every time I get arrested I am grabbed and thrown in by the same kind of policemen . . . and every time I talk to them: "Why are you arresting me? Do you not know that Putin is a thief?" And every time I get the same kind of answers – they all hate United Russia, they don't really like Putin – but they throw me into the cell and shout the same thing back at me. "It'll never get any better, mate . . . It'll never get any better."'

He shrugs his shoulders: 'This is the huge problem. It's the way people think.'

CHAPTER TEN

MOSCOW IS NOT RUSSIA

THEY MADE a human chain, they let off hundreds of white balloons, they wore white ribbons in parliament, they made beautiful websites, they stuck stickers denouncing him in grimy metro carriages, then held a writer's walk, then a protest walk and drove round and round the ring road honking 'Down with the dictator' and waving their white ribbons, whilst Navalny yelled into the microphone, 'Down with the party of crooks and thieves, down, down, down with the thieves', until he was exhausted and simply wanted to go home.

Putin won. The opposition rallies dwindled. The marches got smaller. They dried up outside Moscow. In winter 2012, every few weeks they could still pull out thousands in the capital, this certainly being the demographic in Russia with the best English and the most accustomed to skiing in France. This was the core of something and they called themselves the best of the best. But it was only the beginning of a new opposition, one that could challenge the Kremlin another day. It was not lost on them, that in 2004 when Putin lost in Ukraine, Kiev had been swamped by as many as a million Orange protesters.

'We are seeing a certain weariness. People had hoped for a quick result,' said the opposition personality Ilya Yashin, 'But it's not a sprint, it's a marathon.'[1] The movement was not a complete failure. They had torn up the Putin consensus. The new middle class had begun to become political. The old 'stability' was over. It was the beginning of the end of Putinism by consent, not the Putin regime. However, though the government was almost illegitimate in the eyes of the Muscovite bourgeoisie, for all their tweets and thunderous speeches they had failed to dislodge him.

The protests failed because Moscow is not Russia. Statistically speaking, the capital is another country. Most people live in drab cities about two to three nights away from the Kremlin by train, where the level of human development is somewhere between third-world Peru and Jamaica.[2] Not

Moscow – it is comparable to South Korea, has higher salaries than Poland, a bigger GDP than Hong Kong and more billionaires than New York, or anywhere else in the world.[3] Most 'federal subjects' are economically the size of Ethiopia, Tanzania or other African countries.[4] Not Moscow – with about 22 per cent of all Russian GDP, it is a city worth more than Shanghai, Beijing or Istanbul.[5] It has become a megacity, culturally and economically, dominating the country like London dominates Britain, or even Stockholm Sweden, but not demographically – even if one accounts for the unregistered and throws in the whole of the wider Moscow region, no more than 20 million out of 142 million Russians are living here.

Defining the mood of the megacity matters enormously. Yet cut off from the rest of the country, the opposition failed to break out and become a national movement. This reflects Moscow's accelerating economic disconnection with Russia. The incomes of the richest one-fifth of the capital, the protestors on the streets, are over twenty times the income of the poorest one-fifth of Russians – a Latin American disparity.[6] If you are a foreigner, Moscow is the third most expensive city in the world.[7] If you are working class from the provinces, moving to Moscow is unaffordable. If you are from Siberia or the Far East, a ticket to Moscow would cost you months of wages.[8]

Cut off economically, means cut off socially and cut off culturally. The new Facebook and white-ribbon opposition mirrored Moscow as a whole. It disdains the hinterland, viscerally, like eighteenth-century Paris. This is because those from the sticks have come here to escape, whilst the 'creative classes' that throng the opposition, be they e-workers, globalizers, students or designer-journalists, live like an offshore elite. When they go to the airport they only fly to the south and the west – the oligarchy spend their summers in Tuscany, the 'creative classes' spend weekends in Berlin, and those they both call the 'office plankton' go to Turkey.

The Moscow elites today are as different from Russians as the tsarist elites of St Petersburg, who spoke in a pretentious pidgin French, took the waters in Baden-Baden and tried to marry into the English aristocracy. This has revived a nineteenth-century dialectic between the intelligentsia and the masses. They speak in the name of a people they are cut off from and do not know; they claim to know what is best for them but actually unnerve these same masses. This leaves them powerless and anguished. 'I've never been to those places. . . I've never been anywhere in Russia really,' remarked the admin of the main opposition Facebook group, who did his degree in London – 'I spend my time going from my house to the Red October district and back again, which you know is the place to be.'

They are even more cut off from the hinterland than their tsarist forbears. They never travel 'to Russia' and this is a break with the past.

The tsarist elite had its estates in Russia – huge lands in Tambov or Rostov to spend the summer on. Chekhov's three aristocratic sisters longing for the capital ('*To Moscow, to Moscow*') could not be Russian aristocratic characters today. The truly wealthy today are 99 per cent centred on the capital. But they could be working class, of course – or dreaming of somewhere else ('*To London, to London*'). Then, even if the estates disappeared, the communist elite also often found itself out of Moscow for years on end – Brezhnev and Chernenko in Chisinau, Andropov in Karelia, Khrushchev in Kiev, Yeltsin in Sverdlovsk. The same went for lowly workers in the military–industrial complex and for anyone in lengthy military service. Not to mention the years of exile that the dissidents – the conscience of the intelligentsia – spent in outer Siberia.

No longer. The new Russian state does not send people on multi-year-long assignments to drain the marshes along the Volga, build institutes in Khabarovsk or settle the Taiga. This is a far less romantic country – but one that is losing its knowledge of self. You get a sense from their blogs and conversation that what these 'creative classes' really want is to turn the whole of Moscow into an ersatz London (or Shoreditch), with bicycle lanes and pedestrianized streets, which has sprung up in the cafes they frequent (Bar John Donne, Café Jan-Jak). They do not want to go out, like the Bolsheviks, to convert the people.

The circles around the opposition leadership threw themselves into online elections for their own leadership, plus a busy social calendar promoting these newly found roles as 'icons'. With few exceptions, the hipster counter-elite were more interested in preaching to the choir in Jan-Jak than riding to the end of the metro lines to agitate in estates, supermarkets or for social rights. 'The regions? What do I know about the regions? I have no answer for them,' sneered the popular opposition activist Max Katz, a young man with long greasy hair, as we talked one evening in a 'space' where one paid by the minute as pretty people strummed guitars. 'I'm from Moscow. When the people from the regions do something for themselves, I'll support them.' He then went back to talking about his ideas for cycle paths though the big city. 'I have no answers for the regions.' At least he was honest.

The Moscow Follies

Behaving like an 'iPhone only' social club, interested above all in themselves, they could not overcome the fact that Russia is a country of broken links. These stopped the protest movement in the capital from spreading. The regions are extremely cut off geographically, socially and culturally from the Moscow megacity. But 38 per cent of Russians are living in small towns or in the countryside.[9] Here, there are African male life expectancies and the human development levels of Central America.[10]

The opposition couldn't spread beyond Moscow, as sociologically that is where the wealth and the well-travelled are concentrated. They couldn't overcome the class and regional gulfs this lopsided development entailed. These mean broken links between classes, which each distrust the other as 'backward' or 'treacherous'. The workers of the tank factories in the Urals disdain the e-workers of Moscow, just as much as the latter look down on these grubby factory hands. They lacked the leaders to heal the broken links between generations – the young disdain the old as 'Soviets', the old disdain the young as 'office plankton', every family is divided between those nostalgic for the Soviet Union and those nostalgic for a future Medvedev failed to deliver. All the links that normally tie a country together: elections, functioning institutions, free media, a real public space – have all been broken by Putin.

The brightest in the movement knew that this fragmented, shattered Russia held back change. 'The main problem with our society,' said Filip Dzyadko, one of the movement's most adored journalists and activists, 'are these broken links. Everything that ties us together between regions, generations, past and present, has been shattered by the Soviet Union, the collapse of the Soviet Union and the successor regime to the Soviet Union. We will only become a healthy society once we have rebuilt those connections, somehow.'

But there is something else the opposition could not cut through. Russia is the country of hidden links. Over 40 per cent of the new middle class works for the state or the companies its controls.[11] This means only a very small amount of the new middle class is actually independent from the state – most are either bureaucrats, doctors, teachers or working for companies that either operate, offer services or depend on natural resources – i.e. on the companies answerable to Putin.[12]

So where the new middle class may be around 20–30 per cent of the population, only a very small proportion of that feels secure enough to go out and protest. This way, huge swathes of those who naturally would have something to gain by deposing the regime actually have something to lose. One afternoon I sat with some successful friends drinking coffee, looking out the window of their apartment at the belching smokestacks that spew steam over central Moscow, to keep it warm. A beautiful accountant for Gazprom looked out the window, fed up of questions about Navalny and his ilk. 'Putin's Russia is not the best Russia. But we work. We eat. It's not the worst Russia out of the ones I have lived in. It could be so much worse and our lives are not yet terrible. Do you really think Putin is the worst leader? Compared to the others we followed from time to time?'

For this segment, the state-dependent middle class, you hear this old question across Russia – 'why should I bite the hand that feeds me?' And it is quickly followed by this answer: 'As long as I'm all right, Putin can't be that bad.' Crucially, this is held together by the hidden links of black cash and corruption. Russia is as corrupt as Papua New Guinea on indexes – because millions are tied into corruption rackets.

The new opposition could not cut through this. Culturally, they lacked the tools. Russian political culture always divided the country into the vanguard that has the right to rule, and the people who must be led – like cattle. It has endlessly resurfaced since Peter the Great, be it as Bolsheviks or 'young reformers'. Putin, dreaming of pipelines, behaves as if he has no interest in crowds of Muscovites, whilst Moscow – dreaming of Europe – is disdainful of the rest of Russia.

The opposition counter-elite reacted to defeat childishly. They simply insisted that all those who supported Putin were the least dynamic, most backward and ill-informed parts of society. In reality, things were more knotted and complicated. They, as the leaders of the 'creative classes', would win sooner or later. They were the wave of history – online and globalized, middle class and modernized. The way they talked about provincials, their words derogatory and their tone mocking, left one convinced that most of them think they are 'poor cretins'. It stems from the same belief that the Moscow elites have the right to determine the country's course, the root of managed democracy in the first place.

Worse still, opposition leaders refuse to spend time over the Volga to make up for this – 'People are telling me you're very Moscow based,' I said to Navalny. 'I am very Moscow based,' he snapped back. He repeatedly turned down suggestions from his (at times frustrated) team to take a regional tour, until it was too late. The state, under the guise of an embez-zlement investigation, then banned him from leaving Moscow. The old opposition that he supplanted spends its time on the European think-tank tour scene at conferences, not in the industrial cities where Putinism is a grim affair. Kasparov, Nemtsov, Kasyanov are constantly rushing to the airport – and flying out West. When Putin claims these three men are not 'real Russians', the fact that they are barely in Moscow only helps.

There is no one like Yeltsin – who in 1991 spoke like a real Russian – or even like Lenin, who craved taking 'the light', 'the revolution' and 'electri-fication' into every corner. The opposition says they are limited by money: this is not entirely true. What is missing is desire. If Navalny found the time for a holiday in Cancun and a pit stop in New York between the 2012 parliamentary and the presidential elections, before he was banned from leaving Moscow, he could have found the time to take the night train to Kazan. I know many cheap places to stay there. This is why

Leonid Parfyonov, another culprit who failed to speak at the Sakharova rally despite public appeals as he was enjoying a European city break, remarked: 'Navalny is not the leader. He is just very popular. That's different.'

Figures like this from the opposition may not be present in the regions, but the truly rich, the truly powerful are only half present in Moscow. There cannot be enough pressure on them to make them desperate for change. The oligarchs with resources to throw into battle – their lives are already half-offshore in London, Tel Aviv or Geneva. With half their lives comfortable and secure, it takes the sting out of authoritarianism. It lowers the stakes for risking everything. Why bother, when your children are at an English public school or an American university and your money is in an Austrian or Cypriot bank account? 'If only we were as far away as Brazil,' I have heard more than one sigh. Rather than being too far away from Europe, people have come to fear that those who could force change are too integrated and at home in it to modernize Russia. As long as Domodedovo Airport is always there and the border is always open, what is wrong with Russia now will not be enough to push those with real resources into something truly dangerous. How desperate can this super elite ever become when they have mansions in Kensington?

Only Putin is everywhere and ubiquitous. Only Putin with his retinue and his jet is in every region at once. The TV tells a never-ending story: his hand is kissed by a monk in northern Karelia; he is visiting the tank factories in Nizhny Tagil; he is swimming in the rivers of Tuva; and opening the summit of Asia-Pacific Economic Cooperation (APEC) forum in Vladivostok. This is one of the secrets of Putinism as telepopulism. He has the most punishing travel schedule of any Russian leader in history. It is a permanent campaign – but it does not bring him any closer to the people. The scene is set (faked, cleaned-up, choreographed) before his every appearance. Insulated from any dissenting comment or unpleasant sight, Putin spends his life visiting a Potemkin Russia. The last time this man went for an unescorted walk or took public transport was the last time he had a job without maximum security – as far back as 1998, before he became head of the FSB.

Managed democracy is insulting to provincials in a way snide comments from the opposition could never be. It does not bemoan them as idiots; it classifies them as cattle, not adult enough to vote. Nor is Putin anymore connected in Moscow, increasingly 'working from home' in his palace off the Rublevka as much as possible. He drives from the Kremlin to this palace in an escort that resembles the visits of Western leaders to occupied Baghdad. For Putin to pass, the roads must close. For Putin to spin round the Kremlin, the traffic must stop. On the day of his inauguration in 2012 there was no need for Muscovites. The streets were emptied and sealed. As the black ZIL limousine neared the gates of the power castle, it looked as if Putin was not the tsar, beloved by his people, but the Khan who had conquered Moscow.

While the rest of Russia dreams of Moscow – of the yellow stone Stalin towers lit up like casinos, of the shopping streets that slope towards the Kremlin – Moscow is dreaming of London, New York, Berlin and Tel Aviv. No topic is more popular than emigration. No one is cool unless he has spent time and shopped abroad. To see this as a political act is a mistake. For some it is – but for many it is a consumer act. There is nothing trendy about the Urals, and 'Siberian' is positively an insult. The only places elite Muscovites want to go to are St Petersburg (for the weekend), the beach at Sochi on the Black Sea or the resort islands of Solovki in the Arctic.

'Moscow without Putin', read a placard held by a pretty girl at the protest in June 2012. It meant something. This free city of Moscow, having unmoored itself from Putinism culturally during the 2000s – rejecting Nashi, sneering at members of United Russia and sniggering at photos of Medvedev – has found itself feeling caught. Moscow had shown it was unhappy. The protest movement had brought its cultural elites to the podium, rallied 100,000 of its best-paid and best-informed consumers and shown that Putin no longer had a majority in his capital. It had started a culture war – but Moscow was trapped in Russia.

Putin Riot

To stay in power Putin must divide the nation. He realized that he must box the opposition into Moscow and make Russia see them as a bunch of elitist sexual deviants, led by a Yale-educated American spy, a gaggle of mink-coat-wearing hipsters with criminal intent. Kremlin telepopulism was overhauled – to turn the working class against this bourgeoisie. The Putin consensus, the leader as all things to all Russians, was buried. The Kremlin fought back with a conservative culture war.

The seemingly looped TV footage of the Medvedev years that had shown the official 'president' ordering an iPad 2, visiting Twitter's Californian headquarters, opening Davos 2011, was all dropped. Putin dressed up as a working-class hero. On one broadcast he was wearing a bomber jacket on the factory floor, on another channel he was screeching out lines from Molotov in a puffer jacket in front of thousands of pensioners, whilst on the evening news he was attending mass with the Patriarch. His slogans were nostalgic – 'Russia must restore the aristocracy of labour',

Russia needed to 'carry out the same powerful, all embracing leap forward of the defence industry as the one carried out in the 1930s'.[13]

Quietly, Vladislav Surkov was brought back in after his dismissal as Kremlin deputy chief of staff at the height of the protest movement. For a while, the new deputy prime minister, whose responsibilities included modernization, demographics and religious affairs, was mocked by those who once feared him for having such a vague portfolio. Then the campaign of religious anger started. To quote Deacon Alexander Volkov, spokesman for the Patriarch: 'From Kaliningrad to Vladivostok the real Russia, supports stability and is against the agitation of the creative classes.' In a country sickened by high rates of TB and HIV, alcoholism and aggression, where people have been turning to the Church for guidance – they now found the Kremlin.

Hipster Moscow fell into a trap. On 21 February 2012 a bunch of women dressed in brightly coloured balaclavas stormed into the unlovely white marble Cathedral of Christ the Saviour. Bulldozed by Stalin, its resurrection under a glinting golden-leaf dome is for the Orthodox Church their banner on the Moscow skyline. It incarnates their resurgence to power and grace. The women rushed to its altar, terrified a priest and began gyrating up and down with guitars. They called it a 'punk prayer':

Maria, Mother, Virgin,
Drive Putin away, drive Putin away!
Black robes and epaulettes of gold,
Parishioners are crawling and bowing.

The spirit of liberty is up in Heaven,
Gay Pride's been sent to Siberia, chained.
Their chief saint is the head of the KGB,
Who sends protesters under escort to prison![14]

Three of the women were arrested and charged with 'hooliganism'. They thought they had made a wonderful art attack. In fact they had handed Surkov something very precious. He could not have concocted a video more riling. The Kremlin political technologists threw themselves with relish into whipping up the Orthodox Church into a frenzy of anti-protester fury. Putin was painted as a defender of the faith; installing chapels in some Moscow metro stations, making sure even 'missionaries' were on site in the underground. This turned the religious into their anti-protester faithful, where all their youth movements had failed over the winter. This also snapped any chance of the Patriarch playing the role of negotiator between the Kremlin and the protesters he had flirted with, the role of the Church in Central Europe in the imploding Eastern bloc. This tugged back Orthodox believers from following an opposition anticorruption agenda for a 'purer Russia'.

The Pussy Riot show trial caught everything that was wrong with the Moscow opposition cultural elites and everything that was dangerous and inflammatory about the Kremlin game. The opposition rushed to give endless speeches, write op-eds and make court appearances defending the girls. Putin's men laughingly edited them into nightly TV packages. Their verbose performances suggested the opposition were in fact just a Pussy Riot. Putin's propagandists were overjoyed, mixing in images of protesters shouting 'Free Pussy Riot' with informative clips on how the Voina art-group they had split from, which means war, had staged a public orgy in a botanical museum, extensively photographed bits of a raw chicken being shoved up a vagina in a supermarket and hung an effigy of a dead Uzbek in the aisle of a food store.

Rather than being the new Solzhenitsyn, who spoke to everyone with clear moral actions in the USSR, the group captured the vanity and, ironically, the unpolitical nature of the radical art scene. They were interested in protest, not politics. Pyotr Verzilov, 24, the husband of Nadia Tolokonnikova, 22, the lead singer in the 'band', pranced around the court grinning, with a scraggly pubic beard, visibly thrilled to be in the floodlights of fame. We talked one afternoon by the courtroom door. I asked him if he realized that so many people I was speaking to in the regions now believed that the opposition was in fact Pussy Riot: 'Well, if they believe that, there is absolutely nothing that can be done for them.'

One of the three girls on trial, Yekaterina Samutsevich, barely understood what was going on. 'We were so confused, tired and not sure what was happening,' she remembered. 'We did it to show that the Church is now all a bunch of paid-up bureaucrats controlled by the state.' This was not the first of her stunts. She had been filmed grabbing policewomen in the marble halls of the Moscow metro trying to force-kiss them. 'We really didn't understand what was happening during the trial, especially with the lawyers.' In a squalid signal of how embezzlement permeated all corners of Russian life, some of the girls' lawyers had been asking for cash to be handed over by journalists for access and even tried to register Pussy Riot as a trademark.[15] Nor did Samutsevich appear to have grasped the political repercussions of the stunt. Her two other brightly coloured rioters were sent to prison camps. Luckily, after byzantine negotiations, Samutsevich was freed. We met one evening after her release to talk. She had brown circles under her eyes and the pallor of late nights, or jail cells:

'Did you think that you might create propaganda for Surkov?' I asked

'I don't know. Maybe. We didn't think about that,' she mused looking upwards.

'So what about the people in the regions that now think the opposition is against the Church?' I asked.

'They are not our audience. What people don't understand is that we are not just a political anti-Putin group. We are an art group. But I do see we created a conflictual situation though.'

The Kremlin, though, had thought things through. Surkov must have been delighted when he checked the polls. Only 10 per cent of Russians felt no punishment was in order and just 30 per cent disapproved of the Church's new politics.[16] It seemed such good fortune that conspiracy theories swirled. Regardless, the show trial captured how vicious, manipulative and devoid of legal basis the Russian legal system had become. It showed that the law only existed as Putin's weapon. This, of course, was the whole point.

'They got what they were asking for,' smirked Putin.[17] They may have turned a serious issue into a joke, but their sentence was no laughing matter. Two of the 'singers' were sent to a penal colony for two years' hard labour, one aged twenty-two and the other twenty-four, both mothers of toddlers. Sending half-children with children of their own to places where beating and rapes are routine – as punishment for a silly song – was unspeakably cruel. Nevertheless around that time in Moscow, you could almost hear Surkov's laughter in the dark that a 'punk prayer' they thought was feminism in action, had been inverted into a Putinist dagger to chop up the country.

This sentence was a small part of the wider crackdown. OMON in tundra camouflage and crash helmets burst into opposition bars and grabbed men with white ribbons and T-shirts, others were beaten by them at rallies and detained pending imprisonment. They were more vicious than usual; their salaries had been doubled. Disloyal members of the establishment were more discreetly punished. The dissenting deputy Gennady Gudkov was expelled from the Duma, then forced to fire-sell his business. As he was a former KGB general, the deputies from United Russia shouted 'Judas! Judas!' over his final speech. The minor oligarch Alexander Lebedev, who had donated money to opposition causes, was charged with 'hooliganism' – the same crime as Pussy Riot, for assaulting someone on TV.

As Putinism by consent eroded, the legal infrastructure for authoritarian rule was put into place. A law passed under Medvedev that had decriminalized libel was reversed, the legal definition for treason was ominously widened to include threatening Russia's 'constitutional order', a list of harmful websites drawn up, huge fines passed for 'illegal protests' and any NGO that received funding from abroad was forced to carry the label of 'foreign agent'. Navalny was charged with embezzling on a timber transaction and confined to the capital. He was stunned; if found guilty he could be jailed for ten years. Historians were speechless – crimes with lumber were amongst those Stalin chose with which to prosecute Bukharin in 1932. It was as if the Medvedev years had never occurred. Now prime minister, even Medvedev himself talked like his presidency had been an illusion. 'They often tell me you're a liberal,' he said to a United Russia audience, 'I can tell you frankly: I have never had liberal convictions.'[18]

Russia seemed to be going backwards. Slowly, repression grew darker. 'The good news is – I don't have a sister,' wrote Navalny when the police searched his parents' business for the first time, then opened a criminal investigation into his younger brother.[19] Internet surveillance systems and a new law that effectively allowed the FSB to spy on Russian citizens without restrictions were put in place. Out in the open, 'Cossack brigades' were put on patrol in Moscow and a 'purge of the elite' endlessly discussed on state TV. Starting with Anatoly Sverdyukov, the defence minister, dismissals swept throughout the bureaucracy. Their crime: 'corruption'. Sounding ever more conservative, Putin started to say that Russia would resist 'any outside interference in our affairs'.[20] Russia, he expounded, was 'a unique civilisation' – different from Europe.[21] He was on the offensive again. On the streets, protestors were outnumbered by thousands of OMON. He was winning again. 'The opposition,' Putin scoffed, 'they ask for the impossible and then never do anything.'[22]

Moscow had come full circle. The 'creative classes' sunk into the anguish they had felt when Putin announced his return. It had really happened. Even the apparent concession that Khodorkovsky would be freed two years early in 2014 was only interpreted as a way to divide the opposition, by throwing in a new, divisive leader to undermine Navalny. The gigantic expectations of the protest movement had crashed against the old repressive routine. The opposition busied itself electing a coordination council to represent itself, but even in its own bars and hangouts, hope had given way to disappointment, even disorientation as it sank in the system had not changed. The polls made dreary reading: a majority of Russians were both unhappy with the Putin regime and felt the protest movement had failed.[23] Amongst those elected to a new coordination council was Navalny's deputy Vladimir Ashurkov, the man organizing all his initiatives. We met for breakfast in a cheapish coffee chain and ate burnt eggs and chewy salmon. 'What did people expect?' he sighed. 'The expectations were just enormous. But we have come so far. When I met Alexey he was just one man on his own. First we turned him into a public figure. Then we created a team.

Then we led a movement. Then we created this coordination council. This will take time.' He picked at the salmon, imagining his future. 'There are two fixed trends here. The declining popularity of those that hold power and our rising popularity.' He then asked for my pen and, in my notebook, drew a biro line going exponentially up and another crashing down. Neither of us had any idea if those lines were years, or even decades long, 'but sooner or later, they cross.' Six weeks later his apartment was raided. They even searched his vitamins. Ashurkov could only tweet, nervously.

Precarious Putinomics

The Putin consensus had been replaced by class and culture wars. It implicitly acknowledged having lost the most advanced part of the nation; they would have to rally the most backward. The other Russia that Putin was now appealing to were the 'vengeful losers' who had suffered the most in the 1990s: pensioners, state employees, factory workers, war veterans and bureaucrats. There are a lot of them. Though Russia buzzed with talk of a new middle class in 2011, as many as 53 per cent of people were living off the state budget either as state employees, pensioners or on benefits.[24] Even the most inflated measurements show over 100 million Russians cannot be considered middle class.

Putin's aggressive politics meant new economics. The announcement of his return triggered the departure of the fiscal conservative Alexey Kudrin from the finance ministry, grumbling about not having been chosen as prime minister and worried about reckless loosening of the public purse strings totally dependent on the oil price. This meant there was now nobody trying to restrain Putin's big spend. Ever since the hiss of dissatisfaction had grown audible in mid-2011, the regime had responded by making more and more astounding spending increases in pensions, military and police salaries.

Putin was spending like a Gulf sheik. These states had paid their way out of the 'Arab spring' exactly as the Kremlin was now doing. Payouts had risen drastically since the financial crisis first sent ripples of unrest. Between 2007 and 2010 funding to the regions leapt by $58 billion from 5.7 per cent to 9.2 per cent of GDP.[25] The same year pensions were hiked 50 per cent.[26] In 2011 pensions were raised by 10 per cent again, with a 6.5 per cent across the board increase in public-sector wages.[27] Simultaneously, a gigantic $613 billion ten-year plan for the military was announced.[28] This was not to fight a war but to keep the single-industry armament towns quiet, employed, and the military–industrial complex onside. Surrounding the campaign Putin doubled military and police salaries and promised $160 billion worth of giveaways.[29]

In Russia, as was happening in the Gulf States, this big spend meant the necessary price of oil to balance the budget grew dramatically. The government's break-even price had been less than $40 a barrel in 2007 but stood at over $110 by 2012.[30] Even the head of the central bank had warned this is 'too high'.[31] Instead of making itself secure Putin had bought social calm at the cost of vast exposure should the price of oil tumble from its historically unprecedented highs. This seemed reckless when long-term trends such as an unreformed pension system, slowing growth and a shrinking trade surplus were undermining accounting certainties. The unreformed pensions system alone would see government expenditure here rise from 9 per cent of GDP to 14 per cent of GDP by 2030, which if financed by borrowing would send Russia's debt to GDP ratio up from 14 per cent of GDP to 70 per cent the same year.[32]

To support Putin, state finances were becoming ever more precarious. Even his finance ministry warned spending levels might be unsustainable. The same could be said for the propaganda. With his new image of a working-class hero utterly dependent on fulfilling the new expanded social contract, ostracizing the new middle class would leave the Kremlin without a constituency, should the oil price fall and rip a hole in the budget. Putin's Russia is not cohesive or stable enough for austerity. Any fiscal tachycardia disrupting social payouts could send his new 'support base' into the streets, with bourgeois elites no longer there to buttress him.

However, there are grounds for Putin to feel secure about making such a spending increase: the country had amassed the third largest reserves in the world and has the lowest debt to GDP ratio of a G-20 member state at a mere 14 per cent debt, far behind most Western countries.[33] Reforms were started on pensions. Nevertheless, the collapse of oil prices, no pension reform and a large return to international borrowing amid political risk could send Russian bond yields shooting up before it reached deep levels of debt. Russian stability was now as precariously balanced on market favour. Putin had rebuilt his 'stability' on the one thing in Russia he had no control over whatsoever – the price of oil.

In western Siberia, however, all is not well. Here, in the resource rich wastelands that produce two-thirds of Russian oil, the crushing majority of old Soviet fields are in production decline. The technological revolution pioneered by Khodorkovsky that jacked-up oil production has run out of steam. The 1990s problems of fields with falling production are re-emerging. Even if prices stay high Russia is slowly running out of cheap oil. Its current reserves are of declining quality and its huge potential fields lie in extremely difficult terrain in eastern Siberia or under the Arctic Ocean. At the very moment Putin needs more oil profits, oil production risks entering a long-term stagnation, even decline, unless a radical over-haul in techniques, taxation and import of new technologies gets under way. His own energy minister has warned that without a delicate, but feasible policy turn, oil production could fall from 505 million tons per year in 2010 to 388 million tons per year in 2020.[34]

This can be avoided through extensive investment, tough and expen-sive prospecting and intrusive tie-ups with foreign companies – but the whole industry could be forced to invest not $25 billion upstream but $50 billion annually to keep production steady.[35] It is hard to imagine that the Kremlin will have as much money to play with as in the past if it wants to rejuvenate the sector it depends on. The easiest way to avoid production falling is to lower oil taxes in order to give the companies the money they need to revitalize and drill for new wells.

Yet this will be difficult for the state to do at the very moment it has become more dependent than ever on high oil taxes. Similar problems are looming in the gas sector as LNG and shale pose long-term problems for Gazprom's business model. Russia is set to stay an energy superpower – but the best years of the boom are behind it, even if the oil price continues its ever-volatile rise. The era of both a production and price boom that defined the best years of Putin's regime are likely over. Putin had bet the Kremlin on a challenged industry, where prices are as unpredictable as the hand of a drunken card sharp. This uncertainty means that Russia is not only exporting huge amounts of raw materials – but money and people. As many as 38 per cent of the wealthiest Russians want their children to emigrate, and capital flight hit $80.5 billion in 2011.[36] The two most sensitive assets in any country were fleeing Russia.

Vertical of Discontent

Sustained opposition in Moscow has not gone beyond 100,000, but discon-tent is national. The government claims that only those protesting resent the regime. If this were true, United Russia in the 2011 parliamentary elections would not have fallen below 50 per cent, despite industrial rigging. In most regions dominated neither by oil, gas or ethnic cliques, the party got far less than in Moscow – around 35 per cent.[37]

They are not the 'great ignorant', nor are they apathetic. They are the silent Russian majority that polls show fear the police, do not feel protected by the law, think corruption is greater than in the 1990s, want a strong opposition and disapprove of this government. They are the majority who know and use the slogan 'the party of crooks and thieves'. These are the seething people who, should Putin cut his promises in an oil tumble, would start to shriek with almost physical pain.

Travelling around Russia is like using a time machine. The botched vertical has left a country that once aimed for homogenous Soviet living standards as a patchwork quilt of regions. Each one is run as its own patronage network, some modernizing nicely, others in sociological collapse; some run by competent cadres who look to China, others by crooks in Gucci suits. It has left some cities with glass tower blocks, but others without airports; some with high-speed trains and 3D cinemas, others still single-industry rust heaps overrun by neo-fascists and gangs, where you can only have fun with a needle – a country where the capital has the human development of South Korea but many regions have life male expectancies below the Central African Republic.

Only in government propaganda is there a 'real Russia' and a 'fake Moscow'. This is a fragmented country. Some say that the regions are defined by their demography, others say by geography. In Russia it is usually geology. The territories that thrive are cogs in the hydrocarbons mega-complex, giving them a cut in taxes. Oil and gas do not just create oligarchs, but regional gulfs as great as the social ones between Russia's eighty-three regions – nine produce more than half of Russia's GDP, but in 2010 over forty received more in federal aid than all the profits of their local enterprises.[38] What this means is that gaseous Yamalo-Nenets, Tyumen and Khanty-Mansi regions technically have GDP per capita higher than the United States, but men in Pskov, Novgorod or Chita can expect to live barely beyond fifty-five years of age.[39]

In these geologically unlucky lands, the political variable is personality. 'The governor decides everything,' said one Kremlin aide. 'They really have the power to make the difference in our system.' Each United Russia chieftain determines to what degree his region will be managed or pillaged. Russia is a feudalized entity, a place where the governor is personally dependent on Putin, but without a 'dictatorship of law' it leaves every boss to build up his own regime, his own financial–political holding, the way he wants. It could turn out like Barnaul in Siberia, where no protest permits were handed out and the opposition left protest teddy bears and Lego in the snow, which were duly 'arrested' for their 'illegal public event'; or like liberal Novosibirsk where thousands marched against Putin under colourful banners after United Russia scored just 27 per cent.[40]

Let's take two regions with nothing in their subsoil, whose military-industrial roles in the Soviet plan were scrapped, one near St Petersburg and the other next to Moscow. Pskov, to the south of Putin's home town, has a governor who was not even a member of infamous Yarva-Neva judo club of which the 'national leader' is the honorary president; he is the son of a member. His qualifications are scant and his record dismal. Pskov has lost one-third of its population since 1989 and has one-third of Russia's dying villages.[41] This kind of depopulation normally occurs only in times of war or plague. Despite sharing a border with the EU, no modern economy was built here to replace its socialist role, leaving the youth to be sucked into St Petersburg.

Kaluga near Moscow, however, is actually doing rather well. It makes such a difference who is in charge; there is even a modicum of decent administration here. The governor, Anatoly Artamonov, admires Lee Kuan Yew and jokes that he would like to erect a statue of him and one of Deng Xiaoping. He is seen as the most dynamic of Putin's governors and the 'national leader' himself said of his work: 'if we all go this way, the progress will be very significant.'[42] He has a lot to be proud of. Regional GDP has grown 130 per cent in a few years and Kaluga had the country's fastest growing industrial production of any region in 2011.[43] The accountancy firm KPMG judged that Kaluga was 'the only example where a business climate was created expressly for foreign investors.'[44] The governor thinks he has pulled this off as he is a Kaluga native, not an implant. Yet even a man awarded by Putin with the 'Order of Services to the Fatherland 3rd class', is exasperated by his vertical:

'The vertical of power is not what it appears. Now I am certain that I have more authority than a European governor, thanks to Putin. I can go to China and sign contracts. I don't have to ask him to do that. But I would be happy actually to feel extra control by Putin. I'm in need of that – more estimation, judgement – I'd really like to have that. I'm really free to the point that I'd like to have some constraints. So, I have to call Putin to ask to meet him and Putin always says: "What's the problem?" So, I say: "There is no problem. I'm just coming to tell you what I am doing." He then says: "There is no need. I am sure you are doing good work."'

As we talked, Artamonov began to gesture ironically with his eyebrows:

'This is as far as central control is concerned. So comparatively this works for me but not for everyone. I know there are other governors who are not governing and are only interested in pursuing . . . their hobbies. The centre should more forcefully control them. This is surprising for me – it's Putin's preference. If I was Putin I would be far more decisive and centralizing. Power should not make business. Twenty years ago the political system changed. And we still have not become a fully functioning, efficient, cooperative and clean state . . . the state is really still carrying a Soviet way of thinking inside it. We have a joke in Kaluga that makes me think of the Russian state. "The hedgehog is a proud bird. It will not fly unless you kick it."'

This mess has left Russia in fragments. Moscow elites love making sweeping statements about 'the state of the nation'. However, things are so different from town to town, that Russians live with very different problems, despite the same bad roads and corrupt officials. Authoritarian modernization is working in Kaluga under the United Russia franchise, but take a night train north of Moscow and in Yaroslavl the United Russia cadres have been chased out by the ballot box. Kaluga shows what might have been, had Putin been more competent; Yaroslavl hints at how he could lose control.

The chance conjunction of a catastrophe in the air, official callousness and the electoral cycle detonated the local 'bears'. It was Medvedev's sinking of the Kursk moment. Then 'president' he had wanted to make the city synonymous with his name, to be his Davos. To do this he sponsored the Yaroslavl Policy Forum, which billed itself as 'a permanent international platform for ongoing intellectual discussions and practical definitions and development of the modern state and its role in ensuring stability and security in the modern world'. In reality, like most policy conferences, it was a banquet, this one in the honour of the visiting Italian prime minister, then Silvio Berlusconi, and his Japanese and Korean counterparts.

Yaroslavl is a sporty town, obsessed by hockey. And on the night before the policy forum opened the plane carrying its hockey team, Lokomotiv, crashed at the airport killing all of the players on board. It had been forced to use an inferior landing strip due to Berlusconi's imminent arrival. Grief-struck, the city was soon convinced that ambulances had been blocked so Berlusconi could use reserved lanes to make his way to the conference. Blubbing masses rushed into the squares of this pretty tsarist city of onion domes and sugar-icing stucco, but felt they were treated callously by OMON guarding the forum. They wanted the 'president' to be with them, but Medvedev neither consoled them nor called off the banquet.

This is 'deep Russia' not hipster-land – but this cack-handed performance pulled the plug on Putin's legitimacy. The 'national leader' saw his rating plunge to less than 30 per cent and in the parliamentary elections the party scored just 29 per cent.[45] When unrest broke out in Moscow in December 2011, local Facebook protests flared. 'We had seen the real face of United Russia,' said the e-organizers. Luck gave them the hook-up that never happened in the capital, sealing the fate of the Yaroslavl 'bears'. Evgeny Urlashov, a local defector from the establishment, joined the Facebook protests and was tweeted to victory in mayoral elections. This was not an isolated ballot, but the tenth out of fifteen mayoral votes that the Kremlin lost that season.

This scenario on a national level is not unthinkable, though only mayoral elections can be lost so easily as an 'escape valve' for discontent. However, the new stubbly mayor, smoking a shisha pipe like the mad hatter in a hockey-themed bar, is as frustrated with the Moscow opposition as some governors are with the Moscow government:

'The opposition is quite simply scaring people. I think that if the opposition in Russia is trying to pursue some kind of "revolution" then I am against it. I am positive that us Russians are united on one thing. We don't want to have a revolution. We don't want war, we don't want bloodshed, we don't want slaughter.'

This is a huge problem as he is convinced that the vertical is unworkable:

'Before, when I was a party member, United Russia wouldn't let me do anything without orders from Moscow. I wouldn't do a single thing without waiting for Moscow to say so. I ended up doing nothing at all. Now I can do all kinds of things with power. Look, I can build a kindergarten. But the party of power would do nothing at all without the most explicit directions even for the tiniest of things. The huge problem with this vertical of power is that it has become a vertical of corruption. The vertical prizes loyalty not effectiveness.'

The mayor suddenly had urgency in his voice:

'Putin needs to be stronger! Putin needs to battle the corrupt thieves. If Putin wants to be the good tsar, to be the great tsar, which I know is his intention . . . He needs to change the vertical of power. He needs to do battle with the thieves, with free courts, fair elections and with tough rough methods against the corrupt bureaucrats inside the system.'

United Russia is exceptional in Kaluga because it gets things done; United Russia is exceptional in Yaroslavl because it has lost control. Most cities sit somewhere with the 'bears' in the middle – incompetent, but in charge. Yet it would be a mistake to think only outliers talk scathingly about the vertical of power. So do the middling conformists. I found the same resentment when I met with the head of a rigging machine that returns over 70 per cent for Putin and his party.[46] The blue-eyed Rustem Khatimov, the president of Bashkortostan, an oil-rich and Islamic republic of Russia, claimed he could not think of a single thing about the balding action hero in the Kremlin that displeased him. He spoke about the man as a 'genius', and how he was ready to vote for him in 2018. This did not stop him sniping at the system. Read between the lines:

'I lived in Moscow for a long time and I know sadly, with many Moscow businessmen they begin the conversation with one question – how big is the bribe? We need more responsibility as a region – in terms of the budget, in terms of the control of our natural resources and in controlling the big building projects.'

The vertical that exasperates him has grown stronger in his capital of Ufa. This concrete place is really two towns, a Bashkir-Tatar city of minarets and hard round flatbread, beside a Russian-Soviet town of beer tents and dilapidation. This is a wealthy territory. It calls itself 'the Muslim capital of Russia', but it is clean and quiet like authoritarian Minsk, the capital of Belarus. Even this republic was long run like a family business by the president's predecessor, Murtaza Rakhimov. His son was the biggest Bashkir oil magnate and he stuffed the apparatus with Bashkirs only. He tried to resist the vertical. Those in charge had 'never commanded as much as three chickens', Rakhimov snarled, before growling:

'Right now, everything is decided from above. The level of centraliza-tion is worse than it was in Soviet times. With respect to local people, they carry out a policy of distrust and disrespect.'[47]

Rakhimov's political career was over. Yet the vertical has not grown more legitimate in his old concrete headquarters. Officials' whisper, when the president is out of sight, that his going means non-Bashkirs have only just started to be employed again and the 'local censor' is softer. In private, though, government advisors are frank about the future: 'We cannot be independent, so we want to be autonomous, really autonomous, because Moscow is taking all the oil money for itself.'

The vertical feels at its weakest in Siberian Tuva. This is the Russian territory with the lowest level of human development, at the level of Uzbekistan. It has the country's highest alcohol and murder rates and a male life expectancy lower than Gabon. Annexed by Stalin in 1944, it is over 82 per cent ethnic Tuvan, a Mongol people, and still to be connected to the Russian railway system. Politics amounts to local clans linked to a half-Tuvan Putin ally wrangling rents amongst themselves. In its drab capital, Kyzyl, even those who wear leather jackets are too frightened to step out after dark because of the number of murders. Tuvans lack the metabolism for alcohol but, addicted to vodka, they fight frequently with knives. The city is all shacks and dust tracks, a place where people have fallen back into believing in magic. Without any medical infrastructure for mental health, counselling or psychologists, there were lines outside the Tuvan Shaman's hutch and the cabin of the Russian-Tatar witch. I asked both what they talked about when locals asked about Russia. 'It will collapse,' said both the seer and the witch. The shamans, they said, have long seen the signs. 'Tuva will not always be part of Russia.' The witch had hung up a stuffed black eagle to ward off the sprits and, as it happened, was a Navalny supporter. 'Putin will fall. They will all be washed away.'

Tuva is the size of England, but outside this one town there is almost no state. At the very end of the vertical, in a wood cabin of Russians of 'old believers', a breakaway sect that split under Peter the Great, perhaps a day from a paved road, in a village without drainage, without fully functioning electricity, where the children stop going to school at fourteen, then marry right away, all its villagers living subsistence lives, I met a senior member of the United Russia central committee.

I was tired. To reach the village had taken a day by car down a dirt track, past dead hamlets and a brush with a gang of Tuvan gunmen on horseback, through forests thicker than jungles, that made no sound, to a point where the river is shallow. Here there is a pontoon, where an 'old believer' with a long beard ushers you over, telling me he was here instead of a bridge – 'to keep out Asiatics'. Then hours of cratered track, to a bend in the river where the car could go no further. A motorized canoe then carried me over the night black Yenesei, one of the mother-rivers of Siberia. The 'captain' was a shirtless drunk with white chest hair and a sailor's cap. The old man told me it was here, in this valley that Putin had gone on holiday and posed topless, hunting, swimming and fishing: 'We saw him go by down the river in a huge speed boat.'

I stumbled exhausted into the wooden cabin that was the 'lodge'. A woman in home-spun clothes cooked me a reindeer stew, and poured tea made of purple flowers I had never seen before. Her husband, a hunter, couldn't hold back his enthusiasm for a foreign visitor a moment longer and grabbed his photo album. Seven years ago he had got a throwaway Kodak by chance. After two years he had saved up enough to go to town to get the pictures developed. He had the teeth of a man who had never used a toothbrush and the album of an eighteenth-century Cossack. We went slowly through the photographs. On horseback with guns. On horseback pointing at a wooden village. By the campfire with the pelts of four dead lynx. With the wild-eyed boys holding up the warm bloodied carcass of a bear. I asked; 'How does a man feel when he is alone in the forest and shoots a bear?' 'Alive'. And what do you think of the government? 'It's corrupt.'

In places like this you understand how Russia can have African male life expectancies and Central American murder rates. You understand why it is so lawless. As I thought that, the politician walked in. He was wearing a World Wildlife Fund fleece. It was a craze in the Kremlin, he explained, to come and take photos like Putin, posing like Putin, in the 'Putin places'. And we both ate the reindeer soup, realizing it was actually chopped up reindeer lungs, with what tasted like bitter scones. The peasants sat at the head of the wooden table, her in home-sewn floral patterns, him in hunter's camouflage. So, the politician chose to speak in English. And throughout the evening a hundred micro-moths came in through the cracks in the cabin. Some got in my eyes. In this muddy hole, the politican felt free to speak:

'You see they live so wildly here. Soviet power was a myth, like the myth of the vertical of power today. All the regional barons are just living like feudal lords. This means that here in Tuva there was a battle between the clans over who could control the local United Russia. It was a bitter fight and there was nothing that we could do about it. The local ethnic Tuvans run the administration and cut all ethnic Russians out. In the towns they live like an ethnic minority. Here in this valley they are defending themselves, to live like a majority.'

He told me he was leaving the United Russia central committee and taking up a job in the Kremlin, so the political conversation came back to him, what he was going to do, like they always do:

'It was very clear to us, that for him [Putin], there really was just nobody else. It really was his decision and his conviction that the country would collapse without him. You could leave like a hero in 2012 or leave like a loser in 2018. Hah. That's what he chose.'

The next day the politician was gone. Driven out by a gigantic four-wheel drive. So, I walked through the woods into the village, which is called Erjei. There were a lot of butterflies. The wooden cabins sunk into dirt tracks. Pigs wandered around. Aryan children played in the mud. Here there was no modern toilet, no computer, no doctor and only one TV; they had been having problems with it. This was what social scientists call 'natural exchange'. There was no economy, only the river and only the forest, which leered over the wood-stick crosses in their cemetery. I walked up to some men sharing a cigarette by the waterside. They had the faces of men who lived outdoors, thick knuckled hands and beards that smelt of fish:

'Putin? What do we think of Putin? He never did anything good for the country. He just took all the money from oil and gas production and took it for himself and his mates and did nothing for the country. Why the hell would we support Putin? Who do you think we are?'

Stop Feeding the Caucasus

Nowhere did the vertical fail so completely as in the North Caucasus. You feel this everywhere in Moscow. You see it in the black Mercedes driven by Chechen hoodlums breaking traffic. You see it in the dark posse of leather jackets hanging around the metro. You see it the restaurants, in the fights the football hooligans have. You hear it in the constant racist chatter about the 'blacks' in Russian mouths, in their suspicion and distrust. You see it in the gutter press, where every murder is a Chechen murder.

The Caucasus looms over Moscow: everyone knows that money is transferred to keep the peace with the local elites. The government and the liberals call it 'reconstruction' and 'federal funds', whilst the national-ists and the men who fought in Chechnya, the kind you meet smoking or drinking in train carriages called it 'tribute'. Everybody outside the United Russia machine talks about the relationship between Putin and the Chechen leader Ramzan Kadyrov as purely feudal.

The region has long ceased to be 'in social union' with Russia. They are seen as foreigners: if you marry a North Caucasian (frowned upon) you marry a foreigner; they are seen as 'immigrants' in the major cities, as alien as Azeris. Visiting the North Caucasus is to go to an 'internal abroad', in Russian minds – you 'leave Russia' and 'come back to Russia'.

The tsars annexed this Muslim region in the late nineteenth century. It was never fully pacified until Stalin – infuriated by endless cut-throat rebellions by the Chechens and the Ingush, worried they would greet Hitler as a liberator – who ordered them to be deported to Central Asia. It was genocide: one-third to half of them died. Returning under Khrushchev these 'punished people' never had their own collaborating Soviet nomenklatura like the Tatars or the Bashkirs. This meant that when the collapse came, those who took control were not used to politics, and their games with Moscow ended in two wars and at least 50,000 dead.[48] Conflict de-Russified these republics. Today Chechnya, Dagestan and Ingushetia are less than 5 per cent ethnic Russian – a figure less than in independent Moldova, Kyrgyzstan or Estonia.[49] War brought enmity into a million social ties. With the destruction of the 'social union', the paradoxical situation of the early 2000s – when normal Russians wanted Chechnya in Russia, but not to have a single Chechen living outside of Chechnya – has unravelled. Today post-conflict bitterness has fused with a fury at the excesses of the 'vertical of corruption' in Grozny. Russians find Putin's Caucasian 'stability' demeaning and exorbitant. When Putin goes – the popular will would come to bear on this. Chechnya is in personal union with Putin – not Russia. And in the North Caucasus it is the linchpin republic. Most Russians I have spoken to want Muslim Chechens, Ingush and Dagestanis out. A powerful opposition leader (he asked not to be quoted by name) speaks for the majority: 'They are already basically independent in Chechnya. We don't want to pay for them anymore. They are worthless provinces that contribute nothing to us.'

Reading opinion polls is to come face to face with a damning verdict. Despite Putin's self-styled 'historic role' in the North Caucasus, a full 51 per cent of Russians would not even care if their borders were redrawn to exclude Chechnya.[50] The nation is angrier, more nationalist and exclusivist, than it was when he took over – as many as 59 per cent concur with the slogan 'Russia for Russians'. This is now a country where 56 per cent expect ethnic clashes will soon occur.[51] Over one-third feel irritation, dislike or fear at the sight of North Caucasians in their home towns. These are not the statistics of successful reintegration, but frozen disintegration.[52]

The difference is that today no one thinks that letting Chechnya go will Balkanize Russia. Stability has done the opposite of what Putin expected. Polls show an appetite for a new nationalism that rejects expansionism, in the name of a smaller, purer Russia. It fascinates Navalny. He wants to ride this wave to power. 'A very interesting thing occurred in the past ten years,' he said thoughtfully, 'the nationalists went from being dictatorial and imperialist, rejecting the idea of one inch being given up in the Caucasus, to being pro-democracy and anti-imperialists, wanting to give up on the Caucasus.' Ironically, it is now Russian liberals who have gone from urging Moscow to give it up, to urging Moscow to think of its 'commitments' and 'civilizing role'.

Navalny is a leader of the smash-hit viral campaign 'stop feeding the Caucasus'. Together with extremist nationalist fronts (which have a subtext of neo-Nazism) the campaign has hosted rallies in Moscow, pumped out YouTube videos ('We give them money, they give us death!') and made the demand 'Stop Feeding' part of standard political vocabulary.[53] Navalny repeatedly asks his mantra question: 'Why should they get more than Smolensk region?' Then writes things like this on his blog:

> Stop feeding the Caucasus. Stop feeding Ramzan Kadyrov. Stop feeding the loathsome gang of thieves known as the 'leadership of the North Caucasus!'[54]

Many say he is a neurotic, knee-jerk Caucasophobe. I do not see anything exceptional about him. This is the new normal. His campaign hit a raw nerve in post-recession Russia – with even a poll on the very specific, highly liberal, audience of *Ekho Moskvy* showing 89 per cent agreed with the call to 'Stop the Feeding'.[55] This view is not only that of street leaders like Navalny. The urbane former deputy energy minister Vladimir Milov is onside. 'The thing is,' he said, 'with less than 5 per cent ethnic Russian populations these provinces are de-Russifying. It's a shock to see a Russian there now. There is something inevitable about it. Demographically they are on the way out.'

Putin is not listening, as he correctly believes the only lasting peace is economic peace. In 2011 the state announced its intention to triple funding to over \$141 billion for the North Caucasus 2011–25 regional development programme. It absurdly includes several high-quality ski slopes. With infrastructure budgets being raided by corrupt officials in central Russia, leaving the roads in cities like Bryansk in such appalling state – such that one afternoon a mother pushing a baby in a buggy down a street there felt it collapse beneath her, pulling the child down a drain, where it drowned in the sewers – there is fury at huge transfers to the North

Caucasus, especially to rebellious regions whose exports are migrants, coffins and bombs.

Moscow has already handed over more than $30 billion to the North Caucasus, home to only 9 million people, with a tenfold increase in subsidies since 2000.[56] They reached over $1,000 per capita in Chechnya in 2010.[57] This is more than six times the national average.[58] Grozny's budget has been more than 90 per cent covered by federal funds – almost double the national average.[59] This may be lower in per capita terms than funding for remote Kamchatka, in line with subsidies for other poor ethnic regions in Asia such as Tuva or Buryatia, but it is what Kadyrov appears to be spending the money on that enrages ethnic Russian taxpayers.[60]

Grozny now has the largest mosque in the world, blue-glass skyscrapers and a $280 million football stadium, but half the population is officially unemployed. At night Kadyrov likes to drive his sports cars as fast as he can up and down the new Vladimir Putin Avenue, occasionally pulling up to the curb to heckle any women he sees not wearing their headscarves. Makhachkala, the capital of Dagestan, which registers 90 per cent youth unemployment, in a republic where 824 people were lost or wounded to armed conflict in 2011, somehow found the money to sign the world football star Samuel Eto'o – as the planet's most expensive player – for $20 million a year.[61] Understandably, taxpayers in Ivanovo and Chita feel they are being fleeced – and by the same people who are killing their conscripts. In Chechnya, casualties are down, but endemic conflict has flared in Dagestan. Across the North Caucasus there were 1,378 killed or wounded in 2011.[62]

Denied the satisfaction of peace, the country is riled by the video clips that keep rolling in of Kadyrov at play: throwing dollars into the air, playing with his tigers 'that calm him down' in a private zoo, relaxing on top of a sports car or hosting paid-for Hollywood actors at his birthday. He is behaving like a bandit celebrating after a bank robbery. In a sense, he is. This man inherited power from his father, a rebel who came over to Putin, whose official salary is less than $130,000 a year, but who keeps a stable of fifty stallions that costs $900,000 a year.[63] The same Mr Kadyrov, who publicly stated his approval of honour killings, was observed by one US diplomat at a tribal wedding giving the newly-weds a five kilo lump of gold, whilst the guests threw $100 bills at child dancers, gorging on vodka and enjoying 'water-scooter jaunts on the Caspian sea'.[64] When asked where the money comes from, he smiled: 'Allah gives. I do not myself know how it is possible . . . or where the money comes from.'[65]

It comes from Russian taxpayers. In the North Caucasus, the vertical of corruption has reached such absurd proportions that it has undermined what the vertical was established for: national unity. 'Why should they get more money than Smolensk?' This was exactly the same attitude that saw Russia jettison most of the SSRs. In Gorbachev's 1991 referendum Muslim Central Asians voted to stay in the USSR, but were not even invited to a secret meeting between Ukraine, Belarus and Russia that killed that Union. There was embarrassment when the leaders realized they had 'forgotten' to invite the Kazakh leader Nazarbayev, whom Gorbachev had hoped would be his successor. Nobody cared for the others. In the end it was simple: nobody wanted 'not to eat' for Uzbeks and Tajiks.

The fate of the Muslim Soviet Union was thus decided not in the republics, but by the Russians themselves – I feel it will be the same way with the North Caucasus. And these words from a check-out girl I met on the minibus back from Nizhny Tagil, all flaxen hair and green come-hither eyes, captures much of the mood towards them:

'The Caucasus – I don't want to go there . . . I don't even want them in the minimarket where I work. I don't want to pay for them. They can go their own way. I hate seeing them around. I don't want to pay for ski slopes for them . . . It's tribute, you know? We should stop feeding them and throw them away . . . they are all violent tribes.'

Russia has not found its borders. Frontiers are regarded as temporary or unresolved. The majority feels this way as new borders are already developing, with the governor of Krasnodar calling in 2012 to raise 'Cossacks' to patrol his territory to keep out Caucasians.[66] Instead of stability, what Putin has laid in the North Caucasus is a time bomb. Kadyrov is his vassal, not integrated into the United Russia system. Should Putin fall, with peace depending on the ties between two men alone, catastrophe beckons. 'The end of subsidies for Kadyrov means death,' says Orkhan Jemal, Russia's leading expert on the North Caucasus, son of a Muslim leader, 'which is why he will do whatever he can to keep the regime going.' This is why no one can quite kill the rumour in Moscow, that 'Putin's Chechens', will put down the protests should they ever breach the Kremlin walls.

Stability in the North Caucasus is an illusion. Russians realize this, with only 5 per cent thinking that the government fully controls the situation there.[67] There is a real risk of renewed conflict in a post-Putin era. There are few ways to imagine that the rulers in Grozny could be made to accept anything other than the 'vertical of corruption', even at gunpoint. The North Caucasus is a mosaic – there is no easy way to imagine a new border being drawn. Not all the republics would want to leave. Fewer would be capable of credible statehood. Awfully, the embrace seems as necessary as it is poisonous. Nor is this bitterness just directed at them. The incompetence of the vertical means it is not just the Caucasus that Russians want 'to stop feeding' – but Moscow itself.

CHAPTER ELEVEN

MOSCOW THE COLONIALIST

'MOSCOW IS not Russia.' Wherever you travel from, Kaliningrad to Magadan, they tell you the same thing. 'Moscow is another country.' They tell you that Moscow is a bloodsucker: 'It sucks out all our resources, turns them into petro-dollars and stashes them into the West.' They tell you that Moscow is an imperialist: 'The capital takes all our tax returns and gives us only decrees and corruption in return.' All across the empire 'federalism' is a dirty word – it means rule by Moscow.

The first anti-Putin protests were not in Moscow. They were on the extreme edges of Russia. These pre-tremors of discontent were mistaken for isolated incidents during the Medvedev 'presidency'. First in 2008, thousands demonstrated in Vladivostok and Khabarovsk in the Russian Far East against Kremlin decrees. The crowd reached almost 10,000 strong, shivering by the Pacific portside. Flanked by police, the deputy prosecutor tried to make them leave. 'Go home, they are not sending our OMON, they are sending their OMON, they will hurt you.' The Moscow riot troops landed within hours. They broke up the rally, dragged the steadfast along the pavement and chucked them into vans. They were sent because Putin could not trust the local police. Then in 2010, after the recession, in the Baltic enclave of Kaliningrad between EU Poland and EU Lithuania, over 10,000 came out to demonstrate against a Muscovite governor. The banners read: 'United Russia, Go Back to Russia'.

In both Kaliningrad and Vladivostok, a continent apart, the men and women on the streets had come out in proportional terms to the Moscow protesters. They were not protesting against Putin, an almost abstract entity, but against his vertical – that had passed economic decrees without any considerations as to how they made their money and reduced their business plans to naught.

In 2008 in Vladivostok, anger boiled over when a new tariff was smacked on importing cars from Japan, in a city that lives off importing them and had brought in some 534,000 that year.[1] The sudden decree to favour Russian auto manufacturers looked set to kill this business in one fell swoop. What angered those in the Far East the most was that whoever had signed and drafted it, appeared neither to know nor care that their economy was based on car imports. It enraged them that the vertical had robbed them of any veto-points to reverse it.

Despite everything, the party of power secured only 33 per cent of the vote in the Far East during the 2011 elections, far lower than the 'official' Moscow result.[2] However there was no unrest, because the FSB, the OMON and the local prosecutor's office treat provincials in ways they would never dare treat Muscovites. The heads of these structures are all selected by the Kremlin and almost always non-natives. They are sardonically called the 'Vikings', a nod to Scandinavians who ruled Slavs in medieval Kievan Rus. 'Moscow treats us like a colony,' groaned Andrey Dudenok, the man who had led the car protests in the grim Amur city of Khabarovsk. 'But protests don't change a thing.' He had now given up. Not because he was apathetic during the elections, but because he had been intimidated out of protesting. This is what happened when he got involved in politics.

- The FSB phoned ten times to tell him to stop organizing protests. They threatened him unless he 'stopped this'.
- He was arrested twice. Once he was held in a cell for over twenty-four hours.
- The FSB then threatened his boss with a 'tax inspection' unless Dudenok was sacked. He was immediately.
- The authorities then started two court cases against Dudenok for parking fines.
- Police 'discovered drugs in his car' and threatened to open narcotics charges against him.
- Dudenok then fled Khabarovsk from March to May 2009.
- The FSB then raided his flat. They seized dozens of books and computers.

When he came back to the city, Dudenok decided to quit politics. 'When I returned to Khabarovsk,' he says, 'I made a deal with the FSB. I would stop, providing that they left my family alone.' The most dispiriting thing of all is that Dudenok and his opposition friends resent the haughtiness of the Moscow movement almost as much as United Russia. They have had no contact with its leaders, with its Facebook groups, no visits from them and blame them for being missing in action when the car protests happened. It was as if they too viewed the economic livelihood of the Russian Far East as a 'yawn' issue.

In Kaliningrad in 2010, over 9,500km to the west, its own protest movement similarly erupted only to fizzle out, leaving only resentment. Life in this enclave had become increasingly claustrophobic since neighbouring Poland and Lithuania joined the EU. As they left Russia behind, they happily put up visa restrictions for them. At first it was as difficult to get a visa to Vilnius as it was to Madrid. Economic ties were chopped, locals were furious that Moscow was refusing to compromise on visa negotiations. 'We have been left behind in the ghetto,' croaked a chain-smoking hospital director, 'they promised us we'd catch up with them but we've fallen further behind.'

Kaliningrad feels Moscow has boxed it out of Europe and modernity. They feel cheated when they see that Lithuania can change but they cannot. This city lives on shuttle-trade with its neighbours, but every time they drew up in the EU 'new member states', they felt themselves the poorer. Life was getting cleaner there but in Kaliningrad dirty streets were filled with wild dogs, there was a brisk trade exporting blondes, the police collected dead drunks out of the snowdrifts in the morning and the trams still ran on German tracks. Then, the Muscovite governor decided in 2010 to increase taxes by 25 per cent on car imports from the EU.[3] He detonated unrest. The streets filled with 10,000 protesters who shouted, 'United Russia, Back to Russia'.[4]

The protests fizzled out, its leader 'leaving the movement' in a cloud of FSB harassment and financial suspicion. Blind decrees did not stop. In 2012 a sudden redrafting of import regulation laws left thousands of businesses struggling in this cross-border trade city. There was nothing they could do about it. 'The reason this whole country could collapse,' says the national celebrity-reporter Oleg Kashin, a native of Kaliningrad, 'is that everyone outside Moscow thinks they are just a Moscow colony.' The city gave Putin just 44.5 per cent in 2012 and is very proud of itself.[5]

Moscow (as synonym for Kremlin, as synonym for elite) is resented everywhere. In Vladivostok, I was told by civil servants with gritted teeth how Moscow doesn't give a damn about the time difference and wakes them up in the middle of the night, expecting them to work their business hours – there is a +7 hour time difference. In Irkutsk, I spoke to students who moaned how they would love Navalny to come and speak but they thought he never would, no matter how many comments they left on his blog asking him to – because they were hicks. In Krasnoyarsk, I smoked with officials who sighed how in an economy based entirely on digging out metals, fights between Moscow aluminium oligarchs decided Kremlin metal decrees, leaving them impotent over the regulations that mattered most to them. In Yakutsk, I drank 'KGB' cocktails with local businessmen who snarled that they had been cut out of massive investment projects in the region and that all the contracts had been awarded to 'Muscovites'. In Ussuriysk, I drank gin and tonic in cans with nationalists who told me Moscow was cross-dressing as a European. In St Petersburg, I ate sponge cake with cultural critics who acidly remarked that Moscow was an Asian monster holding them back from Europe.

Russia has swung from craving a tough hand, to resenting it. Every corner has its own story of failed protests that the Moscow opposition had been unsuccessful in knitting into a national opposition. Even in Petropavlovsk-Kamchatsky on the remote north Pacific shore, over 3,000 rallied against decrees changing the time zone. They waved loud banners – 'we refuse to live in the dark' – only to be ignored.[6]

Indifference to waking hours is one thing, money quite another. Everywhere you can send men 'in the know' apoplectic by asking them about company registration. In the Far East locals threw their hands up in disgust that the Far Eastern Shipping Company had its headquarters in Moscow, and was paying its taxes in the capital.[7] In Siberia, I saw the same reaction when asking why oil and gas giants have their headquarters in St Petersburg.

This slogan is popular everywhere: 'Stop feeding Moscow'. Across the country 'federalism' has become a dirty word, synonymous with the dirty wars in the Caucasus for which Moscow wants their sons, with dirty deals that Moscow does with its governors, with their resources extracted to be sold in the electronic markets inside the blue-glass skyscrapers of Moscow city, leaving them to only hope Putin will throw a kindergarten or two into their begging bowls.

Putin says: 'From the very beginning Russia was created as a super-centralized state. That's practically laid down in its genetic code, its traditions and the mentality of its people.'[8] He is wrong. A new form of anti-bureaucratic, anti-federal resentment is fizzing. It is turning into viciously anti-official, anti-Putin anguish, which looks at the prancing Moscow oppositions as but a faction of an elite that sucks them dry. 'Russia has never been a democracy,' said a middle-aged man in Vladivostok, 'and we have always been a colony.'

The rejection of the vertical is written in the polling data. It stems from the idea that central authority is corrupt authority – only 1 per cent believe in officials' income declarations.[9] It shows itself in the routine polls from the late 2000s showing that more than 65 per cent of Russians wanted the return of elected governors, growing to more than 85 per cent of those in the big cities.[10] Only 8 per cent said they were happy with the current system.[11] It is a rejection of the very desire for centralization that accompanied Putin to power. This is why the only concession that the Kremlin was in the long run willing to make to the protest movement was the piecemeal return of governors' elections with a 'Presidential filter'.

The Moscow opposition – speaking the language of romance and rights whilst the regions' protest banners are scrawled in the language of decentralization and efficiency – has missed the real concerns of Russians. They are desperate for a state that will actually do something for them. This is why Russia has a catchphrase when it comes to politics at the moment: 'If not Putin, who?'

This anguish has been picked up in surveys. The Centre for Strategic Research, originally founded to advise Putin, found that in winter 2012 a majority of those in its focus groups across Russia spoke of revolution.[12] It showed the popularity of the government slipping, as well as the opposition. For now, Navalny and his allies are seen as a Pussy Riot opposition that cannot give them what they want – a modern state. Time is on their side, but a fragmented and feudalized country only helps the Kremlin snap anything before it coheres. In fact, Russian regions are so isolated one from another, feeling the enormity of their country, that each place feels they are engulfed by an ocean that backs the regime, caring naught for them. Even Moscow. This is why the Kremlin invented Nizhny Tagil.

We're so Different It's Frightening

Putin is trying his best to look relaxed, to pull the same wisecracks that he always has in front of the cameras, to show complete, untroubled authority in his four-and-a-half-hour-long 'phone in', straight 'from the people' live on national TV.

This is December 2011 and the protest movement has yet to peak. Things look deeply uncertain. The live-link to the regions jumps from the Caucasus to the Pacific to the north, each with a different message to Putin, almost all of them supportive. Now to the Urals, to the industrial plants of Nizhny Tagil. Five men in black overalls are standing in front of a tank on their shop floor. Their tired-eyed foreman in a silver tie starts to speak to power. The men are unflinching:

'I want to say about these meetings, if our militia – or as they're known now the police – are no longer able to work, can no longer cope then we are ready with the lads to come out and defend our stability . . . but of course, within the law.'[13]

Putin seems touched, genuinely surprised and seems to sigh with appreciation, smiling: 'Not yet . . . hopefully it won't come to that.'[14]

It was through this message from 'the workers committee to support Vladimir Putin' that Moscow learnt about Nizhny Tagil, and that this city was the one that the Kremlin PR department had chosen to represent their supposed support in 'real Russia'. Again and again images of 'workers' protesting for Putin in the sleet were shown on federal TV. There were printed placards announcing:

Don't Allow the Country to Go back to the '90s!
We want Stability and Development!
Stop DESTABILIZING the country!

The 'Workers Committee' of Nizhny Tagil was supposed to say that the 27 per cent of the Russian workforce employed in industry, and especially the over 2.5 million workers in the military–industrial complex had none of the doubts about Putin that the cosmopolitan elite had contracted.[15] It was the centrepiece of the campaign to firm up the regime's support base amongst the working class.

Nizhny Tagil became the poster-boy for Putin's 'heartland support'. This is a city with history. It was here, 18km over the theoretical border with the Asian continent, that Stalin evacuated the Kharkov tank factory. It was the mass production of tanks here that enabled the Soviet Union to hold off Nazi armour on the edge of the great Eurasian steppe, at the fringes of the heartland near Kursk and Stalingrad.

They call the Urals, 'the spine of Russia'. As the cracked, uneven motorway jolts the minibus to Putin's bastion, past the ridges and the birch forests of the Urals, it is impossible not to think of Hitler. Nizhny Tagil is an alternate ending to the Second World War. Hitler had wanted these ridges to be where a generation of Germans would fight a guerrilla war against the Slavs – pushed into Asia forever. The distance – 1,800km from Moscow – is a testament to the absurdity of his imperial dream, the one that Albert Speer only grasped when he saw a thick line in pencil, cutting down the Urals, on the Führer's globe in the Berghof. I am hungover, half imagining German troops on the road north (would they have been exhausted, elated, completely lost . . . could they ever have even got here?) when the minibus passes a lonely election poster: 'Strong Country – Strong Leader'. It is for Putin.

Had the Germans ever arrived in Nizhny Tagil they would have found a starving population of Gulag inmates and those only technically 'free' slaving in the plants. Not that they would have cared, their Generalplan-Ost for the next 25–30 years after victory included the extermination of 50–60 per cent of Russians with 15 per cent marched into Siberia, and 75 per cent of Belarusians and 65 per cent of Ukrainians also sentenced to death in the 'big plan'.[16] As the rain obscured the forests and made the windows run, my mind wandered.

Nizhny Tagil is now the codename of a disinformation campaign – 'real Russians' are behind Putin. As the minivan pulls into the rutted mud lanes, at the outskirts of this city of 350,000, it starts to feel like the Kremlin has made an off choice. This is no showcase of the successes of Putinism – or was every other industrial town vastly worse? The roads are so cracked and potholed they look as if they have come under attack. Rotten wooden cottages sink into the mud by the roadside before giving way to a gypsy colony and a crumbling train station. Behind it, belching smokestacks, flares and industrial metal works spew chemicals and pollutants into the town. The air tastes metallic, thick, like toast. Inside, everything in the dingy hotels and government buildings of Nizhny Tagil appeared to be broken. As I'm sure it had been on the day they opened.

The life of the town is completely dominated by the two giant industrial works erected during the Soviet period. There is the massive iron and steel works of NTMK and the enormous train and tank factory, Uralwagonzavod. All employment and the entire economy are entirely dependent on these two plants. In this respect Nizhny Tagil has a diversified economy: a study by the Russian Ministry of the Economy at the start of Putin's rule classified two out of five of all cities, home to 25 million people, as 'mono-gorods', dependent on a single industry.[17] 'They are our most serious economic problem,' as a deputy minister privately put it, 'people are just trapped in them.'

They are also a social problem. Those who live in them will never be able to lead truly modern lives. It is easy to understand why people in these cities feel nostalgic for Soviet power. The bulk of the labour force is still working in the same government-dependent mega-enterprises, the only difference is that the profits of the mega-works are privatized, with all pollution socialized. The local government is still run by a monopoly party of power – not a totalitarian but a tawdry one.

I had come to Nizhny Tagil to find these ardent supporters of the regime who had threatened to come to Moscow to beat up the opposition. They were nowhere to be seen. The 'workers committee' had disappeared, nor could I find a single worker who had taken part in it. Full of anguish and riled at having been taken for a ride, every factory man I spoke to sighed that it was a fiction invented by the plant's management in order to please Putin. The 'workers' in the video-clip were managers and one of the organizers was a PR agent who had previously been the judge of 'Miss Nizhny Tagil in Bikini'.

'It was a complete joke,' grumbled my new friend, Vasily, a chain-smoker in his forties. He had worked all his life in the gigantic Uralwagonzavod works, the same factory as the so-called 'committee'. 'There was no mass worker movement . . . we were not going to come and beat people up. There were only a dozen of them . . . bosses and PR men the lot of them!'

Vasily, like most of the men who worked in the factory, was paranoid of enemy agents. He knew full well that the plant he worked in had built a tank armada to fight World War Three and that if the CIA were really after Russian secrets, they would be snooping around here. 'All your documents, I need to be sure,' he said to me. But after a while he relented. 'You see, I have to be careful . . . I didn't vote for *him* . . . I'm opposition you see.' The workers told me that to make sure everyone voted for Putin, they had been given lectures inside the plant. 'They said we'd all go home starving if Putin didn't win . . . because then the opposition would come to power and they'd cancel all our orders.' The workers were then issued with a barcode and told on the election day that a van would be waiting outside each polling station – and if they handed it in, having voted for Putin, they would get a 'bonus': 'Those idiots didn't realize that you give it in anyway and get the bonus and not vote for Putin. They are all frightened. If you lose your job at the two factories – you're finished here really.'

Vasily and his sons took me for a drive around Tagil in their clapped out Lada car. 'Five years ago I thought Putin was a hero,' he snarled as the car bumped and swerved over huge potholes the size of children on the main street. 'Then he refused to go. He's greedy for power. And I know all the people in his party are crooks in this town. So why should I think he's not like that too?'

Vasily had never heard about the huge corruption scandals that implicate the Kremlin, which have never been shown on TV, all he knew was the behaviour of the local predatory United Russia cadres. We stopped by the war memorial. We stopped by a tank on a plinth. 'I think the problem here,' muttered Vasily, 'is the mentality.' He went a bit quieter. 'Not everyone who came here was free. The grandparents, the parents . . . were in camps. There were camps here. It takes generations to go.'

The gulags, even though no one ever talks of them, are in the blood, in a hundred gestures, in a hundred thousand – 'I'm not sure that's such a good idea.' We stopped by the roadside in his part of town – the Derzhinsky district, named after the founder of the Cheka and thus the KGB. 'You see that spot?' There is nothing there but punctured old tarmac. 'That is where my grandmother starved to death in the war . . . I just wanted to show you that.'

We drove a bit more. We stopped by the dirt track that the tanks roll off towards the train tracks. Women were wandering down it. They had been picking berries in the pristine unpolluted forests close by. Vasily lights another cigarette and sighs: 'In this factory I think about 25 per cent of people are alcoholic wrecks . . . it's really sad. They drink. They work. They drink. They are real wrecks. Then about 50 per cent only think about one thing – fishing. They are fishing fanatics. Rods . . . that's all they talk about. They could not give a damn about politics or Putin. About 25 per cent of people watch the news. They are not Putin fanatics. They like stability, but they hate corruption too. But I don't know anyone who'd go to Moscow to beat people up, or anyone who trusts the opposition in Moscow for that matter.'

The actual election results showed that Vasily was in fact in the majority. Less than a third of those in Nizhny Tagil had in fact voted for United Russia back in December 2011.[18] But he felt completely alone: 'The thing is I think 100 per cent . . . 110 per cent . . . 130 per cent all believe in the 'good tsar and the bad boyars'. They think all the awful things happening in Nizhny Tagil have nothing to do with Putin . . . and that he doesn't know how bad it is here.'

And really terrible things have been happening in Nizhny Tagil. The worst of it all was dug up by a dog. It was 2007, the height of public confidence in 'stability', in a village 40km from the city that a stray found as many as thirty decomposing bodies of young girls tossed into a mass grave. 'As many as thirty', as it is impossible to say exactly how many there were – because they had rotted past the point of being easily identified. This pit seemed like the tip of an iceberg: in the previous two years alone 462 people had gone missing in Nizhny Tagil and these cases remain unsolved.[19] It pointed to a pattern of police indifference, carelessness or even (as most locals believe) complicity in a murder ring of the kind usually found not in Russia but in Central America, or Roberto Bolaño novels.

For years the families of missing girls had been putting up home-printed posters, phoning the authorities and appealing to the police to help them find their daughters – and nothing had happened as a criminal ring preyed on the city. The criminals had been using an eerily attractive, blue-eyed young man to lure girls as young as thirteen back to an apartment. There they would then gang-rape them on the floor. If they refused to become prostitutes, they would be killed.

This is how the bodies had ended up in the pit. The gang was so confident that no one was coming after them that they had barely bothered to cover the latest bodies with much earth. They just tossed them into the pit. Some reports suggested that the mob leader gang-raped, then murdered, his own fourteen-year-old daughter. Distraught families begged the police for help but got none. In one telling case, the police even actually began to investigate the brother of the missing teenager, however unlikely it was that he had murdered her. When the gang was finally arrested they were linked to fourteen murders and suspected of up to fifty in total. Yet they were not even the biggest killers in Nizhny Tagil. They were nothing compared to the tidal wave of drugs and addiction that had hit the Urals after Gorbachev started 'restructuring'.

The collapse hit Nizhny Tagil harder than most. Everything – from the roads to the factories and the hospitals received no investment and fell into disrepair. The collapse of the Soviet Union is something very literal here. It was the collapse of public services. Workers went unpaid and mafia gangs brazenly shot each other on the streets. With the bureaucracy and the economy in breakdown, the city was at its most vulnerable to a tidal wave of heroin from Central Asia. Russia found itself with open borders with Tajikistan and Kyrgyzstan, which turned into trafficking routes for Afghan heroin as the farmers of these former Soviet states and satellites turned to the drugs trade to make up for the loss of agricultural subsidies from Moscow.

Socially, it was as if the city had been hit by a plague. The population fell by almost 100,000 between 1989 and 2002. Heroin addiction and Aids had been rarities in the Soviet Union. They now became ubiquitous. Drug use exploded by 400 per cent between 1992 and 2002.[20] The number of heroin addicts climbed during the Yeltsin and Putin years from virtually nil to almost 2.5 million.[21] There are today a minimum of 1 million Aids cases in Russia, which also consumes almost one-fifth of the world's heroin.[22] Alcoholism rose, with as many as 0.5 million drinking themselves to death every year.[23]

Nizhny Tagil and the rest of the Sverdlovsk region were amongst the hardest hit of all 'oblasts' in Russia. The addiction rate in the province did not double or treble, but jumped more than seventy-four times over, between the years 1990 and 2000. One of the many who turned into a junkie was the brother of Vasily Sigarev, a playwright from Nizhny Tagil. He wasn't a playwright in those days but was driving whores around at night. He would wait outside in the car until they came back. Luck brought him to Ekaterinburg; talent found him a stage in Moscow, for plays that combine the despair of Samuel Beckett with the brutality of a Russian cop-thriller. They are about boys drinking the night before being sent to Chechnya, about an abusive couple lost at a clapped-out railway station, but essentially they are all about this one speech, in one play, that an actor yells out at the audience:

> When you get back to your capital you can tell them how people live in Russia, 'cause they don't have the faintest idea. Even if God was supposed to knock us out equal, we're only equal on the outside. Two arms, two legs and a head with a body. Every other way we're different. We're so different it's frightening.[24]

Why had people ever voted for Putin in the first place, then? I began to ask Vasily this question as we went into his apartment. Outside children were playing in a skip. 'Go on . . . take a picture of our poverty then, if you're so interested in it!' These two-room apartments were mostly bought on mortgages from the plant. We sat on his balcony and drank beer and smoked a packet of tarry Apollo-Soyuz. 'I voted for Putin twice,' he explained. He had four main arguments.

- Workers' salaries had risen from 2,500 rubles a month to 35,000 rubles a month.
- Street killings had stopped (more or less).
- He had gone on holiday to Egypt (once).
- He had bought a computer (for his son).

In fact Vasily's decision to stop voting for Putin and choose Prokhorov, the liberal-minded oligarch asked to run by the Kremlin to catch protest votes – 'He's the best manager in the country. He'd manage all this mess really well' – caught two themes that he shared with the other workers in the factory I spoke to. In industrial Russia there was a similar sense of angst at the dysfunctions of Putinism, but it was not phrased around rights like in Moscow, but inefficiency. There was complete indifference to the freedoms of the media, Khodorkovsky ('That Jew deserves jail!') or the right to compete fairly in the elections, but real anger at the squalid state of public services.

'In the 1990s it was so much worse. It was a dangerous time,' sighed Vasily. 'Things have got better. But Navalny that provocateur is right – things will not get any better as the United Russia party is the party of crooks and thieves. All the policemen and the judges and the bureaucrats that I know that are stealing in Nizhny Tagil are members of that party . . . But there's one guy you have to meet. Go meet Bychkov. He's the leader of the opposition here. Good lad.'

So I went to meet Egor Bychkov. This man in his early twenties represents a trend that obsesses Moscow intellectuals for good and ill. The watchword for the post-Soviet intelligentsia has been 'civil society'. The Soviet Union, with all under the control of the state, infantilized Russians by giving them nothing to take responsibility for. In Yeltsin's Russia, when the state suddenly declared it no longer assumed the responsibility to provide for them, it created a social vacuum in the country. The post-Soviet state was responsible for nothing, whilst post-homo Sovieticus was also responsible for nothing. The metaphor for this sorry state of affairs became the stairwell. The privatized flats people lived in were immaculate, but the common stairwells, for which the state no longer held responsibility were neglected, filthy and almost always foul. They stood for the complete disregard for public space in a privatized Russia.

Hope, for the intelligentsia, was supposed to lie amongst 'civil society'. Average Russians were expected to slowly emerge from a post-totalitarian mindset and assume responsibility through NGOs, charity and activism. Though part of such thinking, like in the USA, was the hint that people should 'do for themselves' what the state had chosen not to pay for, there was also a distinctly post-Soviet absence of social engagement by the older generation and the new middle class. 'At first we didn't understand the country was falling apart,' as Surkov put it.[25]

Egor Bychkov and the 'City Without Drugs' was both exactly the kind of organization the intelligentsia had been waiting for and the kind of movement they deeply feared. Like most things in Putin's Russia this 'NGO' was born at the crossroads of seemingly contradictory forces. It is a 'civil society initiative', but at the same time it carries many of the aggressive, paranoid and nationalistic memes of Putinism itself. It is an organization that describes itself as anti-authoritarian, but born not out of the fight against social oppression, but from where the state is weak.

The 'City Without Drugs' began at the beginning of Putin's reign, in 2000. The drugs rate had exploded 500 per cent since 1992.[26] In Sverdlovsk region the streets of its capital Ekaterinburg, the locals say, had turned into 'shooting galleries' and dealers hovered in every stairwell. Its founder is a man who captured the shift in a generation of young men in the Urals from the wanton, often joyful embrace of 1990s chaos and criminality to an overwhelming rejection of it and craving for moral, political and social order. That man was Evgeny Roizman. He is a social activist with a criminal past, a Russian nationalist proud to be half-Jewish, who leads an 'NGO' fighting the drugs trade and aiming to cure addicts with the methods of a criminal gang, who runs a system of private 're-education' camps, whilst also an icon-collector and a loving father of three.

His machine is notorious, provoking pained shivers when mentioned amongst the 'democratic aristocrats' of the capital. Not only do Roizman and his men intimidate drug dealers, taking them to the police, they try to cure people in several 'clinics' where no medically grounded treatment is practised. Addicts were chained to their beds, fed only on garlic, bread and water, then made to do work restoring ruined churches. The cuffs have now been dropped, but the clinics still operate without a single heroin substitute and are clouded in rumours and court cases concerning beatings and murders. This approach makes no sense according to modern medicine. Roizman's enemies said that instead of clinics he had built a private labour-camp system based on quack counter-narcotics.

With a few exceptions, almost all the leaders of the Russian opposition have told me privately they would let the North Caucasus go. The issues that obsess them are efficiency and immigration, public health and honesty

– coming together in hysteria about corruption. The health and purity, not the territorial integrity of the nation: the next national leader will have to bring these together in a way that resonates nationally in the manner that Roizman has done locally. He will have to be someone who somehow speaks to the regions.

The future of Russian politics sounds like Roizman. He, not Putin, is the most popular politician in Nizhny Tagil. To say this man has an odd office is an understatement: his headquarters in nearby Ekaterinburg are in a carved, wooden tsarist building on a street of nondescript blocks with no sense of history, that could be anywhere in Moscow, or anywhere in the developed world. But out in front Roizman has a made a graveyard. It is for buildings. The twenty-odd orthodox crosses are there to remember, and to express his rage, that such beautiful, tsarist wood architecture, the wood cut like frost-flowers, could be demolished by lawless developers.

His hallways are covered by his clumsy paintings of gouache woodlands and moon-eyed peasants in primary colours, his office a cluttered jumble, the colliding emblems of a political agitator and the mementos of a Jewish poet. Above a banner advertising his blog – 'Strength in Truth', printed out a dozen times in red and blue – are his framed portraits: a poster of Yuri Gagarin beside a photo of the Russian Patriarch, a sword hanging between them and the fading mugshots of two fallen comrades. An old election poster of his unshaven stare, 'Peace Upon All', doubles as a calendar. To the left the glint of an embossed gold Torah, to the right three huge files labelled Gypsies, Tajiks, Drugs.

How this all began, he says: 'When you see what is happening to your country and you see it like a house in flames. I wanted to put out those flames and stop the fire. The government wasn't doing it. So I decided I had to do it.'

The vigilante king passed me a leaflet that was covered in photos of scabbed children and half-dead young women entitled 'Russians Killing Russians', and he wasted no time in telling me why he was at war:

'We are a dying nation. The biggest threat to the country is power that lives for power itself. The Russians are dying out. The demographic situation is worsened by immigrants, then by emigrants, then made sicker still by alcoholism, drugs and the continued collapse of medical care. We are a dying country.'

This is also – as his files suggest – an ethnic battle in a country flooded with a tidal wave of Muslim migrants from the Caucasus and Central Asia. 'The City Without Drugs' began quite simply as a war – there were lots of Gypsies, lots of Tajiks selling drugs on every street corner. I rose up and fought back.' And nothing through his eyes has changed since the war began. 'Of course all the drugs in this city are sold by Gypsies and Tajiks.'

At my doubtful expression, he shrugs: 'You should go to the Gypsy village and see how they live there.'

Roizman is on the same page as the average Russian and on the opposite one to Putin when it comes to empire – he rejects the idea that Muslim Central Asia is part of one 'post-Soviet space' that should be preserved. Those out there – Tajiks, Kyrgyz, Uzbeks – are not part of the family like those from Ukraine and Belarus. They are not welcome in their millions in Russia. He urgently wants a visa wall erected against them, as do most popular opposition figures and a majority of Russians I have spoken to. He snarls: 'The whole problem is that we have no border with Central Asia. We have no visa regime. The clans that run Tajikistan live by the drugs trade. This means that Russia was hit by a drugs tsunami in the 1990s when drugs began to flood north from Tajikistan and Afghanistan after the collapse of Soviet power and Soviet borders. It hit society when it was at its very weakest.'

As we speak, the Roizman 'men' slip in and out of the room as he reclines in an armchair to expound on the failure of the state. They bring photos of stacks of heroin on their iPhones and mutter into his ear about the junkies – 'Boss, Boss'. If you did not know he was fighting drugs, blink and it would look like Roizman was dealing them. These are his personal army, many of them 'cured' by him, and who substitute for the state in Ekaterinburg's heroin wars. 'The government simply cannot operate against this. The government cannot deal with this . . . The country is a dinosaur. This is why I have taken the war on drugs into my own hands – and this is not wrong, simply because there is no war being waged by the authorities.'

On the edge of anger: 'My biggest mistake was to think that once I had shown I could have an impact that the government would come and join me. But no . . . The deciding factor as to why the system is not fighting drugs is not corruption. The system just doesn't want to change. There is no political will.'

Roizman's winning cocktail of Russian nationalism, vigilante policing and civil society is tinged by resurgent Orthodoxy, in a city with several boxy new churches and newfound church power. With a gesture of the head he takes me to his icon museum next door. Then in the stairwell he falls into a silent funk at the questions: 'How can someone half-Jewish be a Russian nationalist? Do you consider yourself a Jew or a Christian?'

He seemed not to want to answer – maybe because professing Jews are said to be unelectable to the highest office in Russia, maybe because these were the personal tectonics that had made him want to be a hero for his city. 'I couldn't say if I was one religion or the other. I don't know . . . I don't know . . . I will always say that I am Roizman. I go to church to make some confessions sometimes. I couldn't say.'

The vigilante had suddenly gone quiet as we sprinted up the stairs to the icons themselves. Maybe because he was trying to *show me* the answer, we went to look at these pieces of a lost Russia: gold, carved, wooden, ancient. He had dozens of them in a medicinally white room in a modern block next to his office. We walked to the main one – 'take this, look' – Roizman had affixed a magnifying glass just below it. 'Can you see? Can you see . . .? All those tiny carvings . . . you cannot see them with the naked eye.' We looked through the magnifying glass together, at the incredible intricacy in the gold leaf on the robes of the priests as they hailed the messiah. He was smiling.

Roizman – unlike almost any other leader of the Russian opposition, maybe even more so than Navalny in Moscow – is the 'King over the Water' here. If there was a democratic election in the Urals he would win it, to be the mayor, the governor or even more. One 2012 poll showed 26.5 per cent of Ekaterinburg want him as mayor – far ahead of anyone else.[27] But more ominously, he is a symbol of how under Putin a new, active Russian society had evolved, twisted and disfigured by Putin's failure to impose order and his harsh, brutal outlook on those that break it. The meaning of Roizman is not lost on the country's brightest political minds such as Vladimir Milov. 'This is Russia! What did you think democratic politics would look like here? It will look like Israel or Turkey at best. Post-Putin politics will be competitive, but it will be aggressive too.'

This brings us back to Egor Bychkov, one of his men. This young man from Nizhny Tagil was highly attracted to Evgeny Roizman and he got what he wanted – barely into his twenties he became the head of the 'City Without Drugs' in Nizhny Tagil. His mission was to bring drug addicts to Roizman's clinics where they could then be cured. This is when Bychkov's enemies claim that the kidnappings started: 'I did what I did as there is no war on drugs in Nizhny Tagil at all. The police are doing absolutely nothing to fight this.'

When he arrived to meet me I felt nervous as I got into his car. The clattering vehicle cannot have been less than twenty years old. It smelt of petrol and cigarettes. We drove to the only modern standard cafe in Tagil. Noticing my name he asked: 'So are there many Semites where you're from?' Bychkov is my age and proud of his town. The restaurant served cappuccino; out of the glass window you could see the huge belching industrial works sending pillars of pollution into people's lungs. 'There is no war on drugs here as the police are all corrupt. And there is no visa regime with Central Asia so all these Tajiks and other immigrants are migrating here and selling drugs. The Tajiks and the Gypsies are selling drugs here.'

'So did you kidnap people?' I asked him.

'Well it depends on your definition of kidnapping,' grinned Bychkov. 'What we used to do is we used to wait outside the houses of the drug dealers and when the addict came out we would jump him and go . . . unless you work with us we'll send you to prison. They always agreed to work with us. Then we would get them to go into the dealers' homes first . . . and then we'd storm the dealers' apartments.'

Bychkov says they stopped 300 drug dealers this way. He claims (his facial expressions are unconvincing) that they did not use guns. Then the addicts would be sent to Roizman's clinics. 'We'd get the parents to sign consent.' There they would be forced onto a cold turkey regime and fed only bread, water, onions and salt. They would often be set to work renovating churches and handcuffed to their beds.

Bychkov was charged by the police with seven abductions and accused of forcing them into Roizman's centres, where they were then alleged to have been starved and abused. He was sentenced to three and a half years in a prison colony. This arrest sparked something very rare in the Urals – a public outcry. Over five hundred protested in Ekaterinburg for his release and, after being pressured by pop-stars and politicians to pardon him so that the 'City Without Drugs' could continue its good work, President Medvedev himself ordered him released.

'Putin is a tsar,' he says. 'I am certain of this. Maybe he even thinks of himself as a god.' Convinced that the police are to blame for the squalid drug addiction of his city, he claims: 'If they wanted to fight drugs they could stop it in a single day. They don't want to. That is why this fund exists. Putin could change it all in one day if he wanted to . . . but he doesn't. He doesn't want to fight a war on drugs or on alcoholism. He couldn't give a shit about the country. I don't believe Putin doesn't know what is happening here.'

This is how Bychkov came to be the leader of the local protest movement. He arranged two rallies for fair elections – where he claims over 200 people turned up at each one and tried to observe the elections, driving around from polling station to polling station in his clapped-out car, to see how the fraud was taking place. 'The workers were told to vote for Putin. They were too scared in the polling booths to vote for somebody else. They didn't realize that they were not going to find who exactly you had voted for.' Bychkov is also a symbol – as his huge popularity amongst the workers attests to – that 1,800km east from Moscow in the city Putin signalled out as his citadel of support, opposition feeling is tangled together with vigilante policing, a certain thrill in beating the weak and racist hooliganism.

For the rest of my time in Nizhny Tagil I was looking for workers who were 'ready, ready to come to Moscow to beat up the protesters there'. I found men ready to beat up Tajiks, to smash in the faces of drug dealers, to hit traffic policemen and beat corrupt officials and, of course, the Gypsies. Not protesters, and not for him. I found a city where wages had gone up but lawlessness, degeneration and abuse remained. These wages had legitimized the regime for a decade, but they had not made these men love it indefinitely. But in Nizhny Tagil I did not find uninformed idiots. The criminalization of the local bureaucracy, and United Russia, the 'party of bureaucrats' was apparent to all. What I found were people who said they had voted for Putin because they saw 'no alternative', the very 'alternative' he had taken away from them.

CHAPTER TWELVE

CHINESE NIGHTMARES

RUSSIA IS not truly sovereign. It is a territory overshadowed by two superpowers – the European Union and China. In the western provinces, the cars people drive are German second-hand, the economy exists off pipelines pumping into the EU and the symbol of success is a multi-entry Schengen visa. Both the Moscow protesters and the Moscow powerbrokers are dreaming of London. The shadow assets of the Kremlin are hidden in European tax havens and its children at British public schools. Those waving anti-Putin placards are exasperated that their home appliances are increasingly from IKEA but their institutions come closer to Kazakhstan.

Putinism is so dysfunctional that in Russia's most western province, Kaliningrad, those who live there are quietly trying to Europeanize themselves. They are proud that they have bicycle lanes – and Asiatic Moscow does not. They are proud that 60 per cent of them have Schengen multi-entry visas, in a country where 80 per cent have never travelled abroad.[1] The best thing money can buy is a European passport. Local experts predict that at current growth rates half its population will by hook or by crook have become EU citizens by 2040.[2] This rejection of Russia even applies to the name – almost a quarter want to rename Kaliningrad as Konigsberg, as it was known before the city was conquered and annexed out of German East Prussia in 1945.[3]

Knowing how they are tied into Europe, the Russian elite has become paranoid about its eastern territory. Since the outbreak of the financial crisis, white men all over the world have become hysterical about China. The 2008 market crash pricked the Brussels delusion-bubble that Europe would be a normative superpower and the Washington fantasy 'Project for a new American century'.[4] In their disorientation, the Western political class became obsessed about Chinese GDP figures, which they read as a synonym for power, and saw in the glass-tower cities that sprang up overnight in the Pearl Delta shimmering reflections of the eclipse of the West. *When China Rules the World* became a best-seller.[5] In Russia, the policy wonks were also worried, especially Sergey Karaganov, a bald authority, consulted by both Yeltsin and Putin. He warned: 'If the current economic trends persist, it is very likely that Russia east of the Urals and later the whole country will turn into an appendage of China – first as a warehouse of resources, and then economically and politically. This will happen without any 'aggressive' or unfriendly efforts by China, it will happen by default.'[6]

The entire hysteria about whether Putinist stagnation or opposition-induced anarchy would lead the country to disaster was not just about the West – but Siberia. The entire conversation in Moscow took place in hysterics. Claims of migrant invasions and Chinese gobbling up of resources filled the newspapers. There was an insecure tinge in the jokes Russians were telling.

'Optimists learn English, pessimists learn Chinese and realists learn how to operate a Kalashnikov.'
'The good news in 2050 is that the Ukrainian Euro and the Russian Yuan are trading one to one.'

The 'yellow peril' was in the air. Yet none of the political class seemed to have been to the eastern provinces. Nobody could give you a firm answer if this ramshackle Russia could live in the shadow of a rising China. It was impossible to work out from Moscow if talk of migrant invasions, resource robberies and losing Siberia reflected the anguished uncertainty that Putin's return and mass protests created – or an emerging reality the vertical would be unable to prevent.

Losing Siberia

The Trans-Siberian from Irkutsk, where men die in their early fifties, to impoverished Birobidzhan on the Chinese border, was claustrophobic with Russian fears. For three nights, through the incessant rocking and screeching of the rails, I chatted with the workers, state employees and military men travelling home on this most remote and least inhabited stretch of the railway. In the restaurant-wagon some young conscripts returning home were drinking. The first lashed out: 'Navalny . . . he's only in it for himself. He never came to the city of Chita. He never talked about Chita! He does not care about Chita! He only cares about Moscow.' The second groaned: 'The opposition is all men like . . . Boris Nemtsov . . .! The former deputy prime minister. They just want to be Europeans not

Russians. They just want to drink oil again.' Yet neither of them had voted. 'Putin is just a billionaire and all politicians are just crooks.'

In the smoking area I befriended a nervous military epidemiologist. For hours he had incessantly walked up and down the carriage looking over his shoulder, taking on and off his glasses. This is how he spent his life, travelling between Irkutsk and Khabarovsk to inspect sites in the Taiga for disease. He said that in his small unit everyone had been too frightened not to vote for Putin: 'They could have sacked us. And I do not know how to be a private sector epidemiologist!' As the train pulled past the Siberian forests, so huge and uninterrupted that it seemed to come from a different geological era of time, he went on: 'There is the big eye. They would have found out if I'd not voted for him.' The military epidemiologist lit up again. 'Life has got better under Putin. But the state has not got better. The schools have not got better. The police have not got better.' At dusk the train passed a tumbledown village. 'China is so much more modernized. I like it. Lots of big glass buildings.'

At night the express pulls into stations where its departure is called out by primitive loudspeakers, making me think of history. It booms metallically: 'Mosvka – Khabarovsk, Mosvka – Khabarovsk', before the clattering and lurching of the carriage begins again, for hours and hours. The loudspeakers, which once called out Stalinist slogans, remind you that for decades this railway shunted cattle-trucks full of humans being deported to the Gulag camps.

Over a day from Irkutsk the train reaches Chita and the villages become fewer and fewer. From here it is over 1,400km to the next major town. They come every hour, then every two hours, then up to every three. They are squalid little wooden wrecks without paved roads, with carved roofs and weak foundations half sunk into the earth. They are dying. You can easily make out that many of them are abandoned. Tangled electric wires bent by the wind tie them into the Russian grid. In the third-class carriages, a long dormitory, all the men lounge shirtless and unwashed, playing cards and drinking beer in the morning. Their tiny gold baptismal crosses glint as the sun comes through the trees. Somewhere near is the camp where they sent Khodorkovsky.

The train passes a whole day without any major settlement. It is so remote, that like ghosts on the rails Yukos is still branded on passing oil wagons. But this is not the edge of the earth . . . it is a mere several hundred kilometres from heavily populated and industrialized northern China, the empire of mass production. The poverty and emptiness of the landscape in the Russian Far East is the geopolitical weakness of the state.

In Siberia it is all too evident that Russia is no longer 'sovereign' economically. As the country produces so little and depends for its livelihood on exporting raw materials, it is now in the trading spheres of influence of other powers. The lives of middle-class Russians in Europe are lived out culturally in the shadow of America and Britain, economically in that of Germany and the rest of the Eurozone. Russians in Asia live in the shadow of China, Japan and South Korea. Instead of taking holidays to Turkey, they go to the visa-free island of Hainan in China. Instead of driving second-hand German cars, they drive second-hand Japanese ones.

From Krasnoyarsk onwards you begin to feel the shadow of China and your distance from Europe. In Krasnoyarsk is the first of the Chinese markets of Siberia, selling everything from electricals to crockery. In Irkutsk you start to see signs in Chinese. In official taxis a welcome sign with a picture of the lightly bearded mayor greets visitors for 'business or rest' in Russian, English and Mandarin.

If you begin to look closely you can see Chinese characters on household appliances, plastic bags, packets of frozen food and countless trucks. This economic aura is exactly the same thousands of miles beyond China in every direction into the continent: into Central Asia, South East Asia and Russian Asia – the areas you can reach by truck and make a profit selling the cheapest stuff with the simplest operation. By Irkutsk you have left the European economic sphere of influence and entered that of East Asia. The further east, the cars are more likely to be right-hand drives. They are second-hand cars from Japan that drives on the left – colonizing Russian roads on which you drive on the right. These 'foreigners' make up as much as one-third of all cars in the country.[7]

In the Caucasus, the Chechens would dream of independence as there is no Turkish empire that could swallow them up. In Europe, the state system is so strong that even peasant Moldova can become independent without fearing German or Romanian armies. In Asia, the age of empires is not over. In Yakutsk, the coldest city in the world, I sat with some nationalistic ethnic Yakut officials in a beer hall where at one end was a bronze Russian figure, at the other a bronze Yakut. 'You see . . . very tellingly they are sitting apart,' snorted one. These men wanted as few Russians as possible in their region but were scared of independence. Even if Russia collapsed: 'that would be a disaster. The Chinese would march in and help our "young democracy". They would flood us with settlers.' They dreamed of a Russia too weak to really control them, but one still strong enough to keep China out. In Tuva, even the local underground nationalists did not want independence. To quote one of their leaders: 'It's better to be part of a weak empire than a strong one. China would swallow in weeks what Russia could never digest.'

Across the paranoid continent you see very few actual Chinese, but they are already in people's heads. In the third-class and second-class cabins of the Moscow–Khabarovsk, people talk about China when you ask them about politics. They tell you how much more efficient China is, how much healthier China is, how much more powerful China is. They are worried that one day it will be more than Chinese products that will come to Russia. The numbers make them worried: Chinese male life expectancy is seventy-one, but in Russia it is only sixty-four.[8] China spent $143 billion on its military, but Russia mustered just $72 billion in 2011.[9]

The second-class carriage is dark brown, this plasticated brown you find only in countries that were once socialist. It is half empty by now. In one compartment some men drink, sing and play cards. There is no shower. No one in this carriage had washed for days. In my own compartment sat two mothers and their three babies. For a few hours in the evening we talked about Putin, politics and the Chinese. One mother is young and attractive. Her name is Katya, she has a missing tooth and a working-class drawl. The other, Vera, has the short hair of a man and the clipped, universal accent of someone with a Soviet higher education, the kind of clear voice that all schoolteachers seem to have, with which the propagandists once read out 'Moscow Calling, Moscow Calling', to the third world.

Is it just me? Or are there more children in Russia these days? In 2006, when I had last journeyed on the Trans-Siberian, the jarring absence as you travelled of many children marked out Russia from the West. 'There are more children because of Putin,' this is the clipped voice of Vera, 'you could say they are Putin's children. He gave money for a second child that made it easier. The country stabilized. In the 1990s people didn't want to have children. It was a terrible time in our country – they closed most of the kindergartens.'

I asked about politics. Katya, the younger one, giggled as if I had asked about UFOs. She was right to do this – asking provincial people in eastern Siberia their political opinions, when they have no political impact, is faintly ridiculous. 'My husband is a soldier. So I didn't protest. We have a baby.' That baby is playing and jumping and chewing the wheels off a toy car. 'There was an idea in Khabarovsk to start a "train army" to go to Moscow for the big protests. Can you imagine – a train army? Everyone rushed to buy tickets. Then they arrested the guy who was organizing it. That was the end of that. Things are good if you have a man in the army. It's a state within a state with better benefits.'

'The railways used to be like that,' sighs Vera, 'but not anymore.'

As we talked more about politics I could sense that Katya was ashamed to talk about such complicated things in front of Vera: she has a Soviet education, she is so much better educated, she knows so much more. In European Russia the younger generation has a better grasp on politics, here in Asian Russia the breakdown of the state schooling system in the

1990s shows. Today, only one-third of Russians feel their children or grandchildren will get a good education. Half do not.

Regardless, they both want to get across their annoyance at inefficiencies – all politics is local, as so are the problems of Putinism: 'All the local officials and policemen are members of United Russia. We know that they steal and that this is the party of the state. About Moscow, what happens there, we are not so sure.'

The older woman tells me a little bit about her town, Oblyche. There had been nine kindergartens, the 'young reformers' had cut them to three, now they were filled 'with Putin's children'. In her town the young people were fleeing to work in Khabarovsk, while the old people were dying. There was no industry. It was a small town of over 1,000 people that lived off the railway. 'The Chinese already feel at home. There are more and more of them every year. They come by boat over the Amur. In China they tell us they are hungry and there is no land and no work.'

But the Russians, she said, were also going to China, 'It's cheaper for us to get there than to get to the Urals, let alone anywhere on the Black Sea for a holiday.' Russians, she said, were increasingly using 'good natural' Chinese medicines and holidaying in Chinese resorts. 'All the technical stuff they produce is great,' she added. 'They are a very hard-working people, unlike us.' They had never been to Moscow.

'It's becoming a Chinese state – eventually it will be one. We've always been a colony, you see. We always will be . . . just maybe belonging to someone else.'

This is a statement one hears repeated like a mantra in the Russian Far East. It contradicts what people say when you question them for 'signs' of this takeover. Everyone states that in their respective cities in Siberia (Irkutsk, Khabarovsk, Birobidzhan, Vladivostok) the amount of Chinese has gone down and the Russian birth rate has gone up. Immigrants are flooding in not from China but from Muslim ex-Soviet republics. Ownership of raw materials is firmly in control of Russian oligarchs and state corporations. Siberians say there are very few Chinese concerns where they come from other than vegetable farms and markets.

It is a statement without any link to the current demographic trends. There are less than 500,000 ethnic Chinese in Russia of which the majority are actually in Moscow.[10] The number of yearly Chinese labour migrants into Russia has declined and both Russian and Chinese experts attest that the border guards have become more effective at keeping unwanted intruders out.

Nor are the numbers of Chinese migrants coming into Russia likely to grow. Siberia is deeply unattractive for Chinese labour migrants compared to the factories in the Pearl River Delta or any number of other countries in South East Asia or even the West. Furthermore, by 2020, as a result of the 'one child' policy China will begin to age as a society at phenomenal speed. By 2025 the country will no longer be meaningfully exporting labour but will be in short supply of workers itself.[11] Unlike the West, China will struggle socially to accept mass migration. It will face a shortfall that there may not be enough migrants in the world to fill.

It seems that in the moment of Russian weakness in the 1990s neither was the Chinese state weak enough for large numbers of hungry settlers to cross the borders, nor strong enough to make Moscow give up control over major natural resources. Only if the massacre on Tiananmen Square had unleashed a collapse of Chinese communism with similar effects to what happened in Russia, might this mass-migration have taken place. The same goes if China had been as strong as it is now during the 1990s. It could have pushed for ownership over the resources it wanted. In Asia, Yeltsin's Russia was not weak enough.

Yet people still talk about losing Siberia, even if the overall number of Chinese around them is not rising dramatically. This is because the source of their fear is not demographic trends, but the weakness of the Russian state. They know that any renewed breakdown could change the racial balance and the ownership of raw materials across the region overnight. Russians are like Israelis. The Jews will tell you – even as Israel is stronger in the Middle East than ever before – that they fear the new Holocaust. The Russians are also a historically shocked nation. If the Holocaust could happen once, it could happen again. If the Soviet Union collapsed, it means that the Russian Federation can collapse. The nation feels that Russia is a fragile thing.

In the train carriage, the conversation drifts to whether people in her town support Mr Putin: 'At first people closed their eyes,' she put her hands in a praying position and lifted her eyes, 'and pretended not to see. They wanted to believe in Putin's power. To see him as our "saviour". But people had already stopped believing in him by 2008. Then we ended up in a war in Georgia, there was a crisis . . . things started getting harder for people again. Now nobody trusts and believes in his power.'

'So who did you vote for?'

She gave a short, embarassed laugh: 'I voted for Zhirinovsky. I think that he says what's right and what's wrong. He sees a problem and says it's a problem. Most of my friends voted for the Communist Party. Yet in our town the results were over 50 per cent for Putin. I don't believe this. In the villages around they say they all voted 100 per cent for Putin on the electoral returns. Am I supposed to believe this too?'

It is important not to think that Russians who vote for Zhirinovsky and Zyuganov are fools. They are not nostalgic for 'empire' or for the days that Russian tanks ruled in Prague. Those who vote for the Russian Communist

Party are nostalgic for the welfare state. Those who vote for Zhirinovsky are frightened of being overwhelmed by millions of Muslims and Chinese. If you live in a tiny town on the Trans-Siberian both seem more immediate issues than liberal economic reform.

She lowered her voice: 'We can't buy the liberal newspapers like *Kommersant* in our town. People who go to Khabarovsk buy them and share them. People in our town are frightened of the FSB . . . unlike in Moscow. We are starting to get some more information. It's seeping in through the Internet. Anybody who wants to know can learn – we know there is an opposition, we know there is this Navalny. But we know very little about it.'

The noise of slamming doors and the screeching of train wheels echoes down the corridor. Inside this carriage and in the minds of these two women, faith, trust and hope in the Putin state has gone, but the power of the Putin state remains. Outside, more oceans of trees on small hills. There is nothing, nothing here.

There is something unsettling looking at their children, playing on the floor of the compartment and toddling up and down past the compartments – these little people that do not know who Putin is – that if his foes continue to be as weak and ineffective as they have always been, that in the year 2024 they will be old enough to talk politics and to question how he ruled their entire lives. But in Russia with what people call 'the Stalin time', then 'the Brezhnev time', it is historically how things tend to play out.

Days go by, with more vague talks about the Chinese 'threat'. It is clear that the Russians of Siberia do not feel themselves the 'bear' of European imagination, but a tiny nation on an enormous and weakly defended territory atop of the teeming masses of Asia. They feel more like a huge Mongolia, a sparsely populated and easily overrun territory inhabited by a backward tribe, towards the new China, than a small India, a fallen-behind peer competitor who smarts at being overtaken.

Part of the reason is historical. Slavs did not always inhabit these lands. In the beginning, the Russian empire was built by bandits and greed. The Cossacks, half-criminal horsemen living beyond the rule of the law, travelled ever further east from the sixteenth to nineteenth centuries in search of furs and then more furs. On their way they trampled on the weak Khanates who ruled over what had been the core of Genghis Khan's empire. This state system was so weak as it was not just Romanov Russia that was expanding, but to the south, the Chinese Qing dynasty was expanding into the north and west. It is a myth that China has never been expansionist. As Moscow conquered Siberia, the Qing emperors added Xinjiang, Tibet, Mongolia and their native Manchuria to its tributary imperium.

In the seventeenth century these alien empires met in the fertile valley of the Amur. Today, the Chinese nationalist narrative claims that these lands were under Chinese sovereignty. In fact the land was on each bank of the river under the sovereignty of the ethnically Manchu Qing dynasty, who made the Han Chinese wear pigtail queues on pain of death. The Qing separated this territory from areas inhabited by Han by one of the last 'great walls' built on the orders of the Forbidden City – the 'willow palisade'.

This was a series of earthworks, moats and ditches begun in 1648 and lined with a wall of willow trees that marked an internal border between Manchu and Han areas. The Manchu, feeling themselves separate to the Han, did not want them flooding their ancestral lands. In 1668 the Kangxi Emperor even forbade Han from settling to the north of the willow palisade by imperial edict. This was not as if the Han were being amputated from their homeland. The 'willow palisade' was actually built along parts of the old 'great wall' built by the Ming dynasty that failed to defend China from barbarians such as the Manchus in the frozen north.

The construction of the 'willow palisade' was a historical error by Beijing of the first order. It meant that when the Cossacks arrived in the Amur they found not lands heavily populated by Han peasants but barren lands inhabited by a scattering of stone-age natives. The story of the rise and fall of the 'willow palisade' is the same as that of Russian annexation in the area. The year after Han were banned from the area in 1668, the Qing dynasty was forced to define its borders with the Tsar. Only when Russia tore up this treaty, to annex all of 'outer Manchuria' in 1858–60 did the Qing realize their world-historic mistake. Imperial officials began to encourage the migration of Han settlers to the north. A land-rush followed, as an estimated 8.7 million settlers arrived from the south in the late nineteenth century.[12] Had they been permitted to migrate earlier there could never have been a Russian majority in the areas that are now the provinces around the cities of Birobidzhan, Khabarovsk and Vladivostok – whose name in Russian taunts them as 'the lord of the east'.

Moscow's Asian power peaked on the eve of the 1905 Russo-Japanese war. It was in this campaign that the last willows on the palisade were hacked down by Russian and Japanese troops as they fought for control of Manchuria. Yet losing the first modern war where Asians defeated whites may have been a piece of historical good luck. Had Moscow won the war it might have annexed Manchuria with its large Han population, which would have spread all over Siberia and the Russian Far East.

As a result of a Manchu error and a Russian defeat in the early twentieth century, the Chinese presence in these territories was only limited. There were perhaps fewer than 100,000 Asians in the whole region and an

Asian majority in Vladivostok, who were overwhelmingly ethnic Koreans. Stalin corrected this by deporting them all to Central Asia, but he could do nothing to remove the geopolitical fault line that is the border between Christianity and China. Neither did shared communism close the huge distance between either country, across the short few kilometres over the Amur.

The wars that had been fought between Russia and China in the eighteenth century for control of these lands reignited in modern form in the Sino-Soviet split. The border between the Socialist brotherhood of the Soviet Union and the People's Republic was as militarized as the Iron Curtain in the West. Yet the gulf between the cultures on either side, in terms of understanding, contact and empathy was wider still. What for the Cossacks who settled the region had been the border between Orthodoxy and paganism, stayed a racial, cultural fissure. And unlike the wall through Europe, this was a border people fired across. Incidents occurred in the early 1960s as the ideological empires began to fall out. Border guards would fire sporadically, then halt. At some points on the Chinese side loudspeakers blasting out the propaganda of the Cultural Revolution were installed to scream into Russia.

As tensions rose in the forms of ideological epistles and accusations of 'revisionism' so too did the number of incidents, or border shootings, climbing 150 per cent from late 1964 to March 1969.[13] It was then that China, having lurched into the convulsions of the Cultural Revolution, resolved to take a tougher stance on clashes with the Soviets. In internal Chinese Communist Party meetings officers of its People's Liberation Army claimed that the Red Army had been found 'clandestinely moving the border markers in our direction'.[14] Their determination to make them pay for this had escalated into a Chinese ambush at the beginning of March 1969, then into two all-out battles with Soviet forces almost two weeks later. The Soviet side believed, according to one internal report, that during the provocation:

> The wounded were shot by the Chinese from close range [and/or] stabbed with bayonets and knives. The faces of some of the casualties were distorted beyond recognition; others had their uniforms and boots taken off by the Chinese.[15]

Moscow responded by sending a small force with tanks backed up by an artillery barrage. The USSR claimed it lost 58 troops, Beijing claimed it had killed 239 Soviet troops and taken 60 prisoners, whilst the former director of the CIA claimed that American satellite photos showed that 'the Chinese side of the river was so pockmarked by Soviet artillery that it looked like a moonscape.'[16]

This began one of the most serious nuclear attack scares of the Cold War. China was whipped into anti-Russian hysteria with the *People's Daily* running the editorial 'Down with the New Tsars'.[17] The Chinese politburo debated the possibility of Soviet bombing, with Mao twice warning of the need to prepare for war. In the Chinese provinces in the last quarter of 1969 follow-up on such declarations was visible with air-raid shelters being built, militias organized and command posts set up. Plans were also drawn up to evacuate schools and colleges from the cities. More severe incidents took place on the border of Xinjiang in western China and Soviet Kazakhstan.

The USSR, meanwhile, approached the USA about the possibility of a 'surgical strike' with atomic weapons on China's nuclear force. The USA had approached the USSR several years before about such a possibility. Symmetrically, Washington rebuffed Moscow, like Moscow had rebuffed Washington. In the end there was no war, but a process of rethinking what had happened on the banks of the Amur began in Beijing. This change in attitudes towards Chinese security saw Mao move towards inviting Nixon to China and the state's eventual opening to the West. The USA proved so receptive to this as Henry Kissinger, then secretary of state, had grasped something essential during the war scare. China could frighten Russia the way America never could. He noted in his memoirs:

> No compromise of Chinese boundary claims could alter the fact that sometime in the next generation the disparity between Soviet and Chinese power in Asia would first narrow and then tilt the other way; from then on, Siberia's future would depend increasingly on Peking's goodwill, which no Chinese government could ensure for eternity.[18]

On the third night, east of Irkutsk, we are closer to Beijing than to Moscow, the noise from the rails is now maddening, and in the gloom-filled corridors of the Trans-Siberian I thought continually about the conversations I have had there. For centuries, a weak China underwrote Russian expansion and Russian security in Asia. A strong China would never have allowed Russia to take this shape. Today, the tables have turned and Russia is now the less-developed state. Even Putin, when visiting the Russian Far East in 2000 warned the locals that unless there was improvement to the economy their children would be speaking Chinese.[19] Medvedev in 2008 also warned that unless Russia invested in the region Moscow could 'lose everything'.[20]

Putin himself is extremely interested in improving Russia's ties with China. Like the Tsar in Sorokin's *Day of the Oprichnik*, his daughter studied and speaks Mandarin and he travels frequently to Beijing. Yet friendship is the only option that Russia today really has. Russia may have legally agreed borders with China, but only with 'this' China. The Republic of China (Taiwan) doggedly claims Tuva in Russia and all of Mongolia as Chinese lands. This is, of course, not the China that matters – but what China will exist in twenty or fifty years, that might well be much more nationalistic, and which Russia of course has no agreement with whatsoever.

One conversation in Beijing comes back strongly. 'So what does China think of Russia?' My question was to the editor of a powerful Chinese foreign policy journal on the steps outside the Chinese Academy of Social Sciences, the party's most powerful think-tank. The smog is enveloping, a combination of humidity and heat that gives the air the qualities of a solid. The main highways of Beijing resemble triumphal motorways, a grid around the Forbidden City lined by the glassy trophies of our times: five-star hotels, oil majors and banks. The central traffic axis is the work of none other than Albert Speer Jr., the son of Hitler's chief architect. His plan bears striking resemblance to what his father made only in 'maquette' form for the Führer's post-war Berlin – the magnificence of inhuman verticals.

'We learnt a lot from Moscow's mistakes,' responds the editor. Since 1991, China and Russia have been mutual utopias and dystopias. In the early 1980s the two powers chose different exits from the dead end of bureaucratic pseudo-communism. For Russia, China's choices came to look like a utopian success of authoritarianism, capitalism and sovereignty, a triumph over the West that Moscow should have followed. For China, Russia came to look like a dystopian blend of lawlessness, corruption and shrunken power: a litany of every mistake a ruling party can make. During the 1990s Chinese academies studied the collapse of the USSR in order to derive policies to strengthen their own Communist Party. Since 2006 a restricted eight-volume DVD set, *Consider Danger in Times of Peace*, on the Soviet collapse has been mandatory viewing for all central, provincial and municipal party organs. The fall of the USSR has replaced Lenin's revolution as the world-historical justification for the 'dictatorship of the proletariat'.

The editor from the Chinese Academy of Social Sciences, along with other members of the Chinese foreign policy establishment, is dismissive of Russia. He sums up his views this way: 'When we think of Russia we think of Putin, vodka, guns and prostitutes.' They leave me with the impression they view Russians as second-class whites. In the Chinese Centre for International Affairs, a think-tank closely affiliated with Beijing's foreign ministry, the specialists are less rude: 'We think Russia is in love with Europe, but does not know how to express its love . . . other than violently.'

They repeated endlessly that the border has been settled and that this is no longer an issue, but boil at what they view as the mistreatment of Chinese traders in Siberia. In a Chinese think-tank, instead of sitting together around a meeting room table, you recline in armchairs spaced apart and sip tea. This only makes the European in me less comfortable, as I listen to what the Chinese think about Russia. That the border is porous to migrants and influence, these experts do not bother to hide. 'They have an army, customs, police and border guards. Our businessmen are no . . . *angels*. Are the Russians sleeping?'

But does China want this land back? When you confront Chinese experts with this question the usual refrain is: 'this is impossible'. And it is not a priority like it is for Taiwan. But when you phrase the question differently: 'But what if Russia collapsed again? If you could have your wish come true, what country would these territories be in?' The answer suddenly changes. In the office of a leading Chinese Russia specialist in the sticky futurism of Shanghai, the professor refuses to answer the question and refers me to his assistant professor, who refuses to answer the question and refers me to the professor. They then argued in Chinese. Those higher up are more cautious. 'If Russia collapses again China would never annex these territories . . . they would become independent,' says one professor who advises the Politburo expert chamber. 'China would not dare.'

Chinese history is an active volcano. The question of whether China is vengeful and hungry towards Russia struck me as unsettled and undecided, but also unimportant amongst its intellectual elites. It was unclear what their intentions would be when China had 'risen' and was not merely 'rising'. But the same could be said for China's views of the world.

As the Trans-Siberian approaches Birobidzhan it seems painfully clear in Russia today, where half of the country lives in the economic shadow of China while the elites of its European cities dream of the 'civilized order' of London and Berlin, that the tsarist reactionary, Konstantin Leonteyev, was accurate in his predictions of what menaced this state: 'Russia's death will come in either of two ways – from the East by the sword of the awakened Chinese, or through the voluntary merger with a pan-European republican federation.'

The Chinese Autonomous Oblast?

The dawn is the colour of stone and the landscape is different now. There is a mist and under it untouched marshes and bogs that roll towards low, rounded hills under forests and ever more mist. The railway is the only thing that is human. The gloom lingers into the morning. This emptiness is as raw and untouched as I imagine the savannah, but it is certainly more so. To those who live here, the Russianness of these lands is beyond dispute, but the plant life, the dense, busy thickets and the clouds clinging to the hilltops look little like Muscovy and everything like Manchuria. The rocking of the train, the damp chill that has entered the compartment, even on a July morning, reinforces the near absurdity of what I am looking at – that these are the lands Stalin designated as farmland for the Jews.

The train screeches to a halt for three minutes at the station. 'Are you sure? Why is a foreigner coming to Birobidzhan?' mutters the elderly ticket inspector. 'Foreigners never come here!' After three nights on the train, the platform had a 'through the looking glass' absurdity – the name 'Birobidzhan' written in big metal cursive Hebrew script over the red walls of this quintessentially Soviet station. A few steps outside and a column toped by a seven-branched candelabra, like the holy Menorah of the long destroyed Jewish temple, greets the traveller. Unlike in Israel, when as you step out of Ben Gurion Airport to be greeted by a small Menorah, at home and at peace with itself by the minibuses that climb the hills into Jerusalem, this one has the opposite effect of putting one at ease. It seems troubling. It is not just in the wrong place but seems duplicitous, sinister even.

A statue in bronze paint of a 'Jew' driving a cart that could have featured in an anti-Semitic pamphlet from the 1930s only exacerbates this feeling. No Jew would have ordered a statue with such a nose, to greet another at his station.

But I had not come to this incredibly remote region looking for Jews, but for signs of Chinese power. Birobidzhan is the capital of the 'Jewish Autonomous Oblast', a territory larger than Belgium with the population of little more than 170,000 people and falling. Its name is a legacy of one of Stalin's projects to destroy Judaism. Like the Nazis, the Soviets believed that Jewish culture should perish in their territory – not physically, but as a religion. The Politburo dreamed of a day when no Russian-speaking Jew knew the meaning of Yom Kippur. Like Hitler, they almost succeeded.

In the utopian frenzy of the 1930s it was decided that to 'normalize' the Jews they should have a fixed territory like every other Soviet ethnos. Because the USSR was frightened of Japan severing the Trans-Siberian, unwanted and inhospitable land was selected for them on the Manchurian border. The Jews would farm the buffer zone. Birobidzhan is the dream that failed, inside the dream that failed. Its Jewish population never surpassed 12 per cent. This is because in the Potemkin Israel there was never a synagogue, the instruction of Hebrew was banned and the holy scrolls and manuscripts the Jews had brought with them were burned.

The longer you spend in Birobidzhan today you realize just how few Jews there really are here. But what is surprising is that for all the talk in Moscow about the 'migrant invasion', the Chinese are similarly invisible in the city. Everyone in Birobidzhan warned me that the Chinese 'are every-where', but I couldn't see a single one as I walked through the streets named after Yiddish writers. This is surprising because the facts about the Chinese

presence in the region would indicate otherwise. The local authorities estimate that Chinese farmers are tilling 14 per cent of its arable land.[21] This is
the highest reported percentage for any region in Russia and a huge amount
of territory. It is not being carried out by private individuals but by the
state. In 2010 the authorities of the neighbouring Chinese province of
Heilongjiang leased 4,266km sq. of Russia.[22] The same year China rented
another 3,450km sq. of agricultural land in the Far East.[23] Altogether, an
area somewhat smaller than the US state of New Jersey.

Yet this does not appear to have changed the city's racial profile. The
demographics of the town of Birobidzhan really do seem what the Russian
2010 census says – 90 per cent Russian. That is not to say there are no
immigrants in the oblast. It is just not the immigrants one expected. There
are Azeris, Armenians and Tajiks in every cafe, shop, building site or place
that people gather. This is as it is anywhere else in Russia. Locals say there
are next to no Chinese living in the city and that their numbers have
dropped during Putin's rule, even if more land is being leased.

I became friendly with one Muslim immigrant, Azer. 'When my family
moved to this place from the Caucasus,' he remembered, 'I was shocked
and so homesick that I had to be hospitalized.' Now in his twenties he is
part of a local business clan of Azeris who migrated to Birobidzhan in the
1990s and have sewn up the city. It is they, not spectral Chinese, who as a
clan dominate over the local taxis, minimarkets, furniture stores, meat-
packaging business and even politics. He boasts that his cousin is even the
local deputy prosecutor.

Intelligent enough to have become bored out of his mind in a small
Siberian town, Azer took me for a drive in his father's SUV. Even though
it has the lowest HDI for a Slavic majority region in Russia, there is still
development. The city is a muddy jumble of ramshackle estates, smattered
with new low-lying housing projects, that even if new, look exactly like
poor-quality Soviet buildings in Moscow. But many live in squalid wooden
houses, the kind usually seen in villages. Azer sniffs: 'Only the drinkers live
there. But all Russians are drinkers. This nation is dying. It's addicted to
everything it can drink, swallow or inject and it's rotten right through.
There will be no Russians left here one day. Only Muslims and Chinese.'
He sighs. 'If only Russians didn't drink, like Muslims, they would be the
strongest.'

He points out that many people still live in the cheapest, simplest
barracks-like, two-storey blocks of flats dating back decades. They are
made of sodden, worn wood. Built by the USSR as a temporary solution
for the first colonists but never replaced due to lack of funds. 'How can
they not afford to build a decent block of flats, when the country produces
more oil than any other? They do not care about Russia ... the

government are all thieves. They are robbing Russia and buying villas in the south of France.'

But what does he think of Putin himself? The car bumps on potholes and swerves out of the way of a bleeding alcoholic stumbling across the road, but Azer is suddenly worried that he has given the wrong impression of Birobidzhan. For the past hour he has been ranting about alcoholism, inevitable migrant invasions, drug abuse and the death of the nation. 'Don't get me wrong. It's so much better than in the 1990s. I want to show you that good things are happening here too. We may not be China but things are getting better.'

The car speeds back towards the centre down empty roads. We have arrived at a glistening new supermarket, packed. It opened last year. 'You see,' smiles Azer as we walk inside. 'This is why people voted for Putin, even if they know that the party are crooks in this town. Because now you can buy whatever you want.' In the aisles we stop and count: over ninety kinds of beer, over eighty kinds of shampoo, over thirty kinds of frozen prawns, a similar number of frozen pizzas. We lost count trying to work out how many variants of yoghurt. Never, before the opening of this supermarket had there been anything approaching a modern shopping centre here. 'Before Putin you could not go shopping like this,' says Azer. 'So I think he has not been all bad.'

Travelling through Russia is like travelling in a time machine. In Moscow, St Petersburg and Ekaterinburg the 'wild 1990s' have faded from memory and with it the problems that 'the Russian Pinochet' was supposed to solve. Supermarkets have been present for over ten years. After a decade, consumerism alone no longer legitimizes the regime. Here in Russia's least developed region a single supermarket is such a huge sign of progress that Putin's inefficiencies, corruption and dysfunctions – the very things that can cause the poor public services that Azer was ranting about – are excusable. When did the people of a region that was home to forced labour camps and impoverished Stalinist collective farms, fighting off the buzzing of mosquitoes in the Taiga, ever before have the chance to taste thirty kinds of frozen pizza?

'The Chinese want this empty land,' expounds Azer. 'They are everywhere.' But where? In the miserable marketplace where peasants in dirty T-shirts and camouflage pants sell bric-a-brac and vegetables, there are only a handful of Chinese. 'The Chinese own the stalls and the Russians sell for them,' said one macho Kyrgyz crockery vendor. 'They are very clever you see. They don't work for nothing like us.' There are half a dozen Kyrgyz and Tajik market hands. Here, like everywhere else in Russia the fabled mass migration of Chinese is hard to see, but the mass migration of Caucasian and Central Asians is self-evident.

The locals say that Chinese peddlers have been 'dying out' during Putin's rule. First, because the 2000s economic boom has brought a super-market even to Birobidzhan, meaning there is less need for Chinese peddlers on street corners. Second, the local police and interior ministry forces were instructed to chuck out more Chinese illegals. The smaller a town is in Russia, the more likely it is to have Soviet-style policing. Birobidzhan is no exception. Locals say 'one call to the FSB', for suspicious behaviour snuffs out opposition before it begins. 'People are frightened,' says Azer. 'Corrupt police can come and extort your business and try and take it away if they find illegal workers.'

So it is incredibly hard to operate as a foreigner, especially for the Chinese, without getting harassed by the local police. During my stay in the 'oblast', I was detained and under a clock with Putin's face in it, interrogated about my 'activities' in the region. The questions ranged from the sinister, which I refused to answer – 'name every single person you met', to the absurd–'how did you learn of the existence of the Jewish Autonomous Oblast?' Their responsibilities, they explained, included catching illegal immigrants. This gave me a chance to interview the front line in Russia's anti-migrant guard about the Chinese.

'We catch illegal Chinese almost every other day,' explained the officer interrogating me. His face had scars and his hair was in a crew cut. 'In all, we estimate there are about 2,000 Chinese here in the region. We are constantly catching them.'

This number is not particularly high and hardly a 'sovereignty threatening' amount. It is a testament that for all the problems of Putinism, the border police have not broken down under the pressure of corruption and weight of numbers. Indeed if the figure of 2,000 from the migration police was anywhere near accurate, it would mean there are less 'ethnic Asians' in Birobidzhan than there were in the 1930s when a 4,500-strong Korean ethnic minority lived here.[24]

The longer I spent in Birobidzhan the more I realized that my expectations – that business and job opportunities would be blending Russia and China across the Amur, the way the USA and Mexico have melded together across the Rio Grande – were misplaced. In fact, the city might even need more Chinese to take advantage economically of its trading position.

According to the migration police the Chinese were almost all farmers in the countryside. To find them I drove out to the former collective farm of Waldheim, the USSR's failed 'kibbutz'. The drop in development is sharp and instant the moment you leave behind the outskirts of Birobidzhan. In the villages there are no paved roads and only official buildings are not made from wood. With the closing of the collective farms these small societies have tumbled into subsistence farming, alcoholism and a degradation of a darker kind than I had seen elsewhere in Russia. People, often visibly sick, stood by the roadside trying to sell berries and mushrooms they had picked – this, they told me, is the only way of making ends meet in the summer.

A car mechanic drove me to the Chinese border, almost 100km to the south, to finally see the 'takeover'. The man in question is Ilya. He has a sandy unshaven look, and does a bit of everything: trading, driving, smuggling, odds and ends. 'You know what makes a man from Birobidzhan? Cannabis, it's all about the cannabis.' The road to the south has not a single piece of farmland by its sides, only pristine, empty fields. 'But everyone knows the dealers are in big business growing huge fields of cannabis in the Taiga and everyone here is an *expert* smoker.' According to Ilya and local rumour, the SUVs in this city all come from men making their money in narcotics. 'What else do you think it is? Oil? We have none of that.'

About 50km from China, we come to a fork in the road. There is a derelict piece of Soviet roadside sculpture, an exuberant, futurist and cracked hammer and sickle. The forests cast their shadows as they do in Disney movies and come close to the road. 'Which way are the Chinks?', shouts Ilya at a passer-by. A young woman of indeterminate age, sweating alcohol is circling round and round the crossroads on a bicycle. 'That way.'

The jagged trees fall away and for the first time in Birobidzhan we see industrial, efficient, farmland. This crop is low-lying, electric green and clings to the earth like a moss. 'Soya,' breathes in Ilya. 'That's how you know the Chinese are farming the land. Only Chinese farm soya.' We drive past kilometres of electric green agriculture until we reach the village of 'Experimental Fields', in the 'Leninsk District'. A rusty sign says that it has been inhabited since 1848 by Cossack horsemen. This era of settlement seems to be coming to an end.

No Russian tills the land in 'Experimental Fields'. The people who live here subsist only from picking berries or mushrooms and the little money they get from state pensions. The twenty or so wooden cottages that make up the village are uncared for but inhabited, yet nevertheless have an abandoned look. The centre of this settlement is no longer the 'village club', where Soviet dances and propaganda films would have been played when it was a collective farm, but what the villagers call the Chinese 'base'. Protected by metal gates and barbed wire, the Chinese are living in a barracks between huge barns filled with what the Russians seem no longer to have: shiny machinery, trucks, tractors and jeeps. A sun-bleached red flag hangs limply at the entrance.

We push in. Ilya steps out of the car and starts to demand of the few huddled Chinese labourers in the barn, 'Where's your master? Where is a guy that speaks some Russian?' Like any working-class person in Birobidzhan, Ilya knows some basic Chinese; the same words that in Europe Russians know in English from contact with Europeans. 'Hello, yes, no, how much does it cost?' Everything in the 'base' is splattered and pungent. Mud, more mud and piles of manure – but it was alive, unlike the Russian villages. The Chinese labourers claim the 'captain' is not here and only the 'captain' speaks Russian.

We go to speak to the Slavs of 'Experimental Fields'. It is like entering into a scene from a Russian nationalist's 3 a.m. nightmare. The 'privatization' of the collective farm effectively killed the village. Now the lands are 'rented' to the Chinese, but no one seems to know who collects the money. By the roadside we talk to some mushroom sellers. They look like they have the plague – in a sense they do – they are moonshine alcoholics.

'The Russians are finished. They till nothing here. Nothing at all . . . All we do is pick mushrooms and sell them to passing cars,' slurs the younger of the two, a cross-eyed woman with brown hair and crunched eyelids. She seems slightly deformed – as if she has never received anything like modern medical care her entire life. 'All the land is farmed by the Chinese to the border. We work for the Chinese . . . we work in the fields for them. They are cruel masters.'

They are like survivors of an apocalypse. In a sense they are, as for this village that is what the death of the state was. The second mushroom seller has a face so riven by wrinkles it looks like cracked mud on the bottom of a dry lake; she shakes a gigantic mushroom she has picked in my general direction, shouting: 'The Chinese have taken all the farm lands. We are just bums here.'

The hags say they are paid $2 a day by the Chinese to get on their knees and harvest the soya. Behind us some dirty teenage girls are wandering around aimlessly. It is a humiliating testament to the staggering incompetence of the Kremlin that despite being one of the world's largest oil producers, people are living within its borders in conditions more squalid than anywhere in Africa, with the same trickle of new Asian landowners. 'We hope more Chinese will come so there will be more work,' squawk the mushroom sellers.

'Are you worried that in the future the land will not be Russian and will be controlled by China? That there will be no more motherland here?'

'Who gives a fuck about the motherland. There is no fucking motherland.'

They then waved the giant mushroom at me again, plaintively. I wanted to understand what the younger generation of 'Experimental Fields' felt about the motherland. So, I started to talk with three teenage girls sitting by the roadside. They were unwashed with crooked teeth, covered in a visible layer of dirt. All three had brilliant green eyes. According to them, every single Slav in the village of about 200 people was either an alcoholic, sick, dying or violent. Nobody was healthy. The Chinese they said lived 'completely parallel in their base', and had next to no contact with them. They laughed when I asked if the Russians tilled any fields in the border area: 'No, only Chinese.'

Living like this, did they feel that they had a homeland, a country that cared for them, or a future? Nastya, aged sixteen, said: 'What the fuck do I care? Who cares about the motherland? Who cares about the Chinese taking it all over? What the fuck should I care about that? The place is dying. It would be better if more Chinese came here so there would be more people here. What the fuck are you talking about a motherland?'

There is no future in 'Experimental Fields'. There is no evidence of the 2000s economic boom, no evidence of Putin, no evidence of the state. Just sick survivors living in the wreckage of the 'privatization' of Soviet agriculture. It looks like a cartoon come to life of what one would expect an encounter between a rising and declining race to look like. Perhaps the thing that is the most dispiriting is that these old Cossack villages close to the border had been founded in the nineteenth century, by people fleeing in search of a better life.

In the remaining 50km to the border, the number of Chinese bases climbs dramatically. There is one in every village and most of the land by the roadside is electric soya green. In the larger village of Babtsovo the scene is equally bleak. The only building that has been renovated in the past two decades is the town council, where outside five or six cows chew the cud on the dirt track beside it. The 'shop' is just a door into the front room of a small house, which sells cigarettes and petrol. One elderly woman by the roadside echoes the story of social collapse I had heard earlier. 'Not one Russian still farms. We only live off pensions. We drink. We pick berries and mushrooms. Sometimes people work for the Chinese.'

In the dirt tracks of this village I crossed paths with an impressive, clean white car being driven by a wealthy man. Out of it stepped a Chinese businessman in his thirties, leaving a pretty Chinese woman nervously looking out from the front seat. He is a thin, wiry young guy from Harbin region, who goes by the Russian name of Andrei, who explains in perfect Russian that he is the director of one of nineteen Chinese companies operating in this small border region of Leninsk in Birobidzhan.

'I'm almost certain that the Chinese are now the majority in Leninsk, especially if you take into account there are next to no Russians of working age here,' he says. In his opinion there are 1,000 Chinese in this region and just over 6,000 in the whole of Birobidzhan. However, that number has declined 'quite a lot' in recent years. 'The local government wants to cut the quota for Leninsk region. They think there are too many Chinese here. They want it to be just 600. There's nothing I can do about it . . . If they tell us to leave, they throw us out . . . then we're gone, we've been thrown out.'

This isn't his only problem regarding labour. The director explains that in recent years he has found it much harder to convince Chinese workers to come to Russia. 'To be honest, life in China is better than it is in Russia these days. As Chinese wages rise I am going to start having serious problems getting people to come to Russia.' Andrei also feels increasingly undercut by the arrival of large numbers of Central Asian and Caucasian immigrants. 'The government is pleased they are coming as it means they need less people from China.' But this hasn't shaken his faith in business here: 'There is so much empty land in Russia, so much of it is just great for vegetables.' The Chinese director refuses to comment on any matter historical, political or geopolitical but groans suggestively: 'And all the Russians are doing on this empty land is drinking moonshine and picking berries.'

The road is now straight to the Amur and the border, past forests and vast swamplands, Chinese bases and degenerated Russian villages. Suddenly, as if from nowhere, a train track appears out of the wilderness and follows the road. A faded poster at the next turn-off of the main road announced where this leads. This sun-bleached placard of a Russian trooper punching the air with his rifle says this is a 'Tankodrome', a military base for armour. We pass some men in uniform, urinating by the roadside next to a parked camouflaged military truck.

Ahead is their large, run-down base on the hillside: rows of artillery, tanks, military trucks and listening towers stand to defend Russian land from the Chinese should the day ever come. It stares out onto the electric green farmlands of the settlers, then over the Amur onto a row of rounded hills.

They are covered in wind farms. We have reached China – civilization, progress and a roadblock of FSB border guards.

We stop the car to look and listen to the distant whirr of the white wind farms on the other side. The ignition is off and Ilya laughs a little sadly.

'I guess the Chinese . . . built communism differently from us.'

The Potemkin Port-City

They say that the last night of the Trans-Siberian always smells the worst. In Europe, when most travellers spend only a night or two in a carriage; it's never been too long since they last washed. The third-class wagon carrying mostly Tajik and Uzbek migrants and poor Russian families into

Vladivostok smells like no one has washed in a week. Pungent, acidic, somewhere between stale sweat, cigarettes butts and gone off meat.

The migrants are worried about the summer's work in the port-city. They have heard that the construction boom on the back of Putin's orders to rebuild it is already coming to an end. They are ready to work for next to nothing and on this last night of rest they are playing cards and smoking cigarettes in the rocking gloom of the carriage. Some drink, none pray. Everyone is excited – almost a week since it left Moscow behind, the train is coming into a station somewhere wealthy. As I fall asleep to the clattering of the tracks there is still chatter:

'There are so many Uzbeks they say it's an Uzbek town.'

'I wonder what the bridges look like.'

'But the police are bad there?'

Dawn in Vladivostok is misty and humid. This is the season of Asia's monsoon. The pressure is heavy and the air is thick: the atmosphere of the Far East. The city comes as a shock. After weeks on Russia's rotting periphery and along the post-Soviet rustbelt, it is a surprise to see so much development and prosperity. Vladivostok, to the chagrin of its Han and Korean neighbours, means 'the lord of the east' and has been redeveloped at huge cost into a Potemkin port-city to dissuade China of any false notions that Russia might be retreating from here.

Putin has sought out events to showcase Russia's 'resurgence' to the world, the way China staged the Beijing Olympics. In 2006, he succeeded in gaining the right to host the 2012 summit of the Asia-Pacific Economic Community (APEC). The site would be Vladivostok. The summit brought together the economic and political leadership of all Pacific nations. For Putin this was a chance to rebuild this city into an impressive showcase to dazzle the Japanese, American and Chinese leaderships all at once. He also hoped to rebuild an economically vulnerable region that simply could not afford to fall behind for strategic reasons – being so close to China, South Korea and Japan.

As a result, day and night, thousands of Tajiks, Uzbeks and Kyrgyz were drilling, spinning cement mixers and hammering the final nails of the rebuilding programme. It is cheaper and less geopolitically risky to ship semi-illiterate Russian speaking migrants from ex-Soviet Central Asia than to employ Chinese from across the border. It is perhaps ironic then that the city they are rebuilding is excessively, ostentatiously in the image of nineteenth-century Europe – to the point of being un-Russian. The pavements are made with paving stones not concrete like most in Moscow or anywhere else in the country, there are neat fresh flowerbeds, freshly tarmacked roads and restored nineteenth-century tsarist facades.

You can see that this city enjoyed the 2000s as boom years, by losing count of how many supermarkets, car dealerships, designer clothes stores, $100-a-head seafood restaurants or hoardings for flights to Hainan and Thailand there are. New high-rise apartments are perched around the Golden Horn Bay, the city's perfect natural harbour that tsarist officers named after the straits in Constantinople, Istanbul – or *Tsargrad*, which they imagined as the most wonderful bay in the world.

The new Vladivostok surprises by what it does not have. There are hardly any Chinese restaurants, Chinese shops or large amounts of Chinese workers, travellers or tourists. In complete contrast to the border cities of more open countries, on the US–Mexican border, or Marseille in southern France, the city is far 'whiter' than any of the major urban areas of Britain, France or the United States. You have to look closely to realize this city is actually on the Sea of Japan. Most of the food on sale is imported from China, practically every car has its wheel on the right and is imported from Japan and dacha-construction companies advertise they can build you something 'To Korean Quality'. It may be dysfunctional – but Moscow appears nowhere near losing control.

Yet by turning Vladivostok into a showcase of what he could build – Putin's own St Petersburg – he had turned it into a showcase for incompetence, corruption and inefficiency. Huge funds went into the city's redevelopment for arrival of the Pacific elites for the APEC Summit. Estimates are that over $20 billion has been spent – more than the London Olympics the same year.[25]

These funds are over sixty times higher than Vladivostok's usual annual budget. It has been 'spent' on a general infrastructure overhaul, including a new opera house and a new university. It would be more accurate to say that the funds have been 'wasted'. It is unclear why a region of 1.9 million people needs a 4 million capacity airport.[26] Its centrepiece is none other than two bridges to nowhere: one crosses the Golden Horn Bay and the other, the largest cable-stayed bridge in the world, stretches over the sea to reach Russky Island off the coast, a place with less than 2,000 inhabitants. The illogical economics of hosting the summit on a disconnected island that needed a 3km bridge built to it, when cities such as Birobidzhan have no functioning airport, was impossible to miss.

It is apparent to everyone in Vladivostok that though big improvements have been made thanks to this investment in the city's roadworks – there is also excitement about a new university and locals find the new bridges pretty – it is clear to everyone that this does not have a price tag greater than the London Olympics. 'The thing is the more money they put in, the more people could see how much money was being stolen,' says the local politics specialist Andrei Kalachinsky. 'Politics here works like it does in all Russian regions. The local governor gets the funds and distributes them to the companies of his loyalists and then the companies of those who Moscow says are its own Kremlin loyalists.'

The 'vertical of corruption' has swallowed up its own dreams. On no projects was this more evident than on Putin's bridges to nowhere. First, the contract was awarded to a Russian company that had never before built a bridge like this. Second, they cost over 2.6 times more than had they been built in the United States and 5.5 more than had they been built in China.[27]

Instead of creating a symbol for his prowess, Putin had created a symbol of his incompetence – one for Navalny and the opposition to 'audit'. They called it 'one giant act of theft'. Then, with only weeks to go before the APEC summit, the new $1 billion road from the airport to the bridge cracked and began to collapse under heavy rain. This was not due to 'lack of funds', as every kilometre of this road had cost $20 million – when the average for a road in the EU is $6.9 million.[28] It was due to shoddy work and probably the embezzlement of those same funds. The government was forced to admit that the project had resulted in almost $500 million dollars having been stolen.[29]

Incompetent, inefficient, corrupt and outrageously expensive, but the Russian state and not Chinese economic power is lord in Vladivostok. This hit home when I spent a day with a crestfallen Chinese nationalist. This visitor from Shenzhen, a frequent commentator on angry websites demanding China 'stand up', had taken the Trans-Siberian to see the lands to the east of Irkutsk, which he said 'were once Chinese, and should be China's living space in the future'. The dream of this mild-mannered IT specialist with the geopolitical appetite of Genghis Khan, he confided as we strolled along the port side, then past the Memorial to Fighters for Soviet Power, was to live on a ranch as a colonialist on the island of Sakhalin, 'once we make it Chinese again . . . I love nature so much you see . . . . Nature is . . . *so beautiful.*'

His inflated hopes of a Chinese takeover had been punctured by the lack of any visible community of his kinsmen. A short visit together to the Chinese-dominated market would destroy them for good. Moving down the market from a car mat vendor, to a crockery salesman, through a bag peddler and a belt trader, the patriot accosted these poor people from Manchuria: 'Do you know this was China? What do you think about getting it back?' The responses did not enthuse him. Only two market hands were really aware that this territory had been Chinese and said they would like it back, a further four said this was so impossible they didn't think about it, the remaining six we spoke to neither knew, nor cared. 'They are not righteous Chinese,' the nationalist mumbled, visibly deflated and a bit confused. 'They are all business focused. Like most Chinese . . . it makes me . . . . *so sad.*'

The Kremlin is felt so keenly as an overlord in Vladivostok that 'federalism' is a term of abuse. Moscow is seen as a colonial force that dispatches its policemen, its FSB colonels and its prosecutors to control the 'Primorye', or Maritime, province. Here, as in all regions of Russia, 'rotation' means that all the commanding posts in the local 'silovik' structures are held by men chosen by the Kremlin. They are usually 'foreigners' from different Russian regions.

The Russians of the Far East are angry at their paradox – they feel their hinterland is a treasure trove, but because all mining subsoil rights belong to Moscow they will forever be begging the capital for funds that will come from the profits extracted from their own wilderness. Local elites believe Moscow is taking 'their' rightful tax revenues from natural resources. 'It's not just that Moscow takes all the money,' says Andrei Kachalinsky, 'but it takes the best money, like the revenues from the port and the pipeline. This makes people angry. In Primorye we are not separatists . . . but against Moscow.' This is why United Russia only scored 32.9 per cent in the parliamentary elections here.[30] In the local elections the following year only 10 per cent turned out to vote.[31]

China is not exploiting this region as a colony – Moscow is. In the name of defending Russian territory against Asian hordes, the state has decided to launch a whole series of new initiatives to consolidate its 'tough hand' on this resource rich territory. In all the 'frontier regions' it is illegal for foreigners to buy land. They have upgraded the 'tough' governor of Khabarovsk province to head the new Ministry for Far Eastern Development. This is not a process that they trust the locals themselves to be directing, as Moscow is preparing new legislation to tighten its grip on what really matters here: the geology.

A new gigantic 'State Corporation for the Development of Siberia and the Far East', answerable directly to Putin, is being planned.[32] Dubbed the 'Far Eastern Republic' it would have preferential access to resources in all sixteen districts of eastern Siberia and the Far East and have the right to allot licences to mine for natural resources such as gold – currently something only federal or regional authorities can do. Answering directly to Putin, the future mega-corporation's decisions would not be answerable to any regional or federal authorities other than the Kremlin itself.

Moscow, they say here, 'is a colonialist'. Moscow, they say 'only cares about itself'. Resentment against the vertical has fused with resentment against the police, the prosecutor and the interior ministry troops – the local 'silovik structures'. Sent from the capital on 'rotation', often engaged in corruption rackets and violent extortion, many have started to blame corruption on the centre.

On the Pacific, where Russia is so starkly an empire that treats all of its provinces as Kremlin geology-colonies, this fury erupted in 2010 into a crime that shook Vladivostok and the whole country. It was as if Fyodor Dostoevsky's novel *The Possessed* had come to life, in a Putinist form in the remote village of Kirovsky over 300km into the Taiga and the north. It was here in an impoverished, jobless, wreck of a collective farm, without any oil-wealth pumped in to resuscitate it, that a gang of boys barely in their twenties tried to wage a partisan war. Not against imaginary Chinese colonialists, but the police – 'the werewolves in uniform'.

The End of the Vertical

They made the video themselves. The camera shakes and presses unprofessionally close to the 'partisans'. These are four Slavic young men crouched in a damp hutch. Their leader, topless and unshaven, with his fist on the barrel of an AK-47, puffs out his chest and holds forth with the grim pomposity of a YouTube Jihadist, but in the slurred Russian of the working class:

'We are honest people, and you are scum, so we will fight you till the end, until you kill us, or until we win . . . most likely you will kill us. But we are not afraid of you . . . People will be on our side, anyway, because justice is on our side. We have already won. We killed the fear and cowardice in ourselves, you could never do this . . . we don't have any weapons to fight you, but still we are not afraid of you and will fight.'[33]

The boy 'partisans' smile cretinously – one buttoned up in camouflage hunting gear waves a pistol, another grins in a black baseball cap. They seem so excited to be on film. They have been on the run, but two of them barely need to shave. Yet this is not the kind of Internet video that male football hooligans or opposition activists aged eighteen to twenty-two usually post, all sound and fury against the Kremlin, as a prelude to absolutely nothing. Because for the past few weeks they have been on a killing spree. They have shot two policemen and two drug dealers, stolen one police car and robbed a police station, before leaving it in flames. They claim this is politics – not hooliganism, that they are partisans – not brigands:

'And this is not some spontaneous act . . . no, we planned and did it on purpose in order to specifically kill you gangsters. You are the real criminals, you can't be named in any other way . . . You cover drug trafficking, prostitution, you steal the woods . . . everyone perfectly knows about it and everyone is afraid of you because you have all the powers to do that . . . People are afraid of you, but be aware that there are still people who are not afraid of you . . . The only thing you can do is to terrorize helpless and submissive people, who are accustomed to indignity . . . And your mighty so-called empire, the Russian Federation, is entirely based on alcoholism, slavery and cowardice. One day it will collapse, and you will fall into the abyss together with it.'[34]

They called themselves the 'Primorsky Partisans' and this shaky October 2010 video was their attempt to explain themselves. The boys claimed they had been driven to assassinate others, because they could no longer bear the blows of an abusive state, but in the same video they revelled in showing off the ID card of a policeman they had shot, grinning as they recounted how they had found him as 'drunk as a pig', before they ended his life. They damned the police in their village for terrorizing them, for being cold-blooded killers, but shot dead officers from other towns and mocked the 'drunk pig' they slaughtered for only having bottles of vodka and not weapons in his secure safe.

Who these boys actually were and what had actually happened in Kirovsky was clouded in the same uncertainty as anything that happens in Russia's lawless hinterland. In Putin's outback – police being gangsters, mafia pretending to be nationalists, nationalists who are actually police – is nothing abnormal. What was new was that a gang had justified themselves in a political language that had electrified the nation. The Kremlin was horrified that according to an independent poll by the radio station Ekho Moskvy over 60 per cent of respondents were ready to help the partisans and saw them as 'Robin Hood' figures.[35] This could be seen on the streets, as across Vladivostok graffiti started appearing – 'GLORY TO THE PARTISANS'.

The partisan video had hit a raw nerve – exhaustion with police brutality and the fusion of gangsterism and officialdom at the lowest level. According to the Russian Academy of Sciences, 34 per cent of the nation 'always feel like killing' corrupt officials, whilst a further 38 per cent 'sometimes feel like killing' them.[36]

The regime was so frightened that it sent more than 1,000 officers into action to crush these boys, a force numerically larger than some EU states' contributions to the Afghan campaign. Tracked down to a flat in the drab town of Ussurisyk, which lives half the year in snow, the other half in gloom and drizzle, the gang held out for a few hours, firing out of the apartment. Their perceived leader died before the rest were arrested.

In Vladivostok, everyone was shaken by the failed 'partisan insurgency' but most do not blame the boys. They feel they were driven to guns because in 'the depths' the situation is so out of control they had little other choice. There is a sense of satisfaction that somebody, somehow – however deranged – gave the police the sock in the face that it needed in order to see how angry the people were at corruption and official hooliganism.

Normal people in the Far East do not see the 2010 shooting as a bizarre local incident. They see the partisans as part of the same protest wave against the regime, but in its purest, crudest form. Russians in the Far East feel that Navalny and the Moscow opposition are simply the most sophisticated expression of simmering anger at a state that does nothing for them. In their minds Putin's state is now personified by his criminalized policemen. Unlike in Moscow, this is not anger at authoritarianism but anger about inefficiency and incompetence. Putin's failure is that he has not pulled the bureaucracy out of the 1990s, along with the national economy. This is anger at a weak, not a strong state, which cannot stop its agents moonlighting as killers. This is why they call them the 'werewolves'.

It is a drizzly afternoon in Vladivostok and outside the district court, policemen shelter by the door, smoking and telling dirty jokes. Inside, through the security check, an air of oppressive absurdity reigns. This is the trial of the partisans. As it would happen, all the documents that would incriminate the law enforcement agencies in this case have suddenly 'disappeared'. The judges, their secretaries and even the prosecutor himself seem to hold an ironic distance from the proceedings. In the courtroom itself the partisans stand in a cage gormlessly waiting for the case to resume, once a decision is taken concerning the 'disappeared' documents. In the linoleum corridors, their lawyers insist that this is evidence that the Kirovsky police were not only criminals, but viciously persecuting these young men. In the confusion I slipped into the courtroom to speak to the partisans through the bars of their cage. I only had time for one question before the policemen rushed towards me then threw me out of the courtroom. 'Why did you do it?'

The baby-faced killer Roman Savchenko (b. 1992), grabs the bars and shouts: 'Because the police are drug dealers!' The rest start to holler with him out of the cage. 'That's why we did it! Because the police are all drug dealers!'

The door slammed, the truth – if there even was one, would be in the village. That evening, I told the director of the local museum, Victor Shalai, in his favourite hipster bar, the Café Montmartre, that I was planning to go to the village. He was horrified. Like everyone who lives in Vladivostok he considered the villages lawless and dangerous. 'Don't go without protection.' The 'protection' the effete intellectual convinced me to take turned out to be two anti-Semitic 'photographers', formally unemployed, who make ends meet taking pictures of 'girls, most topless'. One beefy, the other lanky – and in possession of a tough Mitsubishi – they agreed to drive me to Kirovsky.

We met at 6 a.m. by the bullying Statue for the Fighters of Soviet Power on the portside and drove north. Though hardly 'opposition' the

photographers despised Putin, admired the partisans and bandied around
Navalny slogans in a slightly unnerving (but in the provinces very common)
manner. 'The party of crooks and thieves', in their minds, was none other
than a mysterious plot against Russia, orchestrated by the Jews. 'We need
a clean Russia', was not a call for government efficiency and anticorruption, but a more systematic purification of undesirables. But as we drove
on the rutted main road to Khabarovsk, practically a farm track in places,
it was clear they were unsure on a lot of the details of 'the plot against
Russia'. The driver shouted into the backseat:

'Moscow is a vampire. It's a bloodsucker. The Soviets would take money
and invest in these places, in the villages, in the cities – now Moscow sucks
up our oil, minerals and gold . . . and leaves us weak, begging them for
some crumbs . . . They steal all our money and send it out to America and
Britain. They've been working inside . . . the plot against Russia . . . for
years you see. But Russia survived a lot . . . We survived the Tatar-Mongol
yoke, we survived the Polish yoke, we survived the yoke of the Yids . . .
we'll survive the Putin yoke.'

The lanky photographer is suddenly a bit confused. 'But didn't you say
that Putin's yoke was the yoke of the Yids the other day?' The conversation
fades into whether or not Putin is a Jew.

We stop before the village. 'We want to show you the kind of Russians
that keep up the sky.' Past empty hills of Taiga and mist we come to the
dying village of Spassk, or 'blessed', on the very edge of China. Here,
down a mud track, lives in unexpected penury a former Soviet zoologist
and his wife, with their bric-a-brac zoo. There are two Amur tigers behind
barbed wire, two bears going crazy in tiny cages that do not fit them, and
shambolic netting thrown over some timid lynx. They came when it was
the future for Soviet science. They ended up feeding the animals off their
meagre pensions and some geese they keep.

'What the hell happened?' half laughs the sad 'zookeeper'. 'We used to
be half the world with all those socialists countries . . . and now what the
hell are we? We are practically enemies with Belarus and Ukraine.'

'Wash your hands, they are covered in tiger shit,' sighs his wife, before
telling us how she tastes disappointment: 'The village is dead. The Chinese
cross the border whenever they want in cooperation with the mafia that
call themselves the border police. This all happened because of the plot!
The enemy within! Those groups that have been working to destroy
Russia from the inside all these years . . . they finally managed.'

The tigers are pacing up and down the makeshift cage; their incredibly
muscular, healthy strides and orange fur jars with the gloomy light and
misery of their keepers. The old man smiles at what he loves: 'God . . . so
that jackal of a president is coming back . . . until 2018 at least. It's such a

long time. It's got so bad this is why we said we'd support the boys . . .
didn't we?' She has given up trying to make him wash his hands and nods
vigorously. 'We were ready to help the partisans. If they had come to us.
We'd have hidden them, fed them . . . I was ready to take them to the
places that only the tigers know in the Taiga where the police would never
find them.'

They never came. We drive further north, through hours of low hills
and Taiga emptiness. We passed a cement factory. Then we got stopped by
the police and were made to hand over money (the car was actually
speeding) for a supposed fine. The conversation comes back to the 'plot
against Russia'. They try their best to convince me the bloodsuckers are
real: 'Look mate . . . look into that forest. There's a *tiger* in it. Just because
you haven't seen him doesn't mean he's not there.'

Eventually, Kirovsky welcomes us with a Soviet-painted placard to the
fallen of the 1941–45 war: 'We Will Never Forget Our Heroes'. The place
is poor but you can still see the outlines of a faintly utopian grid in the leafy
streets and neatly placed 'krushchevki'. They are dilapidated, like uncared
for leftovers of an extinct civilization. On the walls of the tenement where
Roman Savchenko grew up, and who at eighteen in 2010 was the youngest
partisan, is scrawled in English:

'TRUE TILL DEHTH[sic]'

His truck-driver father is standing there in a wife beater waiting for me.
His arms are covered in huge tattoos of Jesus Christ. He has a golden-
toothed smile. It's true, he says, that the police are intimidating locals,
beating them up and cultivating fields of cannabis, which they then peddle
in the locals schools. But there is something sinister about the gang that
took over his son's life. He leans over the bonnet of his vehicle and speaks
softly. 'My son's not guilty . . . all is not as it seems . . . I think this was an
FSB operation gone horribly wrong.' The theory of Vladimir Savchenko
is that some Russian 'Europeans' were sent to the local police force.
Desperate to get out they started to engineer fights with the local kids in
order to frame them as capturing a whole militia. 'These guys were
desperate for a promotion to get back to Europe.'

But it strikes me that this kind of conspiracy theory – the default reaction for a post-totalitarian society – is a way that Vladimir is hiding from
the truth. 'I've driven the whole country in my truck,' he spits. 'And it's the
same lawlessness everywhere. From here to the snows of the Komi.' He
tells me how deep and bitter the shock was, the day he was called by a
friend, when he was working on the APEC buildings to be told, 'Your son
has gone on a shooting spree.'

His wife then appears, a woman clinging onto prettiness in tarty heavy
make-up; she doesn't appear to believe this theory. 'I feel real pride in what

my son did. Because . . . now everyone knows that the police are drug dealers and criminals. That they live like drug lords and kill young people.' Roman's brother was beaten up, killed, and then his body dumped in a forest by the police. 'The boys just cracked.'

They have smuggled a phone into jail thanks to 'special ways' so they can speak to their son. His mother dials him. 'Darling . . . are you all right? Is everything fine? I love you.' She passes the line to me. For a second I am lost for words, until the obvious question hits me – how does a man feel when he shoots a policeman?

'We felt belief and faith in what we are doing. Pride that Russian guys so young could rise up.'

But how does a man feel inside, I asked him, not intellectually?

Roman thinks for a second. 'You feel . . . adrenaline innit. But I'm not a fascist . . . we are not against Muslims or immigrants . . . we did this to rise up against the police. They are drug dealers and drug pushers. They are animals. They had killed so many people. How many had their drugs killed? How many lives had they ruined? They had been beating us, beating us for years and years. They were peddling first weed and then heroin. We had to do something to stop them. Putin is a jackal. . . . Take another route? Take protests? Can you really name one protest in Russian history that has had an effect? Do you really think here, in Russia, there is any other way to stop the police regime than by guns? Do you really?'

I feel I should say something. I don't. He rambles on:

'Have you ever read this book? It is called *The Gulag Archipelago*. It will tell you everything you need to know. The police, Putin and Yeltsin, they are the same thing . . . They are part of the same structure that has been beating and killing Russians for years. When they wanted us to be strong and to work in their factories it was different, now they want us to be weak and lazy, alcoholics and drug addicts – so they sell us drugs. Do you really think anything other than guns can stop them? We are different here, we're far from Moscow, that is why we stood up and I feel pride we did.'

There are some clanks that sound like cell bars and Roman says he has to go. 'Mate, the prosecutor's coming.' The line goes dead. His father seems irritated when I tell him the story that his son the partisan had breathlessly told. 'Let's go to the market. The market director will tell you everything. He really knows everything.'

We drive to the miserable market place and meet a man called Sacha, with a scraggly beard and a few gold teeth. We stand by our cars. My feet crunch on broken glass. Someone in the market is playing Spanish party music. Vladimir Savchenko crosses his Jesus tattooed arms. The fading dyed Christ glares like a warrior, not a saviour: 'I told you. This was a

KGB or FSB operation gone very wrong. I'm off.' And off he went. The market director shakes his head.

'All is not what it seems . . . I couldn't say this in front of him . . . but they were not partisans . . . they were hooligans. Basically, it's like this. If you take a helicopter over the Taiga you will see huge gigantic fields cut there – fields of cannabis. This is what it is all about. The police know. They are the drug dealers. What happened . . . and I know these boys, they were always in this market hanging out . . . they wanted to be in the racket and take over the drugs trade, in place of the police. It got out of control and they ended up saying all this stuff that hit a nerve when they knew they were dead meat. They were hooligans pretending to be partisans. But that's not the most important thing. Basically, here there is no state. And there never was one. And there never will be one until it is taken over by another. All this happens because here there is no state. You see?'

The scraggly bearded market director, his skin a moonscape of blotches and scars, gave me a hint to leave the village. After speaking to a few passers-by – one alcoholic hunter, a former military duvet salesman, a belt trader and a hunting-camouflage stallholder – I did. They seemed divided into those who felt that the boys were hooligans pretending to be partisans or hooligans who turned out to be partisans. In short – I got the impression that nobody really knew.

On the six-hour drive back to Vladivostok the 'photographers' were silent and sulky. They were bitterly disappointed that on closer inspection the people seemed to think the partisans were as tainted as those they hunted. In a sense, so was I. They smoked furiously, then started to swig cans of beer at the wheel.

I drifted in and out of a shallow sleep, half drunk and dispirited about Russia – for me and the 'photographers', for the people who lived here, it had become evident that it was not enough to say 'Down with Putin', or 'Down with United Russia'. Places like this needed much, much more than simply a new president. They needed decades of state building.

In Kirovsky – and a thousand other places – Putin was not really the problem. Here, at the end of the vertical of power, it was starkly obvious how weak his system really was. Rather than just being oppressive – incompetence, dysfunction and the absence of control meant that men right the way through the entire bureaucracy, all the way down, have become venal, extortionate and predatory. Out here the 'werewolves in uniform' were not working on Putin's orders. Russia was not threatened by China, but by being driven insane by its own officials.

CONCLUSION: THE GHOSTS

'Excessive concentration of power is a dangerous thing.'

Dmitry Medvedev

IF PUTIN in his palaces is haunted by any ghost – it is not the senile spectre of Leonid Brezhnev but the pained soul of Nicholas II. Would this most naive of tsars have dwelt after death on his catastrophe, on Russia's screaming train-wreck off the rails of history, would he whisper to Putin as he sleeps, as the unlikeliest of successors sweats, that as the centenary of the revolution nears, they share a similar dilemma – that he must at all costs learn from his calamity? Yet, as we can safely assume is the case, and the Tsar remains as convinced in spirit as he was in the Winter Palace, he would creep closer, bent crooked, beseeching Putin to behave exactly as he did: to hold on, to relinquish nothing, never to abdicate in favour of the quibbling liberals who risk handing the inheritance to hysterics, to rule as he must, to rule alone, in the name of the stability that Russia needs at all costs.

The 'national leader' spends less and less time in Moscow. He has retreated to working as much as possible in his palace in the woods outside. He has also chosen to freeze traffic for his motorcade to the Kremlin only for strictly essential, diplomatic matters. The government seems frightened of Moscow. There are even plans to move it from the city. Theoretically, they are going ahead, and would see the entire bureaucracy and Kremlin staff moved to a new 'administrative quarter' to be built over a complex of drab housing estates near Vnukovo Airport. They say it is clogged traffic that inspired this plan. Muscovites says it is protests.

Putin behaves as if he cannot understand how, in 2008, he had the poll ratings of a movie star and was received like the greatest Russian hero since Yuri Gagarin in the capital, but today the most sophisticated of this city, the very people who have thrived during his reign, talk of him the way they once did about Berezovsky – as a thief who has stolen the state. Putin talks as if he is still loved by Russia, but walks with a paranoid shuffle and the aggression of the insecure. Courtiers say he feels hurt and unappreciated. He is cancelling foreign trips, no longer likes mingling 'with the people', preferring wild animals instead. As he once said: 'I'm a superstitious person'.[1]

Russia has fallen out of love with him and the Putin model he built has started to break down. This book has explored how after Yeltsin a regime was built in Russia that was both highly sophisticated and deeply backward at the same time. This managed democracy brought together clever technologies of power, giving the country the formal institutions of a democracy, but gutted them of any meaning. Machinations and corruption turned the Duma into a puppet show and elections into plebiscite contests fought with clowns. Russia became a videocracy that gave censored TV to the masses but allowed free newspapers and blogs for the intelligentsia. Russia saw its leader turn himself into a telepopulist superstar who exploited modern man's seduction by images, his confusion between a great celebrity and a good politician.

This achieved a hegemony that was the envy of authoritarians, with minimal costs. Fewer journalists were imprisoned than in Turkey, fewer protests occurred than in China and the opposition was less of a threat than in Belarus. Putin looked both authoritarian and legitimate, Europe's most successful post-modern politician who had subverted the very institutions Francis Fukuyama had believed would 'end history'.

Yet behind this televised illusion, the regime was building a defunct and anachronistic power structure. It staged a gigantic transfer of assets, beginning with the robbery of Berezovsky and culminating with the robbery of Khodorkovsky, then consolidating with the creation of the Putin oligarchy. The Kremlin tried to build institutions that were outdated and inefficient even when they were young – a vertical of power restoring the Soviet chain of command, with United Russia as a de facto one-party state. These, they promised, would deliver 'a dictatorship of law'.

These great plans inadvertently planted the seeds of corrosion into the Putin model. They were bad administrators and botched their state building. The vertical of power turned into a vertical of corruption, United Russia turned into a patronage network not a party and the 'dictatorship of law' turned out to be a dictatorship of predatory officials. They left Russia a fragmented and feudalized country in which all corrupt policemen, inspectors and governors had been signed up into Putin's party.

Russia looked the other way. It was in love with its leader as a boom was under way that was nothing less than the greatest upswing in living standards in Russian economic history. A new middle class flourished. It was believed that the incompetence of the state could be overcome. After decades of penury, collapse and loss of status the winners rushed into consumerism and the losers breathed a sigh of relief that the free fall was over. Russia ignored politics.

The boom allowed Putin's telepopulism to cement both a Putin consensus over the elite and a Putin majority over society. It was so successful, that by 2008 when he moved to the post of prime minister, Putin was on his own terms the greatest politician of his generation, not just in Russia but amongst his international peers. Bush, Blair, Berlusconi had all ended in failure; in China, India and Brazil, individual leaders never amassed as much power.

This is when Putinism began to undermine itself. By choosing Medvedev to play the role of president to circumvent a constitutional term limit, and allowing him to drum up support for a 'modernization agenda', the regime built up a narrative, infrastructure and constituency for reform that it bitterly disappointed. Medvedev's great words and the battering of the financial crisis exposed Russia's governance crisis. It became obvious that the vertical of power, United Russia and the 'dictatorship of law' had all failed. Below the surface a shift in values was under way, with Russians no longer wanting centralization or to hear Putin's 'commander's voice' that they had craved a decade earlier.[2]

Putin returned, but to another Russia. His return culminated in the disintegration of the Putin consensus and the Putin majority that had begun under Medvedev. It came at exactly the moment that a quiet, giant change driven by the boom undermined the videocracy and his telepopulism. The new richer, globalized, online Russia was devastated by the news of Putin's return to the presidency as it viewed this as the botched institutions he had built being cemented on to their future forever. This is when the winners of Putinism began to feel like losers.

He had triumphed as a politician, but Putin's old model was bust, his old politics was bust, and this was exposed by the protest movement that erupted in Moscow over the winter of 2011–12 to denounce the rigged elections of managed democracy. The movement did not mark the end of the regime. It exposed the regime's power for what it was – based on controlling gigantic assets, TV media and the security organs, not legitimacy and the acclaim of the elites.

The movement electrified and frightened Russia, tarring United Russia as 'the party of crooks and thieves'. It wounded Putin politically for the first time. It marked the beginning of the end of Putinism by consent. The Kremlin has tried to cobble together a new model, but it is highly precarious. The Putin consensus has been replaced by a culture war and the Putin majority has been replaced by class war. Having lost the support of the most advanced part of society, Putin was forced to find it amongst the most backward. This new model turned the old Putin budget on its head. It ended the economics of restricted spending, a budget surplus and low debt not overly dependent on a high price of oil. This occurred just as serious production and investment problems were mounting in Russia's hydrocarbons industry. Putin embarked on a huge spending spree, his accounting menaced by an unreformed pension system that could send debt skyrocketing, a vanishing budget and trade surplus and the danger he could have to cut dramatically should the price of oil fall from present highs. Economic stability has been replaced by volatility to ensure the survival of the regime.

To stay in power Putin knows he must divide the nation, to keep the Moscow opposition from linking up with the discontent in the rest of the country. It is a myth that in deep Russia he is popular. There is an anguished country out there, furious at corrupt officials, resenting the vertical and appalled at the absence of a 'dictatorship of law'. They crave a modern state – but do not yet see the opposition as being able to deliver that. The anti-Putin movement has so far failed to overcome the broken links between regions, generations and classes that fragment the nation, or cut through the hidden links of corruption and dependence on state corporations that tie the people to Putin. These explain why for the moment, discontent is vast, but resistance tiny. This precarious status quo could easily be pushed into unrest if Putin loses control of his balance sheets and cuts back on his handouts to the working class and poor in the regions. They can barely tolerate the system as it is. This is because in a thousands towns like Kushchevskaya in the west or Kirovsky in the east, Putin's botched state building has turned officials into 'werewolves in uniforms' that prey on the people. This makes people hate the state and makes everything fragile.

For centuries, the state has shaped Russian society, marshalling it out of serfdom, then experimenting on it with communism or capitalism. The civil society that sprang up under perestroika was buried in the rubble of the USSR and broken during the depression of the 1990s. It was so easy for Putin to consolidate his power, as atomized, without strong NGOs, newspapers or moral leaders, there was almost no such thing as Russian society at the turn of the century. Yet Putin has failed to come up with any projects or ideologies – be they Nashi, United Russia or Sovereign Democracy – that could shape society. Now, society is going its own way, driven by megatrends that the Kremlin can only try to steer. The protests began the politicization of the new middle class. People want to make inputs. All across Russia, in every town or stretch of territory, activists, bloggers and citizen initiatives are crystallizing into a civil society. How this evolves will decide everything. Will it emerge obsessed about vigilante policing and beating the weak, such as the City Without Drugs in the Urals? Or liberal and green like the Khimki forest defenders near Moscow? We will know soon enough just how far these hundreds of small deeds share Putin's aggression and paranoia – or reject it.

Russia is one of history's great failures. At the beginning of the last century there was the chance that, had the empire been successfully governed, it could have come to play a role like the United States. In the middle of the last century there was no reason why – had a transition to capitalism begun early enough and been managed effectively – the empire couldn't have come to be something like China is today. At the turn of this century, Russia was faced with a situation similar to post-war France. It had lost its colonies, been humiliated and pushed into anarchic politics – but thanks to De Gaulle and his generation the country became a powerful, independent, even wealthy post-imperial player. Russia can aspire to this.

Putin's return throws this in doubt. Rather than saving Russia, he has come to hold her back, imprisoned in defunct institutions. Like a jealous and abusive lover, he is clasping Russia, telling her she cannot live without him. The old pillars of managed democracy are crumbling. Resistance is rising. There is growing resentment. This is not the stability Putin thinks he has fought so hard to achieve. And this means that to stay in power the regime must either reform or repress. The country can only reach the next stage of its development with proper institutions; it needs to restore the very ones Putin destroyed to consolidate his power, and jettison those he built. Otherwise, at best there will be political stagnation, and Russia will sink yet further down the echelon of states, perhaps even to the irrelevance of post-Ottoman Turkey.

Russia is not at risk of state collapse. It has problems but they are not Soviet. The regime may be unpopular and its finances precarious, but this is not necessarily a death sentence. The Putin clan still controls all the assets that matter. The oligarchy, though they grumbled, still seem to want him there as their arbiter. Russia is still a cautious country that does not want a revolution and is terrified of anarchy. Yet the mood, the op-eds, the way people think is jittery and hysterical.

Putinism is apocalyptic. The power to control the Russian nightmare of total collapse brought him to power and has kept him in power. He will only be driven from office when somebody can steal it from him. The West cannot decide Russia's fate, though it needs to think through how it will respond to Putin's. It is deeply uncertain. He and his clan could rule for decades to come if the price of oil stays in their favour. If they do, Brussels and Washington need to ask themselves how they relate to a more repressive and rigid Russia, with a rising opposition. Putin has imprisoned his opponents before.

The West needs contingency plans. There is no real risk of an implosion. Yet if mass unrest and civil disobedience spiral out of control at some point over the years to come, then the 'party of crooks and thieves' may sacrifice their 'tsar'. Today there are almost incalculable sums riding on Putin continuing in power. But the best interests of money can easily flip. In December 1991 the leaders of Russia, Belarus and Ukraine gathered in the Belovezhskaya forest to cut Gorbachev out of the picture – and retain their political machines. It is not inconceivable that one day the masters of Rosneft, Gazprom and Transneft could do the same. This is where the danger is – that Putin may come to feel he is only safe inside the Kremlin. We do not know this side of Putin. We do not know what he will do when he has his back to the wall. What happened to Khodorkovsky, and in Georgia, gives us little confidence.

The West needs to start thinking about this eventuality. It should ask itself if it would offer him exile to avert blood. We do not know how things will turn out. We know that only 6 per cent of Russians say they can imagine what the country will be like in five years' time.[3] What is certain is that for the moment, Putin cannot be defeated politically, only economically – but the rise of Navalny shows Moscow hungers for a new leader. We also know lackeys toppled both Thatcher and Khrushchev.

In the Kremlin they have nightmares about Nicholas II. He survived the internal threat in the 1905 revolution only to see his system disintegrate under the pressure of war. Putin is in a similar position – any blows from the outside, that today move on the markets not in uniform, might push him from a fragile throne. Though it would be wrong to think of regime change as anything inevitable. In the West we are tempted to think authoritarian regimes' decay in a metaphor similar to climatology, that simply by growing a middle class or the Internet by such and such a date, the Kremlin will simply melt. In Russia, people do not think like that. They think in the metaphor of plate tectonics. The regime is fragile and has cracks running through its foundation – it will be damaged by an earthquake, but nobody knows when, how strong or even if that will come.

There are nightmares too, amongst the intelligentsia. Listening to their debates, the commentator Maxim Trudolyubov, the opinion-page editor of Russian's leading broadsheet *Vedomosti*, laments: 'There is this feeling in the air that Russia is somehow cursed . . . . Cursed to an endless cycle of revolution, stagnation and collapse, to be repeated forever.'

There is paranoia everywhere and a presence in Putin's office, one whose shadow is so huge it encompasses everything, to the point it cannot be seen. The ghost of Boris Yeltsin. All Putin's career has been about not being Yeltsin. To not be Yeltsin, he had to become Berezovsky, then to become Khodorkovsky. To not be Yeltsin, he had to build the vertical of power. To not be Yeltsin, he exercises, plays hockey and for the cameras even flies with storks. To not be Yeltsin, he controls TV. But he has made a mistake. In consolidating power, his gigantic transfer of assets means he cannot step down. He has become Boris Yeltsin. Putin cannot leave power for fear of arrest. History is inescapably repeating itself. He will inevitably need a protector, either in 2018 or 2024, because any real transfer of power will be a transfer of assets. His return to the Kremlin, demoting Medvedev to prime minister, hints that he has no confidence anyone in Russia can do that for him.

Russia is not yet unstable, but its future has become uncertain. Something medieval hangs over Moscow, even when you try to hide from it with Wi-Fi or the restaurants that serve imported Italian food, cooked for you by imported Italian chefs. In one of these places I drank beer with the commentator Kirill Rogov, a liberal and a researcher. At first we talked about polling data, but as we picked at a calamari ciabatta that went badly with the drink, the numbers gave way to fears from the past. It was gloomy, and some trashed oil men brayed and ordered more wine at another table:

It has happened many times here before. That the nation comes to believe, hysterically and all of a sudden, that the tsar in the Kremlin is not the true tsar, that he is a fraud, a fake tsar . . . and that the true tsar is elsewhere. And the people then chase him from the castle. This is what Putin is afraid of. The moment when everyone turns on him as an imposter and he is all alone. This is what terrifies him. And you know this has some basis in statistics? In polling it is far easier to go suddenly from eight out of ten believing something, to two out of ten, in a flash, than going slowly down from eight, to seven, to six, to five, to four . . .'

NOTES

Unless otherwise stated all quotes are from interviews with the author. As the purpose of these notes is to make my sources accessible to the widest possible audience, I have used an English language source over a Russian one whenever it is available.

Introduction: The Weakest Strongman

1. 'The State of Russia: Frost at the Core', *The Economist*, 9 December 2010.
2. 'Putin Situatziya V Kushchevskoi I Gus Khrustalnom – Proval Pravokhranitelnoi Sistemi', available at http://www.vesti.ru/doc.html?id=414405&cid=85093.
3. Valery Zorkin, 'Konstitutsiya Protiv Kriminala', *Rossiskaya Gazeta*, 10 December 2010.
4. Gleb Bryanski, 'Russian Patriarch Calls Putin Era Miracle of God', *Reuters*, February 2012.
5. William Maudlin, 'Russia's Rulers Popularity Declines as Elections Loom', *The Wall Street Journal*, 25 August 2011.

Chapter One: The President from Nowhere

1. Allen Lynch, *Vladimir Putin and Russian Statecraft* (Washington DC, 2011), p. 9.
2. Available at http://md-prokhorov.com/vybory/178-vladimir-putineto-zhestkaya-ruka-nachnet-nas-ochen-skoro-dushit.html.
3. Anders Aslund and Andrew Kuchins, *The Russia Balance Sheet* (Washington DC, 2009), p. 39.
4. Jonathan Daniel Weiler, *Human Rights in Russia: The Dark Side of Reform* (Boulder, CO, 2004), p. 36; Branco Milanovic, *Income, Inequality and Poverty during the Transformation from Planned to Market Economy* (Washington, DC, 1998), p. 186.
5. Stepan Opalev, 'Karta Myasoedov Rossii: V Srednem 63 Kilogramma Za God', *Slon*, 12 October 2011, available at http://slon.ru/economics/myasnaya_karta_rossii_v_srednem_63_kilogramma_za_god-687903.xhtml.
6. Vladimir Putin, *First Person: An Astonishingly Frank Self-Portrait by Russia's President* (London, 2000), p. 79.
7. Ibid., p. 42.
8. Steven L. Solnick, *Stealing the State: Control and Collapse in Soviet Institutions* (London, 1998) p. 56.
9. Andrei Sinyavsky, *The Russian Intelligentsia* (New York, 1997), p. 17.
10. Brian D. Taylor, *State Building in Putin's Russia: Policing and Coercion after Communism* (Cambridge, 2011), p. 1.
11. Sergey Polotovsky and Roman Kozak, *Pelevin I Pokolenie Pustoti* (Moscow, 2012).
12. 'Anatoly Sobchak', *The Economist*, 24 February 2000, available at http://www.economist.com/node/286742.

13. Allen Lynch, *Vladimir Putin and Russian Statecraft* (Washington DC, 2011), p. 40.
14. The ghost of Pyotr Stolypin has hung over post-Soviet intellectual debates. He was Nicholas II's most effective minister, under whose watch the economy boomed, but dissent was repressed. His commitment to authoritarian modernization in the run-up to the First World War earned him a reputation for savage effectiveness.
15. Andrei Sinyavsky, *The Russian Intelligentsia* (New York, 1997), p. 30.
16. Anders Aslund, *Russia's Capitalist Revolution* (Washington DC, 2007), p. 72; Tony Wood, 'Collapse as Crucible', *New Left Review*, March-April 2012, available at http:// newleftreview.org/II/74/tony-wood-collapse-as-crucible#_edn35.
17. Ibid.
18. Daniel Treisman, *The Return: Russia's Journey from Gorbachev to Medvedev* (New York, 2011), p. 279.
19. Andrei Sinyavsky, *The Russian Intelligentsia* (New York, 1997), p. 58.
20. Olga Khrystanovskaya and Stephen White, 'Putin's Millitocracy', *Post-Soviet Affairs*, vol. 19, no. 4, available at http://www.scribd.com/doc/19406036/ Putins-Militocracy-Olga-Kryshtanovskaya-and-Stephen-White.
21. In Russian hierarchies the title of deputy mayor or prime minister simply designates a leading role on a policy portfolio. The title of first deputy mayor or first deputy prime minister is the equivalent of deputy mayor or deputy prime minister.
22. Footage available at http://www.twitube.org/show.php?v=Or17Un5Go0k.
23. Interview with Yury Vdovin, June 2012.
24. Putin, *First Person*, p. 44.
25. Sinyavsky, *The Russian Intelligentsia*, p. 29.
26. Putin, *First Person*, p. 99.
27. Stephen Kotkin, 'Stealing the State: The Soviet Collapse and the Russian Collapse', *The New Republic*, no. 15 (1998).
28. It has been calculated that the 'seven bankers' controlled no more than 15 per cent of Russian GDP: see Daniel Tresiman, 'Loans For Shares Revisited', NBER Working Paper 15819, March 2010.
29. Lynch, *Vladimir Putin and Russian Statecraft*, p. 41.
30. The Kremlin strongly denies this was said at the off-record meeting with opposition leaders, to the forceful denial of those present: see http://www.newsru.com/ russia/22feb2012/baburikremlin.html.
31. The 'Democratic-Choice of Russia – United Democrats' faction headed by Yegor Gaidar only received 3.86 per cent of the vote in the 1995 legislative elections and failed to make it into parliament.
32. Lynch, *Vladimir Putin and Russian Statecraft*, p. 42.
33. '84 per cent Inflation', *The New York Times*, 1 January 1999.
34. 'Interview with Alexander Solzhenitsyn', *Der Spiegel*, 30 August 2007.
35. 'Viktor Chernomyrdin', *Literaturnaya Gazeta*, no. 37 (1998).
36. Daniel Treisman, *The Return: Russia's Journey from Gorbachev to Medvedev* (New York, 2011), p. 68.
37. Richard Sakwa, *Russian Politics and Society*, 4th edn (London, 2008), p. 271.
38. Ibid., p. 266.
39. Polling by the Levada Center, available at http://www.levada.ru/press/2011011802. html.
40. Official crime statistics should be taken with extreme caution. They may be an underestimate. Glenn E. Curtis (ed.), *A Country Study: Russia*, Federal Research Division Library of Congress (Washington DC, 1998), available at http://memory.loc.gov/frd/cs/rutoc.html.
41. Ibid., p. 42.
42. Thane Gustafson, *The Wheel of Fortune: The Battle For Oil And Power in Russia* (London, 2012), pp. 186–9.
43. Tony Wood, 'Collapse as Crucible', *New Left Review*, March-April 2012, available at http://newleftreview.org/II/74/tony-wood-collapse-as-crucible#_edn35.
44. Tina Burrett, *Television and Presidential Power in Putin's Russia* (London, 2011), p. 11; Perry Anderson, 'Russia's Managed Democracy', *London Review of Books*, 25 January 2007, available at http://www.lrb.co.uk/v29/n02/perry-anderson/russias-managed-democracy.

45. Lynch, *Vladimir Putin and Russian Statecraft*, p. 56.
46. Ibid., p. 13.
47. Putin, *First Person*, p. 141.
48. John B. Dunlop, *The Moscow Bombings of September 1999: Examination of Russian Terrorist Attacks at the Onset of Putin's Rule* (Stuttgart, 2012), p. 66.
49. Ibid.; However Dunlop's view is fiercely challenged by Andrei Soldatov, Russia's leading expert on the FSB. He believes these allegations of confirmation by French intelligence to be fictitious. Soldatov argues that Western scholars and journalists have repeatedly reported tabloid Russian reporting on the apartment bombings without checking sources.
50. Treisman, *The Return*, p. 91.
51. Dunlop, *The Moscow Bombings*, p. 27.
52. Ibid., p. 85.
53. Ibid., p. 82.
54. 'Over Forty Percent Russians Link Secret Service, Bombings: Poll', *Agence France Presse*, 17 April 2002.
55. For further discussion of the apartment bombings I suggest the reader consults Dunlop's *The Moscow Bombings*. Whilst Dunlop provides many accounts detailing complicity on behalf of the authorities I do not feel he has firmly proved regime culpability in a full 'false flag attack' – but strongly enhanced the case for some degree of involvement. The jury is still out and possible alternatives and mixed scenarios to either outright innocence or regime terror attacks have not been fully explored. In Russia events are either interpreted as either 'conspiracy' or 'incompetence', when most often they are a mix of both.
56. Treisman, *The Return*, p. 92.
57. Boris Kargalitsky, *Russia under Yeltsin And Putin: Neo-liberal Autocracy* (London, 2002), p. 230.

Chapter Two: The Videocracy

1. Vladimir Putin, 'Rossia Na Rubezhe Tishyacheletnie', 29 December 1999, available at http://www.ng.ru/politics/1999-12-30/4_millenium.html.
2. Ibid.
3. Ibid.
4. Mikhail Kasyanov, *Bezputina: Politichiskie Dialog S Evgeny Kiselyevim* (Moscow, 2009), p. 53.
5. Yulia Latynina, 'Macroeconomic Pilfering Won't Work,' *The Moscow Times*, 9 August 2000.
6. John Pearce Hardt (ed.), *Russia's Uncertain Economic Future*, Joint Economic Committee Congress of the United States (Washington DC, 2003), p. 252.
7. Steven Eke, 'Profile: Mikhail Kasyanov', *BBC News*, 22 January 2008, available at http://news.bbc.co.uk/1/hi/world/europe/7202708.stm.
8. Vladimir Putin, *First Person: An Astonishingly Frank Self-Portrait by Russia's President* (London, 2000), p. 139.
9. Rupert Wingfield Hayes, 'Scars Remain Amid Chechen Revival', *BBC News*, 3 March 2007.
10. Andrei Illiaronov interviewed in *Putin, Russia and the West*, Episode 1, 'Taking Control', 2012.
11. Robert Coalson, 'Babitsky's Crime and Punishment', *Committee to Protect Journalists*, 28 February 2000, available at https://cpj.org/reports/2000/02/main.php.
12. Masha Gessen, *The Man without a Face: The Unlikely Rise of Vladimir Putin* (London, 2012), p. 33.
13. Putin, *First Person*, p. 139.
14. Angus Roxburgh, *The Strongman: Vladimir Putin and the Struggle for Russia* (London, 2012), p. 25.
15. Mikhail Kasyanov, *Bezputina: Politichiskie Dialog S Evgeny Kiselyevim* (Moscow, 2009), p. 165.
16. Ibid., p. 126.

17. Andrew Jack, *Inside Putin's Russia* (London, 2004), p. 136.
18. Ibid., p. 135.
19. Ibid., p. 136.
20. Ibid., p. 152.
21. Boris Berezovsky, 'Oligarchs as Nation's Saviors? Berezovsky Justifies Himself', *The St Petersburg Times*, 20 October 2000.
22. David Hoffman, *The Oligarchs: Money And Power in the New Russia* (New York, 2004), p. 475.
23. Richard Sakwa, *Putin: Russia's Choice* (Oxford, 2004) p. 143.
24. Jack, *Inside Putin's Russia*, p. 148.
25. Andrei Soldatov argues that in an investigation he conducted into the NTV documentary he found 'witnesses' had been paid to say the FSB was behind the bombings. He argues that the documentary provides no concrete evidence of FSB involvement.
26. Hoffman, *The Oligarchs*, p. 485.
27. Ibid., p. 409.
28. Gessen, *The Man without a Face*, p. 170.
29. Allen Lynch, *Vladimir Putin and Russian Statecraft* (New York, 2011), p. 78.
30. Tina Burrett, *Television and Presidential Power in Russia* (London, 2011), p. 57.
31. Ibid., p. 12.
32. Ibid., p. 14.
33. Gleb Pavlovsky, *Genialnaya Vlast* (Moscow, 2012), p. 84.
34. Ben Judah, 'Letter From Moscow', *Prospect*, 25 May 2010.
35. This observation is frequently cited in Russia. The importance of it was first brought to my attention in the following exceptional essay. Perry Anderson, 'Russia's Managed Democracy', *London Review of Books*, vol. 29, no. 2, 25 January 2005.
36. Gleb Pavlovsky, *Genialnaya Vlast* (Moscow, 2012), p. 84.
37. Lyudmila Romanova and Ilya Zhegulev, *Operatsiya Edinaya Rossiya: Neizvestnaya Istoriya Partiya Vlasti* (Moscow, 2011), p. 267.
38. Gleb Pavlovsky, 'Privichka K Obazhaniu U Putina Voznikla Ranshe', *New Times*, 26 March 2012, available at http://newtimes.ru/articles/detail/51401/
39. Gleb Pavlovsky, *Genialnaya Vlast* (Moscow, 2012), p. 73.
40. 'Zachem Putiniu Upravlaemyaya Demokratiku', *Sova Centre*, 1 April 2005, available at http://www.sova-center.ru/democracy/publications/2005/04/d4152/.
41. Vladimir Radchenko, 'Samii Negumanii Sud – Dlya Predprinimateli', *Forbes*, 11 April 2012, available at http://www.forbes.ru/sobytiya-column/vlast/80917-samyi- negumannyi-sud
42. 'Putin's "Rape Joke" Played Down', *BBC News*, 20 October 2006.
43. This point is often discussed in Russia. The full importance of it was only rammed home to me though by the following deeply insightful book. Emanuel Carrère, *Limonov*, (Paris, 2011).
44. 'The Long Life Of Homo Soveiticus,' *The Economist*, 10 December 2010.
45. 'Russian Macro View: Consumption to Remain Strong for Now', *Citi Economics*, 21 October 2011.
46. Jonathan Brent, *Inside the Stalin Archives: Discovering the New Russia* (New York, 2008), p. 267.
47. Victor Pelevin, *Babylon* (London, 2000), p. 28.
48. Ibid., p. 6.

Chapter Three: The Great Turn

1. Vladimir Putin, *First Person: An Astonishingly Frank Self-Portrait by Russia's President* (London, 2000), p. 11.
2. Masha Gessen, *The Man without a Face: The Unlikely Rise of Vladimir Putin* (London, 2012), p. 49.
3. Erich Schmidt-Eenboom, 'Putins Schatten an der Elbe,' *Sachsische Zeitung*, 10 Noveember 2011; Alexander Mannheim and Daisy Sindelar, 'A Spy In The House Of Putin,' *Radio Free Europe*, 7 November 2011.
4. 'Interview with Alexander Solzhenitsyn', *Der Spiegel*, 30 August 2007.
5. Ibid.

6. Ibid.
7. Ibid.
8. 'Excerpts from Solzhenitsyn's Article on the Soviets', *The New York Times*, 19 September 1990.
9. Anna Malpas, 'Putin Warns against Despotism, Chaos in Russia', *Agence France Presse*, 22 January 2010.
10. Dominique Moisi, *The Geopolitics of Emotion: How Cultures of Fear, Humiliation and Hope are Reshaping the World*, (London, 2009), p. 125.
11. Allen Lynch, *Vladimir Putin and Russian Statecraft* (Washington DC, 2010), p. 37.
12. Ibid., p. 38.
13. Ibid., p. 37.
14. Putin, *First Person*, p. 168.
15. In 2012 the Yuganskneftegaz fields that formed the heart of Yukos have proven oil reserves of over 11 billion barrels. This is almost double the Norwegian proven reserves of 5.67 billion barrels.
16. Cyril Tuschi (ed.), *Khodorkovsky*, 2012, film.
17. Steven L. Solnick, *Stealing The State: Control and Collapse in Soviet Institutions* (Cambridge, 1998), p. 7.
18. David E. Hoffman, *The Oligarchs: Wealth and Power in the New Russia* (New York, 2002), p. 121.
19. Mikhail Khodorkovsky, 'Krizis Liberalizma V Rossii', *Vedomosti*, 29 March 2003, available at http://khodorkovsky.ru/mbk/articles_and_interview/12296.html.
20. Ibid.
21. Ibid.
22. Khodorkovsky, 'Krizis Liberalizma V Rossii'. 'Choose with the Heart' was the slogan of Yeltsin's 1996 re-election campaign.
23. Ibid.
24. Thane Gustafson, *Wheel of Fortune: The Battle for Oil and Power in Russia* (London, 2012), p. 217.
25. Ibid., p. 186.
26. Ibid.
27. Ibid., p. 196.
28. Ibid., p. 188.
29. Martin Sixsmith, *Putin's Oil: The Yukos Affair and the Struggle for Russia* (New York, 2010), p. 57.
30. Ibid, p. 53.
31. Ibid.
32. Mikhail Kasyanov, *Bezputina: Politichiskie Dialog S Evgeny Kiselyevim* (Moscow, 2009), p. 207.
33. Hoffman, *The Oligarchs*, p. 107.
34. Richard Sakwa, *Russian Politics and Society* 4th edn (London, 2008), p. 443.
35. Sixsmith, *Putin's Oil*, p. 66.
36. Ibid., pp. 61–2.
37. Tuschi (ed.), *Khodorkovsky*.
38. Angus Roxburgh, *The Strongman: Vladimir Putin and the Struggle for Russia* (London, 2012), p. 82.
39. Sixsmith, *Putin's Oil*, p. 122.
40. Mikhail Khodorkovsky, 'Krizis Liberalizma V Rossii'.
41. Keith Gessen, 'Cell Block Four', *London Review of Books*, vol. 32, no. 4, 25 February 2010.
42. Mikhail Kasyanov, *Bezputina: Politichiskie Dialog S Evgeny Kiselyevim* (Moscow, 2009), p. 222.
43. Ibid., p. 226.
44. Anders Aslund, *Russia's Capitalist Revolution: Why Market Reform Succeeded and Democracy Failed* (Washington DC, 2007), p. 251.
45. Ibid., p. 253.
46. Gustafson, *Wheel of Fortune*, p. 264.
47. Ibid., p. 23.

48. Lynch, *Vladimir Putin and Russian Statecraft*, p. 83.
49. Daniel Treisman, 'Loans for Shares Revisited', NBER Working Paper, No. 15819, March 2010; James Sherr, 'Putin is Slipping', *Prospect*, 19 September 2012.
50. Kasyanov, *Bezputina*, p. 241.
51. Lynch, *Vladimir Putin and Russian Statecraft*, p. 68.
52. Ibid.
53. Ellen Barry, 'Putin Speaks His Mind, and Then Some, on Television', *The New York Times*, 16 December 2010.
54. Brian D. Taylor, *State Building in Putin's Russia: Policing and Coercion after Communism* (New York, 2011), p. 87.
55. 'U Bivshik Zalozhnikov Nabludaetsya Astenichiski Sindrom', *newsru.com*, 31 October 2002, available at http://www.newsru.com/russia/31oct2002/astenichesky.html.
56. Evidence for the use of flamethrowers was found by a commission undertaken by the North Ossetian parliament. 'State Forces Blamed Over Beslan', *BBC News*, 29 November 2005.
57. 'Boris Gryzlov Izban Spikerom Gosdumi Chetvortovo Soyuza', *Leningradskaya Pravda*, 29 December 2003.
58. Aslund, *Russia's Capitalist Revolution*, p. 263.
59. Taylor, *State Building in Putin's Russia*, p. 92.
60. Mikhail Shevelev, 'General-Mayor Militsii Vladimir Ovchinskii – O Patriotakh I Liberalakh', *Svabodanews.ru*, 29 October 2012, available at http://www.svobodanews.ru/content/article/2262376.html.
61. Graeme E. Robertson, *The Politics of Protest in Hybrid Regimes: Managing Dissent in Post-Communist Russia* (New York, 2011), p. 196.
62. Ibid., p. 148.
63. Andrew Monaghan, 'The End of The Putin Era?', *The Carnegie Endowment for International Peace*, July 2012.
64. Roxburgh, *The Strongman*, p. 146.
65. Mark Leonard, Ivan Krastev and Andrew Wilson (eds), *What does Russia Think?* (London, 2009), p. 11.

Chapter Four: The Vertical of Power

1. This description is based on photos taken by Ilya Varlamov, a photographer who associates himself with the opposition. After these photos were taken he was found to have received money from Nashi to post certain blog posts that made Putin look intelligent. The photographs are available at http://zyalt.livejournal.com/347515.html.
2. Peter Pomerantsev, 'Putin's Rasputin', *London Review of Books*, vol. 33, no. 20, 20 October 2011.
3. Natan Dubovitsky, *Okolonolya: Gangsta Fiction* (Moscow, 2009).
4. Vitaly Leibin, Viktor Dyatlikovich, Dmitry Kartsev and Andrei Veselov, 'Surkov: Neizvestnaya Istoria Putinskoi Rossii', *Russki Reporter*, 30 January 2012.
5. Charles Clover and Daniel Dombey, 'Oil Trading Group Gunvor Denies Putin Links', *Financial Times*, 3 December 2010.
6. Ilya Zhegulyev and Ludmila Romanova, *Operatsiya Edinaya Rossiya: Neizvestnaya Istoria Partii Vlast* (Moscow, 2012), p. 26.
7. Ibid., p. 27.
8. David E. Hoffman, *The Oligarchs: Wealth and Power in the New Russia* (New York, 2002), p. 123.
9. 'Interview with Kremlin Boss Vladislav Surkov', *Der Spiegel*, 20 June 2005.
10. Zhegulyev and Romanova, *Operatsiya Edinaya Rossiya*, p. 110.
11. Valery Panyushkin, *Twelve Who Don't Agree: The Battle for Freedom in Putin's Russia* (New York, 2011), p. 232.
12. Sean P. Roberts, *Putin's United Russia Party* (New York, 2012), p. 3.
13. Ibid.
14. Ibid., p. 155.
15. Ibid.
16. Ibid.

17. Ibid., p. 73.
18. Ibid., p. 76.
19. Ibid., pp. 3, 80.
20. 'Interview with Kremlin Boss Vladislav Surkov', *Der Spiegel*, 20 June 2005.
21. Ibid., p. 3.
22. Clifford G. Gaddy and Andrew C. Kuchins, 'Putin's Plan', *The Washington Quarterly*, Spring 2008.
23. Zhegulyev and Romanova, *Operatsiya Edinaya Rossiya*, p. 237.
24. Ibid.
25. Ibid., p. 96.
26. 'Interview with Kremlin Boss Vladislav Surkov', *Der Spiegel*, 20 June 2005.
27. Sean P. Roberts, *Putin's United Russia Party* (New York, 2012), p. 150.
28. Mikhail Kasyanov, *Bezputina: Politichiskie Dialog S Evgeny Kiselyevim* (Moscow, 2009), p. 173.
29. Richard Sakwa, *Russian Politics and Society*, 4th edn (New York, 2008), p. 260.
30. Gleb Pavlovsky, *Genialnaya Vlast* (Moscow, 2012), p. 19.
31. Thane Gustafson, *The Wheel of Fortune: The Battle for Oil and Power in Russia* (London, 2012), p. 391.
32. Maria Lipman and Nikolay Petrov (eds), *Russia in 2020: Scenarios for the Future* (Washington DC, 2011), p. 327.
33. Andrei Soldatov and Irina Borogan, *The New Nobility: The Restoration of Russia's Security State and the Enduring Legacy of the KGB* (New York, 2010), p. 5.
34. Yevgeniya Albats, *The State within a State: The KGB and Its Hold on Russia's Past, Present and Future* (New York, 1994), p. 23.
35. Brian D. Taylor, *State Building in Putin's Russia: Policing and Coercion after Communism* (New York, 2011), p. 48.
36. Ibid., p. 38.
37. Soldatov and Borogan, *The New Nobility*, p. 70.
38. Available at http://cpj.org/killed/europe/russia/.
39. 'Interview with Kremlin Boss Vladislav Surkov', *Der Spiegel*, 20 June 2005.
40. Lilia Shevtsova, *Lost in Transition: The Yeltsin and Putin Legacies* (Washington DC, 2007), p. 174.
41. Vladislav Surkov, 'Russkaya Politichaskaya Kultura: Vzglyad Iz Utopii', *Russkiy Jurnal*, 15 June 2007.
42. Yury Pavlov, *Da Gospodin Prezident* (Moscow, 2005).
43. Roberts, *Putin's United Russia Party*, p. 87.
44. Ibid., p. 160.
45. Julia Ioffe, 'Net Impact: One Man's Cyber-Crusade against Russian Corruption', *The New Yorker*, 4 April 2011.
46. 'Vtoraya Partiya Vlasti Poyavilis S Podachi Surkova', *Lenta*, 16 August 2006.
47. Arkady Ostrovsky, 'Bribery in Russia up Tenfold in Four Years', *Financial Times*, 22 June 2010.
48. Ibid.
49. One of the reasons for the sharpness of this drop was the expansion of the number of countries included in the Corruptions Perception Index. However, Elena Panfilova, the head of Transparency International in Russia, insists even if no countries had been added Russia would still have deteriorated on the index. Available at http://archive.transparency.org/policy_research/surveys_indices/cpi/2001.
50. Available at http://archive.transparency.org/policy_research/surveys_indices/cpi/2006.
51. Vladimir Radchenko, 'Samii Negumanii Sud – Dlya Predprinmateli', *Forbes*, 11 April 2011.
52. Allen Lynch, *Vladimir Putin and Russian Statecraft* (Washington DC, 2011), p. 89.
53. Anna Nemtsova, 'Zakhar Prilepin: a modern Leo Tolstoy', *Russia beyond the Headlines*, 13 April 2012.
54. Zakhar Prilepine, *San'kia* (Paris, 2009), p. 90.
55. Ibid., p. 92.
56. Yevgenia Albats, '"Une Generation Insaisissable", Russie: Un Autoportrait', *Courrier Internationale*, September 2011.

57. 'Russia's Regions: Facts And Figures', *United Nations Development Programme*, available at http://www.undp.ru/index.phtml?iso=RU&lid=1&pid=1&cmd=text&id=187.
58. The girl in question was 17 years old at the time. Evidence comes from screenshots of an online conversation in which he appears to acknowledge intercourse. Available at http://dobrokhotov.users.photofile.ru/photo/dobrokhotov/115822366/139283934.jpg.
59. Available at http://www.youtube.com/watch?v=24XBX0Wkmpw.
60. Elizabeta Maetnaya, 'Sudba Barabanshitsi', *Izvestia*, 20 December 2011.
61. Pavlovsky, *Genialnaya Vlast*, p. 90.
62. 'Putin Attacks Jackal Opponents', *BBC News*, 21 November 2007.
63. 'Putin deplores collapse of USSR', *BBC News*, 25 April 2005.
64. 'Putin regrets that USSR did not fight', *Agence France Presse*, 15 December 2011.
65. Natalia Ziganshina, 'Nashi Uchebniki Formiruyut Kulturni Rasizm', *Gazeta.ru*, 13 December 2012.
66. Steven Lee Myers, 'Hazing Trial Bares Dark Side of Russian Military', *The New York Times*, 13 August 2006.
67. Ibid.
68. Daniel Treisman, *The Return Russia's Journey from Gorbachev to Medvedev* (New York, 2011), p. 121.

Chapter Five: Putin's Court

 1. Available at http://www.youtube.com/watch?v=oEsO6HorDro.
 2. Sergey Kolesnikov provided full documentation for his claims to the *Financial Times*, which verified them for the following article: Catherine Belton, 'A Realm Fit for a Tsar', *Financial Times*, 30 November 2011.
 3. 'Gunvor: Riddles, Mysteries and Enigmas', *The Economist*, 5 May 2012.
 4. Gennady Timchenko, 'Gunvor, Putin and Me – The Truth about Russian Oil Trader', *Financial Times*, 22 May 2008.
 5. Andrew E. Kramer and David M. Herszenhorn, 'Midas Touch in St Petersburg: Friends of Putin Glow Brightly', *The New York Times*, 1 March 2012.
 6. 'Gunvor's Roots', *The Economist*, 5 May 2012.
 7. 'In Search of Putin's Money', *Al Jazeera*, 20 April 2012.
 8. Vladimir Milov, Boris Nemtsov, Vladimir Ryzhkov and Olga Shorina (eds), *Putin Itogi* (Moscow, 2011). Available at http://www.putin-itogi.ru/putin-i-korruptsiya/.
 9. *Forbes* 2000 and 2008 billionaires list, available at http://stats.areppim.com/listes/list_billionairesx00xwor.htm and http://www.forbes.com/lists/2008/10/billionaires08_The-Worlds-Billionaires_Rank.html.
10. Ibid.
11. Ibid.
12. Ibid.
13. Ibid.
14. Ibid.
15. Boris Nemtsov and Leonid Martinyuk, *Zhizn Rab Na Galerakh* (Moscow, 2012). Available at http://graphics8.nytimes.com/packages/pdf/world/2012/120827_Russia_Pamphlet.pd.
16. Ibid.
17. Caleb Melby, 'Moscow Beats New York, London, in List of Billionaire Cities', *Forbes*, 16 March 2012.
18. Tony Wood, 'Collapse as Crucible: The Reforging of Russian Society', *New Left Review*, vol. 74, March–April 2012.
19. Ibid.
20. Vladimir Putin, *First Person: An Astonishingly Frank Self-Portrait by Russia's President* (London, 2000), p. 182.
21. Dmitry Zhdannikov, 'Russia Davos Party Has Unusual Opposition Flavor', *Reuters*, 28 January 2012.
22. Available at http://files.vpro.nl/wikileaks/cable/2009/03/09MOSCOW532.html.
23. 'Dokhodi Semi Pervovo Vitze-Premera RF Igor Shuvalov', *RIA Novosti*, 28 March 2012. Available at http://ria.ru/society/20120412/624180449.html.

24. Ibid.
25. Ibid.
26. Ibid.
27. Catherine Belton, 'Shuvalov Case Raises Croneyism Questions', *Financial Times*, 27 March 2012.
28. These allegations were made by Alexey Navalny who posted documents backing up his claims online, which were confirmed as real by a Moscow law firm. Available at http://navalny.livejournal.com/697198.html#cutid1; Andrew Kramer, 'Activist Presses For Inquiry Into Senior Putin Official', *The New York Times*, 30 March 2012.
29. Alexey Kudrin, 'Otveti na Voprosi'. Available at http://akudrin.ru/news/otvety-na-voprosy.html#.T4Szz3lJri8.twitter.
30. 'Letters', *The Economist*, 2 September 2010.
31. Viktor Cherkesov, 'Nelziya Dopustit, Stobi Voini Prevratilis V Torgovets', *Kommersant*, 9 October 2007.
32. Vladimir L. Inozemtsev, 'Neo-Feudalism Explained', *The American Interest*, March–April 2011.
33. 'Wife Serenades Russia's NATO Envoy about "Making Love"' (video), *Agence France Presse*, 6 November 2010.
34. Simon Shuster, 'Vladimir Putin: When Family Is Virtually A State Secret', *Time*, 16 June 2011.
35. Letter from Karl Marx to Arnold Ruge, Cologne, May 1843. Available at http://www.marxists.org/archive/marx/works/1843/letters/43_05-alt.htm.
36. Gleb Pavlovsky, *Genialnaya Vlast* (Moscow, 2012), p. 7.

Chapter Six: Dizzy with Success

1. Vladimir Sorokin, *Journée d'un Opritchnik* (Paris, 2000).
2. Andrei Shleifer and Daniel Treisman, 'A Normal Country: Russia after Communism', *Journal of Economic Perspectives*, vol. 19, no. 1 (Winter 2005).
3. Ibid.
4. David Hoffman, *The Oligarchs: Wealth and Power in the New Russia* (New York, 2002), p. 411.
5. IMF and World Bank Data, available at http://siteresources.worldbank.org/DATASTATISTICS/Resources/GDP_PPP.pdf; http://www.imf.org/external/pubs/ft/weo/2011/01/weodata/download.aspx; http://data.worldbank.org/indicator/NY.GDP.MKTP.PP.KD?order=wbapi_data_value_2005+wbapi_data_value+wbapi_data_value-last&sort=desc&page=1.
6. Ibid.
7. Ibid.
8. Thane Gustafson, *Wheel of Fortune: The Battle for Oil and Power in Russia* (London, 2012), p. 360.
9. Ibid.
10. Ibid.
11. Ibid.
12. Charles Clover, 'Lunch with the FT – Alexander Lebedev', *Financial Times*, 27 July 2012.
13. *The Economist Pocket World in Figures 2012 Edition*, (London, 2011), pp. 50–60.
14. Konstantin Rozhnov, 'Russia attracts investors despite image', *BBC News*, 30 November 2007.
15. Anders Aslund, Sergei Guriev and Andrew Kuchins (eds), *Russia after the Global Economic Crisis* (Washington DC, 2010) p. 20.
16. Marshall Goldman, *Petrostate: Putin, Power and the New Russia* (Oxford, 2008), p. 81.
17. Mikhail Dmitriev and Daniel Treisman, 'The Other Russia: Discontent Grows in the Heartland', *Foreign Affairs*, September–October 2010; Aslund, Guriev and Kuchins (eds), *Russia after the Global Economic Crisis*, p. 12.
18. World Bank. Data, available at http://data.worldbank.org/indicator/NY.GDP.PCAP.PP.CD?order=wbapi_data_value_2011+wbapi_data_value+wbapi_data_value-last&sort=asc.

19. Aslund, Guriev and Kuchins (eds), *Russia after the Global Economic Crisis*, p. 12.
20. 'Putin's Russia: Call Back Yesterday', *The Economist*, 3 March 2012.
21. Ibid.
22. Ibid.
23. 'Surkov: Inovatzii Pozvalyat Zarababativat Bolshe', *Vesti*, 21 March 2010, available at http://www.vesti.ru/doc.html?id=348412.
24. Gustafson, *Wheel of Fortune*, p. 4.
25. Ibid.
26. Sergei Belanovsky, Mikhail Dmitriev, Svetlana Mishikhina and Tatyana Omelchuk, *Socio-Economic Change And Political Transformation in Russia*, (Moscow, 2011), p. 30.
27. Natalia Zubarevich, 'Four Russias: Rethinking The Post-Soviet Map', *OpenDemocracy*, 29 March 2012.
28. 'Putin's Russia: Call Back Yesterday', *The Economist*, 3 March 2012.
29. Natalia Zubarevich, 'Four Russias: Rethinking the Post-Soviet Map', *OpenDemocracy*, 29 March 2012.
30. Mikhail Dmitriev and Svetlana Misikhina, 'Good-bye poverty – Russia's Quiet Social Revoltuion, *Baltic Rim Economies*, 15 October 2012.
31. Ibid.
32. Sergei Belanovsky, Mikhail Dmitriev, Svetlana Mishikhina and Tatyana Omelchuk, *Socio-Economic Change And Political Transformation in Russia*, (Moscow, 2011), p. 31.
33. Aslund, Guriev and Kuchins (eds), *Russia after the Global Economic Crisis*, p. 14.
34. Ibid., p. 15.
35. Mikhail Dmitriev and Alexey Yurataev, *Strategia-2010: Itogi Realitastsi 10 Let Sputsya* (Moscow, 2010), p. 6.
36. Bruce Etling, Karina Alexanyan, John Kelly, Robert Faris, John Palfrey and Urs Gasser, *Public Discourse in the Russian Blogosphere: Mapping RuNet Politics And Mobilization* (Cambridge, MA, 2010), p. 17.
37. Ibid., p. 13.
38. Floriana Fossato and John Lloyd with Alexander Verkhovsky, *The Web that Failed: How Opposition Politics and Independent Initiatives are Failing on the Internet* (Oxford, 2008).
39. Dmitriev and Treisman, 'The Other Russia'; International Telecommunications Union, *Key Global Indicators 2011*, available at http://www.itu.int/ITU-D/ict/statistics/.
40. Ilya Arkhipov and Henry Meyer, 'Putin Faces Anti-Migrant Tide as Opponents Tap Resentment', *Bloomberg*, 7 November 2012; Ben Judah, 'Russia: A Magnet for Migrants', *Prospect*, 20 October 2010.
41. Ibid.
42. Ariel Cohen, 'Domestic Factors Driving Russian Foreign Policy', Backgrounder on Russian Eurasia, no. 2084, The Heritage Foundation, 19 November 2007.
43. Tony Wood, 'Russia Vanishes', *London Review of Books*, vol. 34, no. 23, 6 December 2012.
44. Ibid.; Arkhipov and Meyer, 'Putin Faces Anti-Migrant Tide'.
45. Khristina Narizhnaya, 'Slave Labor on The Rise in Russia', *GlobalPost*, 27 May 2012. Available at http://www.globalpost.com/dispatch/news/regions/europe/russia/120525/slave-labor-the-rise-russia.
46. 'Rabstvo V Moskve', *Boslhoi Gorod*, 31 October 2010, available at http://bg.ru/society/rabstvo_v_moskve-15482/.
47. Available at http://www.patriarchia.ru/db/text/541724.html.
48. Thomas de Waal, 'Springtime for Patriarchs', *The National Interest*, 27 January 2011.
49. Yury Maloveryan, 'Neschitanie Bogatsva Russkoi Pravoslavnoi Tserkvi', *BBC Russian Service*, 30 August 2011.
50. Sophia Kishkovsky, 'Russia to Return Church Property', *The New York Times*, 23 November 2010.
51. Andrei Zolotov, 'Orthodoxy, Oil, Tabacco and Wine: Do They Mix?', *East-West Church and Ministry Report*, vol. 5, no. 1, Winter 1997.
52. John Anderson, 'Putin and the Russian Orthodox Church: Asymmetric Symphonia', *Columbia Journal of International Affairs*, vol. 61, no. 1, Autumn-Winter 2007.
53. Alexey Malashenko and Sergey Filatov, *Pravoslavnaya Tserkov Pri Novom Patriarkhe* (Moscow, 2012), p. 261. Figures in English in press release available at http://carnegie.ru/publications/?fa=46251.

54. Peter Pomerantsev, 'Patriarchy Riot', *London Review of Books Blog*, 16 August 2012, available at http://www.lrb.co.uk/blog/2012/08/16/peter-pomerantsev/patriarchy-riot/.
55. Michael Schwirtz, '$30,000 Watch Vanishes up Church Leader's Sleeve', *The New York Times*, 5 April 2012.
56. Tom Esslemont, 'Russian Orthodox Church defiant over Pussy Riot trial', *BBC News*, 11 August 2012.
57. Sophia Kishovsky, 'In Russian Chill, Waiting Hours for Touch of the Holy', *The New York Times*, 23 November 2011.
58. Ibid.
59. 'Head of Russian church opposes "mindless copying" of western values', *RT*, 28 September 2011.
60. 'G-8 Interview with Vladimir Putin', *Der Spiegel*, 6 April 2007.
61. Gleb Pavlovsky, 'Privichka K Obozhaniu Voznikla Ranshe', *Novaya Vremya*, 26 March 2012.
62. It is extremely hard to measure the scale of protests in both Russia and China due to obvious unreliability of government statistics. However, the Chinese Communist Party's leading think-tank – the Chinese Academy of Social Sciences – became increasingly alarmed of 'mass incident' in its hinterland in the 2000s. These reached over 87,500 a year in 2005. There was not in Putin's first presidency comparable unrest in Russia. See John Fewsmith, 'Social Order in the Wake of Financial Crisis', Hoover Institution, 8 May 2009, available at http://media.hoover.org/sites/default/files/documents/CLM28JF.pdf.
63. Available at http://www.afisha.ru/Afisha7files/File/mediakit/Afisha-mag_mediakit_2011-02_ENG_.pdf.
64. 'Russia Media: Parfyonov's Magic Touch', *The Economist*, 29 November 2010, available at http://www.economist.com/blogs/easternapproaches/2010/11/russian_media.
65. Goldman Sachs intention with the BRIC report was not to engage in scholarly research but to encourage investment in their emerging markets division. Jim O'Neill, 'Building Better Global Economic BRICs', Goldman Sachs Global Economics Paper No. 66, 30 November 2001.
66. It is unclear what measurement of GDP he was referring to. Ben Judah, Jana Kobzova and Nicu Popescu, *Dealing with a Post-BRIC Russia* (London, 2011), pp. 15–16.
67. 'Russian Economy Booming', *The Washington Times*, 29 October 2007.
68. Ben S. Bernanke, 'The Great Moderation, Remarks at the Meeting of the Eastern Economic Association', 20 February 2004; Milton Friedman, 'Why the American Economy is Depression-proof', University of Chicago Industrial Relations Center, 1956.
69. Anders Aslund and Andrew Kuchins, *The Russian Balance Sheet* (Washington DC, 2009), p. 40.
70. Tom Shanker and Mark Landler, 'Putin Says U.S. Is Undermining Global Security', *The New York Times*, 11 February 2011.
71. Tom Shanker, 'Gates Counters Putin's Words on U.S. Power', *The New York Times*, 11 February 2007.
72. 'Putin Asked to Follow FDR's Example', *Kommersant*, online English version, 9 February 2007, available at http://www.kommersant.com/p741228/r_500/Putin_Roosevelt_Third_Term/.
73. Doug Struck, 'Gorbachev Applauds Putin's Achievements', *The Washington Post*, 5 December 2007.
74. Jonathan Powell, *The New Machiavelli: How to Wield Power in the Modern World* (London, 2010), p. 310.
75. Sergei Markov, 'Chto biet po demokratii', 30 September 2006, available at http://dom.viper§son.ru/wind.php?ID=499115&soch=1?17f1fd40.
76. Yury Pavlov, *Da Gospodin Prezident* (Moscow, 2005)
77. 'Russian NATO envoy sees "genocide" in South Ossetia', *Reuters*, 9 August 2008.
78. William Maudlin, 'Russia's Rulers Popularity Declines as Elections Loom', *The Wall Street Journal*, 25 August 2011.

Chapter Seven: Servant Medvedev

1. Vladimir Putin, *First Person: An Astonishingly Frank Self-Portrait by Russia's President* (London, 2000), p. 202.
2. Valery Panyushkin, *12 Who Don't Agree: The Battle for Freedom in Putin's Russia* (New York, 2011), p. 235.
3. Daniel Treisman, *The Return: Russia's Journey from Gorbachev to Medvedev* (New York, 2011), p. 126.
4. Ibid. Anastasia Ustinova, 'Medvedev Says He and Putin Have Same Blood, Make Good Team', *Bloomberg*, 25 February 2010.
5. Speech at Inauguration Ceremony as President of Russia, 7 May 2008, available at http://archive.kremlin.ru/eng/speeches/2008/05/07/1521_type82912type127286_200295.shtml.
6. Richard Sakwa, 'Dmitry Medvedev's Challenge', *OpenDemocracy*, 7 May 2008, available at http://www.opendemocracy.net/article/governments/dmitri_medvedev_s_challenge.
7. Katherine Hendley, 'Who Are the Legal Nihilists in Russia', *Post-Soviet Affairs*, April-June 2012.
8. Available at http://eng.da-medvedev.ru/.
9. Maxim Shishkin, 'Rossiya Vybiraet Ostrovnoyu Taktiku', *Kommersant*, 24 January 2008.
10. Ben Judah, Jana Kobzova, Nicu Popescu, *Dealing with a post-BRIC Russia* (London, 2011), p. 18.
11. Anders Aslund, Sergei Guriev and Andrew Kuchins (eds), *Russia after the Global Economic Crisis* (Washington DC, 2010), p. 27.
12. Ibid., p. xi.
13. Ibid.
14. Steven Pifer, 'President Medvedev Rocks at Brookings', Up Front, Brookings Institution, 15 April 2010, available at http://www.brookings.edu/blogs/up-front/posts/2010/04/15-medvedev-pifer.
15. Konstantin Gaaze and Darya Guseva, 'Lezte s Meste', *Russky Newsweek*, 16 March 2009.
16. Aslund, Guriev and Kuchins (eds), *Russia after the Global Economic Crisis*, p. xiv.
17. 'Financial Times Launches Crisis in Capitalism Series', *Financial Times*, 9 January 2012, available at http://aboutus.ft.com/2012/01/09/financial-times-launches-capitalism-in-crisis-series/#axzz2As88YIMp.
18. Dmitry Medvedev, 'Go, Russia!', 10 September 2010, available at http://eng.kremlin.ru/news/298.
19. Ibid.
20. Ibid.
21. Judah, Kobzova and Popescu, *Dealing with a post-BRIC Russia*, p. 20.
22. 'Vse Vzyatki Moskvi', *Bolshoi Gorod*, 21 February 2011.
23. 'Korrupstionnaya Podstavlayushya,' *Kommersant*, 1 December 2012. Available at http://www.kommersant.ru/doc/2082860
24. Interview with Russian Embassy, London.
25. 'Natural catastrophes 2010, Analyses, Assessments, Positions,' *Munich Re Topics Geo*, February 2011.
26. 'Putin, Pikalyovo and The Failure of the Vertical of Power', United States Embassy Moscow, 15 June 2009. Available at http://wikileaks.org/cable/2009/06/09MOSCOW1562.html.
27. C. J. Chivers, 'Below Surface U.S. Has Dim View of Putin and Russia', *The New York Times*, 1 December 2010.
28. David Hearst, 'Putin We Have Lost Russia's Trust', *The Guardian*, 12 November 2011.
29. Gleb Pavlovsky, *Genialnaya Vlast* (Moscow, 2012), p. 48.
30. Vera Kholmogorova and Anastasia Kornya, 'Medvedev Seeks List of Punished Officials', *The Moscow Times*, 23 June 2010.
31. 'Prezident Dmitri Medvedev Ne Dovolen Arkhaichnoi Sistemoi Upravlenia, Kotoraya, Po Evo Mneniu, Seichas Sushetvuyet V Rossii', *Ekho Moskvy*, 7 June 2011, available at http://echo.msk.ru/news/782067-echo.html.
32. 'Putin Situatziya V Kushchevskoi I Gus Khrustalnom – Proval Pravokhranitelnoi Sistemi', http://www.vesti.ru/doc.html?id=414405&tid=85093.

33. Valery Zorkin, 'Konstitutsiya Protiv Kriminala', *Rossiskaya Gazeta*, 10 December 2010.
34. Ibid.
35. Ibid.
36. Ibid.
37. Anders Aslund and Andrew Kuchins, *The Russian Balance Sheet* (Washington DC, 2009), p. 96.
38. Ibid.
39. Mikhail Dmitriev and Daniel Treisman, 'The Other Russia: Discontent Grows in The Heartland', *Foreign Affairs*, September-October 2012.
40. Ibid.
41. Sergei Guriev and Ekaterina Zhuravskaya, 'Why Russia Is Not South Korea', *Journal of International Affairs*, Spring 2010.
42. Adam Balcer and Nikolai Petrov, *The Future of Russia: Modernization or Decline* (Warsaw, 2012), p. 86.
43. Yulia Fedorovina and Henry Meyer, 'Putin Cabinet Endorses Deputy Premier's Son for Farm Bank Job', *Bloomberg*, 12 May 2011.
44. Vladimir Milov and Boris Nemtsov, *Putin Itogi 10 Let* (Moscow, 2010).
45. 'Son of Rosneft CEO Joins Novatek', *The Moscow Times*, January 2010; Vladislav L. Inozemtsev, 'Neo-Fedualism Explained', *The American Interest*, March–April 2011.
46. Rinat Sagdiev, 'Im Prosto Pozvelo', *Vedomosti*, 25 April 2011.
47. Alexandra Odynova, 'Medvedev Questions Power Vertical', *The Moscow Times*, 16 May 2011.
48. Ellen Barry, 'Satirizing Putin with Boldly Poetic Flair', *The New York Times*, 18 November 2011.
49. Available at http://www.youtube.com/watch?v=-BmnSDoU1Z0.
50. Ibid.
51. Amy Knight, 'The Concealed Battle To Run Russia', *The New York Review of Books*, 13 January 2011.
52. Catherine Belton and Charles Clover, 'Putin to Return as Russia's President', *Financial Times*, 24 September 2011.
53. Ellen Barry, 'Putin Once More Moves to Assume Top Job in Russia', *The New York Times*, 24 September 2011.
54. Ibid.
55. 'Putin Denies Russia Has Authoritarian System', *Agence France Presse*, 20 December 2012.

Chapter Eight: Navalny and the Evolution of the Opposition

1. Anton Stepanov, 'Life News Publikuyet Tanie Peregovori S Oppositianami', *Life News*, 19 December 2011, available at http://lifenews.ru/news/77459.
2. Available at http://rutube.ru/video/5124ebfc40afdcf40314e95ae3eec85e/#.UND6OVH7V8d.
3. Konstantin Voronkov, *Alexey Navalny: Groza Julikov I Vorov* (Moscow, 2012), p. 12.
4. Ibid.
5. Ibid., p. 23.
6. Ibid., p. 24.
7. Ibid., p. 28.
8. Boris Kargalitsky, *Russia under Yeltsin And Putin: Neo-liberal Autocracy* (London, 2002), p. 174.
9. Ibid., p. 175.
10. Ibid.
11. Ibid., p. 176.
12. Voronkov, *Alexey Navalny*, p. 37.
13. Ibid.
14. Ibid., p. 38.
15. Ibid., p. 42.
16. Keith Gessen, 'The Parable Of A Fascist Writer', *Slate*, 20 February 2003.
17. Zakhar Prilepin, *Sank'ia* (Paris, 2009), p. 180.

18. Available at http://navalny.livejournal.com/139478.html.
19. Ibid.
20. Available at http://www.youtube.com/watch?v=oVNJiO10SWw&feature=youtu.be.
21. Voronkov, *Alexey Navalny*, p. 68.
22. Available at http://navalny.livejournal.com/756675.html.
23. Ibid.
24. Ilya Zhegulyev and Ludmila Romanova, *Operatsiya Edinaya Rossiya: Neizvestnaya Istoria Partii Vlast* (Moscow, 2012), p. 94.
25. Available at http://navalny.livejournal.com/242897.html.
26. Ibid.
27. Available at http://navalny.livejournal.com/185724.html.
28. Ibid.
29. Ibid.
30. Ibid.
31. Available at http://navalny.livejournal.com/225726.html.
32. Olga Alexeeva, 'Russia Historic Growth in Private Giving', *Philanthropy UK Newsletter*, no. 34, September 2008.
33. Ibid.
34. The exact figure depends on how one defines an NGO. The 100,000 figures is a conservative definition and estimate based on interviews with experts to discuss official data. The assumption is that many of the 'registered' NGOs are either commercial, inactive or duplicates. Higher figures suggest as many as 600,000 NGOs in Russia. The figures are available at http://yaleglobal.yale.edu/content/russian-civil-society-will-find-it-harder-breathe.
35. Ibid.
36. David Remnick, 'The Civil Archepelago: How far Can the Resistance to Vladimir Putin Go?', *The New Yorker*, 19 December 2011.
37. International Telecommunications Union, *Key Global Indicators 2011*, available at http://www.itu.int/ITU-D/ict/statistics/.
38. Anders Aslund, Sergei Guriev and Andrew C. Kuchins (eds), *Russia after the Global Economic Crisis* (Washington DC, 2010), p. 2010.
39. Available at http://navalny.livejournal.com/profile.
40. Available at http://www.cablegatesearch.net/cable.php?id=09MOSCOW821.
41. Voronkov, *Alexey Navalny*, p. 136.
42. Navalny's account is available to follow at https://twitter.com/#!/navalny.
43. Available at http://navalny.livejournal.com/526563.html#cutid1.
44. Available at http://www.youtube.com/watch?v=hreCylU9O_4&feature=player_embedded.
45. 'Vso Vzyatki Moskvi', *Bolshoi Gorod*, 21 February 2011.
46. Ibid.
47. Ibid.
48. Available at http://www.youtube.com/watch?v=hreCylU9O_4&feature=player_embedded.
49. 'Aleksaya Navalnovo Zaniut 6 per cent Rossiyan', Levada Center, 6 April 2011, available at http://www.levada.ru/06-05-2011/alekseya-navalnogo-znayut-6-rossiyan.
50. Interview with Sergei Guriev, August 2011.

Chapter Nine: The Decembrists

1. Daniel Treisman, *The Return: Russia's Journey from Gorbachev to Medvedev* (New York, 2011), p. 24.
2. Masha Gessen, *The Man without a Face: The Unlikely Rise of Vladimir Putin* (New York, 2012), p. 62.
3. Vladimir Isachenkov, 'Putin Recalls KGB Career with Pride', *Associated Press*, 10 March 2000.
4. Available at http://navalny.livejournal.com/.
5. Available at http://www.youtube.com/watch?v=rj-ZR0Za75I.
6. 'Putin says cannot criticize late president Yeltsin', *RIA Novosti*, 23 August 2010.

7. Ellen Barry, 'Satirizing Putin with Boldly Poetic Flair', *The New York Times*, 18 November 2011.
8. Henry Meyer, 'Moscow Sets Plan to Fight World's Worst Traffic Jams', *Bloomberg*, 10 November 2010.
9. Charles Clover, 'Rising Chorus of Boos Greets Russia's Leaders', *Financial Times*, 24 November 2011.
10. Ibid.
11. Ben Judah, Jana Kobzova and Nicu Popescu, *Dealing with a Post-BRIC Russia* (London, 2011), p. 22.
12. Available at http://www.youtube.com/watch?v=tsIEoAZr1ok.
13. 'Analiz Regionalnikh I Mestnikh Vyborov 14 Oktyabrya 2012', *Komitet Grazhdanski Initiativ*, 16 October 2012, available at http://komitetgi.ru/news/news/250/#. UJGNyFH7U4Y
14. Ibid.
15. Sergei Shpilkin, 'Statistikii Isledovala Vybory', *Gazeta.ru*, 10 December 2011.
16. Ibid.
17. Ibid.
18. 'Voting, Russian Style', *The Economist*, 10 December 2011.
19. Gregory L. White and Rob Barry, 'Russia's Dubious Vote', *The Wall Street Journal*, 28 December 2011; The NGO Golos gathered all evidence of fraud and electoral violations during the 2011 parliamentary elections. The results are available at http://www. kartanarusheniy.ru/.
20. Infographic of results and regional scores of United Russia, available at http://en.rian. ru/infographics/20111208/169491066.html.
21. White and Barry, 'Russia's Dubious Vote'.
22. Infographic of results and regional scores of United Russia.
23. Lilia Shevtsova, 'Implosion, Atrophy or Revolution', *Journal of Democracy*, July 2012.
24. 'Resultati ER Po Moskve Pochti Vdvoe Previshaiut Resultat Exit Poll', *Argumenti I Fakti*, 5 December 2011, available at http://www.aif.ru/society/news/102856. Yulia Taratuta, 'Nash Durdm Golosuyet "Za,"' *Vedomosti*, 6 December 2011.
25. Denis Volkov, 'The Protestors and the Public', *Journal of Democracy*, July 2012.
26. Available at http://www.youtube.com/watch?v=nPXteOAtSwc.
27. 'Medvedev's Twitter obscenity provokes shock', *Reuters*, 7 December 2011.
28. Gleb Bryanski, 'Putin: On the pulse or out of touch with Russia', *Reuters*, 15 December 2011.
29. Volkov, 'The Protestors and the Public'.
30. '102 Tishyacha 486 Chelovek. My Schitali Po Golovam', *Novaya Gazeta*, 24 December 2011, available at http://www.novayagazeta.ru/society/50265.html.
31. Ibid.
32. Available at http://www.newstube.ru/media/naval-nyj-na-mitinge-my-est-vlast.
33. Ibid.
34. Ellen Barry, 'Architect of Russia's Political System under Putin is Reassigned', *The New York Times*, 27 December 2011.
35. Available at http://anti-orange.ru/post/cat/6.
36. 'Russian Tycoon Prokhorov Ready to Be PM wants to join euro zone', *RIA Novosti*, 11 August 2011.
37. The video 'Rossiya Bez Putina Welcome to Hell' was removed from YouTube for breaking its code of conduct, available at http://vimeo.com/36281503.
38. Ibid.
39. Available at http://www.sergeyeva.ru/.
40. Timothy Heritage and Guy Faulconbridge, 'Tearful Putin Wins Back Presidency', *Reuters*, 4 March 2012; Yevgeniya Albats, 'Golosovanie Kak Eto Bilo', Novaya Vremia, 5 March 2012, available at http://www.newtimes.ru/articles/detail/50512.
41. Ibid.
42. Available at http://www.youtube.com/watch?v=30oMuEo4eDw.
43. Available at http://kmartynov.livejournal.com/1692439.html.

Chapter Ten: Moscow Is Not Russia

1. Max Seddon, 'Russian Opposition Fights To Stay Relevant,' *Associated Press*, 16 December 2012.
2. For breakdown of regional HDI levels, see Alexander A. Auzan and Sergei Bobylev, *National Human Development Report For the Russian Federation 2011: Modernization And Human Development*, United Nations Development Program (Moscow, 2011), pp. 138–40, available at http://www.undp.ru/documents/nhdr2011eng.pdf.
3. Ibid.; Oleysa Geresamenko, 'Budet Bedno, No Chisto I Krasivo, Kak V Belorussi', *Kommersant Vlast*, 10 September 2012; Caleb Melby, 'Moscow Beats New York, London, in List Of Billiobaire Cities', *Forbes*, 16 March 2012, available at http://www.forbes.com/sites/calebmelby/2012/03/16/moscow-beats-new-york-london-in-list-of-billionaire-cities/.
4. Figures available at http://www.gks.ru/wps/wcm/connect/rosstat/rosstatsite/main/account/#.
5. These figures are for 2008. That year Russian GDP was approximately $1.6 trillion and Moscow's GNP was approximately $340 billion. Figures available at www.gks.ru/free_doc/new_site/vvp/vrp98-10.xls; 'Global City GDP Rankings 2008–2025', *PriceWaterhouseCoopers*, 2009, available at https://www.ukmediacentre.pwc.com/imagelibrary/downloadMedia.ashx?MediaDetailsID=1562.
6. Available at http://www.undp.ru/index.phtml?iso=RU&lid=1&pid=1&cmd=text&id=187.
7. Worldwide Cost of Living Survey 2012, Mercer (London, 2012), available at http://www.mercer.com/press-releases/cost-of-living-rankings.
8. Olesya Geresamenko, 'My Ne Seperatist My Protiv Mosvky', *Kommersant Vlast*, 14 May 2012.
9. Natalia Zubarevich, 'Four Russias: Rethinking the Post-Soviet Map', *OpenDemocracy*, 29 March 2012.
10. For a breakdown of regional HDI levels and life expectancy see Alexander A. Auzan and Sergei Bobylev, *National Human Development Report For the Russian Federation 2011: Modernization And Human Development*, United Nations Development Program (Moscow, 2011), pp. 138–140. Available at http://www.undp.ru/documents/nhdr2011eng.pdf.
11. Sergei Belanovsky, Mikhail Dmitriev, Svetlana Mishikhina and Tatyana Omelchuk, *Socio-Economic Change And Political Transformation in Russia*, (Moscow, 2011), p. 31.
12. Allen Lynch, *Vladimir Putin and Russian Statecraft* (Washington DC, 2010), p. 83.
13. Vladimir Putin, 'Building Social Justice – A Social Policy for Russia', 13 February 2012, available at http://www.russkiymir.ru/russkiymir/en/publications/articles/article0239.html; Gleb Bryanski, 'Russia's Putin calls for Stalin Style "leap forward"', *Reuters*, 31 August 2012.
14. Available at http://www.youtube.com/watch?v=lPDkJbTQRCY.
15. Shaun Walker, 'Pussy Riot Prisoners Sack Lawyers Who "Cashed in on Fame"', *The Independent*, 20 November 2012.
16. Mikhail Dmitriev and Daniel Treisman, 'The Other Russia: Discontent Grows in The Heartland', *Foreign Affairs*, September–October 2012.
17. Miriam Elder, 'Putin Says Pussy Riot "Got What They Asked for" as Jailed Women Appeal', *The Guardian*, 8 October 2012.
18. Ellen Barry, 'Leaving the Presidency in Russia, Medvedev Fights For Relevance', *The New York Times*, 3 May 2012.
19. Available at http://navalny.livejournal.com/758143.html.
20. Steve Rosenberg, 'Putin warns of foreign meddling in politics in Russia', BBC, 12 December 2012.
21. Charles Clover, 'Russian "civilization" stirs resentment', *Financial Times*, 11 December 2012.
22. Max Seddon, 'Russian Opposition Fights To Stay Relevant', *Associated Press*, 16 December 2012.
23. Ibid.
24. 'Russian Macro View: Consumption to Remain Strong for Now', *Citi Economics*, 21 October 2011.

25. Dmitriev and Treisman, 'The Other Russia'.
26. Christopher Granville and Irina Lebedeva, 'The Consequences of Putin's Big Spend', *Trusted Sources Emerging Markets and Consulting*, 4 October 2011.
27. Ibid.
28. Ilya Arkhipov and Lyubov Pronina, 'Russia Boosts Arms Spree to $613 billion, Seeks US Technology', *Bloomberg*, 20 September 2010.
29. Dmitriev and Treisman, 'The Other Russia'.
30. Granville and Lebedeva, 'The Consequences of Putin's Big Spend'.
31. Ksenia Galouchko, 'Russia Must Cut Break-Even Oil Price to $80, Citigroup says', *Bloomberg*, 2 June 2012.
32. Henry Meyer, 'Putin Balks at Pensions Threat as Ageing Russians Hold Trump Card', *Bloomberg*, 21 October 2010.
33. 'Russian State Debt Lowest Amongst G-8 Countries – Putin', *RIA Novosti*, 11 April 2012.
34. Thane Gustafson, *Wheel of Fortune The Battle for Oil and Power in Russia* (London, 2012), p. 458.
35. Ibid., p. 459.
36. Charles Clover, 'Russia: Ascent and Dissent', *Financial Times*, 11 July 2011; Alexander Kolyandr, 'Capital Flight from Russia Still on Rise', *The Wall Street Journal*, 3 October 2012.
37. Infographic of regional results, available at http://en.rian.ru/infographics/20111208/169491066.html.
38. Dmitriev and Treisman, 'The Other Russia'.
39. I use the term technically as the GRP is calculated based on the regions' natural resources. Inhabitants are not living, for the most part, like Americans. Figures available at www.gks.ru/free_doc/new_site/vvp/vrp98-10.xls; Russian Regions: Facts And Figures, *National Human Development Report Russian Federation 2008: Russia Facing Demographic Challenges*, United Nations Development Program, (Moscow, 2009) available at http://www.undp.ru/documents/NHDR_2008_Eng.pdf.
40. Miriam Elder, 'Doll 'Protesters' Present Small Problem for Russian Police', *The Guardian*, 26 January 2012. Olesya Geresamenko, 'Tak Colonia Bilo, Tak I Ostanetsya', *Kommersant Vlast*, April 2012.
41. Simon Shuster, 'Pskov, Russia: Moonshine, Population Crisis Threaten Region', *Time*, 9 May 2011.
42. 'Kaluga: Be Successful', Kaluga Development Corporation (Kaluga, 2012).
43. Ibid.
44. *Doing Business in Russia: Your Tax And Legal Lighthouse* (Moscow, 2012), p. 8.
45. Dmitry Vinogradov, 'Pochemu Yaroslavl Ne Golosuyet Za 'Medvedei' I Shto On Dumaet O Putine', *RIA Novosti*, 13 February 2012.
46. Infographic with regional results, available at http://en.rian.ru/infographics/20120304/171705949.html.
47. Ellen Barry, 'Official Puts Career at Risk with Diatribe on Kremlin', *The New York Times*, 9 June 2009.
48. Daniel Treisman, *The Return: Russia's Journey from Putin to Medvedev* (New York, 2011), p. 284.
49. Russian 2010 Census, available at http://www.perepis-2010.ru/.
50. Michael Schwirtz, 'Russian Anger Grows over Chechnya Subsidies', *New York Times*, 8 October 2011.
51. 'Kak Vy Otnositsiya K Idee 'Rossiya – Dlya Russkih', Levada Center, 9 October 2011, available at http://www.levada.ru/archive/mezhetnicheskie-otnosheniya/kak-vy-otnosites-k-idee-rossiya-dlya-russkikh; Polling from Levada Center also available in Ben Judah, Jana Kobzova and Nicu Popescu, *Dealing with a Post-BRIC Russia* (London, 2011), p. 22.
52. 'Kakie Chustva Vy Lichno Ispitivaet Po Otnosheniu K Vyhotsam Iz Yughnikh Respublik Prozhivayushikh v Vashem Gorode, Raione?', Levada Center, 9 October 2011, available at http://www.levada.ru/archive/mezhetnicheskie-otnosheniya/kakie-chuvstva-vy-lichno-ispytyvaete-po-otnosheniyu-k-vykhodtsam.
53. Available at http://www.youtube.com/watch?v=uxVVN0j54YQ.

54. Available at http://navalny.livejournal.com/627082.html.
55. Available at http://echo.msk.ru/blog/milov/823340-echo/.
56. Mikhail Alexseev, 'Rubles against the Insurgency: Paradoxes from the North Caucasus Countries', PONARS Eurasia Policy Memo no. 157, May 2011.
57. Ibid.
58. Ibid.
59. Schwirtz, 'Russian Anger Grows over Chechnya Subsidies'.
60. Ibid.
61. Figures available at http://www.eng.kavkaz-uzel.ru/articles/19591/; Mark Kramer, 'Prospects For Islamic Radicalism and Violent Extremism in the North Caucasus and Central Asia', PONARS Eurasia Policy Memo no. 28, August 2008; 'Eto'o Signs with Anzhi', *Agence France Presse*, 25 August 2011.
62. Figures available at http://www.eng.kavkaz-uzel.ru/articles/19641/.
63. Kadyrov Russia's Most Charismatic Regional Leader, Is Marking Birthday, *Itar-Tass*, 5 October 2011; 'Pressa Uznala, Skolko Kadyrov Travit Na Elitnikh Konei – Dengi Vidmo Daet Allah', *Newru.com*, 15 December 2011, available at http://www.newsru.com/russia/15dec2011/loshad.html.
64. Luke Harding, 'WikiLeaks cables: Chechnya's ruler, a three-day wedding and a golden gun', *The Guardian*, 1 December 2010.
65. Svetlana Emalyanova, 'Ramzan Kadyrov: Dengi Chechne Daet Allah', *Rossiskaya Gazeta*, 6 October 2011.
66. 'Alexander Tkachev Uznala Kazakam Na Kavkaz', *Kommersant Vlast*, 6 August 2012.
67. 'V Kakom Mere Federalnie Vlasti Seichas Kontroliruyet Polozhenie Del V Chechne', Levada Center, 1 September 2010.

Chapter Eleven: Moscow the Colonialist

1. Olesya Geresamenko, 'My Ne Za Seperatism, My Protiv Moskvi', *Kommersant Vlast*, 14 May 2012.
2. Ibid.
3. Oleysa Geresamenko, 'Budet Bedno, No Chisto I Krasivo, Kak V Belorussi', *Kommersant Vlast*, 10 September 2012.
4. Ibid.
5. Ibid.
6. 'Russie Un Autoportrait: Vingt ans après la fin de l'URSS', *Courier Internationale*, September-October-November 2011, p. 15.
7. Olesya Geresamenko, 'My Ne Za Seperatism, My Protiv Moskvi', *Kommersant Vlast*, 14 May 2012.
8. Vladimir Putin, *First Person: an Astonishingly Frank Self-Portrait by Russia's President* (London, 2000), p. 186.
9. Levada Polls available in Ben Judah, Jana Kobzova and Nicu Popescu, *Dealing with A Post-BRIC Russia* (London, 2011), p. 22.
10. Maria Lipman and Nikolay Petrov (eds), *Russia in 2020: Scenarios for the Future* (Washington DC, 2012) p. 143.
11. Ibid.
12. Mikhail Dmitriev and Sergei Belanovsky, 'Kak My Teper Dumaem: Revolutisia Ne Obzatalno Dolzhna Byt Karvnoi', *Vedomosti*, 24 October 2012.
13. Available at http://www.youtube.com/watch?v=4atPDPKyz2I.
14. Ibid.
15. World Bank Indicators, available at http://data.worldbank.org/country/russian-federation; 'Russian Defence Industry Production up 2.5 per cent in 1Q2009', RIA Novosti, 2 June 2009.
16. Full text available at http://gplanost.x-berg.de/gplanost.html.
17. Russian Economic Report 2010, *The World Bank* (Moscow, 2010), p. 21.
18. Peter Leonard, 'Tank Towns symbolizes Putin's campaign', *Associated Press*, 28 February 2012.
19. 'Taina Kladbusha Seks-Rabnikh: Pochemu Za Pyat Let Evo Ne Nashli', *Komsomolskaya Pravda*, 3 February 2007.

20. Jarett Zigon, 'Russia's Heroin Epidemic; Why the Government Is Ducking the Issue?', *Opendemocracy*, 4 February 2011.
21. United Nations World Drugs Report 2010, available at http://www.unodc.org/unodc/en/data-and-analysis/WDR-2010.html'; Russia Blames US for "Heroin Tsunami Sweeping Russia"', *BBC News*, 1 April 2010.
22. 'Russia and HIV/AIDS: Opportunities for Leadership and Cooperation', Brookings Institution, May 2005, available at http://www.brookings.edu/research/reports/2005/05/russia; 'Russian Health and Demography: A Sickness of the Soul', *The Economist*, 7 September 2006.
23. Rupert Wingfield-Hayes, 'The Heroin Epidemic Sweeping Russia', *BBC News*, 3 April 2010.
24. Vasily Sigariev, *Black Milk* (London, 2012) p. 35.
25. 'Interview with Kremlin Boss Vladislav Surkov', *Der Spiegel*, 20 June 2005.
26. Figures available at http://www.gks.ru/dbscripts/Cbsd/DBInet.cgi?pl=2322048.
27. 'Yakob – 6.5 per cent, Porunov – 3.3 per cent, Roizmann – 26.5 per cent', *Ura.ru*, 21 November 2012, available at http://ura.ru/content/svrd/24-09-2012/articles/1036258447.html.

Chapter Twelve: Chinese Nightmares

1. Oleysa Geresamenko, 'Budet Bedno, No Chisto I Krasivo, Kak V Belorussi', *Kommersant Vlast*, 10 September 2012.
2. Ibid.
3. Ibid.
4. Mark Leonard, *Why Europe Will Run the 21st Century* (London, 2005); 'Statement of Principles', Project for a New American Century, 3 June 1997, available at http://www.newamericancentury.org/statementofprinciples.htm.
5. Martin Jacques, *When China Rules the World* (London, 2009).
6. Sergey Karaganov, 'Russia's Asian Strategy', *Russia in Global Affairs*, 2 July 2011.
7. Andrei Kalachinsky, 'The Russian Far East', *Russian Analytical Digest*, 12 July 2010.
8. Data available at https://www.cia.gov/library/publications/the-world-factbook/rankorder/2102rank.html.
9. Available at http://www.sipri.org/databases/milex.
10. Ben Judah, Jana Kobzova and Nicu Popescu, *Dealing with A Post-BRIC Russia* (London, 2011), p. 39.
11. Available at http://csis.org/node/24824/multimedia.
12. James Reardon Anderson, *Reluctant Pioneers: China's Expansion Northwards 1644–1937* (Stanford, 2005), p. 89.
13. Roderick MacFarquhar and Michael Schoenhals, *Mao's Last Revolution* (Cambridge, MA, 2006), pp. 309–11.
14. Ibid.
15. Ibid.
16. Ibid.
17. Ibid., p. 312.
18. Henry Kissinger, *Years of Upheaval* (London, 1982) p. 48.
19. Judah, Kobzova and Popescu, *Dealing with A Post-BRIC Russia*, p. 39.
20. 'Dalniy Vostok Dolzhen Stat' Blizhnim', *RBK Daily*, 26 September 2008, available at http://www.rbcdaily. ru/2008/09/26/focus/382248.
21. Judah, Kobzova and Popescu, *Dealing with A Post-BRIC Russia*, p. 39.
22. 'Heilongjiang leases land, grows crops in Russia', *China Daily*, 29 May 2010, available at http://www.chinadaily. com.cn/china/2010-05/29/content_9907873.htm.
23. Andrew E. Kramer, 'China's Hunger Fuels Exports in Remote Russia', *The New York Times*, 9 June 2010, available at http://www.nytimes.com/2010/06/10/business/global/10ruble.html.
24. 'Birobidzhan, Stalin's Soviet Zion: An Illustrated History', Swarthmore College (2001), available at http://www.swarthmore.edu/Home/News/biro/.
25. 'Russia's APEC Summit in Vladivostok', *British Embassy Moscow*, 21 September 2012, available at http://www.ukti.gov.uk/export/countries/europe/easterneurope/russia/premiumcontent/376980.html.

26. Anna Nemtsova, 'Shrinking Siberia: Why Young People Are Fleeing Russia's Far East', *Newsweek*, 17 September 2012.
27. 'Grazhdanski Aktivisit Vyyasnyat, Kak Razborvali Dengi Sammit Ates', *Globalsib.ru*, 23 July 2012.
28. Ibid.
29. '15 Billion Rubles Stolen During APEC Summit', *The Voice Of Russia*, 13 November 2012.
30. Oleysa Geresamenko, 'Budet Bedno, No Chisto I Krasivo, Kak V Belorussi', *Kommersant Vlast*, 10 September 2012.
31. 'Russian Elections Marred By Low Turnout', *RIA Novosti*, 14 October 2012.
32. 'Russian Government Plans Far Eastern Republic – Paper', *RIA Novosti*, 20 April 2012.
33. Available at http://globalvoicesonline.org/2010/10/18/russia-new-video-from-primorsky-krai-guerrillas/.
34. Ibid.
35. Lucy Ash, 'Why Russians backed anti police rage', *BBC News*, 25 November 2010.
36. 'A third of Russians wish they could shoot dead corrupt officials', *RT*, 23 June 2011.

Conclusion: The Ghosts

1. Vladimir Putin, *First Person: An Astonishingly Frank Self-Portrait by Russia's President* (London, 2000), p. 139.
2. Ellen Barry, 'Putin Once More Moves to Assume Top Job in Russia', *The New York Times*, 24 September 2011.
3. 'The State of Russia: Frost at the Core', *The Economist*, 9 December 2010.

SELECT BIBLIOGRAPHY

Akunin, Boris, *The State Counsellor* (London: Weidenfeld and Nicolson, 2008)
Albats, Yevgeniya, *The State within a State: The KGB and Its Hold On Russia's Past, Present and Future* (New York: Farrar Straus Giroux, 1994)
——, '"Une Génération Insaisissable", Russie: Un Autoportrait', *Courrier Internationale*, September 2011
Amalrik, Andrei, *Will the Soviet Union Survive until 1984?* (London: Allen Lane, 1970)
Anderson, James Reardon, *Reluctant Pioneers: China's Expansion Northwards 1644–1937* (Stanford University Press, 2005)
Artomonov, Anatolii, *Kaluzhskii Vektor: Opit Razvitya Regiona* (Moscow, 2011)
Aslund, Anders, *Russia's Capitalist Revolution: Why Market Reform Succeeded and Democracy Failed* (Washington DC: Peterson Institute for International Economics, 2007)
—— and Kuchins, Andrew, *The Russian Balance Sheet* (Washington DC: Peterson Institute for International Economics, 2010)
——, Guriev, Sergey and Kuchins, Andrew (eds), *Russia after the Global Economic Crisis* (Washington DC: Peterson Institute for International Economics, 2010)
Auzan, Alexander A. and Bobylev, Sergei, *National Human Development Report for the Russian Federation 2011: Modernization and Human Development* (Moscow, 2011)
Balcer, Adam and Petrov, Nikolay, *The Future of Russia: Modernization or Decline?* (Warsaw, 2012)
Bashkirov, Valeria, Solovyev, Aleksandr and Dorofeev, Vladislav, *Geroi 90-x: Ludi I Dengi: Noveishaya Istoria Kapitalizma V Rossii* (Moscow, 2012)
Belanovsky, Sergey and Dmitriev, Mikhail, *Politicheskii Krizis V Rossii I Vozhmoshie Mekhanizm Evo Razvitya* (Moscow, 2011)
Belanovsky, Sergey, Dmitriev, Mikhail, Misikhina, Svetlana and Omelchuk, Tatyana, *Dvuzhenyushchie Sili I Perspetivy Politicheskoi Transformatsii Rossii* (Moscow, 2011)
Belton, Catherine, 'A Realm Fit for a Tsar', *Financial Times*, 30 November 2011
Benjamin, Walter, *Moscow Diary* (Harvard University Press, 1986)
Billington, James H., *The Icon and the Axe: An Interpretive History of Russian Culture* (New York: Knopf, 1970)
Bremmer, Ian and Charap, Samuel, 'The Siloviki in Putin's Russia: Who They Are and What They Want', *The Washington Quarterly*, vol. 30, no. 1 (2007)
Brent, Jonathan, *Inside the Stalin Archive: Discovering the New Russia* (New York: Atlas, 2008)
Burrett, Tina, *Television and Presidential Power in Putin's Russia* (London: Routledge, 2011)
Carrère, Emmanuel, *Limonov*, (Paris, 2011)
Centre for Strategic Research, *Changes in the Political Sentiments of Russian Citizens after the Presidential Elections* (Moscow, 2012)
Colton, Timothy, *Yeltsin: A Life* (New York: Basic, 2008)
Curtis, Glenn E. (ed.), *A Country Study: Russia* (Washington DC: Federal Research Division, Library of Congress, 1998)

Dmitriev, Mikhail and Yurataev, Alexey, *Strategia–2010: Itogi Realitastsi 10 Let Sputsya* (Moscow, 2010)

Dmitriev, Mikhail and Treisman, Daniel, 'The Other Russia: Discontent Grows in the Heartland', *Foreign Affairs*, vol. 91, no. 5, September–October 2010

Dovlatov, Sergei, *The Suitcase* (London: Oneworld, 2011)

Dubovitsky, Natan, *Okolonolya: Gangsta Fiction* (Moscow, 2009)

Dunlop, John, *The Moscow Bombings of September 1999: Examination of Russian Terrorist Attacks at the Onset of Vladimir Putin's Rule* (Stuttgart, 2012)

Ericson, Edward Jr., and Mahoney, Daniel, *The Solzhenitsyn Reader: New and Essential Writings 1947–2005* (Wilmington: ISI Books, 2008)

Erofeev, Benedict, *Moscow Circles* (London: Writers and Readers Publishing Cooperative, 1981)

Etling, Bruce, Alexanyan, Karina, Kelly, John, Faris, Robert, Palfrey, John and Gasser, Urs, *Public Discourse in the Russian Blogosphere: Mapping RuNet Politics and Mobilization* (Cambridge, MA: Berkman Center for Internet & Society, 2010)

Fawn, Rick and White, Stephen, *Russia after Communism* (London: Frank Cass, 2002)

Fitzpatrick, Sheila, *Everyday Stalinism: Ordinary Lives in Extraordinary Times: Soviet Russia in the 1930s* (Oxford University Press, 1999)

Fossato, Floriana and Lloyd, John with Verkhovsky, Alexander, *The Web that Failed: How Opposition Politics and Independent Initiatives are Failing on the Internet* (Oxford: Reuters Institute for the Study of Journalism, 2008)

Gaidar, Yegor, *Collapse of an Empire: Lessons for Modern Russia* (Washington DC: Brookings Institution Press, 2007)

Gammer, Moshe, *The Lone Wolf and the Bear: Three Centuries of Chechen Defiance of Russian Rule* (London: Hurst and Company, 2006)

Garadzha, Nikita (ed.) *Suvrenitet* (Moscow, 2006)

Garrard, John and Garrard, Carol, *Russian Orthodoxy Resurgent* (Princeton University Press, 2008)

Gelman, Vladimir and Ross, Cameron, *The Politics of Sub-National Authoritarianism in Russia* (Farnham: Ashgate, 2010)

Geresamenko, Oleysa, 'Budet Bedno, No Chisto I Krasivo, Kak V Belorussi', *Kommersant Vlast*, 10 September 2012

——, 'Kak Kolonei Bila, Tak Ostanetsya', *Kommersant Vlast*, 16 April 2012

——, 'My Ne Seperatist My Protiv Mosvky', *Kommersant Vlast*, 14 May 2012

Gessen, Masha, *The Man without a Face: The Unlikely Rise of Vladimir Putin* (London: Granta, 2012)

Glazunov, Oleg, *Kitaiskaya Ugroza* (Moscow, 2010)

Goldman, Marshall, *Petrostate: Putin, Power and the New Russia* (Oxford University Press, 2008)

Graney, Katherine, *Of Khans and Kremlins* (Plymouth: Lexington, 2010)

Gurevich, Vera, *Vladimir Putin: Roditeli, Druzya, Uchitelya* (Moscow, 2004)

Guriev, Sergei and Zhuravskaya, Ekaterina, 'Why Russia Is Not South Korea', *Journal of International Affairs*, vol. 63, no. 2, Spring–Summer 2010

Gustafson, Thane, *Wheel of Fortune: The Battle for Oil and Power in Russia* (Harvard University Press, 2012)

Hardt, John Pearce (ed.), *Russia's Uncertain Economic Future* (Washington DC: M.E. Sharpe, 2003)

Hill, Fiona and Gaddy, Clifford, *The Siberian Curse* (Washington DC: Brookings Institution Press, 2003)

Hoffman, David, *The Oligarchs: Wealth and Power in the New Russia* (New York: PublicAffairs, 2003)

Holmes, Stephen, 'Simulations of Power in Putin's Russia', Carnegie Endowment for International Peace, 1 October 2001

Hosking, Geoffrey, *Rulers and Victims: Russians in the Soviet Union* (Harvard University Press, 2006)

Idov, Michael, 'The New Decembrists', *New York Magazine*, 22 January 2012

Ioffe, Julia, 'Net Impact: One Man's Cyber-Crusade against Russian Corruption', *The New Yorker*, 4 April 2011

Inozemtsev, Vladislav L. 'Neo-Feudalism Explained', *American Interest*, vol. 6, no. 4, March–April 2011

Jack, Andrew, *Inside Putin's Russia* (Oxford University Press, 2005)

Jacques, Martin, *When China Rules the World* (London: Penguin, 2009)

Judah, Ben, Kobzova, Jana and Popescu, Nicu, *Dealing with a Post-BRIC Russia* (London, 2011)

Judah, Ben and Wilson, Andrew, 'The End of the Putin Consensus', *European Council on Foreign Relations*, ECFR 50, March 2012

Kalachinsky, Andrei, 'The Russian Far East', *Russian Analytical Digest*, no. 82, 12 July 2010

Kapuscinski, Ryszard, *Imperium* (London: Granta, 1995)

Kargalitsky, Boris, *Empire of the Periphery: Russia and the World System* (London: Pluto, 2008)

——, *Russia under Yeltsin and Putin: Neo-liberal Autocracy* (London: Pluto, 2002)

Kasyanov, Mikhail, *Bezputina: Politichiskie Dialog S Evgeny Kiselyevim* (Moscow, 2009)

Khodorkovsky, Mikhail and Nevzlin, Leonid, *Chelovek S Rublyom* (Moscow, 1992)

Khrystanovskaya, Olga, *Anatomiya Rossiyskoi elity* (Moscow, 2005)

—— and White, Stephen, 'Putin's Millitocracy', *Post-Soviet Affairs*, vol. 19, no. 4

Kissinger, Henry, *Years of Upheaval* (London: Phoenix, 1982)

Korzhakov, Alexander, *Boris Yeltsin: Ot Rassveta Do Zakata* (Moscow, 1997)

Kotkin, Stephen, *Armageddon Averted* (Oxford University Press, 2001)

Layard, Richard and Parker, John, *The Coming Russian Boom* (London: Free Press, 1996)

Ledeneva, Alena, *Russia's Economy of Favours: Blat, Networking and Informal Exchange* (Cambridge University Prses, 1998)

Leibin, Vitaly, Dyatlikovich, Viktor, Kartsev, Dmitry and Veselov, Andrei, 'Surkov: Neizvestnaya Istoria Putinskoi Rossii', *Russki Reporter*, 30 January 2012

Leonard, Mark, *Why Europe Will Run the 21st Century* (London: Fourth Estate, 2005)

—— and Popescu, Nicu, *A Power Audit of EU–Russia Relations* (London: European Council on Foreign Relations, 2007)

——, Krastev, Ivan and Wilson, Andrew (eds), *What Does Russia Think?* (London: European Council on Foreign Relations, 2009)

Lermontov, Mikhail, *A Hero of Our Time* (London: Norilana Books, 2001)

Lieven, Dominic, *Empire: The Russian Empire and Its Rivals from the Sixteenth Century to the Present* (New Haven and London: Yale University Press, 2003)

Lipman, Maria and Petrov, Nikolay, (eds), *Russia in 2020: Scenarios for the Future* (Washington DC: Carnegie Endowment for International Peace, 2011)

Lucas, Edward, *The New Cold War: How The Kremlin Menaces both Russia and the West* (London: Bloomsbury, 2008)

Lynch, Allen, *Vladimir Putin and Russian Statecraft* (Washington DC: Potomac, 2011)

Macfarquhar, Roderick and Schoenals, Michael, *Mao's Last Revolution* (Harvard University Press, 2008)

McFaul, Michael, *Russia's 1996 Presidential Elections: The End of Polarized Politics* (Stanford: Hoover Institution Press, 1996)

McKinsey Global Institute, *Lean Russia: Sustaining Growth through Improved Productivity* (Moscow, 2009)

Mankoff, Jeffrey, *Russian Foreign Policy: The Return of Great Power Politics* (Landham, MD: Rowman & Littlefield, 2009)

Mendras, Marie, *Russian Politics: The Paradox of a Weak State* (London: Hurst, 2012)

Milanovic, Branco, *Income, Inequality and Poverty during the Transformation from Planned to Market Economy* (Washington DC: World Bank Publications, 1998)

Milov, Vladimir, Nemtsov, Boris, Ryzhkov, Vladimir and Shorina, Olga (eds), *Putin Itogi* (Moscow, 2011)

Moisi, Dominique, *The Geopolitics of Emotions* (London: Bodley Head, 2009)

Monaghan, Andrew, 'The *vertikal*: power and authority in Russia', *International Affairs*, vol. 88, no. 1, January 2012

——, 'The End of the Putin Era?', Carnegie Paper, Carnegie Endowment for International Peace, July 2012

Nemtsov, Boris and Martinyuk, Leonid, *Zhizn Rab Na Galerakh* (Moscow, 2012)

Panyushkin, Valery, *12 Who Don't Agree: The Battle for Freedom in Putin's Russia* (New York: Europa, 2011)
——, *Mikhail Khodorkovsky: Uznik Tishiny* (Moscow, 2006)
——, *Mikhail Khodorkovsky: Uznik Tishiny 2* (Moscow, 2009)
Pavlov, Yury, *Da Gospodin Prezident* (Moscow, 2005)
Pavlovsky, Gleb, *Genialnaya Vlast* (Moscow, 2012)
Pelevin, Victor, *Babylon* (London: Faber and Faber, 2000)
——, *Omon Ra* (London: Faber and Faber, 1996)
——, *The Lives of Insects* (London: Faber and Faber, 1999)
——, *The Yellow Arrow* (New York: New Directions, 1993)
Pipes, Richard, *Russia under the Old Regime* (London: Penguin, 1974)
Poliakov, Leonid (ed.), *PRO Suverennuyu Demokratiyu* (Moscow, 2007)
Politovskaya, Anna, *Putin's Russia: Life in a Failing Democracy* (London: Harvill Press, 2005)
Polotovsky, Sergey and Kozak, Roman, *Pelevin I Pokolenie Pustoti* (Moscow, 2012)
Pomerantsev, Peter, 'Putin's Rasputin', *London Review of Books*, vol. 33, no. 20, 20 October 2011
Powell, Jonathan, *The New Machiavelli: How To Wield Power In the Modern World* (London: Bodley Head, 2010)
Prilepin, Zakhar, *San'kia* (Paris, 2009)
Putin, Vladimir, *First Person: An Astonishingly Frank Self-Portrait by Russia's President* (New York: Public Affairs, 2000)
Raleigh, Donald, *Soviet Baby Boomers: An Oral History of Russia's Cold War Generation* (Oxford University Press, 2012)
Reddaway, Peter and Glinski, Dmitri, *The Tragedy of Russia's Reforms: Market Bolshevism against Democracy* (Washington DC: United States Institute of Peace, 2001)
Reid, Anna, *The Shaman's Coat: A Native History of Siberia* (London: Weidenfeld and Nicolson, 2002)
Remnick, David, *Lenin's Tomb: The Last Days of the Soviet Empire* (London: Penguin, 2004)
——, 'The Civil Archipelago: How Far Can the Resistance to Vladimir Putin Go?', *The New Yorker*, 19 December 2011
Roberts, Sean P., *Putin's United Russia Party* (New York: Routledge, 2012)
Robertson, Graeme E., *The Politics of Protest in Hybrid Regimes: Managing Dissent in Post-Communist Russia* (Cambridge University Press, 2011)
Rose, Richard, Mishler, William and Munro, Neil, *Popular Support for an Undemocratic Regime: The Changing Views of Russians* (Cambridge University Press, 2011)
Rotislav, Antonov, *Primorskie Partizany* (Moscow, 2011)
Roxburgh, Angus, *The Strongman: Vladimir Putin and the Battle for Russia* (London: IB Tauris, 2012)
Rybakov, Vladimir, *The Burden* (London: Hutchinson, 1984)
Sakwa, Richard, *Russian Politics and Society* (London: Routledge, 2008)
Schlögel, Karl, *Moscow* (London: Reaktion, 2005)
Shambaugh, David, *China's Communist Party: Atrophy and Adaptation* (Berkeley: University of California Press, 2008)
Shevtsova, Lilia, *Putin's Russia* (Washington DC: Carnegie Endowment for International Peace, 2005)
——, *Lost in Transition: The Yeltsin and Putin Legacies* (Washington DC: Carnegie Endowment for International Peace, 2007)
——, *Lonely Power* (Washington DC: Carnegie Endowment for International Peace, 2010)
Shleifer, Andrei and Treisman, Daniel, 'A Normal Country: Russia after Communism', *Journal of Economic Perspectives*, vol. 19, no. 1, Winter 2005
Sigariev, Vasily, *Black Milk* (London: Nick Hern Books, 2003)
Sinyavsky, Andrei, *The Russian Intelligentsia* (New York: Columbia University Press, 1997)
Sixsmith, Martin, *Putin's Oil: The Yukos Affair and the Struggle for Russia* (London: Continuum, 2010)
Skinner, Gerald, *At the Kremlin Gates: A Historical Portrait of Moscow* (Oxford: Signal Books, 2011)
Sloterdijk, Peter, *Critique of Cynical Reason* (Minneapolis: University of Minnesota Press, 1987)

Sobchak, Anatoly, *Dyuzhina Nozhei V Spinu* (Moscow, 1999)

Soldatov, Andrei and Borogan, Irina, *The New Nobility: The Restoration of Russia's Security State and the Enduring Legacy of the KGB* (New York: Public Affairs, 2010)

Solnick, Steven, *Stealing the State: Control and Collapse in Soviet Institutions* (Harvard University Press, 1998)

Solzhenitsyn, Alexander, *Rebuilding Russia: Reflections and Tentative Proposals* (London: Harvill Press, 1991)

——, *The Gulag Archipelago 1918–1956* (London: Harvill Press, 2003)

Sorokin, Vladimir, *Journée d'un opritchnik* (Paris, 2006)

Svanidze, Nikolai and Svanidze, Marina, *Medvedev* (Moscow, 2008)

Taylor, Brian, *State Building in Putin's Russia: Policing and Coercion after Communism* (Cambridge University Press, 2011)

Terziani, Tiziano, *Goodnight, Mister Lenin: A Journey through the End of the Soviet Empire* (London: Picador, 1993)

Tishkov, Valery, *Chechnya: Life in a War Torn Society* (Berkeley: University of California Press, 2004)

Treisman, Daniel, 'Loans for Shares Revisited', *Post-Soviet Affairs*, vol. 26, no. 3 (2010)

——, *The Return: Russia's Journey from Gorbachev to Medvedev* (New York: Free Press, 2011)

Trenin, Dmitri, *Getting Russia Right* (Washington DC: Carnegie Endowment for International Peace, 2007)

——, *Odinochnoe Plavanie* (Moscow, 2009)

——, *Post-Imperium* (Washington DC: Carnegie Endowment for International Peace, 2011)

Tsygankov, Andrei, *Russia's Foreign Policy: Change and Continuity in National Identity* (Landham, MD: Rowman and Littlefield, 2010)

Vishnevsky Anatoly, *Rossia Pered Demographicheskim Vyborom* (Moscow, 2007)

Volkov, Denis, 'The Protestors and the Public', *Journal of Democracy*, vol. 23, no. 3, July 2012

Volkov, Vadim, *Violent Entrepreneurs: The Use of Force in the Making of Russian Capitalism* (Ithaca: Cornell University Press, 2002)

Voronkov, Konstantin, *Alexey Navalny: Groza Julikov I Vorov* (Moscow, 2012)

Weiler, Jonathan Daniel, *Human Rights in Russia: The Dark Side of Reform* (Boulder, CO: Lynne Rienner, 2004)

Wilson, Andrew, *Virtual Politics: Faking Democracy in the Post-Soviet World* (New Haven and London: Yale University Press, 2005)

Winters, Jeffrey, *Oligarchy* (Cambridge University Press, 2011)

Wood, Tony, *Chechnya: The Case for Independence* (London: Verso, 2007)

——, 'Collapse as Crucible', *New Left Review*, no. 74, March–April 2012

Yeltsin, Boris, *Midnight Diaries* (London: Phoenix, 2001)

Yurev, Dmitri, *Regim Putina: Postdemokratiya* (Moscow, 2005)

Zhegulyev, Ilya and Romanova, Ludmila, *Operatsiya Edinaya Rossiya: Neizvestnaya Istoria Partii Vlast* (Moscow, 2012)

Zubarevich, Natalia 'Four Russias: Rethinking the Post-Soviet Map', *OpenDemocracy*, 29 March 2012

INDEX